TOURISM AND HOSPITALITY DEVELOPMENT AND MANAGEMENT SERIES

ECOTOURISM: MANAGEMENT, DEVELOPMENT AND IMPACT

TOURISM AND HOSPITALITY DEVELOPMENT AND MANAGEMENT SERIES

Competitive Strategies and Policies for Tourism Destinations: Quality, Innovation and Promotion
Flora Maria Diaz-Perez (Editor)
2010. ISBN: 978-1-60876-475-4

Ecotourism: Management, Development and Impact
Anton Krause and Erich Weir (Editors)
2010. ISBN: 978-1-60876-724-3

TOURISM AND HOSPITALITY DEVELOPMENT AND MANAGEMENT SERIES

ECOTOURISM: MANAGEMENT, DEVELOPMENT AND IMPACT

ANTON KRAUSE
AND
ERICH WEIR
EDITORS

Nova Science Publishers, Inc.

New York

LIBRARY OF CONGRESS CATALOGING-IN-PUBLICATION DATA

Ecotourism: management, development and impact / Anton Krause and Erich Weir, editors.
   p. cm.
 Includes bibliographical references and index.
 ISBN 978-1-60876-724-3 (hardcover : alk. paper)
 1. Ecotourism--Management. 2. Ecotourism--Planning. I. Krause, Anton. II. Weir, Erich.
 G156.5.E26E354 2009
 910.68--dc22
                 2009036292

Published by Nova Science Publishers, Inc. ✛ *New York*

CONTENTS

PREFACE

Ecotourism can be conceptualized as a reconciliation of tourism and environmentalism. The environmentalist dimension of ecotourism involves environmental education and financial support of nature conservation. Extensive and intense human activity has altered the balance of ecosystems to the detriment of the natural environment. The movement of people, capital, goods and services has caused different types of ecosystem changes, including deforestation. Marine ecotourism offers contemporary attractive alternatives to marine resource use within marine protected areas (MPAs). This book reviews our current state of knowledge on the development, effects and management of ecotourism in MPAs, identifies factors affecting the appropriateness, success and sustainability of ecotourism in MPAs, and highlights research and practice priorities in the future. Also summarized in this book are the documented impacts of recreational uses on the coastal marine environment of the Mediterranean. These range from the impact of recreational boating on seagrass meadows, the effects of scuba-diving on hard-sessile benthic invertebrates, and the possible disturbance of marine mammals by whale and dolphin watching activities. Other chapters in this book analyze the current state of the art of ecotourism in Cameroon, an overview of present status quo of ecotourism and its educational activities with its utilization of wild animals in Japan, the effects of coastal ecotourism and water quality in the Yucatan Peninsula and the impact of tourism management on a population of infant monkeys. The findings suggest that tourism leads to high levels of stress, aggression and infant loss at this site. Several recommendations are offered to minimize harmful effects to help ensure that natural behavioral patterns are fostered.

Chapter 1 - Marine ecotourism offers contemporary attractive alternatives to marine resource use within marine protected areas (MPAs). The article reviews our current state of knowledge on the development, effects and management of ecotourism in MPAs; identifies factors affecting the appropriateness, success and sustainability of ecotourism in MPAs; and highlights research and practice priorities in the future.

Although an evolving tourism market sector regarding its definition, principles, and practice, marine ecotourism has infiltrated MPAs due to conformity between ecotourism principles (environmentally benign, socio-culturally empowering, and economically viable) and MPAs objectives (conservation and development). A growing body of literature has demonstrated both positive and negative effects of ecotourism on the natural, the socio-cultural, and the economic environment of MPAs. The advancement of the relationship between ecotourism and MPAs from co-occurrence to symbiosis requires the integration of ecotourism principles in a sustainable manner.

We need a world-wide, comprehensive assessment of the level, nature, and intensity of ecotourism penetration to MPAs. Ecotourism incentive, development and practice are expected to differ depending primarily on the socio-economic status of the countries with MPAs. In any case, self-regulation and safeguard of its distinctiveness from other types of tourism are the responsibility and interest of the ecotourism industry. Concurrently, monitoring and enforcement are the responsibility and best interest of the MPAs management authorities, if MPAs are to be able to accommodate a next attractive alternative to marine resource use in the future.

Chapter 2 - Tidal mudflats and coastal swamps are distributed along the sea-land ecological transition in humid tropical and subtropical regions. They are among the most endangered ecosystems on Earth, and have been intensively impacted both from water and land during the last 50 years. These transitional systems play a key-role in the homeostasis of inshore waters and whole watersheds, being natural buffers between the land and the sea, and establishing a network of connections between terrestrial and marine systems. Rational management has been frequently attempted; however, the vast majority of such initiatives proved to be largely unsustainable. Furthermore, since human impact is highest from land, frequently only a narrow coastal belt is managed, allowing only for the conservation of the most marine portion of these ecological transitions. More recently, zoning and multiple-use strategies offer promising perspectives of both survival and sustainable profit. It is here proposed that parks and rehabilitation projects are planned and designed to include wider portions of the ecological sea-land transition, incorporating subtidal, intertidal and supratidal systems, in a more holistic perspective. The economic and ecological value of these natural systems is still often misunderstood, and the obsolete misconception of unhealthy and unproductive wastelands still survives among politicians, economists and stakeholders, while political decision is almost invariably the main obstacle to ecosystem-based management. In this respect, ecotourism has a considerable potential, although particular care must be taken to correctly direct its goals and monitor its effects. Surprisingly, few if any flagship species have ever been proposed for these ecosystems, which might symbolize projects and raise public sympathies and awareness during environmental campaigns. The fauna and flora living in these habitats include several conspicuous and evolutionarily unique potential flagship species, which make an obligatory use of these systems during at least part of their life cycle. To facilitate the observation of these organisms in natural parks, different structures can be built, such as lower plank walks to improve the observation of relatively small macrofauna ("mud-watching"); observational bunkers to observe smaller animals at close distance; and boats and towers to observe larger animals in the distance. The focus on biodiversity promoted by flagship species and a correctly implemented ecotourism may elicit changes in the present political and institutional attitude, facilitating a more holistic perception of these ecosystems and of their immense ecological and socio-economic value.

Chapter 3 - Ecotourism can be conceptualized as a reconciliation of tourism and environmentalism. The environmentalist dimension of ecotourism involves environmental education and financial support of nature conservation. In this regard, environmental education has the potential to enhance visitor environmental knowledge and prompt change of visitor environmental behaviour. For instance, one of the main challenges for ecotourism is to move visitors from a passive state to an active contribution to the sustainability of protected areas. Indeed, previous research showed that there is a significant potential of ecotourists financing environmental conservation and providing voluntary work in the frame of the protected area management. However, a considerable number of studies highlighted a significant inefficiency of educational programs to support nature conservation. Most ecotourism activity seems to foster a frivolous understanding of particular megafauna and does not aspire to transform visitor behaviour. The prevalent circumstances at most ecotourism destinations, including non-captive audiences and a limited time frame, challenge even the goal of effective interpretation. Superficial learning opportunities are usually concentrated on flagship species, which may be easier to provide and guarantee visitor satisfaction. The objective of this paper is to show how environmental education can support a comprehensive approach in ecotourism development, which wishes to foster a deep understanding of natural and social characteristics of ecotourism destinations and endeavors to transform visitors' and locals' behaviour. We recorded baseline information of visitors and local people in the National Marine Park of Zakynthos, Greece, including demographic information, self-reported environmental behaviour, pro-environmental behaviour intention, consensus estimates for pro-environmental behaviour intention, environmental knowledge, and environmental concern. The crucial questions to be addressed are (1) how can baseline information derived by the present study inform the development of aims and specifications of environmental education interventions targeting ecotourists who visit protected areas as well as local people residing in ecotourism destinations (2) how can the potential effects of environmental education programs contribute in protected area management.

Chapter 4 - In the tourism industry, Cameroon has often sold itself as "Africa in miniature" because of its rich biocenoses representing almost all ecotones found in Africa including a very wide variety of landscape patterns. About 75 percent of the flora is still virgin. The fauna diversity includes rare carnivores, herbivores, primates and a diversity of birds. On gaining independence, the government of Cameroon realised the strong socio-economic potential of the tourism and of course the ecotourism industry as a source of revenue and therefore tried to geared efforts towards its promotion. However, the discovery of oil in the late 70s as a cheap source of revenue led to the neglect of this sector as well as some other important ones thereby provoking the well documented Dutch disease in the country. Of late, there has been a resurgent in the ecotourism business and government policy in this domain are aimed at fostering the sustainable development and co-management of the ecotourism potentials, involving local communities as well as some international and local NGOs. Some ecotourism potentials in Cameroon include; national parks, reserves and world heritage sites. However, these efforts have bore little fruits in terms of attracting tourist to the country and thereby boasting its foreign exchange earnings. This paper analyses the current state of the art of ecotourism in Cameroon, its challenges and prospects to serve the dual purpose of conservation as well as income generation to the local communities. Some comparison has been made with Kenya, which is one of the most popular ecotourism destinations in Sub-Saharan Africa.

Chapter 5 - This chapter summarizes the documented impacts of recreational uses on the coastal marine environment of the Mediterranean. These range from the impact of recreational boating on seagrass meadows, the influence of recreational fishing on littoral species (particularly the vulnerable ones), the effects of scuba-diving on hard-sessile benthic invertebrates, the human trampling's effects on rocky shallow areas or the possible disturbance of marine mammals by whale and dolphin watching activities. Considering all these effects, a shift from the actual mass tourism model to an ecologically responsible marine tourism model involving sustainable practices is urgently needed in all Mediterranean border countries. This model implies the management of physical stresses produced by tourist activities on the marine environment including energy and waste minimization and wider environmental impacts cited before.

To implement this responsible model, coastal integrated management plans should consider specific policy tools (described in this chapter) to safeguard the vulnerable (threatened) Mediterranean species and habitats. It is also concluded that recreational fisheries could be reconverted into sustainable practices if a list of new regulations and management actions are implemented to avoid the environmental problems associated with this type of fishing

If responsible tourist practices should be implemented all along the Mediterranean coast, the learning orientation concept should be considered as well, at least in marine protected areas to allow the development of marine ecotourism there. This chapter proposes a list of practices that create awareness on the impacts of human uses on the marine environment. In particular, the long-term consensus building with all stakeholders is necessary to establish marine ecotourism.

Overall, this chapter concludes that the sustainability of the tourism industry and the marine environment in the Mediterranean are closely linked to each other and depend upon the urgent adoption of sustainable environmental practices all along the Mediterranean coast as well as the establishment of a marine ecotourism model, at least in marine protected areas.

Chapter 6 - Establishing marine protected areas (MPAs) comes along with restrictions on biological resources extraction in the concerned zones. It is one of the conditions for reaching biodiversity conservation objective. These restrictions can engender high costs for the local communities. It can be particularly true when these communities are strongly dependent on the uses affected by the MPAs. However, MPAs by achieving biodiversity conservation objectives can also generate monetary and non monetary, social and economic benefits. This paper analyses the relevance of ecotourism as a way to share these benefits with local populations in order to establish a sustainable trade-off between conservation and social, economic and cultural development. Using the recent results of a research program (Biodivalloc) related to biodiversity conservation in Southern countries, we study the case of three MPAs in Western Africa: the Banc d'Arguin National Park (Mauritania), the Saloum Delta Biosphere Reserve (Senegal) and the Bolama-Bijagos Biosphere Reserve (Guinea Bissau). These MPAs shelter high diversities as well from a biologic point of view as sociocultural. In these three countries, many projects intend to develop ecotourism in MPAs. However, the concept of ecotourism is very often merged with the other forms of nature-based tourism like fishing and hunting. Are these last ones really ecotourism or could be ecotourism if practiced according to a sustainable way? How communities living inside the concerned MPAs benefit or could benefit from tourist activities in their livelihood? Our casework tries to assess all these questions. It suggests that if the local communities are well involved in the management of ecotourism development programs and projects in MPAs which affect them, they can benefit from their social and economic effects and would better accept the MPAs conservation strategies. In that case, ecotourism can be perceived as a means to share benefits from biodiversity conservation.

Chapter 7 - Rural tourism is often considered an economic alternative for rural areas facing decreasing profits and requiring a second or third economic footing. However, like other tourism activities, rural tourism results in a full range of environmental impacts. In particular, accommodation, one important element of the tourism system, generates various environmental loadings. Some obvious impacts are the following: architectural pollution owing to the effect of inappropriate hotel development on the traditional landscape, and the resort infrastructure becoming overloaded and breaking down in periods of peak usage. An Eco-inn, the environmentally friendly accommodation, is proposed to reduce the negative impacts from tourism.

However, no evaluation indicators and related assessment criteria for the Eco-inn are investigated up to now. Hence, the purpose of this study is to explore the indicators that can be used for evaluating the Eco-inn in Taiwan. This evaluation indicator system is based on the findings from literature review, and then the Delphi Method is employed to collect experts' opinions. Finally, 50 of the 109 candidate indicators were selected after three rounds of the Delphi method. These indicators can be categorized into the following sectors: green building, sustainable landscape construction, organic agriculture, environmental education, local benefit and others. Hence, the five core principles of eco-inns are: (1) green building, (2) sustainable landscape construction, (3) organic agriculture, (4) environmental education, and (5) local benefit. Furthermore, the eco-inn can be linked with ecotourism development and may be the low-impact accommodation choices for ecotourists.

Chapter 8 - Here the authors summarize research on the impact of tourism management on a population of wild Tibetan macaques. They compared long term data on infant mortality and adult aggression rates before, during and after a single group was used for tourism, and investigated short term effects of tourist presence and behavior on the behavior of the monkeys in the same social group and in an additional group. Long term results strongly suggest causal links between infant loss and management for tourism, and raise the hypothesis that artificial range restriction jeopardized infants by raising levels of aggression in the provisioning area. Infant mortality was significantly higher in the 11 years of tourist management than in the 6 preceding years, but was similar before and after management. Although few infanticides were witnessed, many infant corpses were found with wounds, and serious attacks on infants by adults were observed following outbreaks of aggression among adults in the provisioning area. Yearly rates of infant mortality were positively correlated with adult aggression rates in the provisioning area, and both factors were strongly associated with the degree to which the group's range was artificially restricted. Analysis of immediate responses of monkeys suggested multiple ways in which tourist behavior may cause monkeys stress and aggression in the provisioning area. Threat rates increased when tourist noise levels were high and when tourists directed behavior towards the monkeys, especially when tourists pointed or slapped the rail. Increases in tourist density were associated with increases in self-directed behavior by the monkeys, a behavioral index of stress. Collectively these results suggest that tourism leads to high levels of stress, aggression and infant loss at this site. The authors offer several recommendations to minimize harmful effects and help ensure that natural behavioral patterns are fostered.

Chapter 9 - Extensive and intense human activity has altered the balance of ecosystems to the detriment of the natural environment. Human migration has occurred throughout history. The movement of people, capital, goods, and services has caused different ecosystem changes, including deforestation. Coastal urbanization is a challenge for conservation, as people moving away from rural and protected areas has increased per capita demand for energy, goods, and services. Nowadays, most people migrate either temporarily or permanently to tropical coastal tourist areas. In the Yucatán Peninsula, migration has been taking place since the 1970s, with differing environmental impacts. The tourists are increasing every year, which demanding ecotourism facilities and industrial development increases to support population and business activities. Coastal water quality is also affected by increasing tourism development. Environmental awareness is lagging as efficient waste treatment systems are lacking. The water quality of the aquifer and the coast are threatened. This area has no rivers because of its karst geomorphology, the coastal freshwater comes from springs or seeps, and aquifers are the only freshwater source. Domestic garbage and wastewater are the main sources of pollution. The Yucatán Peninsula coast is undoubtedly an important economic resource for México, which requires the implementation of integrated coastal management, keeping in mind that continental human activities have a direct impact into coastal environment. It is unquestionable that successful coastal management of ecotourism must be implemented on the basis of efficient waste treatment, which requires more in-depth knowledge of the area. There should be permanent water quality monitoring programs, as well as long-term studies on the oceanographic and biogeochemical processes that control water quality dynamics, which are probably driven by stochastic events and by probable climate change. These factors will also complicate both conservation and migration flows. Also, this will involve fostering agreements among people, industrialists, and government to execute preventive and corrective actions. Water quality conservation is important for two reasons: first, for the preservation of coastal water quality and the beautiful scenery for ecotourism; and second, for freshwater quality protection. Taking action will contribute to the sustainable development of this region of México.

Chapter 10 - Regarding the natural and cultural backgrounds of Japan, ecotourism to gain access to wild animals will be developed more in the future, and so adequate utilization of the animals for tourism is needed because the wild animals are valuable tools and should continue to be sustainable resources. But, some wild animals are regarded as a public/captive animal/ecosystem health risk factor due to their carrying agents of infectious/parasitic diseases. Therefore, before or in performance of the ecotourism with utilization of the animals on the site, educational opportunities are needed. To start a discussion, a case of Rakuno Gakuen University in Hokkaido was given. There have been suspicious infectious and parasitic diseases in wild and zoo/exotic animals since the 1990s, and to provide facilities for conservation medicine research and education, the Wild Animal Medical Center was established. The facility has helped indirectly to accelerate the creation of solid relationships between zoological gardens and aquariums' directors/wildlife officers and researchers/exotic veterinarians, etc., and the facility. Such relationships provide not only clinical benefits with its positive diagnoses but also educational activities as byproducts of exchanging information between the organizations and university staffs. Also, to maintain ecotourism, some potential strategies including monitoring with consideration of ecology of the agents will be continued because the agents related to the diseases could infect not only humans but also captive animals. Finally, education related to wildlife or nature is one of the developing businesses in Japan, and we will discover a new business field between the ecotourism and wildlife education in the future.

Chapter 11 - Over the last 50 years, land use has dramatically changed. Over the past two decades, Remote Sensing imagery and its capacity to observe detailed land use patterns has facilitated a deeper understanding of historical land development patterns. Hence, the goal of this chapter is to shed some light on the possibilities of recovering ancient landscapes, by using spatial analysis combined with statistical methodologies applied to archaeological Roman sites in Portugal. The investigation of Roman land use patterns in the Algarve is carried out using density patterns of site propensity based on geographic and topological characteristics. Such a methodology allows a more accurate assessment of what might have been past land use during the Roman period in the Algarve. This experiment is also useful to better comprehend and make a more appropriate interpretation of predictive modelling scenarios. In particular, in the authors' case-study area, to have a share in the Algarve's archaeological legacy value may be very interesting to the tourist industry because of the possibility to explore more sustainable tourism options rather than the 'sun and beach' mass tourism offered traditionally in that region. This may lead to the development of an eco-history tourism product, by recycling existing built environments and creating an opportunity to generate revenues related to historico-cultural assets.

Chapter 12 - Mainstream tourism eco-certification programmes focus with varying success on "brown" aspects of environmental management, such as energy efficiency, resource consumption and waste treatment, whereas the impacts of tourism on "green" aspects, i.e. on the species and habitats that attracted nature-based tourism in the first place, are still largely being ignored. As the growth of nature-based tourism is expected to continue, it is important not only for ecological but also for economic sustainability to minimise any associated negative human impacts. Currently, managers are forced to operate without the information necessary for appropriate and anticipatory management decisions. The authors believe that effective mitigation of potentially harmful effects that accompanies any human activity in natural environments will arise only from detailed site- and species-specific guidelines derived from rigorous research. Such research is resource hungry so it becomes increasingly important that costs will be borne by end users.

Chapter 13 - Rural tourism in Spain has relied heavily on quality as a competitive strategy. However, some aspects of this sector make the buying process complex for consumers, which may compromise their ability to achieve their quality expectations. Facilities' variability in terms of their type and quality distinctions, as well as the important use of the Internet and the presence of illegal facilities, all contribute to this complexity.

In: Ecotourism: Management, Development and Impact   ISBN: 978-1-60876-724-3
Editors: A. Krause, E. Weir, pp. 1-42   © 2010 Nova Science Publishers, Inc.

Chapter 1

ECOTOURISM IN MARINE PROTECTED AREAS: DEVELOPMENT, IMPACTS AND MANAGEMENT – A CRITICAL REVIEW

*Angela Dikou**

Dept. of Ichthyology and Aquatic Sciences, University of Thessaly, Volos 38446, Greece

ABSTRACT

Marine ecotourism offers contemporary attractive alternatives to marine resource use within marine protected areas (MPAs). The article reviews our current state of knowledge on the development, effects and management of ecotourism in MPAs; identifies factors affecting the appropriateness, success and sustainability of ecotourism in MPAs; and highlights research and practice priorities in the future.

Although an evolving tourism market sector regarding its definition, principles, and practice, marine ecotourism has infiltrated MPAs due to conformity between ecotourism principles (environmentally benign, socio-culturally empowering, and economically viable) and MPAs objectives (conservation and development). A growing body of literature has demonstrated both positive and negative effects of ecotourism on the natural, the socio-cultural, and the economic environment of MPAs. The advancement of the relationship between ecotourism and MPAs from co-occurrence to symbiosis requires the integration of ecotourism principles in a sustainable manner.

We need a world-wide, comprehensive assessment of the level, nature, and intensity of ecotourism penetration to MPAs. Ecotourism incentive, development and practice are expected to differ depending primarily on the socio-economic status of the countries with MPAs. In any case, self-regulation and safeguard of its distinctiveness from other types of tourism are the responsibility and interest of the ecotourism industry. Concurrently, monitoring and enforcement are the responsibility and best interest of the MPAs management authorities, if MPAs are to be able to accommodate a next attractive alternative to marine resource use in the future.

---

* Correspondence author: E-mail: angeladikou@hotmail.com.

A. MARINE ECOTOURISM

The Eco-Label

Environmental concerns and a desire for more nature based tourism experiences (Budowski 1976; Diamantis 1991; Weaver 2001; Fennell 2003) were the impetus for the evolution during the last three decades of ecotourism as the fastest growing sector of the world's largest industry (Fennell 2003). On the basis that individuals who are requiring experiences of an ecotourism nature can be grouped due to their distinct needs, characteristics and behavior, and respond in a similar way to marketing stimuli, it has been argued that ecotourism can be regarded as a distinct segment of the tourism market or else a diversified product of the tourism industry (Mattheus 1993; Blamey 1997; Burton 1998).

Yet, a single agreed definition of ecotourism has remained elusive because of the multipurpose nature of the term. It is used to describe an activity, a philosophy and a model of development (Diamantis 1999). Furthermore, it is based on the premise of a continuum or spectrum: i) from hard to soft ecotourism depending on the rigor of experience and the level of interest in natural history (Laarman and Durst 1993); ii) from shallow to deep ecotourism based on the principles of environmentalism and sustainability (Acott et al. 1998); iii) from hard core through dedicated through mainstream to casual ecotourism based on dedication of and time spend by tourists (Lindberg 1996), and iv) from "pillar" to "lite" products offered (Honey 1999). Thus, subjective decisions cannot be avoided and definitions will be suited to different circumstances (Blamey 1997). The lack of an operational definition of ecotourism, however, impedes the quantification of the relative size of the sector (Fennell 2003). It is also necessary for legal, planning and funding purposes, gathering economic statistics, entrepreneur or community-based initiatives, and product development purposes, such as marketing, operating and accreditation (Blamey 1997). Furthermore, because the "eco" label itself has cachet suggesting special quality, high-value and exclusivity, overuse of the label is not surprising. Orams (1999) referred to many businesses, from small motorboat whale watching in the Canary Islands to giant cruise ships carrying several thousand passengers to the Caribbean, have been described as ecotourism. Thus, Blamey (1997) proposed the operationalization of the term for market and research purposes. Also, Higham and Carr (2003) confirmed the importance of weighting and, in some cases, rejecting defining parameters of ecotourism, as determined by the national or regional context within which ecotourism takes place. Furthermore, even well-established principles of ecotourism may not apply to "urban" marine environments (Lück and Higham 2003). Alternatively, Garrod and Wilson (2004) argued that ecotourism is best thought of not as a type of tourism but as an orientation of tourism towards sustainable outcomes.

There appears to be, however, growing consensus that genuine ecotourism is nature-based, oriented towards sustainable development balancing resource, economy and societal issues, educational/interpretative and local community-involving (Fennell 2001; Weaver 2005). Thus, principles adopted by the Irish initiative to develop West Clare into a marine ecotourism destination (Garrod and Wilson 2004) include: i) interprets marine wildlife and its environment to provide a better quality of experience for tourists; ii) increases appreciation of the marine environment and raises the overall conservation ethic, thereby making a fuller contribution to environmental conservation; iii) decreases and/or minimises the negative impact of tourism on the marine environment; iv) interprets the local marine/coastal culture and heritage; v) genuinely involves the local community in decision making; and vi) is managed according to the principles of sustainable development. In another example, planning for genuinely sustainable marine ecotourism in the EU Atlantic Area (Garrod et al. 2001) is based on seven principles: i) local participation; ii) environmental protection as a priority; iii) balance of statutory and voluntary approaches; iv) education and interpretation; v) collaborative approach; vi) responsible marketing; and vii) continued monitoring of actions against principles.

According to Gibbons (1992) ecotourism distinguishes itself from other forms of tourism because of the natural attraction per se; the underdeveloped area; the small group size; the lower expectations for amenities; the more diverse and participatory types of activities; the greater amount of interaction with locals; the larger contribution to conservation of local resources; the larger amenability of tourists to adaptation; the smaller impact on the environment; and the tourists better behavior. Anak Agung Gde Raka Dalem (2002) presented a comparison of the strengths and weaknesses of ecotourism over nature based and mass tourism and found that ecotourism performs better than mass and nature based tourism in terms of foreign exchange leakage, numbers of locals employed, and conservation of natural resources but required considerable time and extension of all stakeholders involved. Khan (1997) evaluated the potential of ecotourism as a viable option for self-sustaining tourism development in less developed countries against mass tourism, which is heavily dependent on foreign exchange. She purported that ecotourism with its small-scale development, provides opportunities for local empowerment, encourages the use of local knowledge and labour, promotes local ownership, perpetuates local identity, and strengthens economic equity. As such, it may weaken foreign dependence of less developed countries. However, ecotourism cannot replace mass tourism in less developed countries because it involves many stakeholders; mass tourism benefits may outweigh its adverse impacts; and not all tourists are seeking eco-experiences (Khan 1997). In fact, Shepherd (2002) reported that the efforts of two international awards-receiving ecotourism companies have been thwarted by the growth of mass tourism imitators of the original pioneers in South Thailand. Nevertheless, ecotourism offered an appealing alternative as a conservation *and* development tool to complement broader resource management regimes (Salafsky et al. 2001; Kiss 2004).

From Land to Sea

The transition from terrestrial to marine ecotourism is bestowed with unique challenges, such as the connectivity at larger spatial scales (with implications for the dispersion of organisms, diseases, and pollutants and the enforcement of administrative boundaries); the open access to a common pool of marine resources (with implications for the regulation of human uses); and the reliance of humans on equipment (Agardy 2000; Cater and Cater 2007). Yet, marine ecotourism has emerged as a significant industry, practice and developmental tool that involve: i) travel to a marine or coastal setting, which may include some cultural attractions, that benefits local communities, including involvement and financial returns; ii) travel that help to conserve the local (both cultural and natural) environment; iii) travel that minimizes its negative impact on natural environments and local communities; iv) travel that emphasizes learning and interpretation of the local environment to visitors; v) travel that motivates visitors to re-examine how they impact the earth and how they can aid local communities and the environment (Cater and Cater 2007). Modes and targets of marine ecotourism may include water, land or boat-based observation of animals, such as whales, dolphins, sharks, seals, birds, and corals; nature-based sightseeing trips by surface boat or submarine; coastal footpath and beach walking; visiting seashore and sea life centers and may involve swimming, snorkeling, diving, boating, sailing, fishing, kayaking and surfing (Garrod and Wilson 2004).

While there are countries, such as Australia and New Zealand, which are already well-established marine ecotourism destinations, others, such as Malaysia and Indonesia, have realized and started investing in their great potential for marine ecotourism (Anak Agung Gde Raka Dalem 2002; Weaver 2002). Expansion has also resulted in opportunities being sought in the polar (Snyder and Stonehouse 2007) or less exotic regions due to market forces and marketing ingenuity. The growth and diversification of activities in the marine ecotourism sector, however, has been highlighted as an area that should be of principal concern to policy-makers, practitioners and researchers world-wide (Halpenny 2002) since marine ecotourism provides incentives for protection/regulation of the heavily visited coastal zone (Hall 2001; Davenport and Davenport 2006). The highest level of protection/regulation of the coastal/marine environment is expected within Marine Protected Areas (MPAs).

B. DEVELOPMENT OF ECOTOURISM IN MARINE PROTECTED AREAS

What Are the MPAs?

The rate and magnitude of the continued degradation of the marine environment through pollution, habitat degradation, over-exploitation, and species extinction (Norse 1993; Sheppard 2000; GESAMP 2001; Hassan et al. 2005) has prompted the creation of MPAs as a management tool to secure the conservation of fish stocks, habitats, and endangered species without unnecessarily prohibiting human use and development (Agardy et al. 2003). The term MPA is used as a collective, simple, general term that encompasses different strategies for the protection of marine life, such as marine parks, sanctuaries or refuges, reserves, biosphere reserves, nature reserves and others, which in turn reflect different goals, types, and levels of restrictions at different parts of the world (Agardy et al. 2003). Nevertheless, the main goal of MPAs is the preservation *and* enhancement of these areas without unnecessarily prohibiting human use and development.

The first MPAs were established at the beginning of the 20th century and today reach an approximate total of 4,500 worldwide, making up some 0.5% of the total ocean surface (Chape 2005). They have been established either pro-actively to preserve areas of high biodiversity value, such as the Galapagos marine reserve at Ecuador; reactively to resolve existing or future conflicts among resource users, such as the Soufriere Marine Management Area, at St. Lucia Island in the Caribbean; or reactively to restore degraded areas, such as the Everglades in Florida, US (Agardy 2000). Depending on the particular socio-political, historical and economic context of a site, MPA governance may be: i) traditional, based on pre-colonial management systems and traditional ecological knowledge or on taboo systems; ii) community-based, which is led primarily by resource users, is generally small-scale and participatory; and shows promising results when based on Ostrom's (1990) principles for managing long-enduring common property regimes; iii) co-management, based on joint management by resource users and government; iv) centralized, which is led by a government agency and is consultative with resource users; and v) private, which is led by private sector (Christie and White 2007).

The importance of the interconnection of the marine environment through the transport of eggs and larvae by currents (Hjort 1914; Ogden 1997; Roberts 1997) has reinforced the establishment of MPAs with initiatives for the establishment of networks of MPAs (Brunckhorst and Bridgwater 1995; Kelleher et al. 1995; Badalamenti et al. 2000). Therefore, at the Johannesburg Summit on Sustainable Development, national governments agreed upon the creation of networks of MPAs by 2012 (United Nations 2002). Thus, MPAs have evolved from protecting charismatic mega faunal species, such as whales, dolphins and seals, to protecting critical ecosystem processes responsible for the goods and services provided by the coastal and marine environment; from protecting ecosystem structure to protecting ecosystem function; from marine amusement parks to multiple use areas; from isolated "conservation islands" to networks of marine protected areas (e.g. MEDiterranean Protected Areas Network, MEDPAN; CAribbean MPA Management Network, CAMPAMN).

However, despite the progress achieved regarding the establishment of MPAs, the total expanse of MPAs is not adequate; many are being threatened from external sources of impact; the majority of MPAs are not effective (Jameson et al. 2002); and conflicts most often arise when an MPA is established (Stern 2008). National (McField 2000, CANARI 2001), regional (Alder 1996; Mascia 1999; McClanahan 1999, Geoghegan et al. 2001; Burke et al. 2002; Appeldoorn and Lindeman 2003) and world-wide (Kelleher et al. 1995; Leverington et al. 2008) evaluations point to a low degree of effectiveness due to insufficient financial and technical support for the development and enforcement of a management plan; lack of trained staff, data, and community support; imbalanced use of resources within the MPAs; effects and threats from sources outside the MPAs; lack of strict organizational responsibility by the management body; absence of cooperation among involved stakeholders; and limited community involvement.

Existing assessments of marine protection initiatives suggest that successful management requires the active involvement of stakeholders in decision-making and perception of benefits from management (Mascia 1999; Agardy et al. 2003; Pomeroy et al. 2006; South East Asia: Pomeroy 1995; Russ and Alcala 1999; Pollnac et al. 2002; Caribbean: Rudd et al. 2001; Geoghegan and Renard 2002; Africa: Andersson and Ngazi 1995; Latin America: Da Silva 2004). This therefore signals the transition from a paradigm, in which local people are seen as a direct threat to biodiversity, towards a paradigm, in which complementarities and trade-offs are the focus, rather than conflicts between conservation and development (Brown 2002, e.g. see Murray 2005). MPAs interact with the local community (Caldecott 1996; Pomeroy et al. 2006) and may provide benefits to its economy through fisheries enhancement (Roberts et al. 2001, Sanchirico et al. 2002) and tourism development (Post 1992; Dixon 1993; Dixon et al. 1993; Post 1994; Farrow 1996; Mundet and Ribera 2001). Perceived benefits and shared positive attitudes are expected to increase the chances for participation and management compliance, particularly for extractive users, who frequently perceive the least benefits from protected areas' restrictions (Oikonomou and Dikou 2008). Thus, effective local awareness, consultation, and participation are considered as keys to the success of an MPA (Pomeroy et al. 2006).

Why Ecotourism in MPAs?

Ecotourism has great potential to assist MPAs in achieving their main dual goal of conservation and development. This potential lays in the fact that ecotourism principles conform with MPAs objectives. Ecotourism is one of the most important ways with which money can be generated to manage and protect the world's natural habitats and species. Ecotourism can contribute directly to conservation through park admission fees and payments for guiding, accommodation and interpretation centres. In addition, central to the definition of ecotourism is re-investment by the industry in the maintenance of habitats and species (Goodwin 1996).

Furthermore, since ecotourism is seeking a balance between resource, economy and societal issues, it ideally complies with driving marine resource use change within protected areas toward sustainable development alternatives; locals are urged to engage in ecotourism and gain supplementary income (Goodwin 1996; Stem et al. 2003). Collaborative community development is required to further economic diversification and reverse, thereby, adverse trends which deteriorate the social fabric of rural communities, such as rising unemployment rates, aging and declining population due to youth outmigration (Che 2006). Shifting perceptions of natural environments from sources of food and other natural products to potential sources of income from tourism often co-occurs with the designation of marine and terrestrial protected areas (Ceballos-Lascurain 1991; Agardy 1993). Marine ecotourism offers a more sustainable development alternative for local communities as a form of endogenous growth, rather than involving the transplantation of economic activities from the core or the encouragement of foreign-owned firms to locate to areas with MPAs. This is particularly important for peripheral, disadvantageous areas, where the majority of marine protected areas lay (Garrod and Wilson 2004). There is a major source of risk stemming from the possibility that if the net profit drops for some reason, the major international players may pull out of a destination that is investing in marine ecotourism, leaving it high and dry (Garrod and Wilson 2004). Cruz-Trinidad et al. (2009) found that shifts of fishers to tourism-based and other low-capital requirement mariculture (e.g. sea ranching) were more realistic than the expectation of absorbing fishers into current aquaculture businesses at Lingayen Gulf, Philippines. Pollnack et al. (2001) found that important factors, among others, that influence the success of community-based marine protected areas in the Visayas, Philippines, are successful alternative income projects and high levels of participation in community decision making.

Also, ecotourism can offer a means by which people's awareness of the importance of conservation and ecological literacy can be raised, whether those tourists are domestic or international. The clients, on whom the ecotourism section of the tourism industry depends, are potential voters, taxpayers and leaders who may help to build constituencies of support to lobby for conservation (Goodwin 1996).

On the other hand, MPAs constitute platforms of opportunity for the development of ecotourism (Lawton 2001); this high-in-demand diversified product of tourism. The MPA designation becomes a statement of the importance of the area and the diversity of life that lives there, as well as a way to market ecotourism products. Furthermore, experiencing the underwater environment may be more enjoyable than visiting aquaria (Corkeron 2004). For those who believe that sustainable tourism is an important part of conserving marine ecosystems, MPAs provide a powerful, convincing method for marketing the marine environment and the value of its conservation. Ecotourists will be more inclined to visit well-managed protected areas where species diversity is high, water quality is good, and has helped to instill or protect an existing sense of pride, stewardship, and involvement in management of the local inhabitants. The fostering of these attitudes, in turn, acts to make the area both more attractive and more hospitable for interested groups (Agardy 1993). Williams and Pollunin (2000) showed that protected reefs of the western Caribbean possessed attributes valued by dive tourists, e.g. abundance and variety of fishes, number of 'unusual', and number of 'large' fish. The Saba Marine Park, Netherland Antilles, benefits both the environment and the island's economy because it is highly influential in making divers decide to visit (Fernandes 1995). Shivlani and Suman (2000) found in the Florida Keys, that areas already enjoying protection attracted more trips and divers than those that had no such name recognition. Nearly half of 459 scuba diving and snorkelling tourists surveyed in St. Lucia, said they chose to visit because of the MPA (Barker 2003).

Hoyt (2005) advocated that one of the most valuable ways to promote and manage successful wildlife ecotourism is through the establishment of an MPA. MPAs with cetaceans have also played a small but growing role in terms of establishing a framework for managing ecotourism and making sure it remains sustainable (Hoyt 2005). Saba Marine Park demonstrates that it is possible to fund protection at sustainable levels of use and that the principles of ecotourism can be achieved in reality (Fernandes 1995). Cater (1997) purported that sustainable ecotourism can more readily occur in MPAs with environmental protection resulting both from and in enhanced local livelihoods, sustained visitor attraction, continued profits for the industry and revenue for conservation.

Actually, conserving the "environmental amenities" of a region and "advancing regional development through tourism" are increasingly considered interdependent aims. Many tropical island countries have begun to include development of MPAs in their national strategies for tourism and for sustainable development. From a purely commercial perspective, a system of legally protected areas has been called an "essential prerequisite for ecotourism' (Gibbons 1992). Tourism has been a force for establishing protected areas in Brazil, Ecuador and Costa Rica (Pappim de Oliveira 2005) either as environmental safeguards or because of ecotourism demand (Weaver 2002). Belize's growth in tourism has coincided with the designation of a national network of MPAs spanning the length of the Belize Barrier Reef (Diedrich 2007). Furthermore, there are regional conservation agreements pertaining to cetaceans and MPAs with an impact on ecotourism in the Mediterranean and the Caribbean regions (Hoyt 2005). Depondt and Green (2006) found that MPAs in South-East Asia, like the Wider Caribbean, present a high potential to raise revenue for conservation via the implementation of diving user fees, although this potential is largely unexploited.

Apparently, a number of mechanisms have led to the infiltration of ecotourism into MPAs (Figure 1). The symbiotic relationship (Budowski 1976) between ecotourism and MPAs can be perceived (Figure 2). Whether this is materialized (Figure 3) could be examined through documentation of the effects of ecotourism on MPAs.

C. EFFECTS OF ECOTOURISM ON MARINE PROTECTED AREAS

Environmental

The impact of tourism on the coastal environment is considerable and is extremely difficult to manage or limit (Miller and Auyong 1991; Kenchington 1993; Miller 1993; Bellan and Bellan-Santini 2001; Hall 2001; Craig-Smith et al. 2006; Davenport and Davenport 2006). It involves: i) coastal erosion; ii) habitat degradation; iii) pollution; and iv) waste, sewage and marine litter. Construction of roads, airports, hotels and other tourist infrastructure has led to increased coastal erosion, siltation and degradation of near shore habitats in many parts of the world (Maragos 1993; Hawkins and Roberts 1994; Shackley 1999). The demand for tourist amenities and ambition of local tourism authorities and businesses can result in concentrated development along narrow coastal areas that not only threaten the integrity of near shore landscapes and resources but also the serenity and wilderness factor that are the foundation of this sector. Nowhere was this more evident than in Pulau Sipadan, where all six resorts on the tiny 16 ha island were recently removed in light of the negative effects resort-based tourism was having on the island's fragile ecosystem (in Teh and Cabanban 2007). Tourists may consume disproportionate quantities of local resources. For example, the average tourist in Barbados consumes eight times the amount of water the average resident does (in Gibbons 1992). This may lead to decrease in groundwater reserves (Gössling 2001), exhaustion of local fisheries (Hockey 1987; White and Rosales 2001) and resource (seafood or souvenirs) depletion driven by tourist demand (Orams 1999). Wastes generated by tourists often overwhelm local sanitation systems (in Gibbons 1992) and lead to decline in groundwater quality (Kahoru and Yap 2001). Much of the toxic waste discharged into recreational waters represents (motorboat) crankcase drainage (in Gibbons 1992) and greenhouse gas emissions (Byrnes and Warnken 2006). Heavy tourism in the Outer Banks of North Carolina has adversely altered the ecology of the barrier islands in a dramatic fashion (in Gibbons 1992).

While the impact of tourism on the marine and coastal environments depends on scale of development and concentration of tourists, even ecotourism requires basic services and infrastructure, and even ecologically minded tourists consume resources (energy, water, land, food), generate waste (sewage and litter) and impact on pristine destinations (Gibbons 1992). It has been warned that effects on pristine ecotourism destinations may be more severe than in tourist destinations which have been already developed and hardened while the high environmental cost of travelling by airplane to ecotourism destinations is often not calculated in parochial local accounts of ecotourism impacts (Lück and Higham 2003). Wall (1997) elaborated on four good reasons suggesting that ecotourism has the potential to be environmentally disruptive: the locations visited, the timing of visits, the nature of use– impact relationships and the distances travelled.

As yet, there are no formal assessments of the environmental impacts of ecotourism on the marine and coastal environment (Cater 1993; Lindberg and McKercher 1997; Lück and Higham 2003). Okello and Kiringe (2004) interviewed protected area officers in order to identify and assess the relative importance of threats against biodiversity and conservation in Kenya and concluded that tourism was not a major threat; paradoxically some of the other threats identified, may be a threat to Kenya's tourism industry in protected areas. Christie (2005) found that MPAs, embedded within an Integrated Coastal Management framework, have had positive environmental impacts on coral reefs in Mabini, the Philippines and within tourism-reserved zones of the Bunaken National Park (BNP), Indonesia as indicated by both field observations and locals perceptions. Alterations in the quality and quantity of local natural resources due to tourism development within MPAs usually occur outside the borders of an MPA at proximal human settlements. The larger body of knowledge on tourists impacts on MPAs focus on non-consumptive wildlife tourism.

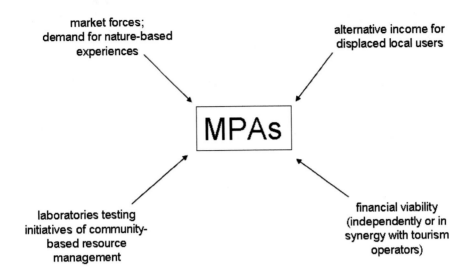

Figure 1. Mechanisms of ecotourism infiltration within MPAs.

Higham (1998) found that site users, the marine North Albatross focal species and the natural habitat at Taiaroa Head wildlife reserve, New Zealand, have all changed from 1972 to 1998 and concluded that in the absence of deliberate management intervention, wildlife tourism attractions evolve over time to the detriment of both the visitor experience and the focal wildlife species since wildlife species may appear to be perfectly tolerant of tourists while significant impacts still occur. However, seabird (and seal) colonies can have their breeding activities disrupted by intensive tourism (e.g. Yorio et al. 2001). A recent study by McClung et al. (2004) at beaches in New Zealand indicated that the presence of tourists delays post-foraging landing, and, therefore, affects fledging weight and survival, in the endangered penguin *Megadyptes antipodes*. Also, moving motorboats create visual and acoustic disturbance for birds.

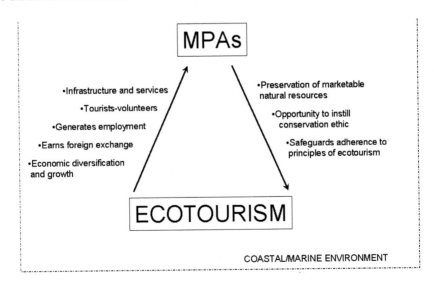

Figure 2. Depiction of the symbiotic relationship between ecotourism and MPAs in the coastal/marine environment.

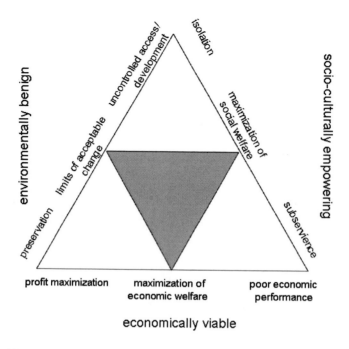

Figure 3. Sustainable ecotourism as the viable form of tourism within MPAs (adapted from FAO 1992).

Sorice et al. (2006) in reviewing studies that have examined human–marine mammal encounters concluded that boats seem to affect significantly the behaviour of marine mammals and manatees. Laist et al. (2001) showed that the numbers of incidents of ship strike by whale watching boats (second only to the US navy in importance) are a major cause of death and injury to whales. Stensland and Berggren (2007) purported that behavioural changes due to intense non-regulated boat-based tourism centred around the Indo-Pacific bottlenose dolphins *Tursiops aduncus* off the south coast of Zanzibar may lead to a shift in habitat use by nursing females and ultimately reduce fitness at both individual and population levels. Richter et al. (2006) documented small-size, most likely not of biological importance, indicating habituation, responses of male sperm whales to commercial whale watching activities off Kaikoura, New Zealand over three years of monitoring. Theberge and Dearden (2006) analysed long-term (10 years) whale shark *Rhincodon typus* sightings collected by ecotourist operators along 300 km of coastline, at Phuket, Thailand, and documented a 96% drop in whale shark sightings during 1998-2001 after data was corrected for effort. Carrera et al. (2008) found that both the average number of dolphins and the foraging activity of the threatened, coastal, exhibiting site-fidelity *Sotalia fluviatilis* were significantly reduced due to vessel's presence at the studied bay, Brazil.

A review of swim programs with cetaceans (whales, dolphins and porpoises) by the Scientific Committee of the International Whaling Commission (IWC 2000) noted that ''the available evidence indicated that swim with programmes in the wild could be considered highly invasive''. It was further noted, however, that ''the impact of swim-with programmes in the wild will vary among species, populations and locations and, therefore, that the impacts of such programmes should be assessed on a case by case basis'' (IWC 2000). Valentine et al. (2004) acknowledged that a number of studies have been conducted on swim activities with small toothed whales, especially dolphins with reviews of potential stress indicators, while information on swim-with activities involving larger toothed whales (beaked whales, sperm whale) and baleen whales were rarer, and often anecdotal or based on limited data. Sorice et al. (2006) concluded that published studies on commercial swim-with wild marine mammals programs have shown changes in behaviour but no overt negative impacts on target species.

Unmanaged human visitation of nesting beaches at night can cause marine turtles to abort nesting attempts (Fangman and Rittmaster 1993; Jacobson and Lopez 1994) or cause a shift in nesting locality (Murphy 1985). Even organised turtle watch groups influenced nesting behaviour of the loggerhead turtle *Caretta caretta* in Florida by reducing the time taken for the turtle to complete the covering and camouflage phases of the nesting process (Johnson et al. 1996). Also, constant lighting from street lights and coastal development (McFarlane 1963; Arianoutsou 1988; Witherington 1992) as well as flashing sources of light (Salmon and Witherington 1995; Lutcavage et al. 1997) can affect marine turtle orientation.

Anchor, trampling and diving damage are well studied human impacts on temperate and tropical benthos. Millazo et al. (2002) reviewed the biological effects of anchoring on seagrass meadows and tropical reefs and of recreational scuba diving and human trampling on marine communities with relevance to Mediterranean MPAs. Anchoring directly affects meadow cover and shoot density (Garcìa-Charton et al. 1993; Francour 1994; Poulain 1996; Francour et al. 1999; Lloret et al. 2008a) and indirectly affects sessile invertebrates leading to changes in both structural and trophic relationships on benthos (Backhurst and Cole 2000). The number of boats and their sizes, weather conditions, substrate firmness, and anchor type may all affect the extent of anchor damage to seagrass meadows (Walker et al. 1989; Francour et al. 1999) while recovery patterns may be related to both season and species (Creed and Amado 1999). Besides causing anchor damage in seagrass beds, motorboats also cause damage to seagrass meadows by propeller action in shallow water. This phenomenon has been particularly well studied in the coastal waters of Florida where an aerial survey in the early 1990s showed that some 70,000 ha of 1.1 million ha of seagrass beds was damaged by propellers (Sargent et al. 1994). Dawes et al. (1997) subsequently showed that regrowth of the seagrass *Thalassia testudinum* in propeller scars took some 3.5-4 years. Anchors cause damage to coral reefs during setting, retrieval, and while at anchor (Dinsdale and Harriott 2004). Corals are broken, fragmented, or overturned as the anchor drops to the substratum. Once set, further damage occurs by the chain dragging across the substratum or wrapping around reef structures. If the anchor lodges under a coral colony, overturning occurs during the retrieval process, particularly if an electronic winch is used.

Human trampling leads to lower biomass, densities and diversities of algae (Addessi 1994; Eckrich and Holmquist 2000; Pinn and Rodgers 2005), to a simpler structural state dominated by low profile and turf-like algae (Brosnan and Crumrine 1994; Schiel and Taylor 1999) and to lower densities and cover of sessile invertebrates (Povery and Keough 1991; Brosnan and Crumrine 1994; Eckrich and Holmquist 2000; Pinn and Rodgers 2005) on rocky shallow areas and intertidal sand flats. Direct impacts of trampling on corals can include mortality, fracturing, and coral tissue damage (Woodland and Hooper 1977; Tilmant and Schmal 1981; Liddle and Kay 1987; Tilmant 1987; Liddle 1991; Rodgers et al. 2003).

SCUBA divers may unintentionally damage stony corals and other benthic reef organisms by breaking their skeletons, abrading their tissues, and causing resuspension of sediments (Hawkins and Roberts 1992; Zabala 1999). Cumulative impacts of direct contact with corals lead to higher proportions of broken and damaged corals and lower percent live coral cover (Riegl and Velimirov 1991; Hawkins and Roberts 1992; Allison 1996; Plathong et al. 2000; Tratalos and Austin 2001; Zakai and Chadwick-Furman 2002; Rodgers et al. 2003), to changes in dominance patterns of corals (Hawkins et al. 1999), to slower growth rates (Meesters et al. 1994; Rodgers et al. 2003), to smaller average coral sizes (Hawkins and Roberts 1992), to susceptibility to disease and other perturbations (Hawkins et al. 1999; Hawkins et al. 2005), and to lower aesthetic value of coral reefs (Dixon et al. 1993; Hawkins and Roberts 1997). Sala et al. (1996) showed that both the size and density of the erect foliaceous bryozoan *Pentapora fascialis* were greater within unfrequented sites than frequented ones. It is logical to expect that smooth-bodied animals probably suffer less damage from frequent diver visits than hard sessile invertebrates, such as corals, gorgonians and bryozoans or coralline algae (Milazzo et al. 2002).

Orams (2002) reviewed the effects of feeding wildlife by tourists and found that it may alter natural behaviour patterns and population levels; lead to dependency of animals on humans for food, habituation to human contact, inter and intra species aggression for offered food, which, in turn, resulted in harming one another and tourists; injury and disease from artificial food sources while only in a limited number of cases wildlife has benefited from interaction with humans. Feeding attracts predators that scare off smaller fish, reducing local biodiversity (probably reversibly over short periods). It also attracts sharks that may damage corals with their abrasive skins whilst seeking prey (Tratalos and Austin 2001). McCrone (2001) regarded changes to fish behaviour through interactions with visitors feeding them as one of the most important problems associated with visitors to marine reserves in New Zealand. Lloret et al. (2008b) found that spearfishing in the Cape Creus Marine Protected Area, Italy, can induce changes in both the trophic structure and the intrinsic vulnerability of taxa (long lived, slow growing, with low reproductive potential species) in the catch.

Social

Social benefits expected through the development of ecotourism in MPAs refer to community empowerment (Sheyvens 1999) and conservation. Community empowerment may be expressed in various ways, including increased cohesion within the local community, participation in management of the MPA, reinforcement of the values of local tradition and upgrade of public facilities. Conservation benefits emanate from raising awareness of ecotourists, the tourism industry itself and the local community of the value and importance of natural resources for a sustainable future and diversion from consumptive to non-consumptive uses of marine natural resources; the latter are presented as "spread" effects in Cater and Cater (1999).

Clifton (2004) examined a dive and a research tourism foreign operation at Wakatobi marine national park in Indonesia. Both operations advertised themselves under the banner of ecotourism with references to economic and social benefits reaching local communities in their vicinity as well as to their strategies regarding marine conservation. She demonstrated contrasting direct and indirect socio-cultural impacts between the two operations. Direct impacts included consequences of interaction between visitors, local communities and the ecotourism operator itself with regard to the maintenance or otherwise of local institutions, traditions and values. Indirect impacts included image of the local community projected by the advertisements of the ecotour operator to local communities. Research ecotourism had a positive socio-cultural contribution to local communities. In particular, close informal interaction could raise local communities' awareness of the distinctive nature of their values and customs in comparison to those of foreign visitors. Research ecotourism could also add to the social capital of the community through improving their knowledge of the natural environment and their expertise in foreign languages. In contrast, the limited potential for contact between local individuals and visitors in the dive ecotourism operation in combination with the relatively limited economic benefits available to local communities had generated an atmosphere of apathy or distrust which needed to be addressed. Furthermore, analysis of publicity material available on the websites of the two ecotourism operators, which was the main source of advertising for these companies, compared the language and images used to describe the local community and visitors' interactions with local individuals. It became evident that visitors to the dive ecotourism operation may had expected to receive samples of local culture if they so required, thereby demoting the local community to a subservient position and implying that local people would be in awe of foreign visitors to some extent. This perspective, which could be characterised as a neo-colonial attitude toward indigenous culture, stood in stark contrast to the ideas projected by the research ecotourism publicity, which was stressing the need for the visitor to adapt to local norms and values and was presenting images assumed to represent daily life amongst everyday Indonesians. Although the research ecotourism depiction was simplistic, with little attention to the widespread problems of poverty, education and healthcare within this region of Indonesia, it was clearly far more congruent with ecotourism principles in terms of respecting local cultural values and ensuring local people are not disadvantaged in any way as a result of ecotourism activities. The author concluded that those contrasting impacts reflected the philosophy of the ecotour operator as well as the nature of the ecotourism activity.

Community empowerment is also particularly important in light of the increasing attention paid in the literature to principles of co-management of protected areas, which are intended to address the lack of managerial capacity through a sharing of responsibility between managers and local communities (Christie and White 1997). With a fragile insular island ecosystem as its physical base, exploding tourism becoming its chief economic base, and development rapidly expanding to keep apace, Roatan, Bay Islands, Honduras, provided a model situation of community based management of a MPA (Luttinger 1997). Based on interviews with the marine reserve Director and many of the local reserve members, Luttinger (1997) concluded that several key elements were responsible for catalyzing community support for this marine reserve: an economic base increasingly dependent on a rapidly expanding reef based tourism industry; community awareness of economic and social links to the marine resource; community awareness of existing serious impacts to the reef; community awareness that the pre-existent policies and system of resource use were unsustainable; that a new system had to be developed; community awareness, through education, of the broad-ranging benefits of establishing a MPA; trust in the community members, who initially organized the reserve; provision of employment alternatives for traditional users of reef resources and the continued right to line fish; and the marine reserve comprised only a limited area.

Through examining local perception data in five coastal communities in Belize, each attracting different levels of coral reef related tourism, Diedrich (2007) explored the relationship between tourism development and local coral reef conservation awareness and support. She demonstrated a positive correlation between tourism development and coral reef conservation awareness and support in the study communities and a positive correlation between tourism development and local perceptions of quality of life; a trend that was most likely the source of the observed relationship between tourism and conservation. She concluded, however, that, because the observed relationship may had been dependent on continued benefits from tourism as opposed to a perceived crisis in coral reef health, Belize must pay close attention to tourism impacts in the future. Failure to do this could result in a destructive feedback loop that would contribute to the degradation of the reef and, ultimately, Belize's diminished competitiveness in the ecotourism market. Young (1999) used a political ecology approach to examine whether ecotourism along the Pacific Coast of the Baja California peninsula in Mexico promoted stewardship of marine resources, which had been devastated by uncontrolled commercial harvesting. This case illustrated how conflicts over access to common-pool resources that fuelled the demise of area fisheries are now emerging in the rapidly growing industry of recreational whale watching. But resource conflicts may not preclude efforts to promote conservation through ecotourism. Along the shores of Baja's gray whale calving lagoons there are nascent, community-based organizations that could serve as vehicles for mobilizing local people into conservation efforts, if local access rights to marine resources were both secure and accorded preference over outside claims to the same. Taylor and Buckenham (2003) reviewed the effects of marine reserve establishment in New Zealand and concluded that there were changes in attitudes towards marine protected areas and found evidence of greater knowledge and acceptance of marine reserves amongst local communities and the wider public once the initial negative impact on commercial and recreational fishing were turned into positive impacts of marked increase in visitors, who, in turn, increased levels of recreation activity, such as swimming and diving.

However, even if ecotourism provides a significant new source of income through environmentally friendly, non-consumptive resource use, it may not be sufficient to discourage local people from engaging in other, more destructive forms of consumptive resource use. Lloret and Riera (2008) tracing the evolution of the marine environment and the human uses in Cape Creus, a Mediterranean coastal area where intense commercial fisheries and recreational uses have coexisted over the last fifty years, found that after the establishment of a marine reserve, the area is evolving from a species-based impact model due to professional fisheries to an ecosystem-based impact model due to recreational uses, which could be in the long term even more harmful for the whole marine environment. The aforementioned case-studies highlight that, if managed appropriately, ecotourism in MPAs may contribute to conservation through change in marine resources use patterns and alleviation of former pressures on marine resources but do not seem to reduce local dependence on parks' resources.

The importance of ecotourism in promoting environmental learning has recently been emphasized by Kimmel (1999) and Weiler and Ham (2001). Kimmel (1999) maintains that ecotourism provides an important opportunity to promote environmental education and that greater attention should be given to appropriate methods and materials to achieve this environmental objective. Weiler and Ham (2001) emphasise that intellectual, emotional and even spiritual connections between people and places are important ingredients of ecotourism experiences, and that interpretation is the key to establishing links between people and places.

As noted by Sorice et al. (2006), participants in marine wildlife encounters can derive cognitive benefits including increases in knowledge, awareness, and pleasure from up-close encounters with wildlife (Schänzel and McIntosh 2000). Kals et al. (1999) found that emotional affinity for and interest in wildlife was equally based on direct experiences in nature. Educational activity is necessary to provide meanings and relationships to people about the places they visit and about the things they see and do there. The 120 ha, "urban", Miramare Marine Reserve in the Gulf of Trieste, Italy, serves an impressive environmental education role. The 16,730 visitors reported during 1989 (Spoto and Franzosini 1992) has been sustained to date while the MPA has expanded into significant research activities (Constantini et al. 2003).

Many studies (Adams et al. 1989; Fishbein and Manfredo 1992; Broad and Weiler 1998; Jacobson and Marynowski 1998; Woods 1998; Orams and Hill 1998; Bradley et al. 1999) further emphasize the significant role of environmental education and experience in fostering pro-conservation values and actions. The benefits derived by tourists can translate into benefits for wildlife as people adopt more pro-environmental behaviours (Kals et al. 1999; McFarlane 1994) or contribute to wildlife conservation efforts (Sekhar 2003). There are two major concerns, however, regarding these interactions (Sorice et al. 2006)). First, direct encounters with wildlife may not positively influence tourist attitudes or behaviours. This, along with a second concern that encounters with wildlife can have deleterious effects on the target species, may eliminate the net benefit to the species. For example, Schänzel and McIntosh (2000) found that although tourists who engaged in an up-close penguin encounter derived cognitive benefits, this did not translate into behaviour change. On the other hand, Tisdell and Wilson (2005) provided evidence that ecotourism (learning and the interaction of tourists with wildlife) can support nature conservation (pro-conservation sentiments and actions) at Mon Repos Conservation Park (an important marine turtle rookery involved in ecotourism) in Queensland, Australia. The authors stress, however, that while knowledge may change environmental attitudes, those who already have pro-conservation attitudes are likely to be more eager to seek environmental knowledge (Bogner 1998).

Working at the same MPA, Tisdell and Wilson (2001) showed that the on-site experiences of ecotourists had positive impacts on the willingness of tourists to pay for the conservation of wildlife, and that willingness to pay was sensitive to whether or not wildlife was seen. It is suggested that *in situ* ecotourism is likely to be a more powerful force for fostering pro-conservation attitudes and actions among visitors than *ex situ* wildlife-based tourism in aquaria and zoos. Benefits to wildlife and habitat also accrue as demand for these types of experiences increase, encouraging local, regional, and national governments to weigh the opportunity costs of wildlife consumption and habitat destruction (Wilson and Tisdell 2001). Tisdell and Wilson (2002) highlighted the importance for conserving a species of thresholds (the loggerhead sea turtle *Caretta caretta*) in the demand for visits by ecotourists to view it, and in turn of thresholds in political and social support for conserving the species, as a function of its abundance. Thus, the significance of Ciriacy-Wantrup's concept of a social safe minimum standard was underlined. This significance often transcends the importance of the biological safe minimum standard. Hoyt (2001) noted that the regional impact of wildlife ecotourism can be significant. For example, communities such as Kaikoura, New Zealand; Provincetown, Massachusetts, USA; and Ogata and Ogasawara, Japan; Canary islands, Spain have been "transformed" by whale watching and its economic, educational, and scientific benefits.

Economic

Economic benefits from the development of ecotourism within MPAs are examined in terms of revenue generated, numbers of people involved, and the extent to which these benefits were distributed within local communities.

There are a number of case-studies that justify MPAs from an economic point of view (Lindberg 1996; Mundet and Ribera 2001; Carter 2003). Asafu-Adjae and Tapswan (2008) presented a selection of studies that have used diving fees or diving costs as a proxy for the value of MPAs and other well-known dive sites and estimated that aggregate benefits associated with scuba diving at Mu Ko Similan Marine National Park, Thailand, ranged between US$31 and US$71 million, using a social discount rate of 3%. Tongson and Digyco (2004) reported that to address the perennial problem of park financing, the Management Board of Tubbataha Reefs Natural Marine Park, a UNESCO World Heritage Site in the Sulu Sea, Philippines, developed a fee collection and permit system in cooperation with the diving community. Using the results of a willingness-to-pay survey conducted among divers in 1999, a two-tiered pricing scheme was developed for foreign and local divers. After two years of fee collection, the total fee collected amounted to US$65,000, which covered 28% of the annual recurring costs and nearly 41% of the core costs to protect Tubbataha. Examples of successful user fee systems can be found in several locations, such as Bonaire (Netherlands Antilles), Saba (Malaysia), Republic of Palau, Galápagos (Ecuador), and other sites in Africa, the Caribbean, and Asia (Lindberg 2001). Important lessons derived from these experiences are: the importance of active participation by the tourism sector; information dissemination; awareness raising; multi-tiered pricing; transparency in fee collection and disbursements; need to monitor visitor arrivals both before and after fee establishment or fee increases; clear agreements on revenue sharing; and earmarking funds for conservation activities. McClanahan (1999), however, when reviewing the effectiveness of coral reef MPAs in the tropics, demonstrated that unless there is a high level of tourism, expenditure for boat and entry fees, and assurance of providing a better nature experience than free-entry unprotected areas, only small-size MPAs are financially competitive against fishing.

The positive economic effect of wildlife tourism can be significant as well (Hoyt 2001; Kerlinger and Brett 1995; Wilson and Tisdell 2001; Garrod and Wilson 2004). Solomon et al. (2004) estimated that the benefits of the long-term endangered manatee protection in Citrus County, Florida greatly exceeded the development benefits foregone by approximately US$8.2–$9 million, primarily related to eco-tourism.

Yacob et al. (2007) contacted an empirical study of the local economic benefits of ecotourism development in the Redang Island Marine Park (RIMP), Malaysia, in terms of employment opportunities provided by the ecotourism sector and other related sectors. He showed that the development of ecotourism in the RIMP had definitely generated local employment opportunities; direct, indirect and induced employment created 938 jobs. Clifton (2004) in her comparison, among others, of the relative economic benefits from research *vs* diving ecotourism at Wakatobi National Marine Park, Indonesia, found that economic benefits from research ecotourism to local communities were both greater and more equitably distributed amongst local communities compared to those of diving ecotourism. Walpole and Goodwin (2000), on the other hand, documented that distributional inequalities favoured external operators and urban gateway residents rather than rural villagers at Komodo National Park, Indonesia. Unequal redistribution of economic benefits in favour of the tourism sector due to the redistribution of uses of natural resources with the establishment of MPAs has been documented in several cases (Fernandes 1995; Van't Hof 1998; Walpole and Goodwin 2000; Geoghegan et al. 2001; Pomeroy et al. 2006; Oikonomou and Dikou 2008). This has led to significant social changes in some instances. Oracion et al. (2005) documented that inherent economic advantages enjoyed by the tourism sector have marginalized the fishery sector in terms of access and control of the MPAs: both sectors helped to establish in the municipality of Mabini, Philippines. In reviewing the socioeconomic impacts of MPAs in the Mediterranean region, Badalamenti et al. (2000) speculated that at isolated places and the economically depressed "south," resident fishers and habitual visitors are expected to be the "losers" while new tourists are expected to be the "winners" from the establishment of MPAs in the Mediterranean. Conversely, at accessible locations and the affluent "north," fishermen often have complementary occupations and tourists include many resident people.

D. Management of Ecotourism in Marine Protected Areas

Integration of Ecotourism Principles

The success of ecotourism in fulfilling all three of its fundamental principles of being environmentally benign, socio-culturally empowering, and economically viable for local communities remains relatively untested in practice. Steyvens (1999) purports that, from a development perspective, ecotourism ventures should only be considered successful only if local communities have some measure of control over them and if they share equitably in the benefits emerging from ecotourism activities. Tershy et al. (1999) concluded that ecotourism to islands in north western Mexico provided no formal direct economic benefits to the conservation of the islands and López-Espinosa De Los Monteros (2002) admitted that operator-based ecotourism activities within the Area de Protección de Flora y Fauna 'Islas del Golfo de California protected area at La Paz bay, Mexico, provided direct economic benefits for conservation that were not comparable to the costs involved in the conservation of the protected area being used. López-Espinosa De Los Monteros (2002), however, reckoned that ecotourism activities may have not met the expectations of the protected area managers but provided other benefits to conservation associated with the promotion, education, and protection of the ecosystems in which ecotourism activities took place. Lindberg et al. (1996) evaluated the extent to which tourism at case study marine protected sites in Belize achieved three ecotourism objectives: generation of financial support for protected area management, generation of local economic benefits and generation of local support for conservation. When they used positive net financial impact as a standard, tourism did not achieve the first objective, but could do so with implementation of a modest user fee. Tourism achieved the second and third objectives. Working at the same sites, Diedrich (2007) confirmed the positive association between local economic benefits and local awareness and support for coral reefs conservation. Clifton (2004) highlighted distinct environmental, economic and social consequences of research and dive ecotourism ventures at Wakatobi Marine National Park, Indonesia, with research ecotourism performing in overall better than dive ecotourism. Stem et al (2003) found ecotourism in Costa Rica to have succeeded in providing viable economic alternatives when diverted pressure from heavily used resources. Its influence, however, on locals' conservation perspectives was minimal. He pointed that other factors, such as indirect tourism benefits and education levels, showed stronger associations with conservation behaviours and perspectives of local communities. De Haas (2002) showed that small-scale ecotourism at Niue, South Pacific, was sustainable only in environmental and socio-cultural aspects; due to insufficient visitor arrivals it was not economically viable.

Garrod (2003) purports that the principle of community participation is downplayed in favour of community involvement in ecotourism projects, although its critical importance to conservation of natural resources has been emphasized (Drake 1991; Brandon 1993; Cater 1994; Beeton 1998). He clarifies that "involvement" may imply gaining the cooperation of local people to enhance the feasibility of the implementation plan or, more often, ensuring that local people are provided with alternative means of employment should existing livelihoods be compromised by the development of ecotourism in their local area. "Participation", on the other hand, implies a much greater level of collaboration in the decision-making processes by which ecotourism planning and management take place. Thus, Garrod (2003) provided a revised model approach to building local participation into the planning and management of ecotourism by basing on Drake's (1991) original approach and incorporating elements of best practice. The model consists of the following eight stages: 1) determine the appropriate participation mechanisms; 2) undertake initial dialogue and educational efforts; 3) create and/or reinforce support mechanisms; 4) conduct preliminary studies; 5) collective decision making as to the scope and nature of ecotourism development; 6) community-based development of action plan and implementation scheme; 7) implementation; and 8) monitoring and evaluation.

Yet, Kiss (2004) and Salafsky et al. (2001) reached the same conclusion after they reviewed community-based ecotourism projects and enterprise strategy to promote conservation of natural resources, respectively; gains to local communities were few and there was dependence on long-term external support. Goodwin (2002) noted that issues of access to tourists and capital, enclaves and bypasses and employment need to be addressed regarding local community involvement in tourism around national parks.

Sustainability

The fact that ecotourism development tends to occur primarily in remote and marginal areas of the world, in pristine natural environments and economically disadvantaged human communities, makes the need for appropriate planning and management all the more critical (Boyd and Butler 1996). *A priori* evaluations can provide a contextual understanding of ecological, economic and socio-cultural forces, which shape the prospects for sustainable tourism development at the host destination, and can avert adverse impacts of tourism. Teh and Cabanban (2007) conducted an *a priori* assessment of the biophysical environment and infrastructure of Pulau Banggi, Saba, Malaysia, and evaluated how these will influence options for sustainable tourism development. They concluded that while Pulau Banggi possesses natural qualities that are attractive for ecotourism, financial and institutional support must be made available to provide facilities and services (water and sanitation infrastructure) that will enable local participation in environmental protection and enhance prospects for future sustainable tourism, while blast fishing can potentially destroy the major attraction for tourists. Caldicott and Fuller (2005) concluded that ecotourism activities are likely to provide potential for economic and human development within remote Australian Indigenous communities if they establish partnerships with other stakeholders within a region to overcome community capacity constraints. Dikou et al. (2009) obtained baseline data on benthic composition and coral community structure at seven reef sites of representative reefs of the Turks and Caicos Islands within the Admiral Cockburn Land and Sea National Park of South Caicos Island and performed *a priori* statistical power analysis to calculate replication requirements for safely and confidently detecting small, medium, and large effect sizes for a number of relevant to anticipated changes, i.e. increase in fishing and tourism pressures, univariate indices and for certain level of power.

Once ecotourism is ventured within an MPA, an armor of strategies, frameworks, procedures and tools for managing marine natural resources, humans (tourists and locals) and the tourism industry may be applied. The zoning strategy subdivides a managed area into two or more sub-areas, define classes of activities, and specify which activities are permitted and prohibited in each zone (Kenchington and Kelleher 1995). Agardy (1993) echoed the accommodation of ecotourism in multiple use planning of coastal and marine protected areas. The Great Barrier Reef Marine Park, Australia uses zoning as the backbone for park management and planning (GBRMPA 2003). Lusseau and Higham (2004) after determining critical habitat through spatio-ecological analysis proposed that the delineation of multi-levelled marine sanctuaries may be an effective approach to managing the impacts of tourism upon marine mammals at Doubtful Sound, New Zealand. Appropriate zoning is facilitated by powerful new technologies, such as geographical information systems and remote sensing image analysis. Fung et al. (2007) used IKONOS imagery classification to identify land cover types, a geographic information system to integrate land cover, ecological, and ecotourism use data, and a multiple objective land allocation model to resolve conflict between recreation and conservation at Yan Chau Tong, Hong Kong. Thus, sites were grouped into: i) those where conservation or recreation should receive the highest priority; ii) those that can be treated as additional recreation or conservation sites; and iii) conflict areas that can serve both purposes.

The carrying capacity strategy has been employed to avoid irreparable damage to the natural resource base through human use. It is based on the concept of critical threshold, i.e. a point or zone where there is a dramatic change in the resource (Luck 2005). Thus, carrying capacity sets a limit to the magnitude of change a natural resource will accept without breaching a critical threshold leading to an undesirable alternate state by placing a limit on the number of users who would be allowed access to the resource. Research on carrying capacity in recreational contexts showed clearly that: i) limits on numbers of users are of little value unless they are placed in the context of management objectives; ii) it is generally accepted that there are a number of measures of user satisfaction for any area, rather than only one and, related to this, that user dissatisfaction may not be simply a mirror image of satisfaction; iii) compatibility or tolerance of different user groups to one another varies with the nature of the resource and other elements, including frequency, place, type and time of encounters; iv) ecological effects of use in an area vary widely, and indicators of change may be numerous; v) the mix of users is as important as, or more so, the actual numbers of users in some situations; vi) the importance of the nature of the resource, vii) the dynamic nature of both the resource base and the human users, and viii) there is a spectrum of recreational activities or opportunities within a site (expanded on Hoyt et al. 2005). Thus, the concept of carrying capacity moved from one of finding optimal numbers of users to one involving the management of resources, user expectations and preferences, and physical parameters of the resource. Hoyt (2005) reported that in ecotourism policy recommendations for Hawaii (Cooper et al. 1998), carrying capacity was divided into ecological or biophysical (the maximum tourist presence beyond which ecological impact will occur in the natural environment), socio-cultural (the maximum use without causing negative effects on the host community and culture) and aesthetic or facility carrying capacity (the level beyond which the visitor satisfaction drops from overcrowding). All three of these aspects of carrying capacity should be considered when considering ecotourism-induced impacts.

Duffus and Dearden (1990) augmented the carrying capacity concept into a temporal dimension with their conceptual framework on nonconsumptive wildlife oriented recreation. The model is based on the premise that wildlife tourism resources exhibit evolution and change in terms of the nature of the users and the sites where the activity takes place. Higham (1998) verified Duffus and Dearden (1990) model using long-term data on the North Royal Albatross Colony, Taiaroa Head, New Zealand. He concluded that site users, contact wildlife species, and the natural habitat of the focal species all demonstrated various dimensions of change over time. He further pointed out that: i) in the absence of deliberate management intervention, wildlife tourism attractions evolve over time to the detriment of both the visitor experience and the focal wildlife species; ii) the impacts of tourism upon wildlife transcend tolerance, or else, wildlife species may appear to be perfectly tolerant of tourists while significant impacts still occur, and iii) research of this nature is both site- and species-specific. Sorice et al. (2006) called in the Duffus and Dearden (1990) model to the management of the endangered Florida manatee at Crystal River, Florida, US.

The ecotourism opportunity spectrum (ECOS) model constitutes specific application to ecotourism, and thus evolutionary development, of models already presented (Boyd and Butler 1996). Eight factors are viewed as important to ecotourism: 1) accessibility; 2) relationship between ecotourism and other resource uses; 3) attractions in a region; 4) presence of existing tourism infrastructure; 5) level of user skill and knowledge required; 6) level of social interaction; 7) degree of acceptance of impacts and control over level of use; and 8) type of management needed to ensure the viability of areas on a long term basis. Of these eight factors that comprise the ECOS framework, the first four can be determined from on-site study. The remaining factors, excluding the last one concerning an appropriate management regime, require input from ecotourists themselves, preferably from those visitors who have experience in the region under consideration. The eighth factor requires dialogue with all the groups and interests involved, both on an individual basis and collectively in order to reach areas of consensus over how ecotourism could be promoted and who should be responsible for overseeing the management of ecotourism within the region.

Stankey et al. (1985) introduced the "Limits of Acceptable Change" (LAC) concept. This concept accepted that, as the solutions to the issues of carrying capacity were likely to have to be found and instituted by resource managers, a process to assist them to identify acceptable use levels was required (Boyd and Butler 1996). Applying a LAC management model consists of: 1) selecting key indicators of setting conditions, 2) specifying quantitative standards of quality for each selected indicator, 3) applying different LAC standards within different zones across a recreational opportunity spectrum, and 4) implementing a range of management actions to maintain selected standards of environmental quality over time (McCool and Cole 1998). The LAC framework is also an iterative, adaptive management process that includes ongoing monitoring and adjustments (Hammitt and Cole 1998; McCool and Cole 1998).

Sustainability of recreational activities in coral reef environments, namely diving and snorkelling, is probably the most extensively researched. Tentative threshold limits of 4000-7000 dives per site per year have been estimated working on reefs around the world (Riegl and Velimirov 1991; Dixon et al. 1993; Scura and van't Hof 1993; Prior et al. 1995; Hawkins and Roberts 1997; Hawkins et al. 1999; Schleyer and Tomalin 2000; Zakai and Chadwick-Furman 2002; Hawkins et al. 2005). Hawkins et al. (2005) confirmed through nine years monitoring that the maximum diving levels of approximately 3,000 dives per site per year at Saba Marine Park, Malaysia, was bellow threshold limits. At this level of diving usage, benthic cover damage was not significantly related to diving intensity and nor did it accumulate over time, indicating sustainable use of resources. Most studies of diver impacts have recorded higher levels of damage in heavily used areas (Hawkins and Roberts 1992; Medio et al. 1997; Roberts and Harriott 1994; Tratalos and Austin 2001; Zakai and Chadwick- Furman 2002; Schleyer and Tomalin 2000). Jameson et al. (1999) and Zakai and Chadwick-Furman (2002) showed that increase in diver use results in an exponentially increasing level of coral damage. Coral reefs in Hahauma Bay in Hawaii are virtually dead after chronic, heavy use by tourists (Wells and Hanna 1992).

The intensity, however, of the impact of recreational activities, such as snorkelling and diving, on coral reefs, depends not only on level of use but also on diver experience, dive characteristics, coral community composition, and history. Although a large proportion (70–90% depending on the study) of divers contact the reef during their dive, a minority cause most of the damage (Talge 1992; Rouphael and Inglis 1995; Harriott et al. 1997). Fins cause most damage to the reef, followed by hands, knees and equipment gauges (Rouphael 1997). Apart from contacts with living substrate, fin kicks can also re-suspend sediment, which then settles on whatever substrate is in the vicinity, including corals (Rouphael and Inglis 1995; Zakai and Chadwick-Furman 2002). Although a study on Australia's Great Barrier Reef failed to find any relationship between diver damage and level of experience, excluding damage caused during diver training (Rouphael 1997), earlier work there on sub-tropical reefs revealed that people who had done less than 100 dives caused greater impacts than those who had done more (Roberts and Harriott 1994). Male divers, camera use, the initial phase of the dive, and night dives are also associated with increased levels of reef damage (Rouphael and Inglis 2001; Walters and Samways 2001; Barker and Roberts 2004; Luna et al. 2009).

Branching corals are particularly vulnerable to breakage (Hawkins and Roberts 1992; Walters and Samways 2001) compared to massive, plate-like, digitate, or submassive corals and dominate through their fast growth rates in low-energy environments. Thus, coral communities in wave-swept or naturally resilient to storms environments may be more resistant to diver impacts. The Florida Keys and Australia are regularly hit by hurricanes in contrast to the "insular" Red Sea. In Florida, divers broke corals about 150 times less frequently than they did in the Red Sea and Australia (Talge 1992) and this was mainly attributable to much lower levels of branching coral cover on Floridian reefs. Meyer and Holland (2009) found that recreation (snorkelling and diving) was low at Hawaiian MPAs because most fragile corals occurred below the maximum depth of the dominant recreational activity (snorkeling) while SCUBA diving was only common at one MPA with physically durable benthic habitats. Yet, massive corals may be more susceptible to disease in heavily dived areas as a result of diver contacts causing tissue lesions that provided sites for infection

(Azueta 1991; Peters 1997). Interestingly, average figures for the number of corals broken per dive have been reported at 4.5 in Australia (Rouphael and Inglis 2001) and about 6 in Egypt (Medio et al. 1997), whereas in Israel, all coral colonies examined in some intensively dived areas showed signs of damage (Zakai and Chadwick-Furman 2002).

Simple measures implemented by dive companies through their dive guides could greatly reduce impacts and increase carrying capacity within an MPA. They include using standard access points, underwater intervention when divers contact the reef, leading by example in keeping fins and equipment clear of the reef, and extra vigilance toward camera users, on night dives and at the beginning of dives, spreading diving over a range of alternative sites, and rotation of diving sites. The size of the dive group will influence the ability of dive leaders to perform their supervisory role, so smaller groups are better for the reef, and are preferred by divers in any case (Barker and Roberts 2004).

Divers at Sipadan, Malaysia, highly valued biodiversity, easy diving access, friendliness and efficiency of the staff (Musa 2002). Pedleton (1994) showed that marine environmental quality, which was measured as percent live coral cover, was a significant predictor of dive site visitation at Roatán, Honduras. A tourist destination, where environment is important, might, however, loses its attractiveness either through deterioration of the environment or as a result of crowding *per se*. A few studies have investigated visitor perceptions in marine environments (Shafer et al. 1998; Inglis et al. 1999; Shafer and Inglis 2000; Petrosillo et al. 2007). These studies have confirmed crowding as one of the major factors contributing to visitor dissatisfaction (Hoover et al. 1985; Musa 2002), with perceptions of crowding depended on a variety of factors, such as visitor characteristics and the location where encounters take place (Schreyer and Roggenbuck 1978; Manning 1985; O'Reilly 1986; Chavez 1993). In particular, crowding norms appear strongly dependent on expectations, with visitors with greater experience of nature being more sensitive to visitor density (Manning 1985; Manning 1986; Inglis et al. 1999). In addition, recreational use impacts, such as litter or damage to plants, trees, or corals, have been shown to reduce recreational enjoyment (Hoover et al. 1985; Lynn and Brown 2003), although individuals with a lower degree of environmental concern appear more accepting of impacts (Priskin 2003). In marine settings, it has been found that snorkelers are more tolerant of crowding above water than below it, and the acceptability of a setting is greatly reduced by the presence of man-made structures, such as buoys (Inglis et al. 1999). Divers appear more susceptible to crowding than snorkelers, with impact on enjoyment being significantly correlated with group size (Barker and Roberts 2004).

Petrosillo et al. (2007) showed that perceptions of environmental quality of visitors at the MPA of Torre Guaceto, south Italy, were highly dependent on education level, the place of visitor residence, and park related attitudes. To investigate how the perceptions and behaviour of visitors to coral reefs are influenced by their prior experience and knowledge of marine life, a questionnaire-based study was undertaken at sites in the Ras Mohammed National Park and at Sharm El Sheikh, South Sinai, Egypt (Leujak and Ormond 2007). It was evident that over the 10–20 years during which these reefs had deteriorated (mainly due to reef-flat trampling), there have been interrelated shifts in the nature of visitors making use of them. First, there had been a shift from experienced divers and snorkelers to inexperienced snorkelers and non-snorkelers with a poorer knowledge of reef biology. Second, there had been a shift in the predominant nationalities of visitors, from German and British, through Italian, to Russian. More recent user groups both stated and showed that they had less experience of snorkelling; they also showed less knowledge of marine life and less interest in learning about it. Visitor perceptions of both the state of the marine life on the reefs and the acceptability of current visitor numbers also varied between groups. More recent visitor groups and visitors with less knowledge were more satisfied with reef health. In general, however, visitor perceptions of reef health did not correlate well with actual reef conditions, probably because more experienced visitors preferred less impacted sites with which they were, nevertheless, less satisfied than inexperienced visitors at heavily impacted sites. More recent visitor groups were also less bothered by crowding on the shore or in the water. Consequently, the apparent "social carrying capacity", defined as the level of use before a decline in users' recreational experience ensues (O'Reilly 1986; Hillery et al. 2001), of sites seems to be increasing to a level well above the likely "ecological carrying capacity", defined as the numbers of visitors that can be sustained without affecting an area's ecological function (Martin and Uysal 1990; Hawkins and Roberts 1997). Both perception and behaviour will influence a reef area's "carrying capacity", defined in the study as the number of visitors it can support without unacceptable impact.

Shafer and Inglis (2000) showed that the number of people on a snorkelling trip and site infrastructure may have the greatest potential as setting indicators of Limits of Acceptable Change in the GBR, Australia. Roman et al. (2007) illustrated how ecological (reef diversity and vulnerability) and socioeconomic (visitor perception and satisfaction) studies in MPAs can be integrated within the LAC framework to craft a zoning plan addressing snorkelling activity at Koh Chang National Marine Park, Thailand.

There are a wide range of management regimes and structures which are used to control the interaction between tourists and wildlife. These regimes can be categorised as marketing, physical, regulatory, economic and educational. Currently, the management of interaction is dominated by physical and regulatory strategies but considerable potential exists to increase the role of education-based management strategies (Hoyt 2005).

Marketing management structures in the ecotourism industry include ecolabeling schemes, environmental certifications and awards, environmental quality assurance and evaluation systems, and guidelines of best practice to protect the natural environment on which the industry depends and to set the course for the environmentally compatible development of the tourism industry (Sasidharan et al. 2002). Sorice et al. (2006) found that the US Fish and Wildlife Service, which is responsible for manatee management at Crystal River, Florida, did not have mechanisms in place to manage the tourism component of the manatee encounter. They claimed that although a regulatory approach can be taken, a better approach would be to create an organization of tour operators to establish "best practices" that reflect the goal of the managing agency to enhance manatee protection, to ensure their livelihood, and to enhance the visitor experience. Sirakaya and Uysal (1998) found that education was more important than deterrence (sanctions and enforcement) in predicting conformance behaviour of tour operators with ecotourism guidelines. Cottrell and Graefe (1997) found that the best predictors of a specific responsible environmental behaviour, i.e. percentage of waste pumped in a pump out station, in the Chesapeake Bay region, Maryland, were knowledge of water pollution issues, knowledge of dumping in bay regulations, knowledge of dumping offshore regulations, and awareness of the consequences of raw sewage on water quality along with three background variables, namely education, boat length and years of boating experience working. Parsons and Woods-Ballard (2003) found that whale-watching operators in British Colombia, Canada, were far more likely to adhere to a code of conduct developed by an association of their peers than to regulations developed by governing agencies. Yet, Sirakaya et al. (1999) found that the view of ecotourism by 282 US based ecotourism operators reflected and confirmed definitions of ecotourism found in existing literature.

Physical management structures in the ecotourism industry include distance and code of contact guidelines between wildlife and tourists. Although closeness of approach by wild life is positively associated with visitor satisfaction (e.g. Valentine et al. 2004) such guidelines are especially beneficial given the adverse effects on wildlife behaviour, especially at locations with high tourism activity and potentially dangerous wildlife. Waayers et al. (2006) reported that 77% of tourist groups breached the voluntary code of conduct with marine turtles attempting to nest in the Ningaloo Marine Park, Western Australia. Lovasz et al. (2008) recommended that the managers of Seal Bay Conservation Park increase the approach distance of the Australian sea lion *Neophoca cinerea* from 6 to 10 m after based on results of the effects of experimental manipulation of human distance and density with sea lions behaviour.

Regulatory management structures in the ecotourism industry involve either restricting the number of participants (use of permits) and/or regulating the activities of participants. Scarpaci et al. (2003) demonstrated non-compliance by operators during 128 commercial dolphin-swim trips in Port Phillip Bay, Victoria, Australia of all four permit conditions studied: approach type, swim time, time in proximity of dolphins and presence of "fetal fold" calves. Shivlani and Suman (2000) found disproportionate dive operator use patterns in the designated no-take zones of the Florida Keys National Marine Sanctuary and proposed the implementation of a carrying capacity plan and a limited-entry system for dive operators.

User fees are both a regulatory and the most important economic management instrument of recreational activities in MPAs (Depondt and Green 2006). Thus, there are MPAs that depend exclusively or heavily on income generation through user fees (Lindberg 2001). Significantly reduced user fees for local compared to foreign visitors in documented cases (e.g. Tongson and Digyco 2004; Asafu-Adjaye and Tapswan 2008) are used to promote domestic recreation in MPAs and weaken foreign dependency.

Education management structures in the ecotourism industry include education centers, displays and exhibits, publications, guided tours, self-guided trails, audio-visual and multimedia technology and briefings. Harriott et al. (1997) found a positive correlation between diver briefings and a lack of environmental damage. Also, Medio et al. (1997) showed that divers did less damage after they were given a 45-min illustrated dive briefing covering reef biology, contacts caused by divers and the concept of a protected area, followed by an in-water demonstration lasting a few minutes. However, dive companies often give briefings that last only a few minutes and, in many instances, those briefings do not include how to avoid damaging the reef. Even if visitors are briefed about avoiding touching the reef, it is not known whether such briefings are sufficient to control their behaviour. Thus, Barker and Roberts (2004) found that briefing divers on the problem during actual operations had no effect. Instead, only divers closely supervised by dive leaders reduced the numbers of their reef contacts. Jacobson and Robles (1993) reported on the results of a pilot tour guide training program involving 12 residents near Costa Rica's Tortuguero National Park. The program was developed to respond to the impacts of the 24-fold increase in park visitation in the past decade, to involve local communities in resource management, and to provide regional environmental education. They found that the program: i) helped mitigate negative tourism impacts on Tortuguero National Park's natural resources, particularly by regulating tourists on the park's 35-km beach used for nesting by endangered sea turtles; ii) provided environmental education to an important segment of the local community not traditionally reached through school or government development projects; iii) provided environmental information to tourists, thus enhancing their visit; and iv) provided local economic benefits through lucrative part-time employment, thereby allowing local people to participate more fully in the tourism system. Orams (1996) developed a conceptual model which clarifies the range of wildlife interaction opportunities (spectrum of tourist-wildlife interaction opportunities). Within this spectrum are both situations where tourists view captive wildlife in facilities such as zoos and circuses and ones where tourists interact with wildlife in the wild (in national parks or the marine environment) and the management regimes (physical, regulatory, economic and educational) used. The model establishes a basis upon which the effectiveness of education can be tested.

Assessing the impact of ecotourism activities on marine natural resources requires the development and application of established and standardized impact assessment protocols and techniques. Although these may be readily available after years of research and experimentation, as in the case of diving impacts on coral reefs, identifying indicators that reflect environmental conditions relevant to management practices has proven difficult. Farrell and Marion (2001) applied rapid visitor impact assessment methods through managers' interviews and trail and recreation site condition assessments at eight protected areas in Belize and Costa Rica. Dinsdalle and Harriott (2004) found that the number of overturned colonies was the single most useful indicator of coral reef condition associated with anchoring intensities by applying an indicator selection framework, which is transparent, cost efficient, and readily transferable to other types of human activities and management strategies. Theberge and Dearden (2006) proposed that ecotourism operators could be used as non-specialist volunteers for data collection for long-term, broad geographic studies on recreational impacts on wildlife. Lloret et al. (2006) used GIS-mediated mapping of both benthic community distribution and vulnerability to scuba diving to design alternative diving routes for the Cabo de Palos-Islas Hormigas Marine Reserve, off the Mediterranean coast of south-east Spain.

Gradually, methods and techniques from other scientific disciplines are being employed to assist management of ecotourism activities. Hakem et al. (2005) offered an analytical assessment of cultural and nature-based tourism trends in Kuwait using environmental indicators within a Driving-Pressure-State-Impact-Response (DPSIR) model (EEA 1999) in order to evaluate sustainability. Hoyt (2005) used cost-benefit analysis (CBA) to evaluate, guide the improvement of the quality, and assure sustainability of whale watching and ecotourism, and help make it sustainable. CBA is usually done by evaluating all the various benefits, values, services, and costs of a particular resource and then comparing with other options for use and non-use in the same or other areas. Kaur (2005) conducted a gap analysis on the ecotourism guidelines developed for the marine parks of Malaysia. The study proposed stricter enforcement of regulations, restriction of the total number of visitors to the park, control of the number of dive groups, restriction of large groups of visitors to certain areas of the parks, increase in the frequency of patrols around the marine park area, increase in the number of staff or officers on duty, putting up more boards sign on dos and don'ts, designation of zones for various recreational activities and enforcement of stricter controls on development projects within the marine parks. The same study advised for greater emphasis on the enforcement of regulations designed to protect marine resources and marine biodiversity and to manage shoreline development and for best ecotourism practices from selected countries, such as Australia, Costa Rica and Cuba, be applied in Malaysia.

E. THE FUTURE OF ECOTOURISM IN MARINE PROTECTED AREAS

Given the momentum of ecotourism and the primarily fragmented, case studies-nature of scientific literature on ecotourism development in MPAs, we need a world-wide, comprehensive assessment of the level, nature, and intensity of ecotourism infiltration to MPAs. An initiative by The International Ecotourism Society (TIES) and available regional MPAs communication networks (e.g. MEDPAN, CAMPAMN) could foster the development and implementation of a pertinent evaluation framework. Information on: i) how many MPAs support ecotourism activities/projects, ii) what types of ecotourism activities/projects are promoted within MPAs, iii) to what extend MPAs rely on ecotourism activities/projects, and iv) to what degree ecotourism activities/projects within MPAs integrate the principles of being environmentally benign, socio-culturally empowering, and economically viable would greatly benefit the ecotourism industry, MPA management, and related (development and conservation) policy initiatives.

Ecotourism incentive, development and practice are expected to differ depending primarily on the socio-economic status of the countries with MPAs. Developed countries with established, strong economic structures and available armor of management competencies are expected to readily assimilate ecotourism in MPAs within their national strategies for development. Less developed countries will need to address weaknesses in their institutional or/and community capacity before ecotourism in MPAs delivers balanced benefits to society, economy and conservation. The least developed countries will need to rely on external support for considerable amount of time before ecotourism in MPAs develop into a sustainable alternative of marine resource use.

In any case, self-regulation through education, best practice guidelines, and update on developments along with safeguard of its distinctiveness from other types of tourism are the responsibility and best interest of ecotourism industry in order to be viable within MPAs. On the other hand, enforcement of regulations, monitoring of its effects and adaptive management of its operation within MPAs are the responsibility and best interest of MPAs management authorities in order MPAs to function as an effective environmental management tool. Ecotourism provides contemporary, attractive alternatives to marine resource use within MPAs. It changes the way people depend on marine resources within MPAs, not their dependence itself, until it is replaced by a next attractive alternative in the future.

REFERENCES

Acott, T. G., Trobe, H. L. & Howard, S. (1998). An evaluation of deep ecotourism and shallow ecotourism. *Journal of Sustainable Tourism, 6(3)*, 238-253.

Adams, C. E., Thomas, J. K., Lin, P. & Weiser, B. (1989). Promoting wildlife education through exhibits. *Journal of Research in Science Teaching*, *26*, 133-139.

Addessi, L. (1994). Human disturbance and long-term changes on a rocky intertidal community. *Ecological Applications*, *4(4)*, 786-797.

Agardy, T. (1993). Accommodating ecotourism in multiple use planning of coastal and marine protected areas. *Ocean and Coastal Management*, *20*, 219-239.

Agardy, T. (2000). Information needs for marine protected areas: scientific and societal. *Bulletin of Marine Science*, *66(3)*, 875-888.

Agardy, T., Bridgewater, P., Crosby, M. P., Day, J., Dayton, P. K., Kenchington, R., Laffoley, D., McConney, P., Murray, P. A., Parks, J. E. & Peau, L. (2003). Dangerous targets? Unresolved issues and ideological clashes around marine protected areas. *Aquatic Conservation: Marine and Freshwater Ecosystems*, *13(4)*, 353-367.

Alder, J. (1996). Have tropical marine protected areas worked? An initial analysis of their success. *Coastal Management*, *24*, 97-114.

Allison, W. R. (1996). Snorkeler damage to coral reefs in the Maldive Islands. *Coral Reefs*, *15*, 215-218.

Anak Agung Gde Raka Dalem (2002). Ecotourism in Indonesia. In: Hundloe T. (ed) Linking Green Productivity to Ecotourism: Experiences in the Asia-Pacific Region. Asian Productivity Organisation. *University of Queensland: Brisbane, Australia*, 85-97.

Andersson, J. E. C. & Ngazi, Z. (1995). Marine resource use and the establishment of a marine park: Mafia island, *Tanzania. Ambio*, *24(7-8)*, 475-481.

Appeldoorn, R. S. & Lindeman, K. C. (2003). A Caribbean-wide survey of no-take marine reserves: spatial coverage and attributes of effectiveness. *Gulf and Caribbean Research*, *14(2)*, 139-154.

Arianoutsou, M. (1988). Assessing the impacts of human activities on nesting of loggerhead sea turtles (*Caretta caretta*) on Zakynthos Island, Western Greece. *Environmental Conservation*, *15(4)*, 327-334.

Asafu-Adjaye, J. & Tapsuwan, S. (2008). A contingent valuation study of scuba diving benefits: Case study in Mu Ko Similan Marine National Park, Thailand. *Tourism Management*, *29*, 1122-1130.

Azueta, J. (1991). Unpublished 3rd year progress report to the World Wide Fund for Nature. *WWF, Washington*.

Backhurst, M. K. & Cole, R. G. (2000). Biological impacts of boating at Kawau Island, north-eastern New Zealand. *Journal of Environmental Management*, *60*, 239-251.

Badalamenti, F., Ramos, A. A., Voultsiadou, E., Sánchez Lizaso, J. L., D'Anna, G., Pipitone, C., Mas, J., Ruiz Fernandez, J. A., Whitmarsh, D. & Riggio, S. (2000) Cultural and socio-economic impact of Mediterranean marine protected areas. *Environmental Conservation*, *27(2)*, 110-125.

Barker, N. H. L. (2003). Ecological and socio-economic impacts of dive and snorkel tourism in St. Lucia, West Indies. Ph.D. Thesis, *University of York, UK*, 220.

Barker, N. H. L. & Roberts, C. M. (2004). Scuba diver behaviour and the management of diving impacts on coral reefs. *Biological Conservation*, *120*, 481-489.

Beeton, S. (1998). Ecotourism: A Practical Guide for Rural Communities. *Collingwood*: *Landlink*.

Bellan, G. L. & Bellan-Santini, D. R. (2001). A review of littoral tourism, sport and leisure activities: Consequences on marine flora and fauna. *Aquatic Conservation: Marine and Freshwater Ecosystems, 11(4)*, 325-333.

Blamey, R. K. (1997). Ecotourism: the search for an operational definition. *Journal of Sustainable Tourism, 5(2)*, 109-130.

Boyd, S. W. & Butler, R. W. (1996). Managing ecotourism: an opportunity spectrum approach. *Tourism Management, 17(8)*, 557-566.

Bogner, F. X. (1998). The influence of short-term outdoor ecology education on long-term variables of environmental protection. *The Journal of Environmental Education, 29*, 17-29.

Bradley, J. C., Waliczck, T. M. & Zajicek, J. M. (1999). Relationship between environmental knowledge and environmental attitude of high school students. *The Journal of Environmental Education, 30*, 19-21.

Brandon, K. (1993) Basic steps toward encouraging local participation in nature tourism projects. In: Lindberg K., Hawkins D. E. (eds) Ecotourism: A Guide for Local Planners. *The Ecotourism Society: North Bennington, Vermont*, 134-151.

Broad, S. & Weiler B. (1998). Captive animals and interpretation – a tale of two tiger exhibits. *The Journal of Tourism Studies, 9*, 14-27.

Brosnan, D. M. & Crumrine L. L. (1994). Effects of human trampling on marine rocky shore communities. *Journal of Experimental Marine Biology and Ecology, 177(1)*, 79-97.

Brown, K. (2002). Innovations for conservation and development. *Geographical Journal, 168(1)*, 6-17.

Brunckhorst, D. J. & Bridgwater, P. B. (1995). Marine bioregional planning: a strategic framework for identifying marine reserve networks, and planning sustainable use and management. Proceedings of the symposium on marine protected areas and sustainable fisheries conducted at the second international conference on science and the management of protected areas. Halifax, Nova Scotia, Canada.

Budowski, G. (1976). Tourism and Environmental Conservation: Conflict, Coexistence or Symbiosis? *Environmental Conservation, 3(1)*, 27-31.

Burke, L., Selig, L. & Spalding, M. (2002). Reefs at risk in Southeast Asia. *The World Resources Institute, Washington DC.*

Burton, F. (1998). Can ecotourism objectives be achieved? *Annals of Tourism Research, 6(3)*, 755-758.

Butler, R. W. & Boyd S. W. (1996). Managing ecotourism: an opportunity spectrum approach. *Tourism Management, 17(8)*, 557-566.

Byrnes, T. A. & Warnken, J. (2006). Greenhouse gas emissions from marine tours: A case study of Australian tour boat operators. *Journal of Sustainable Tourism, 14(3)*, 255-270.

Caldecott, J. (1996). Designing conservation projects. *Cambridge University Press: Cambridge.*

Caldicott, J. & Fuller, D. (2005). The concept and relevance of ecotourism to Indigenous economic and human development in remote Australian communities. Center for Enterprise Development and Research, Occasional Paper No. *6, Division of Business, Southern Cross University, Australia*, 18.

CANARI, (2001). Review of Jamaica's protected areas system and recommendations on the way forward. Caribbean Natural Resources Institute in collaboration with the Negril Area Environmental Protection Trust. *CANARI Technical Report No.*, 296.

Carrera, M. L., Favaro, E. G. P. & Souto, A. (2008). The response of marine tucuxis (*Sotalia fluviatilis*) towards tourist boats involves avoidance behaviour and a reduction in foraging. *Animal Welfare, 17(2)*, 117-123.

Carter, D. W. (2003). Protected areas in marine resource management: another look at the economics and research issues. *Ocean and Coastal Management, 46*, 439-456.

Cater, E. (1993). Ecotourism in the Third World: problems for sustainable tourism development. *Tourism Management, 14(2)*, 85-90.

Cater, E. (1994). Ecotourism in the third world: Problems and prospects for sustainability. In: E. Cater and G. Lowman (eds) Ecotourism: A Sustainable Option? (pp 69-86). *John Wiley and Sons: Chichester*.

Cater, E. (1997). Ecotourism or Ecocide? *People and the Planet, 6(4)*, 9-11.

Cater, C. & Cater, E. (1999). Marine ecotourism: new depths. *Geographical Paper No.*, 139.

Cater, C. & Cater, E. (2007). Marine Ecotourism: Between the devil and the deep sea blue. *CAB International: Oxfordshire*.

Ceballos-Lascurain, H. (1991). Tourism, ecotourism and protected areas. In: Kusler J. (ed) Ecotourism and resource conservation: a collection of papers. *US Army Corps of Engineers, Virginia*, 24-30.

Chape, S. (2005). Systematic assignment of protected area management categories: an opportunity for achieving a measurable framework. *Parks, 14(3)*, 51-62.

Chavez, D. J. (1993). Visitor perceptions of crowding and discrimination at two National Forests in southern California. Research Paper PSW-RP-216. Albany, CA: Pacific Southwest Research Station, Forest Service, U.S. *Department of Agriculture*, 17.

Che, D. (2006). Developing ecotourism in FirstWorld, resource-dependent areas. *Geoforum, 37*, 212-226.

Christie, P. (2005). Observed and perceived environmental impacts of marine protected areas in two Southeast Asia sites. *Ocean and Coastal Management, 48*, 252-270.

Christie, P. & White, A. T. (2007). Best practices for improved governance of coral reef marine protected areas. *Coral Reefs, 26(4)*, 1047-1056.

Clifton, J. (2004). Evaluating contrasting approaches to marine ecotourism: "Dive tourism" and "Research tourism" in the Wakatobi Marine National Park, Indonesia. In: Boissevain J., Selwyn, T. (eds) Contesting the foreshore. Tourism, society and politics on the coast. Center for Maritime Research. *Amsterdam University Press: Amsterdam*, 151-168.

Constantini, M., Spoto, M. & Cid, G. (2003). Miramare A demonstration case. Application of the WCPA-Marine/WWF guidebook on evaluating effective management in MPAs. WCPA-Marine, *WWF International and NOAA-National Ocean Service*, 17.

Cooper, C., Fletcher, J., Gilbert, D., Shepherd, R. & Wanhill, S. (1998). Tourism, principles and practice. *Addison Wesley Longman: Harlow*, UK.

Corkeron, P. J. (2004). Whale watching, iconography, and marine conservation. *Conservation Biology, 18(3)*, 847-849.

Cottrell, S. P. & Graefe, A. R. (1997). Testing a Conceptual Framework of Responsible Environmental Behavior. *The Journal of Environmental Education, 29*, 17-27.

Craig-Smith, S. J., Tapper, R. & Font, X. (2006). The coastal and marine environment. In: Gössling, S., Hall, M. C. (eds) Tourism and global environmental change. Ecological, social, economic and political interrelationships. *Routledge: Oxon, UK*, 107-127

Creed, J. C. & Amado, F. (1999). Disturbance and recovery of the macroflora of a seagrass (*Halodule wrightii* Ascherson) meadow in the Abrolhos Marine National Park, Brazil: an experimental evaluation of anchor damage. *Journal of Experimental Marine Biology and Ecology, 235*, 285-306.

Cruz-Trinidad, A., Geronimo, R. C. & Aliño, P. M. (2009). Development trajectories and impacts on coral reef use in Lingayen Gulf, Philippines. *Ocean and Coastal Management, 52*, 173-180.

Da Silva, P. P. (2004). From common property to co-management: lessons from Brazil's maritime extractive reserve. *Marine Policy, 28*, 419-428.

Davenport, J. & Davenport, J. L. (2006). The impact of tourism and personal leisure transport on coastal environments: A review. *Estuarine Coastal and Shelf Science, 67*, 280-292.

Dawes, C. J., Andorfer, J., Rose, C., Uranowski, C. & Ehringer, N. (1997) Regrowth of the seagrass *Thalassia testudinum* into propeller scars. *Aquatic Botany, 59(1/2)*, 139-155.

De Haas, H. C. (2002). Sustainability of Small-Scale Ecotourism: The Case of Niue, South Pacific. *Current Issues in Tourism, 5(3/4)*, 319-337

Depondt, F. & Green, E. (2006). Diving user fees and the financial sustainability of marine protected areas: Opportunities and impediments. *Ocean and Coastal Management, 49*, 188-202.

Diedrich, A. (2007). The impacts of tourism on coral reef conservation awareness and support in coastal communities in Belize. *Coral Reefs, 26*, 985-996.

Diamantis, D. (1999). The concept of ecotourism: Evolution and trends. *Current Issues in Tourism, 2 (2/3)*, 93-122.

Dikou, A., Ackerman, C., Banks, C., Dempsey, A., Fox, M., Gins, M., Hester, P., Parnes, A., Roach, S., Rohde, J., Spital, C., Tapleshay, M. & Thomas, L. (2009). Ecological Assessment to Detect Imminent Change, Admiral Cockburn Land and Sea National Park, Turks and Caicos Islands. *Marine Ecology (In Press)*.

Dinsdale, E. A. & Harriott, V. J. (2004). Assessing Anchor Damage on Coral Reefs: A Case Study in Selection of Environmental Indicators. *Environmental Management, 33(1)*, 126-139.

Dixon, J. A. (1993). Meeting ecological and economic goals: marine parks in the Caribbean. *Ambio, 22(2/3)*, 117-125.

Dixon, J. A., Scura, L. F. & van't Hof, T. (1993). Meeting ecological and economic goals: marine parks in the Caribbean. *Ambio, 22(2/3)*, 117-125.

Drake, S. P. (1991). Local participation in ecotourism projects. In: Whelan T. (ed) NatureTourism: Managing for the Environment. *Washington DC: Island Press*, 132-163.

Duffus, D. A. & Dearden, P. (1990). Non-consumptive wildlife-oriented recreation: a conceptual framework. *Biological Conservation, 53*, 213-231.

Eckrich, C. E. & Holmquist, J. G. (2000). Trampling in a seagrass assemblage: direct effects, response of associated fauna, and the role of substrate characteristics. *Marine Ecology Progress Series, 201*, 199-209.

European Environment Agency (EEA). (1999). Environmental indicators: typology and overview. In: Smeets E., Weterings R. (eds) *Technical report No., 25*, 19.

Food and Agriculture Organization (FAO). (1992). Integrated Management of Coastal Zones. Fisheries *Technical Paper No, 327*.

Fangman, M. S. & Rittmaster, K. A. (1993) Effects of human usage on the temporal distribution of loggerhead nesting activities. In: Schroeder, B. E., Witherington, B. E. (eds) Proceedings of the 13th Annual Sea Turtle Biology and Conservation. NOAA Tech. Memo. Miami: NMFS-SEFC-341.

Farrell, T. A. & Marion, J. L. (2001). Identifying and assessing ecotourism visitor impacts at eight protected areas in Costa Rica and Belize. *Environmental Conservation, 28(3)*, 215-225.

Farrow, S. (1996). Marine protected areas emerging economics. *Marine Policy, 20(6)*, 439-446.

Fennell, D. A. (2001). A content analysis of ecotourism definitions. *Current Issues in Tourism, 4(5)*, 403-421.

Fennell, D. A. (2003). Ecotourism: An Introduction. *Routledge: New York*.

Fernandes, L. (1995). Integrating economic, environmental and social issues in an evaluation of Saba Marine Park, Netherlands Antilles, Caribbean Sea. Report to Saba Marine Park, Saba Conservation Foundation and Saba Executive Council.

Fishbein, M. & Manfredo, M. J. (1992). A theory of behaviour change. In: Manfredo M.J. (ed) Influencing Human Behaviour. Theory and Applications in Recreation and Tourism Natural Resources. *Sagamore Publishing: Champaign IL*, 29-50.

Francour, P. (1994). Impact du mouillage sur l'herbier à *Posidonia oceanica* dans le baie de Port-Cros (Méditerranée nord-occidentale, France). *GIS Posidonie Publications, Marseille, 51*.

Francour, P., Ganteaume, A. & Poulain, M. (1999). Effects of boat anchoring in *Posidonia oceanica* seagrass beds in the Port-Cros National Park (north-western Mediterranean Sea). *Aquatic Conservation, 9*, 391-400.

Fung, T., Wong, F. K. K. (2007). Ecotourism planning using multiple criteria evaluation with GIS. *Geocarto International, 22(2)*, 87-105.

Garcìa-Charton, J. A., Bayle, J. T., Sànchez-Lizaso, J. L., Chiesa, P., Llauradò, F., Pérez, C. & Djian, H. (1993). Respuesta de la pradera de *Posidonia oceanica* y su ictiofauna al anclaje de embarcaciones en el parquet Nacional de Port-Cros, Francia. *Publ. Espec. Inst. Esp. Oceanogr., 11*, 423-430.

Garrod, B. (2003). Local Participation in the Planning and Management of Ecotourism: A Revised Model Approach. *Journal of Ecotourism, 2(1)*, 33-53.

Garrod, B. & Wilson, J. C. (2004). Nature on the Edge? Marine Ecotourism in Peripheral Coastal Areas. *Journal of Sustainable Tourism, 12(2)*, 95-120.

Garrod, B., Wilson, J. & Bruce, D. (2001). Planning for Marine Ecotourism in the EU Atlantic Area: Good Practice Guidance. META- Project, c/o Centre for Research, Innovation and Industry (CRII), University of the West of England, Bristol, UK.

Great Barrier Reef Marine Park Authority (GBRMPA) (2003). Zoning. Great Barrier Reef Marine Park Authority, Townsville, QLD, Australia. Available from: http://www.gbrmpa.gov.au/corp_site/management/zoning.html.

Geoghegan, T., Smith, A. H. & Thacker, K. (2001). Characterization of Caribbean marine protected areas: an analysis of ecological, organisational and socio-economic factors. *CANARI Technical Report No.*, 287.

Geoghegan, T. & Renard, Y. (2002). Beyond community involvement: lessons from the insular Caribbean. *Parks, 12(2)*, 16-27.

GESAMP, (2001). Protecting the oceans from land-based activities: land-based sources and activities affecting the quality and uses of the marine, coastal and associated freshwater environment. Rep. Stud. No. 71. Available from: http://www.gesamp.imo.org/no71/index. htm

Gibbons, J. H. (1992). Science and Technology Issues in Coastal Ecotourism. U.S. Congress, Office of Technology Assessment, OTA-BP-F-86. *U.S. Government Printing Office: Washington DC.*

Goodwin, H. (1996). In pursuit of ecotourism. *Biodiversity and Conservation, 5,* 277-291.

Goodwin H. (2002). Local Community Involvement in Tourism around National Parks: Opportunities and Constraints. *Current Issues in Tourism, 5(3/4),* 338-360.

Gössling, S. (2001). The consequences of tourism for sustainable water use on a tropical island: Zanzibar, Tanzania. *Journal of Environmental Management, 61(2),* 179-191.

Hakem, S., Abahussain, A. A. & Abdo, A. S. (2005). Ecotourism in the state of Kuwait impact analysis and sustainable strategy. *Journal of the Social Sciences, 33(2),* 291-312.

Hall, C. M. (2001). Trends in Ocean and Coastal Tourism: the end of the last frontier? *Ocean and Coastal Management, 44(9/10),* 601-618.

Halpenny, E. A. (2001). Islands and Coasts In: Weaver D. B. (ed) The Encyclopaedia of Ecotourism. *CABI Publishing: Wallingford,* 235-250.

Halpenny, E. A. (2002). Marine Ecotourism. Impacts, International Guidelines and Best Practice. Case Studies. *The Ecotourism Society, North Bennington, Vermont.*

Hammitt, W. & Cole, D. (1998). Wildland recreation: Ecology and management. *John Wiley and Sons: New York.*

Harriott, V. J., Davis, D. & Banks, S. A. (1997). Recreational diving and its impact in marine protected areas in Eastern Australia. *Ambio, 26,* 173-179.

Hassan, R., Scholes, R., Ash, N. (eds) (2005). Millennium ecosystem assessment. *Island Press: Washington DC.* Available from: http://www.millenniumassessment.org/en/Condition.aspx

Hawkins, J. P. & Roberts, C. M. (1992). Effects of recreational SCUBA diving on fore-reef slope communities of coral reefs. *Biological Conservation, 62,* 171-178.

Hawkins, J. P. & Roberts, C. M. (1994). The growth of coastal tourism in the Red Sea: Present and future effects on coral reefs. *Ambio, 23(8),* 503-508.

Hawkins, J. P. & Roberts, C. M. (1997). Estimating the carrying capacity of coral reefs for Scuba diving. *Proceedings of the 8th International Coral Reef Symposium, Panama, 2,* 1923-1926.

Hawkins, J. P., Roberts, C. M., van't Hof, T., de Meyer, K., Tratalos, J. & Aldam, C. (1999). Effects of recreational scuba diving on Caribbean coral reefs and fish communities. *Conservation Biology, 13,* 888-897.

Hawkins, J. P., Roberts, C. M., Kooistra, D., Buchan, K. & White, S. (2005). Sustainability of Scuba Diving Tourism on Coral Reefs of Saba. *Coastal Management, 33,* 373-387.

Higham, J. E. S. (1998). Tourists and albatrosses: the dynamics of tourism at the Northern Royal Albatross Colony, Taiaroa Head, New Zealand. *Tourism Management, 19(6),* 521-531.

Higham, J. & Carr, A. (2003). Defining Ecotourism in New Zealand: Differentiating Between the Defining Parameters within a National/Regional Context. *Journal of Ecotourism, 2(1),* 17-32.

Hillery, M., Nancarrow, B., Griffin, G. & Syme, G. (2001). Tourist Perception of Environmental Impact. *Annals of Tourism Research, 28(4),* 853-867.

Hjort, J. (1914). Fluctuations in the great fisheries of northern Europe. *Rapport P.-V. Reunion Conseil Permanent pour l'Exploration de la Mer, 20,* 1-227.

Hockey, P. A. R. (1987). The influence of coastal utilisation by man on the presumed extinction of the Canarian black Oystercatcher *Haematopus meadewaldoi* Bannerman. *Biological Conservation, 39(1)*, 49-62.

Hoover, S. L., King, D. A., Matter, W. J., Johnson, R. R., Ziebell, C. D., Patten, D. R., Folliot, P. F. & Hamre, R. H. (1985). A wilderness riparian environment: Visitor satisfaction, perceptions, reality, and management. Riparian Ecosystems and Their Management: Reconciling Conflicting Uses. USDA Forest Service General Technical Report: RM-120.

Honey, M. (1999). Treading lightly? Ecotourism's impact on the environment. *Environment, 41(5)*, 4-16.

Hoyt, E. (2001) Whale Watching 2001: Worldwide Tourism Numbers, Expenditures, and Expanding Socioeconomic Benefits. *International Fund for Animal Welfare, Yarmouth Port, MA.*

Hoyt, E. (2005). Sustainable ecotourism on Atlantic Islands, with special reference to whale watching, marine protected areas and sanctuaries for cetaceans. *Biology and Environment: Proceedings of the Royal Irish Academy, 105B (3),* 141-154.

Inglis, G. J., Johnson, V. I. & Ponte, F. (1999). Crowding Norms in Marine Settings: A Case Study of Snorkeling on the Great Barrier Reef. *Environmental Management, 24(3)*, 369-381.

International Whaling Commission (IWC). (2000). Report of the Scientific Committee, 52nd meeting of the International Whaling Commission, Adelaide.

Jacobson, S. K. & Robles, R. (1993). Ecotourism, sustainable development, and conservation education: Development of a tour guide training program in Tortuguero, Costa Rica. *Environmental Management, 16(6)*, 701-713.

Jacobson, S. K. & Lopez, A. F. (1994). Biological impacts of ecotourism: Tourists and marine turtles of Tortuguero National Park, Costa Rica. *Wildlife Society Bulletin, 22*, 414-419.

Jacobson, S. K. & Marynowski, S. B. (1998). New models for ecotourism management interpretation: target audiences on military lands. *Journal of Interpretation Research, 3*, 1-20.

Jameson, S. C., Ammar, M. S. A., Saadalla, E., Mostafa, H. M., Riegl, B. (1999). A coral damage index and its application to diving sites in the Egyptian Red Sea. *Coral Reefs, 18(4)*, 333-339.

Jameson, S. C., Tupper, M. H. & Ridley, J. M. (2002). The three screen doors: can marine protected areas be effective? *Marine Pollution Bulletin, 44(11)*, 1177-1183.

Johnson, S. A., Bjorndal, K. A. & Bolten, A. B. (1996). Effects of organized turtle watches on loggerhead (*Caretta caretta*) nesting behaviour and hatchling production in Florida. *Conservation Biology, 10(2)*, 570-577.

Kahoru, T. & Yap, S. Y. (2001). A baseline study on water resources of the tourist island, Pulau Perhentian, Peninsular Malaysia, from an ecological perspective. *The Environmentalist, 21(4)*, 273-286.

Kals, E., Schumacher, D. & Montada, L. (1999). Emotional affinity toward nature as a motivational basis to protect nature. *Environment and Behavior, 31(2)*, 178-202.

Kaur, C. R. (2005). National Ecotourism Plan - Assessing Implementation of the Guidelines for Marine Parks. Maritime Institute of Malaysia, 38.

Kelleher, G. C., Bleakley, C. & Wells, S. A. (1995). Global representative system of marine protected areas. Vol. 1: Antarctic, Arctic, Mediterranean, Northwest Atlantic and Baltic. *The World Bank, Washington DC*.

Kenchington, R. (1993). Tourism in Coastal and Marine Environments-A Recreational Perspective. *Ocean and Coastal Management, 19*, 1-16.

Kenchington, R. & Kelleher, G. (1995). Making a management plan. In: Gubbay S. (ed) Marine protected areas: Principles and techniques for management. *Chapman and Hall: London*, 85-118.

Kerlinger, P. & Brett, J. (1995). Hawk Mountain Sanctuary: A case study of birder visitation and birding economics. In: Knight R.L., Gutzwiller K.J. (eds) Wildlife and Recreationists: Coexistence Through Management and Research. *Island Press: Washington DC*, 271-280.

Khan, M. M. (1997). Tourism Development and Dependency Theory: Mass Tourism vs. Ecotourism. *Annals of Tourism Research, 24(4)*, 988-991.

Kimmel, J. R. (1999). Ecotourism as environmental learning. *The Journal of Environmental Education, 30*, 40-44.

Kiss, A. (2004). Is community-based ecotourism a good use of biodiversity conservation funds? *Trends in Ecology and Evolution, 19(5)*, 232-237.

Laarman, J. G. & Durst, P. B. (1993). Nature tourism as a tool for economic development and conservation of natural resources. In: Nenon J., Durst P. (eds) Nature tourism in Asia: Opportunities and Constraints for Conservation and Economic Development. *United States Forest Service, Washington DC*, 1-19.

Laist, D. W., Knowlton, A. R., Mead, J. G., Collet, A. S. & Podesta, M. (2001). Collisions between ships and whales. *Marine Mammal Science, 17(1)*, 35-75.

Lawton, L. (2001). Ecotourism in public protected areas. In: Weaver, D.B. (ed) The Encyclopaedia of Ecotourism. *CABI Publishing: Wallingford, UK*, 287-302.

Leujak, W. & Ormond, R. F. G. (2007). Visitor Perceptions and the Shifting Social Carrying Capacity of South Sinai's Coral Reefs. *Environmental Management, 39*, 472-489.

Leverington, F., Hockings, M. & Lemos Costa, K. (2008). Management effectiveness evaluation in protected areas -a global study. *The University of Queensland, Gatton, IUCN WCPA, TNC, WWF, Australia*.

Liddle, M. J. (1991). Recreation ecology: effects of trampling on plants and corals. *Trends in Ecology and Evolution, 6(1)*, 13-17.

Liddle, M. J. & Kay, A. M. (1987). Resistance, survival and recovery of trampled corals on the Great Barrier Reef. *Biological Conservation, 2*, 1-18.

Lindberg, K. (1996). Ecotourism: a critical overview. *Pacific Tourism Review, 1*, 65-79.

Lindberg, K. (2001). Economic Impacts. In: Weaver, D. B. (ed) The Encyclopaedia of Ecotourism. *CABI Publishing: Wallingford, UK*, 363-378.

Lindberg, K. & McKercher, B. (1997). Ecotourism: A Critical Overview. *Pacific Tourism Review, 1*, 65-79.

Lindberg, K., Enriquez, J. & Sproule, K. (1996). Ecotourism Questioned: Case Studies from Belize. *Annals of Tourism Research, 23(3)*, 543-562.

Lloret, J. & Riera, V. (2008). Evolution of a Mediterranean Coastal Zone: Human Impacts on the Marine Environment of Cape Creus. *Environmental Management, 42*, 977-988.

Lloret, J., Marína, A., Marín-Guirao, L. & Carreño, M. F. (2006). An alternative approach for managing scuba diving in small marine protected areas. *Aquatic Conservation of Marine and Freshwater Ecosystems, 16,* 579-591.

Lloret, J., Zaragoza, N., Caballero, D. & Riera, V. (2008a). Impacts of recreational boating on the marine environment of Cap de Creus (Mediterranean Sea). *Ocean and Coastal Management, 51,* 749-754.

Lloret, J., Zaragoza, N., Caballero, D., Font, T., Casadevall, M. & Riera, V. (2008b). Spearfishing pressure on fish communities in rocky coastal habitats in a Mediterranean marine protected area. *Fisheries Research, 94,* 84-91.

López-Espinosa, De. & Los Monteros, R. (2002). Evaluating ecotourism in natural protected areas of La Paz Bay, Baja California Sur, México: ecotourism or nature-based tourism? *Biodiversity and Conservation, 11,* 1539-1550.

Lovasz, T., Croft, D. B. & Banks P. (2008). Establishing tourism guidelines for viewing Australian Sea Lions Neophoca cinerea at Seal Bay Conservation Park, South Australia. *Australian Zoologist, 34,* 225-232.

Luck, G. W. (2005). An introduction to ecological thresholds. *Biological Conservation, 124,* 299-300.

Lück, M. & Higham, J. E. S. (2003). Marine ecotourism in the New Zealand urban context: Emerging trends, new challenges and developing opportunities. Urban Tourism – Mapping the Future. Travel and Tourism Research Association (Europe) Conference, Glasgow, United Kingdom, 24-27 September, 2003, pp 134-145.

Luna, B., Pérez, C. V. & Sánchez-Lizaso, J. L. (2009). Benthic impacts of recreational divers in a mediterranean marine protected area. *ICES Journal of Marine Science, 66 (3),* 517-523.

Lusseau, D. & Higham, J. E. S. (2004). Managing the impacts of dolphin-based tourism through the definition of critical habitats: the case of bottlenose dolphins (*Tursiops* spp.) in Doubtful Sound. *New Zealand Tourism Management, 25,* 657-667.

Lutcavage, M. E., Plotkin, P., Witherington, B. & Lutz, P. L. (1997). Human impacts on sea turtle survival. In: Lutz, P. L., Musick, J. A. (eds) The Biology of Sea Turtles. *CRC Press: Boca Raton FL,* 387-404.

Luttinger, N. (1997). Community-based coral reef conservation in the Bay Islands of Honduras. *Ocean and Coastal Management, 36,* 11-22.

Lynn, N. A., Brown, R. D. (2003). Effects of recreational use impacts on hiking experiences in natural areas. *Landscape and Urban Planning, 64(1/2),* 77-87.

Manning, R. E. (1985a). Crowding norms in backcountry settings: A review and synthesis. *Journal of Leisure Research, 17,* 75-89.

Manning, R. E. (1986). Density and crowding in wilderness: search and research for satisfaction. *Proceedings of the National Wilderness Research Conference, Fort Collins,* 440-448.

Maragos, J. E. (1993). Impact of coastal construction on coral reefs in the U.S.-affiliated Pacific Islands. *Coastal Management, 21,* 235-269.

Martin, B. S. & Uysal, M. (1990). An examination of the relationship between carrying capacity and the tourism lifecycle: Management and policy implications. *Journal of Environmental Management, 31(4),* 327-333.

Mascia, M. B. (1999). Governance of marine protected areas in the wider Caribbean: preliminary results of an international mail survey. *Coastal Management, 27(4),* 391-402.

Matthews, A. (1993). Ecotourism: Fostering Australia's Biggest Growth Industry. *Australian Environment Review*, *8(5)*, 10-11.

McClanahan, T. R. (1999). Is there a future for coral reef parks in poor tropical countries? *Coral Reefs*, *18*, 321-325.

McCool, S. & Cole, D. (1998). Proceedings-limits of acceptable change and related planning processes: Progress and future directions. USDA Forest Service General Technical Report RMRS-GTR, Missoula MT.

McClung, M. R., Seddon, P. J., Massaro, M., Setiawan, A. N. (2004). Nature-based tourism impacts on yellow-eyed penguins Megadyptes antipodes: Does unregulated visitor access affect fledging weight and juvenile survival? *Biological Conservation*, *119(2)*, 279-285

McCrone, A. (2001). Visitor impacts on marine protected areas in New Zealand. *Science for Conservation*, *173*, 5-61.

McFarlane, R. W. (1963) Disorientation of loggerhead hatchlings by artificial road lighting. *Copeia*, *2*, 153-162.

McFarlane, B. L. (1994). Specialization and motivations of birdwatchers. *Wildlife Society Bulletin*, *22(3)*, 361-370.

McField, M. (2000). Evaluation of management effectiveness, Belize marine protected areas system. Report to the Coastal Zone Management Authority and Institute, Belize.

Medio, D., Ormond, R. F. G. & Pearson, M. (1997). Effect of briefings on rates of damage to corals by scuba divers. *Biological Conservation*, *79*, 91-95.

Meesters, E. H., Noordeloos, M. & Bak, R. P. M. (1994). Damage and regeneration: links to growth in the reef-building coral *Montastrea annularis*. *Marine Ecology Progress Series*, *112*, 119-128.

Meyer, C. G., Holland, K. N. (2009). Spatial dynamics and substrate impacts of recreational snorkelers and SCUBA divers in Hawaiian Marine Protected Areas. *Journal of Coastal Conservation* (In press).

Milazzo, M., Chemello, R., Badalamenti, F., Camarda, R. & Riggio, S. (2002). The impact of human recreational activities in marine protected areas: what lessons should be learned in the Mediterranean Sea? *Marine Ecology*, *23(S1)*, 280-290.

Miller, M. L. (1993). The Rise of Coastal and Marine Tourism. *Ocean and Coastal Management*, *20*, 181-199.

Miller, M. L. & Auyong, J. (1991). Coastal Zone Tourism: A Potent Force Affecting Environment and Society. *Marine Policy*, *15(2)*, 75-99.

Murphy, T. E. (1985). Telemetric monitoring of nesting loggerhead sea turtles subjected to disturbance on the beach. Fifth Annual Workshop on Sea Turtle Biology and Conservation, Waverly, Georgia.

Mundet, L. & Ribera, L. (2001). Characteristics of divers at a Spanish resort. *Tourism Management*, *22*, 501-510.

Murray, G. D. (2005). Multifaceted measures of success in two Mexican marine protected areas. *Society and Natural Resources*, *18*, 889-905.

Musa, G. (2002). Sipadan: a SCUBA-diving paradise: an analysis of tourism impact, diver satisfaction and tourism management. *Tourism Geographies*, *4(2)*, 195-209.

Norse, E. A. (ed) (1993). Global marine biological diversity: a strategy for building conservation into decision making. *Island Press: Washington DC*.

Ogden, J. C. (1997). Marine managers look upstream for connections. *Science*, *278*, 1414-1415.

Oikonomou, Z. S. & Dikou, A. (2008). Integrating Conservation and Development at the National Marine Park of Alonissos, Northern Sporades, Greece: Perception and Practice. *Environmental Management, 42(5)*, 847-866.

Okello, M. M., Kiringe, J. W. (2004). Threats to biodiversity and their implications in protected and adjacent dispersal areas of Kenya. *Journal of Sustainable Tourism, 12(1)*, 55-69.

Oracion, E. G., Miller, M. L. & Christie, P. (2005). Marine protected areas for whom? Fisheries, tourism and solidarity in a Philippine community. *Ocean and Coastal Management, 48,* 393-410.

Orams, M. B. (1996). A conceptual model of tourist-wildlife interaction: The case for education as a management strategy. *Australian Geographer, 27(1),* 39-51.

Orams, M. B. (1999). Marine tourism: development, impacts and management. *Routledge Press: London.*

Orams, M. B. (2002). Feeding wildlife as a tourism attraction: a review of issues and impacts. *Tourism Management, 23,* 281-293.

Orams, M. B. & Hill, G. J. E. (1998). Controlling the ecotourist in a wild dolphin feeding program: is education the answer? *The Journal of Environmental Education, 9,* 33-38.

O'Reily, A. M. (1986). Tourism Carrying Capacity. Concepts and Issues. *Tourism Management, 7(4),* 254-258.

Ostrom, E. (1990). Governing the commons the evolution of institutions for collective actions. *Cambridge University Press: New York.*

Parsons, E. C. M., Woods-Ballard, A. (2003). Acceptance of voluntary whale watching codes of conduct in West Scotland: The effectiveness of governmental versus industry-led guidelines. *Current Issues in Tourism, 6(2),* 172-182.

Pendleton, L. (1994). Environmental quality and recreation demand in a Caribbean coral reef. *Coastal Management, 22,* 399-404.

Peters, E. C. (1997). Diseases of coral reef organisms. In: Birkeland C. (ed) Life and Death of Coral Reefs. *Chapman and Hall: New York,* 114-139.

Petrosillo, I., Zurlini, G., Corlianò, M. E., Zaccarelli, N. & Dadamo, M. (2007). Tourist perception of recreational environment and management in a marine protected area. *Landscape and Urban Planning, 79,* 29-37.

Pinn, E. H., Rodgers, M. (2005). The influence of visitors on intertidal biodiversity. Journal of the Marine *Biological Association of the United Kingdom, 85(2),* 263-268.

Plathong, S., Inglis, G. & Huber, M. (2000). Effects of self-guided snorkelling trails on corals in a tropical marine park. *Conservation Biology, 14(6),* 1821-1833.

Pollnac, R. B., Crawford, B. R. & Gorospe, M. L. G. (2002). Discovering factors that influence the success of community-based marine protected areas in the Visayas, Philippines. *Ocean and Coastal Management, 44,* 683-710.

Pomeroy, R. S. (1995). Community-based and co-management institutions for sustainable coastal fisheries management in Southeast Asia. *Ocean and Coastal Management, 27,* 143-162.

Pomeroy, R. S., Mascia, M. B. & Pollnac, R. B. (2006). Marine protected areas: the social dimension. FAO Expert Workshop on Marine Protected Areas and Fisheries Management: Review of issues and considerations, 12-14 June 2006. pp 149-181. Available from: ftp://ftp.fao.org/docrep/fao/010/a1061e/a1061e03.pdf

Poulain, M. (1996). Le mouillage forain dans le Parc National de Port-Cros. Impact sure le herbiers à *P.oceanica. GIS Posidonie Publications, Marseille*, 1-51.

Post, J. C. (1992). The economic feasibility and ecological sustainability of the Bonaire marine park. Paper prepared for the World Parks Congress Organized by the IUCN, Caracas, 10-21 February, 1992.

Post, J. C. (1994). The economic feasibility and ecological sustainability of the Bonaire Marine Park, Dutch Antilles. In: Munasinghe M. & McNeely J. (eds) Protected area economics and policy: linking conservation and sustainable development. *World Bank and World Conservation Union, Washington DC*, 333-338.

Povery, A. & Keough, M. J. (1991). Effects of trampling on plant and animal populations on rocky shores. *Oikos, 61*, 355-368.

Prior, M., Ormond, R., Hitchen, R. & Wormald, C. (1995). The impact of natural resources of activity tourism: a case study of diving in Egypt. *International Journal of Environmental Studies, 48*, 201-209.

Priskin, J. (2003). Tourist perceptions of degradation caused by coastal nature-based recreation. *Environmental Management, 32(2)*, 189-204.

Puppim de Oliveira, J. A. (2005). Tourism as a force for establishing protected areas: the case of Bahia, Brazil. *Journal of Sustainable Tourism, 13(1)*, 24-49.

Richter, C., Dawson, S. & Slooten, E. (2006). Impacts of commercial whale watching on male sperm whales at Kaikoura, New Zealand. *Marine Mammal Science, 22(1)*, 46-63.

Riegl, B. & Velimirov, B. (1991). How many damaged corals in Red Sea reef systems? A quantitative survey. *Hydrobiologia, 216/217*, 249-256.

Roberts, C. M. (1997). Connectivity and management of Caribbean coral reefs. *Science, 278(5342)*, 1454-1457.

Roberts, L. & Harriott, V. J. (1994). Recreational scuba diving and its potential for environmental impact in a marine reserve. In: Bellwood O., Choat H., Saxena N. (eds) Recent Advances in Marine Science and Technology. James Cook University of North Queensland, Townsville, Australia, 695-704.

Roberts, C. M., Bohnsack, J. A., Gell, F., Hawkins, J. P. & Goodridge, R. (2001). Effects of marine reserves on adjacent fisheries. *Science, 294*, 1920-1923.

Rodgers, K., Cox, E. & Newston C. (2003). Effects of mechanical fracturing and experimental trampling on Hawaiian corals. *Environmental Management, 31(3)*, 377-384.

Roman, G. S. J., Dearden, P. & Rollins, R. (2007). Application of Zoning and ''Limits of Acceptable Change'' to Manage Snorkelling Tourism. *Environmental Management, 39*, 819-830.

Rouphael, A. B. (1997). The temporal and spatial patterns of impact caused by SCUBA diving in coral reefs, and the human and site specific characteristics that influence these patterns. Ph.D. Thesis. James Cook University of North Queensland,Townsville, Australia.

Rouphael, T. & Inglis, G. (1995). The effects of qualified recreational SCUBA divers on coral reefs. CRC Reef Research Centre Technical Report No. 4, Townsville, Australia, 39.

Rouphael, A. B. & Inglis, G. J. (2001). Take only photographs and leave only footprints?: an experimental study of the impacts of underwater photographers on coral reef dive sites. *Biological Conservation, 100*, 281-287.

Rudd, M. A., Danylchuk, A. J., Gore, S. A. & Tupper, M. H. (2001). Are marine protected areas in the Turks and Caicos Islands ecologically and economically valuable? Proceedings of the International Conference on the Economics of Marine Protected Areas. *Fisheries Center Research Reports, 9(8)*, 198-211.

Russ, G. R. & Alcala, A. C. (1999). Management histories of Sumilon and Apo Marine Reserves, Philippines, and their influence on national marine resource policy. *Coral Reefs, 18*, 307-319.

Sala, E., Garabou, J. & Zabala, M. (1996). Effects of diver frequentation on Mediterranean sublittoral populations of the bryozoan *Pentapora fascialis. Marine Biology, 126(3)*, 451-459.

Salafsky, N., Cauley, H., Balachander, G., Cordes, B., Parks, J., Margoulis, C., Bhatt, S., Encarnacion, C., Russell, D. & Margoulis, R. (2001). A Systematic Test of an Enterprise Strategy for Community-Based Biodiversity Conservation. *Conservation Biology, 15(6)*, 1585-1595.

Salmon, M. & Witherington, B. E. (1995). Artificial lighting and seafinding by loggerhead hatchlings: Evidence for lunar modulation. *Copeia, 4*, 931-938.

Sanchirico, J. N., Cochran, K. A. & Emerson, P. M. (2002). Marine protected areas: economic and social implications. Discussion Paper. *Resources for the Future, Washington DC*, 2-26.

Sargent, F. J., Leary, T. J., Crewz, D. W. & Kruer, C. R. (1994). Scarring of Florida's Seagrasses: Assessment and Management. Florida Marine Research Institute Technical Report FMRI 1h/94, St. Petersburg, Florida, 62 pp.

Sasidharan, V., Sirakaya, E. & Kerstetter, D. (2002). Developing countries and tourism ecolabels. *Tourism Management, 23*, 161-174.

Scarpaci, C., Dayanthi, N. & Corkeron, P. J. (2003). Compliance with Regulations by "Swim-with-Dolphins" Operations in Port Phillip Bay, Victoria, Australia. *Environmental Management, 31(3)*, 342-347.

Schänzel, H. A. & McIntosh, A. (2000). An insight into the personal and emotive context of wildlife viewing at the Penguin Place, Otago Peninsula, New Zealand. *Journal of Sustainable Tourism, 8(1)*, 36-52.

Scheyvens, R. (1999). Ecotourism and the empowerment of local communities. *Tourism Management, 20*, 245-249.

Schiel, D. R. & Taylor, D. I. (1999). Effects of trampling on a rocky intertidal algal assemblage in southern New Zealand. *Journal of Experimental Marine Biology and Ecology, 235(2)*, 213-235.

Schleyer, M. H. & Tomalin, B. J. (2000). Damage on south African coral reefs and an assessment of their sustainable diving capacity using a fisheries approach. *Bulletin of Marine Science, 67(3)*, 1025-1042.

Schreyer, R. & Roggenbuck, J. W. (1978). The influence of experience expectations on crowding perceptions and social-psychological carrying capacities. *Leisure Sciences, 1(4)*, 373-394.

Scura, L. F. & Van't Hof. T. (1993). The ecology and economics of Bonaire Marine Park. The World Bank Environment Department, Land, Water and Natural Habitats Division, Divisional Paper No., 1993-44, 48.

Sekhar, N. U. (2003). Local peoples' attitudes towards conservation and wildlife tourism around Sariska Tiger Reserve, India. *Journal of Environmental Management, 69(4)*, 339-347.

Shackley, M. (1999). Tourism development and environmental protection in southern Sinai. *Tourism Management, 20*, 543-548.

Shafer, C. & Inglis, G. (2000). Influence of social, biophysical, and managerial conditions on tourism experiences within the Great Barrier Reef World Heritage Area. *Environmental Management, 26(1)*, 73-87.

Shafer, C. S., Inglis G. J., Johnson, V. Y. & Marshall, N. A. (1998). User experiences and perceived conditions of day use tourism on the Great Barrier Reef: Toward a limits of acceptable change approach to planning and management. Technical Report No. 21, CRC Reef Research Centre, Townsville, Australia, 73 pp.

Shepherd, N. (2002). How Ecotourism can go Wrong: The Cases of SeaCanoe and Siam Safari, Thailand. *Current Issues in Tourism, 5(3/4)*, 309-318.

Sheyvens, R. (1999). Ecotourism and the empowerment of local communities. *Tourism Management, 20*, 245-249.

Shivlani, M. J. P. & Suman, D. O. (2000). Dive Operator Use Patterns in the Designated No-Take Zones of the Florida Keys National Marine Sanctuary (FKNMS). *Environmental Management, 25(6)*, 647-659.

Sirakaya, E. & Uysal, M. (1998). Can sanctions and rewards explain conformance behaviour of tour operator's with ecotourism guidelines? *Journal of Sustainable Tourism, 5*, 322-332.

Sirakaya, E., Sasidharan, V. & Sonmez, S. (1999). Redefining ecotourism: The need for a supply-side view. *Journal of Travel Research, 38*, 168-172.

Snyder, J. M. & Stonehouse, B. (2007). Prospects for Polar Tourism. *Scott Polar Research Institute, Cambridge University, UK*, 336 pp.

Solomon, B. D., Corey-Luse, C. M. & Halvorsen, K. E. (2004). The Florida manatee and eco-tourism: toward a safe minimum standard. *Ecological Economics, 50*, 101- 115.

Sorice, M. G., Shafer, S. C. & Ditton, R. B. (2006). Managing Endangered Species Within the Use-Preservation Paradox: The Florida Manatee (*Trichechus manatus latirostris*) as a Tourism Attraction. *Environmental Management, 37(1)*, 69-83

Spoto, M. & Franzosini, C. (1991). The Natural Marine Reserve of Miramare (Trieste, Italy): Tourism and Environmental Education. *Ocean and Shoreline Management, 16*, 53-59.

Stankey, G. H., Cole, D. N., Lucas, R. C., Peterson, M. E. & Frissell, S. S. (1985). The Limits of Acceptable Change (LAC) System for Wilderness Planning. USDA Forest Service General Technical Report INT-176, *Intermounta*.

Stem, C. J., Lassoie, J. P., Lee, D. R., Deshler, D. D. & Schelhas, J. W. (2003). Community participation in ecotourism benefits: the link to conservation practices and perspectives. *Society and Natural Resources, 16*, 387-413.

Stensland, E. & Berggren, P. (2007). Behavioural changes in female Indo-Pacific bottlenose dolphins in response to boat-based tourism. *Marine Ecology Progress Series, 332*, 225-234.

Stern, M. J. (2008). The power of trust: toward a theory of local opposition to neighboring protected areas. *Society and Natural Resources, 21*, 859-875.

Talge, H. (1992). Impact of recreational divers on scleractinian corals at Looe Key, Florida. *Proceedings of the 7th International Coral Reef Symposium, Guam, 2*, 1077-1082.

Taylor, N. & Buckenham, B. (2003) Social impacts of marine reserves in New Zealand. *Science for Conservation, 217*, 5-51.

Teh, L. & Cabanban, A. S. (2007). Planning for sustainable tourism in southern Pulau Banggi: An assessment of biophysical conditions and their implications for future tourism development. *Journal of Environmental Management, 85*, 999-1008.

Tershy, B. R., Bourillón, L., Metzler, L. & Barnes, J. (1999). A survey of ecotourism on islands in Northwestern México. *Environmental Conservation*, 26:212-217.

Theberge, M. M. & Dearden, P. (2006). Detecting a decline in whale shark *Rhincodon typus* sightings in the Andaman Sea, Thailand, using ecotourist operator-collected data. *Oryx, 40(3)*, 337-342.

Tilmant, J. T. (1987). Impacts of recreational activities on coral reefs. In: Human Impacts on Coral Reefs: Facts and Recommendations. Salvat B. (ed) Antenne Museum EPHE, French Polynesia, pp 195-214.

Tilmant, J. T. & Schmahl, G. P. (1981). A comparative analysis of coral damage on recreationally used reefs within Biscayne National Park, Florida. *Proceedings of the 4th International Coral Reef Symposium, 1*, 187-192.

Tisdell, C. & Wilson, C. (2001). Wildlife-based tourism and increased support for nature conservation financially and otherwise: Evidence from sea turtle ecotourism at Mon Repos. *Tourism Economics, 7(3)*, 233-250.

Tisdell, C. & Wilson, C. (2002). Ecotourism for the survival of sea turtles and other wildlife. *Biodiversity and Conservation, 11*, 1521-1538.

Tisdell, C. & Wilson, C. (2005). Perceived impacts of ecotourism on environmental learning and conservation: turtle watching as a case study. *Environment, Development and Sustainability, 7*, 291-302.

Tongson, E. & Dygico, M. (2004). User Fee System for Marine Ecotourism: The Tubbataha Reef Experience. *Coastal Management, 32*, 17-23.

Tratalos, J. A. & Austin, T. J. (2001). Impacts of recreational scuba diving on coral communities of the Caribbean island of Grand Cayman. *Biological Conservation, 102*, 67-75.

United Nations (2002). World summit on sustainable development. General Assembly. Available from: http://www.earthsummit 2002.org/resolution.pdf

Valentine, P. S., Birtles, A., Curnock, M., Arnoldd, P. & Dunstane, A. (2004). Getting closer to whales-passenger expectations and experiences, and the management of swim with dwarf minke whale interactions in the Great Barrier Reef. *Tourism Management, 25*, 647-655.

Van't Hof, T. (1998). Social and economic impacts of marine protected areas: a study and analysis of selected cases in the Caribbean. *CANARI Technical Report No.*, 252.

Waayers, D., Newsome, D. & Lee, D. (2006). Research Note Observations of Non-Compliance Behaviour by Tourists to a Voluntary Code of Conduct: A Pilot Study of Turtle Tourism in the Exmouth Region, Western Australia. *Journal of Ecotourism, 5(3)*, 211-222.

Walker, D.I., Lukatelich, R. J., Bastyan, G. & McComb, A. J. (1989). Effect of boat moorings on seagrass beds near Perth, Western Australia. *Aquatic Botany, 36*, 69-77.

Wall, G. (1997). Is ecotourism sustainable? *Environmental Management, 21(4)*, 483-491.

Walpole, M. J. & Goodwin, H. J. (2000). Local economic impacts of dragon tourism in Indonesia. *Annals of Tourism Research, 27(3)*, 559-576.

Walters R.D.M. & Samways M.J. (2001). Sustainable dive ecotourism on a South African coral reef. *Biodiversity and Conservation, 10*, 2167-2179.

Weaver D.B. (2001). Ecotourism. *John Wiley and Sons: Australia.*

Weaver, D. B. (2002). Asian ecotourism: patterns and themes. *Tourism Geographies, 4(2),* 153-172.

Weaver, D. B. (2005). Comprehensive and minimalist dimensions of ecotourism. *Annals of Tourism Research, 32(2)*, 439-455.

Weiler, B. & Ham, S. H. (2001). Tour guides and interpretation. In: Weaver D.B. (ed) The Encyclopaedia of Ecotourism. *CABI publishing: Wallingford, UK*, 549-563.

Wells, S. & Hanna, N. (1992). The Greenpeace Book of Coral Reefs. *Blandford Press: London.*

White, A. T. & Rosales, R. (2001). Community-oriented tourism in the Philippines: role in economic development and conservation. In: Gössling S. (ed) Tourism and Development in Tropical Islands: Political Ecology Perspectives. *Edward Elgar Publishing Limited: Cheltenham, UK*, 237-262.

Wight, P. A. (1993). Ecotourism: ethics or eco-sell? *Journal of Travel Research, 31(3)*, 3-9.

Williams, I. D. & Pollunin, N. V. C. (2000). Differences between protected and unprotected reefs of the western Caribbean in attributes preferred by dive tourists. *Environmental Conservation, 27(4)*, 382-391.

Wilson, C. & Tisdell, C. (2001). Sea turtles as a non-consumptive tourism resource especially in Australia. *Tourism Management, 22*, 279-288.

Witherington, B. E. (1992). Behavioural responses of nesting sea turtles to artificial lighting. *Herpetologica, 48*, 31-39.

Woodland, D. D. & Hooper, J. N. A. (1977). The effect of human trampling on coral reefs. *Biological Conservation, 11*, 1-4.

Woods, B. (1998). Animals on display: principles for interpreting captive wildlife. *The Journal of Tourism studies, 9*, 28-39.

Yacob, M. R., Shuib, A., Mamat, M. F., Radam, A. (2007). Local economic benefits of ecotourism development in Malaysia: The case of Redang Island Marine Park. *International Journal of Economics and Management, 1(3)*, 365-386.

Yorio, P., Frere, E., Gandini, P. & Schiavini, A. (2001). Tourism and recreation at seabird breeding sites in Patagonia, Argentina: Current concerns and future prospects. *Bird Conservation International, 11(4)*, 231-245.

Young, E. (1999). Balancing development with conservation in small-scale fisheries? *Human Ecology, 27(4)*, 581-620.

Zabala, M. (1999). Efectes biològics de la création d'una reserva marina: el cas de les illes Medes Island. In: Estudis Cientn&xcs a les illes Medes Islands. Torroella de Montgrmn: Museu del Montgrmn i del Baix Ter. *Centre d'Estudis i Arxiu.*

Zakai, D. & Chadwick-Furman, N. E. (2002). Impacts of intensive recreational diving on reef corals at Eilat, Northern Red Sea. *Biological Conservation, 105*, 179-187.

In: Ecotourism: Management, Development and Impact   ISBN: 978-1-60876-724-3
Editors: A. Krause, E. Weir, pp. 43-87   © 2010 Nova Science Publishers, Inc.

Chapter 2

ECOTOURISM AND FLAGSHIP SPECIES: HOLISTIC APPROACHES AND HIGHER LEVELS OF CONNECTIVITY FOR ENDANGERED TROPICAL MUDFLATS AND COASTAL SWAMPS

G. Polgar[*1] *and A. Sasekumar*[2]

[1] University of Rome "La Sapienza", Rome, Italy
[2] University of Malaya, Kuala Lumpur, Malaysia

ABSTRACT

Tidal mudflats and coastal swamps are distributed along the sea-land ecological transition in humid tropical and subtropical regions. They are among the most endangered ecosystems on Earth, and have been intensively impacted both from water and land during the last 50 years. These transitional systems play a key-role in the homeostasis of inshore waters and whole watersheds, being natural buffers between the land and the sea, and establishing a network of connections between terrestrial and marine systems. Rational management has been frequently attempted; however, the vast majority of such initiatives proved to be largely unsustainable. Furthermore, since human impact is highest from land, frequently only a narrow coastal belt is managed, allowing only for the conservation of the most marine portion of these ecological transitions. More recently, zoning and multiple-use strategies offer promising perspectives of both survival and sustainable profit. It is here proposed that parks and rehabilitation projects are planned and designed to include wider portions of the ecological sea-land transition, incorporating subtidal, intertidal and supratidal systems, in a more holistic perspective. The economic and ecological value of these natural systems is still often misunderstood, and the obsolete misconception of unhealthy and unproductive wastelands still survives among politicians, economists and stakeholders, while political decision is almost invariably the main obstacle to ecosystem-based management. In this respect, ecotourism

---

* Dipartimento di Biologia Animale e dell'Uomo, University of Rome "La Sapienza", 00185 Rome, Italy; gianluca.polgar@uniroma1.it; gianluca.polgar@gmail.com; www.themudskipper.org

has a considerable potential, although particular care must be taken to correctly direct its goals and monitor its effects. Surprisingly, few if any flagship species have ever been proposed for these ecosystems, which might symbolize projects and raise public sympathies and awareness during environmental campaigns. The fauna and flora living in these habitats include several conspicuous and evolutionarily unique potential flagship species, which make an obligatory use of these systems during at least part of their life cycle. To facilitate the observation of these organisms in natural parks, different structures can be built, such as lower plank walks to improve the observation of relatively small macrofauna ("mud-watching"); observational bunkers to observe smaller animals at close distance; and boats and towers to observe larger animals in the distance. The focus on biodiversity promoted by flagship species and a correctly implemented ecotourism may elicit changes in the present political and institutional attitude, facilitating a more holistic perception of these ecosystems and of their immense ecological and socio-economic value.

INTRODUCTION

Tidal Mudflats and Tropical Coastal Swamps

Tidal mudflats are peculiar coastal morphodynamic deposits which can occur in a variety of sedimentological conditions, such as above barrier-enclosed lagoons, in enclosed sheltered bays, or, more typically, at the edge of estuaries (Healy 2005; Dyer et al. 2000). Mudflats are characterized by a high proportion of silt and clays resulting in typical cohesive and plastic properties, a low-gradient morphological surface and a characteristic stratigraphy (Healy 2005). Tidal mudflats occur in the whole tropical and subtropical belt, but the knowledge of their worldwide distribution is fragmentary (Deppe 2000); the first baseline studies on their sedimentology and hydrology were only made in the 1990s (Walker and McGraw 2005). The geomorphology of these systems makes them structurally homogeneous at a macroscopic scale, even if morpho-sedimentary zonation can occur, in association with different hydrodynamic forcing processes (Healy 2005). Mudflats are extremely dynamic ecosystems, being exposed to intense tidal currents and climatic events (Coleman et al. 1970). Organic material is imported from the riverine and marine domains, while in situ production (Healy 2005) sustains rich detritus-based food webs and dense macrofaunal associations (Dittmann 2002). This makes mudflats important feeding and nursery grounds for several species of aquatic and terrestrial vertebrates, such as staging, wintering and breeding areas for both migratory and non-migratory birds (Deppe 2000). Examples of wide tropical and subtropical tidal mudflats throughout the world (Deppe 2000; PEMSEA 1999) include those of Coppename Mouth in Suriname; Merja Zerga in Morocco; the Bijagos Archipelago in Guinea-Bissau; Kuwait Bay and the Khouran Straits, in the Persian Gulf; the flats of the Gulf of Khambhat in Gujarat, India; those along the west coast of Peninsular Malaysia; the extensive system of the Bo Hai and Korea Bays between China, North and South Korea; Roebuck Bay in Western Australia; Isahaya Bay in southern Japan; and the Firth of Thames, along the coasts of the North Island of New Zealand.

At higher levels, above high water neap tides, mudflats are often colonized by halophytic vascular plants. In tropical and subtropical conditions, such plant communities are dominated by mangroves (Tomlinson 1986). Mangrove ecosystems have a pantropical distribution, including two very different biogeographic regions: the Atlantic-Caribbean and East-Pacific region (ACEP) and the Indo-West Pacific region (IWP; Hogarth 2007). The largest and most diverse mangrove systems on Earth grow around large tropical deltas of the IWP, where high rainfall promotes the deposition of mud by fluvial discharge and run-off (riverine and basin mangroves: Hogarth 2007). Nonetheless, mangroves can occur in a wide range of environmental conditions, from tide or wave-dominated estuaries to carbonate platforms (Hogarth 2007; Woodroffe 1992) and on alluvial deposits formed by seasonal torrents in arid regions (wadis; de Lacerda 2002). Examples are the riverine and basin mangroves of the Sundarbans, Bangladesh; the mangroves of the Northern Territory, Australia, characterized by wide salt flats behind the back forest; the swamps of the Rio Negro-Rio San Sun in Central America; the wide formations of the Niger delta in Nigeria; and the stunted mangrove shrubs of the Persian Gulf. Mangroves are found in association with different coastal systems such as mudflats, seagrass beds and coral reefs (Duke and Wolanski 2001), and with terrestrial systems with very different rainfall regimes and geomorphological settings, such as freshwater swamps, saltmarshes, salt flats and sand dunes (e.g. Hogarth 2007).

The intertidal zone is a rich source of food and shelter for a variety of terrestrial and aquatic animals. Nonetheless, only a few species are adapted to such challenging environmental conditions, and live here during the whole tidal cycle (residents). Other species (transients) occupy the intertidal zone on a tidal basis, either during low tide (terrestrial visitors, e.g. birds, monkeys, wild pigs, terrestrial snakes; Noske 1995; Storr et al. 1986; Sasekumar 1980), or high tide (marine visitors, e.g. fishes; Blaber 2007; Gibson 1999). Some species live as intertidal residents or transients only during specific life stages (i.e. as adults, larvae or juveniles), or on a seasonal basis. The colonisation of intertidal deposits by mangroves drastically increases spatial heterogeneity, offering a variety of habitats to complex communities, structured both in time and space (Polgar and Crosa 2009; Nagelkerken et al. 2008). As a result, water and nutrient movements, indirect trophic relationships and animal behaviours maintain a continuous flux of mass and energy between the sea and the land through a complex network of direct and indirect interactions (Lee 2008). Mangrove communities typically cope with environmental stressors acting at different time scales, from hours (e.g. salinity or soil oxygen fluctuations induced by tidal action) to tens and hundreds of years (e.g. lightnings, typhoons, meander diversions, sea-level changes). Such stressors act during the life history of individual trees (Duke 2001, Woodroffe 1992), and probably affect mangrove-associated species in a similar way. Therefore, the strong selection for complex evolutionary adaptations (Hartnoll 1987; Tomlinson 1986), and the improbable culmination of ecological successions in climax communities (Lugo 1980) may explain why mangrove ecosystems typically include heterogeneous assemblies of relatively few and evolutionary unique resident species. The interplay of abiotic stressors and biotic factors determines the spatial structure of mangrove forests (zonations, mosaics: Hogarth 2007; Dahdouh-Guebas 2001, cited in Cannicci et al. 2008), which is also reflected in the habitat distribution of mangrove-associated residents, showing habitat-checkerboards along the intertidal zone (e.g. Polgar 2008; Ashton et al. 2003; Sasekumar 1974). Mudflat and mangrove communities play a pivotal role in the hydrology and sedimentology of coastal areas, interacting with sediment balance (Mazda et al. 2002; Furukawa et al. 1997; Young and Harvey 1996); offshore outflow of organic and inorganic suspended particles (Wolanski 1992); groundwater flow (Mazda et al. 1990); salinity, oxygen and nutrient levels in the sediment (Hogarth 2007); tidal dynamics and residence time of sea water inside the creek network (Mazda et al. 1995; Wolanski 1992); and wave action (Mazda et al. 1997; Wolanski 1995). Primary production can also be relatively high (Hogarth 2007), and the abundant necromass is either exported to the sea, accumulated in the mud, or decomposed by detritivore and microbial action. This latter process is apparently the principal routing of primary products (e.g. Cannicci et al. 2008), and typically varies along the intertidal zone with the intensity of the tidal action and the detritivores' species composition (e.g. crabs).

In tropical and humid conditions in the Neotropics, equatorial West Africa, Indo-Malayan region and New Guinea, supratidal swamps adjoin the landward margin of mangrove forests. Critical ecological factors are the hydroperiod (i.e. the amount of time per year that soils are water-logged), the main source of water, the frequency of fires, and the depth of the accumulated organic matter (Myers and Jewel 1990). In natural conditions, slow-burning and infrequent fires, from once a decade to once a century, burn off accumulated litter and peat during droughts, accelerating the turnover of nutrients. Some species living in these habitats are well adapted to natural fires and have thick, loose and corky bark (e.g. *Melaleuca* spp.; MacKinnon et al. 1996).

When the source of water is mainly from flooding rivers, the freshwater is mineral rich and the pH roughly neutral (> 6). These swamps have a short hydroperiod, a measurable flow rate at least part of the year, and relatively higher water oxygen concentrations: the forest floor is frequently crossed by small streams and small pools (Corner 1978). In such conditions, the accumulation of peat is balanced by the import of fluvial sediments (Bird 2008) and a tropical freshwater swamp is formed. These ecosystems are regulated by periodic flooding events, which redistribute energy and materials from terrestrial and aquatic systems, moving large amounts of nutrients and stimulating the reproductive activities of aquatic animals (Kottelat and Whitten 1996). Soil and vegetation can be extremely heterogeneous, including many species from the neighbouring lowland dry and riparian forests, and the productivity can be relatively high (MacKinnon et al. 1996). Freshwater swamps have been severely decimated in the last decades, and few examples still exist throughout the world, most of which are degraded forests. Less than 20% of the original coverage remains in Sumatra, with less than 3% being protected, while several once luxuriant forests, such as the Irrawaddy swamps in Myanmar, the Sundarbans in Bangladesh, and the Red river in Viet Nam, had almost completely disappeared mainly due to agriculture conversion (Wikramanayake et al. 2001). Few exceptions still survive, such as the vast swamps of northern and southern New Guinea (Wikramanayake et al. 2001), the swamps of the Congo basin in Africa (Sayer et al. 1992), and the Orinoco delta in Venezuela (Harcourt and Sayer 1996). Nonetheless, recent human activities (e.g. oil exploration and extraction, mining) are already starting to affect these once pristine systems (e.g. Townsend and Townsend 2004).

When the forests are only fed by rainwater and shallow groundwater, being water saturated at all times of year, they have no perceptible water flow. Tropical stillwater swamps can accumulate peat deposits 50 cm to 20 m thick, which determine anoxic, oligotrophic and highly acidic (pH< 4) soil conditions. These forests are called peat swamps (e.g. Ng et al. 1994; MacKinnon et al. 1996), and originated as the sea level rose at the end of the Late Pleistocene and Holocene glaciations (Page et al. 2008). More than 62% of the global area of tropical peatlands occurs in South-East Asia (20-30 million hectares), but they are also present in Africa, Central and South America, and New Guinea (Martini et al. 2006). Peat swamps are poorly studied systems, hosting many endemic aquatic species (Kottelat and Whitten 1996). These forests can exhibit a typically zoned concentric pattern: inner zones have more acidic and oligotrophic soils; higher topographical elevation (due to slower decomposition rates); lower biodiversity; and a higher concentration of evolutionary peculiar species (MacKinnon et al. 1996). Not unlike mangroves, many tree species occurring in freshwater and peat swamps show convergent adaptations to anoxic soils, such as prop roots and pneumatophores (Corner 1978). Understory vegetation is relatively sparse, while vines and epiphytes (bromeliads, orchids, ferns) are abundant and diverse. Many animals found here continuously move through different systems (e.g. monkeys); therefore, the neighbouring habitats (mangroves, dry lowland forests, riverine forests) can be of critical importance. Examples of these peculiar systems include the swamps of the Maputoland, in South Africa; those present in the floodplain of the Congo River; and the rich ombrogenous peat swamps of Borneo and Sumatra (Joosten 2004).

Flagship Species

Flagship species (Primack 2004) are species which represent environmental causes. They are chosen for the presence of morphological or behavioural features that lend themselves to provoking public sympathies, and their ultimate function is to raise public awareness of the role and value of whole endangered ecosystems (e.g. World Land Trust 2003). In this respect, they can be strong promoters of ecotourism, as a valuable economic resource for ecosystem management and conservation. They can also be utilised to symbolize environmental or management projects, and to obtain political support. Flagship species can appeal to people because they are useful (e.g. wild relatives of crops), behave like humans (primates), are majestic (tigers), are mysterious (pandas), are ancient (bristlecone pines, coelacanths), or are perceived as strange (penguins) (Given and Harris 1994).

The main objectives of this contribution are 1) to review the current state of art of the relationship between man, tropical tidal mudflats and coastal swamps; 2) to suggest different park designs to preserve the transitional ecological functions of these systems and integrate holistic management perspectives; 3) to suggest a collection of potential flag species of mudflats and coastal swamp ecosystems; and 4) to suggest improvements to park structures to allow a richer experience of conspicuous species, including small peculiar faunas.

MAN, TROPICAL TIDAL MUDFLATS AND COASTAL SWAMPS

Anthropogenic Impact

One third of the world's human population lives in small islands and coastal areas, which only constitute 4% of the Earth's land area (Barbier et al. 2008).

Few estimates of habitat change or global anthropogenic impact are presently available for intertidal mudflats, although isolated cases of long-lasting conservation and management experience do exist, and several areas have been designated as Ramsar sites (i.e. "Wetlands of International Importance", according to the Ramsar Convention; Ramsar Convention on Wetlands 2009; Deppe 2000).

Only 40-50 years ago mangrove forests fringed about 70-75% of low-energy tropical shorelines around the world (Por and Dor 1984). Thirty to forty percent of the global mangrove coverage has been lost during the past 60 years, with extreme cases such as Singapore, which presently retains only 0.5% of the original area (Ellison 2008; Blaber 2007; Wilkie and Fortuna 2003; Alongi 2002). Declining rates are possibly faster than for coral reefs and tropical rainforests, and mangroves are highly endangered or at risk of extinction in several countries worldwide (Duke et al. 2007). As dramatic as they may seem, such figures usually do not take into account the extent of degradation suffered by the remaining ecosystems, nor the differential impact on different habitat types along the intertidal zone (Polgar 2008). Habitat destruction is the most severe type of human impact on mangrove systems, resulting from timber harvesting, mining, urban development (Alongi 2002; Sasekumar 1980) and aquaculture (fish and shrimp farming: Menasveta 1996), this latter one often fitting the well-known process of "roving banditry" (Ellison 2008). Another potentially important yet neglected aspect is the reduction of ecological connectivity caused by anthropogenic habitat fragmentation (e.g. due to inefficient dispersal of mangroves' pollinators, or animal early life stages; Ellison and Farnsworth 2001; Fig. 1).

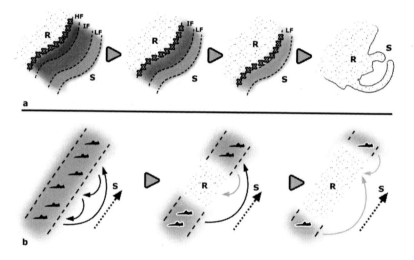

Figure 1. Two diagrams illustrating the possible effects of habitat destruction and fragmentation on coastal swamp resident species; a. Habitat destruction: the coastal swamp is progressively reclaimed from land to sea (from left to right) and the resident species living in different forest zones progressively go extinct; b. Habitat fragmentation: the model assumes that gene flow is maintained between different demes or populations by dispersal of early pelagic/planktonic stages (black arrows) along the prevalent longshore current (stippled arrow), a widespread convergent trait in several resident intertidal species (e.g. Hogarth 2007); in this example: mudskippers (Gobiidae: Oxudercinae), a group of related species which are differentially distributed from sea to land (see text). Similar models can be designed for different modes of dispersal. Progressive habitat fragmentation caused by land reclamation gradually isolates an increasing number of populations (highligthed individuals), limiting gene flow (grey arrows) and inducing inbreeding and genetic erosion. Since habitat destruction comes from land, the species distributed at higher topographical levels (a: HF) are the first to be affected by genetic erosion. R: reclaimed area; S: sea; LF: low forest; IF: middle forest; HF: high forest; red crosses: reclamation bund (modified from Polgar 2006).

Clear relationships between loss of intraspecific genetic diversity (inbreeding and genetic erosion) and a decrease of resistance and or resilience against environmental change have been documented in various groups of organisms (e.g. Hughes and Stachowicz 2004). At the same time, more and more evidence indicates that the usually assumed long range dispersal of shorefishes and other coastal organisms, that would ensure ecological connectivity between geographically fragmented populations, is frequently not taking place (e.g. Rocha and Bowen 2008; Barber et al. 2000).

Mudflats and mangrove ecosystems originate in conditions of positive sedimentary balance, and can facilitate sediment trapping and nutrient sinking, due to hydrologic (Wolanski 1992), sedimentological (Wolanski 1995) and physicochemical processes (Logan and Longmore 2003). For these reasons, these systems tend to accumulate pollutants. In particular, silt, clay and organic particles provide a large surface-to-volume ratio and readily adsorb metals and organic pollutants; only a fraction of these compounds is degraded in anaerobic conditions (Clough et al. 1983) the rest rapidly accumulating in the organisms which feed on tidal mudflats (e.g. Nakata et al. 2002; Srinivasan and Mahajan 1989). If not excessive, freshwater organic sewage probably has a secondary impact in most cases, since mangrove systems are often limited by nutrients and salinity (Hogarth 2007). Most highly impacting pollutants are released either by agricultural (e.g. herbicides, pesticides, fertilizers) or industrial (e.g. heavy metals) activities. In some areas, such as the Strait of Malacca, oil spills are a major threat (Chaw et al. 1993; Sasekumar 1980; PEMSEA 1999) and in many tropical and subtropical countries, mangrove forests located at the periphery of metropolitan areas are used for solid waste disposal (Lacerda et al. 1993).

A main source of degradation that can be particularly destructive in seasonal and drier climatic regions are land-based activities which impair the hydrology of the catchment area (damming, water diversion). The effects of these actions on the coastal zone are often overlooked even by rational management or conservation strategies (Farnsworth and Ellison 1997). River damming deprives the mangrove forests of freshwater, causing dieback and promoting coastline erosion, saline intrusion, nutrient depletion, or even marine sand deposition in the estuaries, and sediment accretion (Lacerda et al. 2001). Abstraction and impoundment of freshwater can also increase the frequency and duration of naturally occurring seasonal closures of estuaries (i.e. by the formation of sandbars). This can have important effects on estuarine species having a marine larval phase (e.g. Papadopoulos et al. 2002). These issues are topical aspects of coastal management, since it is now well known that while deforestation within catchments determines erosion and soil runoff from the hinterland, with consequent deltaic progradation, the reverse is true when sediment availability is reduced due to offshore exploitation, river damming, or flow reduction from longshore drift (Doody 2005). As a result, the outer margins of many formerly river-dominated deltas today become wave-dominated and are being eroded, with saline water intrusions in the underground aquifer. This has obvious implications for agriculture and ground water abstraction.

Another threat to the global survival of mudflats and coastal swamps is what has been described as the "coastal squeeze" (Doody 2005). Mangrove systems are known to migrate towards land keeping up with relatively slow sea-level rise (8-10 cm/100 yr; Ellison 1993). A much higher rate is being currently observed in several coastal regions worldwide, heavily affecting areas with intense coastal development (Pugh 1997). In fact, if we are facing a global acceleration of eustatic sea-level rise (even if scenarios will likely vary at a regional level: Hogarth 2007; Ong and Tan 2008), the general trend would reasonably be a compression of coastal systems between the sea water's edge and urban systems.

Freshwater and peat swamps are severely impacted in several Indonesian countries, with reductions of the original coverage of more than 50% (World Wildlife Fund 2008a,b,c). The main causes are deforestation, reclamation and water diversion for agriculture. Deforestation is usually followed by increased frequencies of natural or human-induced fires. Peat swamp forests are particularly vulnerable to fire (Hoscilo et al. 2009), since fires continue to burn underground, destroying soil and eliminating the seedbank. Furthermore, peat fires produce large amounts of CO_2, dangerous fumes and haze, and kill many animals (Yeager and Russon 1998). Ironically, much of the conversion of peat swamps for palm-oil plantations is driven by the European Community demand for biofuels for "Green Energy" production. Indonesia and Malaysia, which were heavily impacted by these fires, currently account for 85% of the world's supply of crude palm-oil (Murdiyarso et al. 2009).

Direct and Indirect Values

While mudflats and coastal swamps undoubtedly have an economic value, figures are not easily calculated (Hogarth 2007; FAO 1998). Marketed and non-marketed products can be assessed, and regarded as "direct use values". The former include those coming from traditional or sustainable aquaculture (e.g. cockles, *gei wei*, and modern pond systems; Hogarth 2007; Cha et al. 1997; Broom 1985) and sustainable timber or fuelwood production (e.g. sustainable rotational harvesting; Hogarth 2007). Non-marketed products warrant survival and subsistence of peoples living along coast (timber for building, fuel, food, beverages, drugs, medicine, textile, fodder, drugs, honey, wax, etc.: Hamilton and Snedaker 1984). Sustainable ecotourism can be considered as a direct use value.

More difficult to assess, "indirect use values" can be either calculated as the effects on products that are harvested elsewhere such as off-shore fisheries, or as services offered by unimpacted systems that in case of loss would have to be artificially provided. The former figures are often calculated by correlative approaches, since predictive ecological models are particularly difficult to obtain, due to the variable and complex interaction of different combinations of coastal habitats such as mangroves, mudflats, seagrasses and coral reefs (e.g. Nagelkerken et al. 2008; Blaber 2007; Mumby et al. 2004). The latter figures are often much higher and include the costs for substitute artificial defences against coastal erosion or destructive energetic events (Barbier et al. 2008; Cochard et al. 2008), or for the possible loss of the protected resource, such as rice paddy fields and palm-oil plantations. For example, different types of mangrove forests provide different types of services (Ewel et al. 1998): fringing mangroves efficiently protect the shoreline from energetic events, while riverine mangroves and mudflats act as sedimentary traps, protecting seagrass beds and coral reefs from siltation and decreased light availability (Duke and Wolanski 2001). If carefully calculated to balance the impacts on mangrove ecosystem functions, such figures can also include the costs of artificial plants to treat aquaculture or other organic waste effluents (Clough et al. 1983). Basin mangroves are particularly efficient as nutrient sinks (Ewel et al. 1998). Mangroves can also prevent the transfer of pollutants from landfills to adjacent coastal areas, since mangrove roots generate oxidized rhizospheres in the anoxic mud that allow the fixation of heavy metals in non-bioavailable compounds (Lacerda et al. 1993). Indirect use values of freshwater swamps include their importance as traditional fisheries (Kottelat and Whitten 1996); while peat swamps are valued for their capability to mitigate floods by soaking and storing water; buffering coastal lands from the intrusion of salty marine water; filtering pollutants and preventing their dispersal in lakes, rivers and groundwater; and storing high amounts of carbon, acting as some of the most efficient carbon sinks on Earth (Siegert and Jaenicke 2009).

Even more difficult to assess, although often particularly relevant in a socio-cultural perspective, are "non-use values", such as the opportunity for research and education, biodiversity conservation, or the preservation of traditional cultures. In particular, coastal swamps provide critical habitats for several endangered species (see below).

Rational Management: Past Failures and Future Possibilities

The general failure of sustainable management and the rapidly accelerating destruction of coastal swamps worldwide during the last 20 years, has exasperated the conflicts between ecosystem conversion and conservation or rehabilitation (Tan and Ong 2008). For that which concerns mangroves (e.g. Dodd and Ong 2008; Ong et al. 2001), there has been a very conspicuous bias in management strategies all over the world, with IWP mangrove systems in Asia being principally managed for silviculture (timber, fuelwood, pulpwood), and ACEP mangroves in the Neotropics for ecosystem function and wildlife protection (Ellison 2000). Since silviculture considerably reduces the species richness (monocultures or low diverse polycultures), IWP managed forests usually include a number of plant species which is comparable with the much less biologically diverse ACEP ones; surprisingly, animal species are frequently not taken into account (Ellison 2008; 2000), but probably follow parallel trends, especially for resident species, whose diversity is usually positively correlated with the biodiversity of mangroves (Ellison 2008). When management causes consistent biodiversity losses, it can be considered as inherently unsustainable. Furthermore, low diversity silvicultures such as the world-famous Malayan managed forests of Matang (Gong and Ong 1995) and those in the Sundarbans, Bangladesh, are also more susceptible to disturbance (e.g. herbivory, encrustation), and substantial reduction of the productivity occurs in the long term (Ellison 2008; Hogarth 2007). It has been repeatedly demonstrated that populations of intensive monocultures, both plant and animal, undergo frequent and drastic fluctuations, often resulting in considerable economic damage. Such fluctuations are essentially induced by high population densities, which determine favourable conditions for explosive demographic increases of specific predators, parasites, and pathogens (e.g. Karvonen et al. 2006; Risch 1981). In Matang, 35,000 ha forests had been managed by rotational forestry for over a century, and sustainability (especially in terms of biodiversity) could not be achieved. In particular, the lack of concern for the benthic fauna is exemplified by the periodical use of herbicides (pers. obs.), which may accumulate in the substrate or along trophic chains. On the other hand, management could be significantly improved through multiple-use strategies and rehabilitation of parts of this area, that would be probably far easier to accomplish than for alternative types of human use. A recent market analysis shows that this would also lead to greater benefits to local residents (Othman et al. 2004).

Freshwater swamps are being reclaimed all over the world and converted into fertile agricultural systems, e.g. wet-rice fields, pineapple, palm-oil and sago plantations.

Neighbouring riparian forests also produce high quantities of commercial timber, and are intensively exploited (MacKinnon et al. 1996). Sustainable management is rarely attempted: forests are often deliberately burned, to reclaim areas and encourage new growth. Peat swamps are particularly difficult to rehabilitate, since the superficial layer of peat is rapidly oxidized by sunlight when they are reclaimed for cultivation, becoming irreversibly dry and hydrophobic; moreover, water drainage causes soil compaction and subsidence, disrupting the physicochemical structure and zonation of the whole forest (Hoscilo et al. 2009).

A possible direct-use of both freshwater and peat restored swamps is sustainable forestry of native species (Rieley and Page 2005).

The most important issue for the rehabilitation of coastal swamps is the implementation of careful water management plans (Wösten 2009; Lewis 2005). The autoecology of the involved plant species (with particular reference to reproduction and dispersal modes) and the normal hydrologic patterns that control their establishment and distribution must be carefully studied before any action is taken. Relatively pristine sites in the same area, or alternatively, benchmarks and surveys from other sites must be used as a reference for the model. Then the rehabilitation plan can be designed: where necessary, artificial barriers are removed (e.g. reclamation bunds behind mangrove forests) or built (e.g. dams in drainage canals dug in peat swamps) and water inflow calibrated by water gauges both to restore the water regime, and prevent flooding of uplands and not protected areas. The level of the water table and physicochemical values should also be routinely monitored (EMA 2009) and constructive interactions with other resident species which have a relevant impact at ecosystem level (e.g. crabs, gastropods and insects in mangrove systems: Cannicci et al. 2008; Kristensen and Alongi 2006; Botto et al. 2005; Ridd 1996) taken into careful consideration.

More recently, the integration of a multiplicity of objectives is advocated as a more efficient management strategy. In this view, different types of resources are exploited by multiple stakeholders, from shrimp farms to tourist facilities, rotational harvesting and no-access natural sanctuaries (Ellison 2008; Ellison and Farnsworth 2001; Ellison 2000; Fig. 2). To implement this approach, different zones can be used for different activities (zoning), being distributed along the ecological transition from sea to land. This approach can lead to higher biodiversity, higher stability, and much higher profits, up to one order of magnitude (Ellison 2000).

The presence of non-linear relationships between ecosystem structures and functions confirms that higher total economic returns can be obtained by finding trade-off solutions between ecosystem conversion and conservation, in the reconciling vision of ecosystem-based management (EBM; Barbier et al. 2008). Reconciling approaches have also the advantage to take into consideration the local socioeconomic conditions, and meet local community needs (e.g. PEMSEA 2007a; Farnsworth and Ellison 1997). This type of approach is highly promising in a holistic perspective, taking into account the whole catchment area and the highly interacting coastal ecosystems (e.g. ICARM, Integrated Coastal Area and River Basin Management; UNEP 2006).

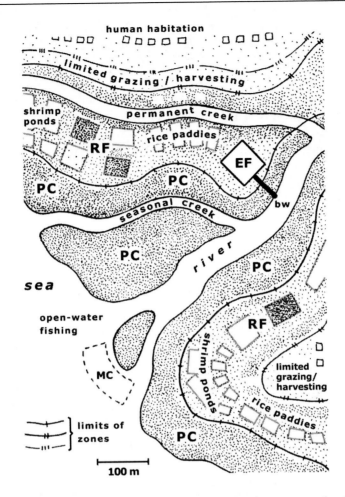

Figure 2. Hypothetical site conservation/sustainable management plan: an example of multiple use of the resources. Note that the mangrove forest is a belt running parallel to the coastline, with trees' density that progressively diminishes (density of spots) from sea to land. Wihout an appropriate water management plan, coastal reclamation bunds, which often demarcate the limits of the different zones of uses, can severely disrupt the forest's hydrology, especially during dry periods. RF: rotational forestry; EF: ecotouristic facility; PC: protected core; MC: mollusk culture; bw: boardwalk. Modified from Ellison and Farnsworth, 2001 (drawing courtesy of E. Farnsworth).

Examples of the gradual implementation of the ICARM approach and its advantages are present in several different countries, such as Sri Lanka, Australia, India, Kenya, and Senegal (UNEP-DHI 2007).

Even if many problems remain, some solutions were proposed to overcome the universally predominant administrative, financial and political obstacles, such as twinning mechanisms and networking between different countries to achieve the goals of policy reform and sustainable financing and investment, a deep involvement of local stakeholders, and the search for more accessible scientific foundations of ecosystem-based management (PEMSEA 2007b).

In this perspective, sustainable ecotourism is an important potential resource for transitional ecosystems, being a potentially low-impact activity, a high source of income, and a precious educational tool. Nonetheless, it is important to stress that ecotourism does impact natural systems. Examples are habitat destruction for resort construction; coastal pollution; structural and community changes due to boardwalk construction (Skilleter and Warren 2000; Kelaher et al. 1998); erosive wakes caused by motorboat traffic which can uproot trees along banks; and noise (Ellison and Farnsworth 2001). Last but not least, ecotourism facilities which start up as low-impact local hotels or small resorts, all too often get bought up by larger chains and expanded, with little benefit to the local community and the lack of any regulated, rational management plan (E. Farnsworth, pers. comm.). Several cases of unsustainable ecotourism have actually contributed to considerable degradation of conserved areas (e.g. Wall 1997).

Careful definition, scientific research and a periodic and systematic monitoring of the limits of acceptable change (LAC) must be conducted within the managed system (e.g. McCool 1996) both to quantify and assess the quality of anthropogenic impacts, ecotouristic activities included.

INTEGRATED COASTAL MANAGEMENT FROM SEA TO LAND: "TRANSECTS" VS. "BELTS"

The network of intimate connections between mudflats, mangrove forests, freshwater and peat swamps is the result of the evolutionary interaction between biotic and abiotic factors on large temporal and spatial scales. Geomorphic structures and communities are shaped by the continuous interplay of biological, hydrological, sedimentological and geological forces, setting out one of the most dynamic system of the biosphere. For these reasons, it is our opinion that the goals of the sustainable management and conservation of these systems cannot be achieved without the acknowledgement of the fundamental ecological and evolutionary continuity between them.

In fact, the economic values of each different ecosystem can be substantial (e.g. Costanza et al. 1997), especially when considered as long-term investments. On the other hand, the holistic properties of the interconnections between these ecosystems have only recently being perceived as an intrinsic economic and ecological value (Yu 2005). Even if the above mentioned considerations suggest that such holistic properties could be even more valuable than isolated systems, these values have not been scientifically quantified, being completely ignored by mainstream economists. Furthermore, such approaches put a disproportionate emphasis on pollution relative to other types of anthropogenic impact, such as habitat destruction and functional impairment of the watershed hydrology (e.g. PEMSEA 2007b).

Since coastal zones are progressively developed from land, rationally managed or conserved coastal areas are frequently characterized by 1) a spatial arrangement as a "belt" along coast of variable width; and 2) a deep alteration of the hydrology of the whole system, if reclamation had occurred. In the few cases where the belt is wider than a few hundreds of metres, the hydrology is rarely restored within the system, with the obvious result of a poor internal connectivity and a considerable loss of ecological functionality and diversity.

Therefore, to restore the homeostasis and aim at the sustainability of the managed system, 1) areas should not be oriented as belts along coast, but as "transects" from water to land (Fig. 3); and 2) the designation of protected areas should always imply the rehabilitation of the hydrological connections by a careful water management plan.

Ecological transitions including mudflats and coastal swamps can be distributed from sea to land; from the river or creek banks landwards; from coast to coast in small islands; and along river, from the mouth to lower or middle tracts (Fig. 3). Transect-like areas will include larger portions of the ecological transition, and each subsystem will contribute to the homeostasis of the other ones. For example, we showed that periodically flooded freshwater swamps and the fluvial discharge provide mangrove forests of the fundamental freshwater input, while peat swamp forests act as water reservoirs for marginal habitats during drier periods. Many species actively move between these systems (e.g. fishes, monkeys, apes, birds), following seasonal, climatic or tidal fluctuations, or during their life histories. In fact, it is well known that the loss of connectivity between different habitats can have consequences as serious as the same reduction of the habitat size (Nisbet 1968).

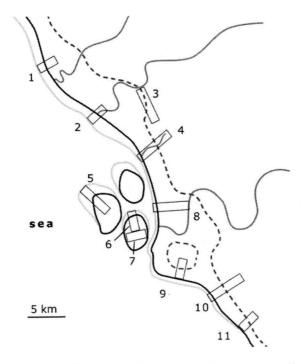

Figure 3. Different examples of possible transect-like conserved/managed coastal areas. The hypothetical coastline is similar to the actual coast of western Peninsular Malaysia (e.g. Coleman et al. 1970); the real distribution of Malayan coastal swamps is now much more fragmented and coastal freshwater swamps almost completely disappeared. Black line: coastline; pale grey line: outline of mudflats during mean low tide; dark grey lines: rivers; interrupted line: contact zone between mangrove forests and freshwater or peat swamps. The geometric shapes of the managed areas are simplifications. Belt transects may include a mudflat and a mangrove forest, with or without the mouth of a river (1, 2, 5, 6); can connect the sea to the banks of a river (8); connect the opposite coasts of a small island (7); include a large portion of a river or a large creek (4); part of the transition from the banks of a river to the flooding plain, including or not the contact zone between different coastal swamps (3); the sea-land transition from mangrove forests to freshwater or peat swamps (9, 11); or wide transitions from mudflats to freshwater swamps (10). Each case would both imply different water management plans, and different ranges of multiple-use conflicts. On the other hand, the connectivity between different types of systems would be greatly enhanced. Drawings by GP.

The described multiple-use management and the zoning strategies may be profitably applied to transect-like designs (Fig. 4). In particular, the strategy to promote the local stewardship and management of sub-basins by local communities (PEMSEA 2007b) particularly fits the zoning concept, and the integrated vision of transitional ecosystems.

However, the conservational effectiveness of transect-like designs greatly depends on its geographical scale. For any given available area, a transect-like design would imply much smaller habitat-specific communities and populations than a belt-like design. On the other hand, in this latter case many habitats would entirely disappear, as it is presently the case.

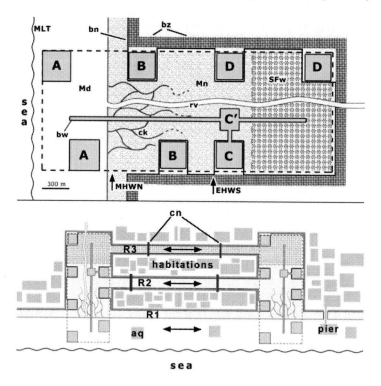

Figure 4. *Above*: hypothetical example of a transect-like conserved/managed coastal area with sustainable multiple uses of the resources. A mudflat (Md), a mangrove forest (Mn), and a freshwater swamp (SFw) are included in an area of 1 km x 3 km. Less than 20% of the total area is managed: the rest is conserved or rehabilitated; the sea is on the left. bn: reclamation bunds/channels to control flooding; bw: boardwalk; bz: buffer zone; ck: creeks' network; MLT: mean low tide; rv: river. A: clam cultivations; B: shrimp farms; C: park ecotouristic facility; C': system of boardwalks connected to the facilities; D: rotational forestry. The river and creeks' network are part of the water management plan and must be carefully designed to provide both the needed tidal flooding and freshwater supply to the mangroves, and the periodical flooding of the freshwater swamp. *Below*: diagram illustrating the connection between two adjacent transect-like coastal areas. Each zone is connected by a corridor (R1-R3) which crosses reclaimed areas with habitations or other human activities and allows gene flow (double arrows) between the protected populations hosted in the two conserved / managed areas. To connect reclaimed areas, roads can be built either on bridges or on underground passages (cn), to preserve the ecological continuity along corridors. A stripe of mangrove vegetation of 100-200 m along coast (R1) acts as a barrier to energetic marine events. Note that gene flow in the lower intertidal zone probably takes place mainly through water and tidal action (first double arrow from below); therefore, a moderate presence of piers and other human activities along coast would not prevent it; aq: aquaculture facility. Drawing not to scale: distances and areas would be determined by a trade-off between the eco-biological needs of the managed communities and human socio-economic issues. Drawings by GP.

Possible solutions could be 1) to scale the transect-like area so as to include minimum viable populations of the hosted species with the largest minimum viable areas (e.g. large mammals or birds); and 2) to create more transects along coast separated by distances determined by the minimum dispersal ranges of the hosted species, and connected by ecological corridors between the different subsystems (Fig. 4: R1-R3). The ecological corridor along the lower forested shore (R1, 100-200 m wide) would also provide a precious ecological barrier to marine energetic events (not unlike many present belt-like conserved areas), and it is strongly recommended also in the absence of multiple transect-like conservational units. Such design would allow terrestrial, marine and aerial gene flow between each conservational unit, eventually creating a mosaic of conserved, rehabilitated, managed and urbanized zones in the whole catchment area (Fig. 4). In this respect, an enhanced research effort of conservation geneticists is urgently needed, to inform and support ecosystem-based management with measures of minimum viable areas, minimum viable population sizes, and dispersal capabilities of the species of these communities.

It is important to note that while such approach is focussed on habitat destruction and fragmentation, pollution issues are equally important and should be addressed with the same philosophy.

The integrated management of whole watersheds, coastal and marine areas issues a harsh challenge to governments, institutions and managers, in the attempt to solve widely debated issues such as the definition and demarcation of landward and seaward boundaries (often completely unrelated to ecological concepts; e.g. PEMSEA 2007a); the integration of multiple-use economic conflicts within and among different sectors; institutional issues and management capacity (lack of human, legal, scientific and financial resources); cross-jurisdictional problems; and the functioning of the administrative framework.

POTENTIAL FLAGSHIP SPECIES OF
MUDFLATS AND COASTAL SWAMPS
THROUGHOUT THE WORLD

Flagship species are charismatic symbols that can stimulate the popular imagination and promote social facilitation around environmental issues. Ideal flagship species or group of species are easily identified as distinctive organisms, have captivating features (shape, behaviour, colouration patterns, etc.) and have the potential to symbolize the environmental issues of whole ecosystems and their connections. For that which concerns transitional ecosystems, another advantageous feature of ecologically or taxonomically related flagship species is to have a differential distribution along the intertidal and supratidal gradient, thus being potential biomonitors of the differential anthropogenic impact from sea to land (Polgar 2008).

Several flagship species are found in coastal swamps, such as primates, e.g. the Orang-utan *Pongo pygmaeus* (Linnaeus, 1760), the Proboscis Monkey *Nasalis larvatus* (Wurmb, 1787) and the White-Handed Gibbon *Hylobates lar* (Linnaeus, 1771); the Sumatran Rhinoceros *Dicerorhinus sumatrensis* (G. Fischer, 1814) and the Javan Rhinoceros *Rhinoceros sondaicus* Desmarest, 1822; different subspecies of tiger, *Panthera tigris* (Linnaeus, 1758); and the Indian Elephant *Elephas maximus* Linnaeus, 1758.

Nonetheless, most of these large and mobile species also occur in other ecosystems (e.g. lowland forests, rainforests) which are differentially impacted by the human action, and none are exclusive of coastal swamps. For instance, up to date no flagship species have been widely publicized to promote the conservation and sustainable management of mudflat and mangrove ecosystems. This is probably due to the fact that with the exception of some reptiles, no large animals live here as residents. Nonetheless, several plants and animals with unique evolutionary adaptations live exclusively in these coastal ecosystems and will surely follow their fate; furthermore, many transient species make a critical use of mudflats and mangrove systems during part of their life history. A selection of these taxa is here proposed as potential flagship species.

Potential Flagship Species for Tidal Mudflats and Mangrove Forests

Shorebirds and Waders

Many species of migratory and non-migratory birds heavily depend on tropical tidal flats, roosting on the adjoining mangrove forests during high tide, and feeding on the open mudflat or along the forest edge and banks of the creek networks during low tide. Some of the most abundant birds' preys found on mudflats are polychaetes, bivalves, gastropods and gobiid fishes (Pepping et al. 1997; Swennen et al. 1982). Several tidal mudflats throughout the world (e.g. South America, Africa, South East Asia, Australasia) are the wintering grounds of large colonies of migratory birds coming from the cold regions of the northern hemisphere such as Siberia and Alaska, where they return to breed when the northern winter is over (Malaysian Wetland Directory 1987); mudflats are also important stopovers along migratory routes.

Shorebirds (e.g. ibises, plovers, sandpipers) and waders (herons, storks) are the most abundant bird predators feeding on tropical tidal mudflats during low tide (Evans 1988; Ardeidae, Ciconiidae, Threskiornithidae, Charadriidae, Haematopodidae, Ibidorhynchidae, Phalaropodidae, Recurvirostridae, Rostratulidae, Scolopacidae), while other species feed on mudflats both during high and low tide (e.g. Laridae, Anatidae: Tadorninae). Birds feeding during low tide search preys either visually (e.g. several species of Charadriidae) or by touch, inserting their beaks into the soft sediment (e.g. several species of Scolopacidae and Haematopodidae); many species have different beak lengths and feed at different depths (Ng et al. 2008). Herons (Ardeidae) instead, are lurking predators which spear large preys (e.g. fish) with their sharp beaks.

Among scolopacids, the Bar-tailed Godwit *Limosa lapponica* (Linnaeus, 1758) breeds in North America and Europe, wintering in South Asia, Africa, Australia and New Zealand. A specimen of *L. lapponica* followed the longest recorded route by a migrant bird: more than 11,500 km in 9 days of non-stop flight across the Pacific Ocean (Gill et al. 2008). The Spotted Greenshank *Tringa guttifer* (Nordmann, 1835) and the Common Greenshank *Tringa nebularia* (Gunnerus, 1767) (Fig. 5) breed in northern Europe and Asia, wintering in Africa, India, South Asia, and Australasia. *T. guttifer* is Endangered (conservational status: BirdLife International 2008), being also included in Appendix I of the CITES (UNEP-WCMC 2009), mainly due to pollution and coastal development.

Figure 5. Shorebirds. *Left*: the endangered Humblot's Heron (*Ardea humbloti*), photographed at Belon'i Tsiribihina, Toliara, Madagascar (photo courtesy of Daniel Vaulot). *Right*: the Greenshank (*Tringa nebularia*) preying on the mudskipper *Scartelaos histophorus*, Changhua, Taiwan (photo courtesy of Chia-Yang Tsai).

Examples of the numerous charadriid species feeding on tidal mudflats are the Wilson's Plover *Charadrius wilsonia* Ord, 1814, which breeds on both coasts of the Americas from the equator northwards and often migrates in Peru and Brazil for wintering; the Endangered endemic New Zealand Dotterel *Charadrius obscurus* Gmelin, 1789, threatened by coastal development and introduced predators (BirdLife International 2008); and the widely distributed Grey Plover *Pluvialis squatarola* (Linnaeus, 1758), which breeds in Arctic islands and coastal areas of Alaska, Canada, and Russia, and winters almost throughout the world, from south-western British Columbia and Massachusetts south to Argentina and Chile; from Britain and south-western Norway south throughout coastal Africa to South Africa; and from southern Japan south throughout coastal South Asia and Australia, sometimes reaching New Zealand (Hayman et al. 1986).

An example of short-distance migrator, the threskiornithid Scarlet Ibis *Eudocimus ruber* (Linnaeus, 1758), is distributed in northern South America, and performs seasonal shifts between different locations in coastal or inland wetlands, often nesting in dense colonies on mangrove trees (Hancock et al. 1992). This species is included in Appendix II of the CITES (UNEP-WCMC 2009). It is a very popular species, and the national bird of Trinidad.

Herons (Ardeidae) frequently prefer to hunt nearby the vegetation (e.g. mangroves), like the Endangered *Ardea humbloti* Milne-Edwards and Grandidier, 1885 (Fig. 5), which lives in western Madagascar on coral islets, in mangrove systems and estuaries. This species is presently threatened by the habitat loss caused by the extensive deforestation and wetland degradation (BirdLife International 2008).

Storks (Ciconiidae) such as the Milky Stork *Mycteria cinerea* (Raffles, 1822), distributed in South-East Asia, and the Lesser Adjutant *Leptoptilos javanicus* (Horsfield, 1821), distributed in South and South-East Asia, frequently feed on tidal mudflats, roosting and nesting on adjacent mangroves, being also found in freshwater swamps. Both of these species are listed as Vulnerable in the IUCN Red List (BirdLife International 2008), and *M. cinerea* is included in Appendix I of the CITES (UNEP-WCMC 2009).

Birds are some of the best studied animal groups, with impressive numbers of recreational associations worldwide ("birdwatching" or birding; e.g. Cordell and Herbert 2002); therefore, their potential as flagship species is very high, especially for the conservation and sustainable management of tidal mudflats.

Mudskippers

Mudskippers are peculiar amphibious gobies (Teleostei: Gobiidae: Oxudercinae: Periophthalmini), which are "fully terrestrial for some portion of the daily cycle" (Murdy 1989). Some species present some of the most extreme morphological and physiological adaptations to semi-terrestrial life among fishes. They belong to four genera (*Boleophthalmus*, *Periophthalmodon*, *Periophthalmus*, and *Scartelaos*) including 30 species distributed from West Africa to the whole Indo-Pacific region, up to the Samoa and Tonga islands. The genus *Periophthalmus* includes 18 species, almost half of the species of the whole subfamily, and is distributed over its whole distributional range.

Figure 6. Mudskippers. *Above*: two fighting *Boleophthalmus dussumieri*, Bandar Abbas, Hormozgan, Iran. *Below*: *Periophthalmus chrysospilos* perching on a mangrove root during high tide, Pulau Kukup, Johor, Peninsular Malaysia. This latter species periodically shuttles back and forth following the tide, feeding on the mudflat during low tide, and looking for shelter in the mangrove marine fringe during high tide (Polgar and Crosa 2009). Photos by GP.

Mudskippers are closely linked to mudflats and mangrove forests, and are differentially distributed along the whole intertidal zone (Polgar and Crosa 2009; Takita et al. 1999). During low tide, several species are abundant on exposed mudflats and along creeks' mud banks, such as the Indo-Malayan Golden-Spotted Mudskipper, *Periophthalmus chrysospilos* Bleeker, 1852 (Fig. 6); The Dussumier's Mudskipper, *Boleophthalmus dussumieri* Valenciénnes, 1837 distributed from the Persian Gulf to West India (Fig. 6); and the Blue Mud-Hopper *Scartelaos histophorus* (Valenciénnes, 1837), distributed from West India to Australia and southern Japan (Murdy 1989).

Figure 7. *Above*: fishermen fishing mutsugoro (*Boleophthalmus pectinirostris*), Saga City, Ariake Sea, southern Japan (photo courtesy of Ben Cook). *Below*: a mudskipper cartoon: a *Periophthalmus* sp. is illustrated; drawing by GP.

Instead, more amphibious species of the genera *Periophthalmus* and *Periophthalmodon* often inhabit forested areas, such as the Weber's Mudskipper, *Periophthalmus weberi* Eggert, 1935, distributed in New Guinea and northern Australia, which is also found in the freshwater swamps adjoining back mangroves (GP pers. obs.).

On open mudflats, mudskippers can form conspicuous and dense associations. Herbivores such as *Boleophthalmus* spp. actively defend their territories and graze algae on the mud surface, exhibiting dynamic courtship behaviours. Carnivores, such as the relatively large Giant Mudskipper *Periophthalmodon schlosseri* (Pallas, 1770) (up to 25 cm of total length) are less active, but capable of powerful bursts of movements to chase their prey (mainly crabs or other mudskippers) or escape predators, such as predatory birds.

The differential distribution of mudskippers along the sea-land transition makes them potential biomonitors for mudflats and mangrove forests, which can be impacted both from the sea (pollution; e.g. Manoj and Ragothaman 1999) and from the land (habitat destruction; Polgar 2008). Some of the species living at higher topographical levels in the intertidal zone may be already locally endangered due to the extensive destruction of coastal swamps, such as *Periophthalmodon septemradiatus* (Hamilton, 1822) in western Peninsular Malaysia (Polgar 2008). Nonetheless, also mudflats' reclamation for coastal development can expose mudskippers to the risk of local extinction, as in the case of the Mutsugoro *Boleophthalmus pectinirostris* (Linnaeus, 1758) in the Ariake Sea, Japan (Takegaki 2008).

Mudskippers are often in close contact with human settlements, and in many countries they are fished with traditional techniques, such as Sierra Leone (Turay et al. 2006), Gujarat (Kizhakudan and Shoba 2005), southern Japan (Fig. 7; Takegaki 2008) and Papua New Guinea (GP pers. obs.), or also aquacultivated, as in Thailand, Taiwan and China (Zhang et al. 1989).

In particular, *Periophthalmus* and *Boleophthalmus* spp. have always inspired popular and scientific imagination (Kemp 2005; Polunin 1972; Linnaeus 1758), and they are frequently reared in public aquaria or kept as pets (Engelmann 2005; Mancini 1991). Their morphological and behavioural characteristics could easily make them very popular: they have big heads and extremely mobile eyes, amphibious habits and highly dynamic and diverse behaviours, including intense and colourful fin signalling, "eye-blinking", "crutching", skipping, jumping, rolling, skating, perching, burrowing, etc. (Clayton 1993; Harris 1961). They are also probably the only fishes that are systematically parasitized by mosquitoes (Okudo et al. 2004). Such characteristics make these fish particularly attractive and somewhat anthropomorphic (Fig. 7) and likely to provoke public empathy and sympathy.

Fiddler Crabs

The 97 species of crabs of the genus *Uca*, or fiddler crabs (Ocypodidae: Ocypodinae; Rosenberg 2001; Crane 1975) are characterized by the conspicuous asymmetry of males, which have a much enlarged claw (from one third to half of the crab's body mass) and a small minor claw. Females have two small claws which resemble in size the males' minor ones. *Uca* spp. are highly territorial (e.g. Pratt et al. 2006), and males use their huge claw during agonistic displays and encounters, and to attract females. *Uca* spp. inhabit several intertidal tropical and subtropical habitats, but the highest levels of biodiversity are reached in mangrove swamps and tidal mudflats. The genus is distributed from the western Atlantic region, e.g. *Uca rapax* (Smith, 1870), *Uca pugilator* (Bosc, 1802) and *Uca pugnax* (Smith, 1870); to south-western Europe and West Africa: *Uca tangeri* (Eydoux, 1835); East Africa, e.g. *Uca inversa* (Hoffman, 1874) and *Uca chlorophthalmus* (Milne Edwards, 1852); the Indo-West-Pacific region, e.g. *Uca annulipes* (Milne Edwards, 1837) (Fig. 8), *Uca triangularis* (Milne-Edwards, 1873), *Uca dussumieri* (Milne-Edwards, 1852) and *Uca forcipata* (Adams and White, 1848); and the Eastern Pacific region, e.g. *Uca brevifrons* (Stimpson, 1860), *Uca intermedia* Prahl and Toro, 1985 and *Uca flammula* Crane, 1975 (Fig. 8).

These relatively small semi-terrestrial crabs are highly specialized deposit feeders which feed during low tide on diatoms, smaller meiofauna, and bacteria (Hogarth 2007). During high tide, the species living on mudflats and mangrove forests look for shelter inside burrows, exhibiting typical tidal rhythms (e.g. Hartnoll 1987).

Having probably evolved in similar ecological conditions, fiddler crabs share surprising ecological and evolutionary convergent features with the already mentioned amphibious oxudercine gobies (mudskippers), including their aquatic evolutionary origins; adults' semi-terrestrial habits and a larval pelagic phase; a differential distribution of species along the intertidal zone; the presence of numerous morphologically similar congeneric species; high-positioned eyes (all *Uca* spp. have elongated eyestalks); territorial and burrowing behaviours; the use of a pocket of air inside burrows during high tide; and intense visual signalling in aggressive and reproductive behaviours. Both groups are closely associated to mudflats and mangrove systems, and include only a single West African species, although mudskippers are not known from the New World.

Figure 8. Fiddler crabs. *Above*: male of *Uca flammula*; Streeter's Jetty, Broome, Western Australia (photo courtesy of Tim South). *Below*: male of *Uca annulipes*; Pulau Ubin, Singapore (photo courtesy of Marcus Ng).

Not unlike mudskippers, fiddler crabs were also used as bioindicators of coastal habitats (e.g. Ashton et al. 2003; Macintosh et al. 2002) and in eco-toxicological studies (e.g. Ismail et al. 1991). *Uca* spp. can reach very high densities (70 ind/m^2; Hogarth 2007): their burrowing activity can have a profound effect on soil hydrology (Ridd 1996) and geochemistry (Botto et al. 2005; Kristensen and Alongi 2006), and, consequently, on forest productivity (Smith et al. 1991; Kristensen et al. 2008).

Hogarth (2007) described fiddler crabs as "the most colourful mangrove invertebrates" and their feeding, territorial and reproductive behaviours can be extremely appealing, both scientifically and aesthetically. Furthermore, they are often more abundant in relatively more open areas along boardwalks. For these reasons, they are excellent subjects of "mud-watching" activities in nature parks.

Mangroves

"Mangroves" are a polyphyletic group of dicotyledonous trees and shrubs that occupy soft-bottom tropical and subtropical shorelines throughout the world (Tomlinson 1986). In favourable conditions, such as those offered by tropical estuaries of large rivers over shallow continental shelves, these plants act as efficient ecosystem engineers, deeply altering intertidal habitat conditions for several resident and transient intertidal species, and forming communities which can extend for tens of kilometres inland, with a gradual transition to more terrestrial coastal forests.

Mangrove associations include major components ("true mangroves"), which almost exclusively occur in tidal swamps and often form monotypic stands; minor components, which are never preponderant elements; and "mangrove associates", which can also occur in other habitats. Major components include about 35 species, of which 25 belong only to the genera *Avicennia* and *Rhizophora*, which dominate mangrove communities throughout the world (Tomlinson 1986; Hogarth 2007; Fig. 9). In the ACEP biogeographic region the most widely distributed species are *Rhizophora mangle* L. 1753, *Avicennia germinans* (L.) Stearn 1958 and *Laguncularia racemosa* (L.) Gaertn.f. 1805; in the IWP widespread species are *Avicennia marina* (Forsk.) Vierh. 1907, *Bruguiera gymnorrhiza* (L.) Lamk. 1797-8, *Heritiera littoralis* Dryand. in Ayton 1789, *Sonneratia alba* J. Smith 1819 and *Rhizophora mucronata* Lamk. 1804 (Tomlinson 1986). The ACEP hosts about one fifth of the IWP region's species richness.

In a recent review (Polidoro et al., under revision), thirteen of the 70 mangrove species (19%) are threatened by extinction: geographical areas of particular concern include eastern Pacific, southern Brazil and the African Atlantic coasts.

Figure 9. *Above*: high mangrove forest flooded by a spring high tide. Most trees are *Rhizophora apiculata*. Note the conspicuous stilt roots of this mangrove species. Pulau Kukup, Johor, Peninsular Malaysia (photo by GP). *Below*: five saplings of *Bruguiera* spp. cultivated in a nursery at the National Institute of Education, Singapore; from left to right: *Bruguiera parviflora* Wight and Arnold ex Griffith 1936; *B. hainesii*; *Bruguiera sexangula* (Lour.) Poir. 1816; *B. gymnorrhiza*; and *Bruguiera cylindrica* (L.) Bl. 1827 (photo courtesy of W.H.J. Yong).

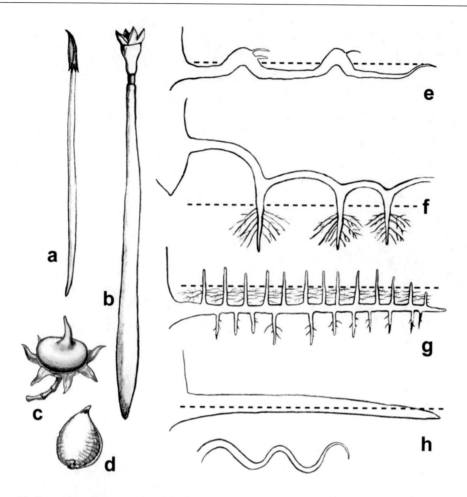

Figure 10. Drawings of some anatomical parts of mangrove trees; a, b: propagules (seedlings) of the viviparous *Bruguiera gymnorrhiza* and *Rhizophora apiculata*, respectively; c: fruit of *Sonneratia caseolaris*; d: fruit of *Avicennia officinalis*; e: cable root with knee roots of *Bruguiera* sp.; f: aerial stilt root and hypogeal anchoring and absorbing roots of *Rhyzophora* sp. (pneumatophores are the vertical portions of the stilt root, immediately above ground level); g: cable root, aerial pneumatophores and hypogeal anchoring and absorbing roots of *Avicennia* sp.; h: plank root of *Xylocarpus granatum* (below: plan view); stippled line: substrate level. All drawings were redrawn and modified by GP from Tomlinson (1986). Drawings not to scale.

Examples are the Critically Endangered *Sonneratia griffithii* Kurz 1871 and *Bruguiera hainesii* C.G. Rogers 1919, distributed in the IWP region; the Vulnerable *Rhizophora racemosa* Meyer 1818, distributed in the Caribbean and along the Atlantic African coasts; and the Endangered *Avicennia schaueriana* Stapf and Leechman ex Moldenke 1939, distributed in southern Brazil. The mangrove species *Avicennia lanata* Ridley 1920 (Chua 1998) and *Sonneratia hainanensis* Ko, Chen and Chen 1985 (World Conservation Monitoring Centre 1998) are already listed in the IUCN Red List respectively as Vulnerable and Critically Endangered.

This taxonomically heterogeneous collection of vascular plants is characterized by major convergent physiological and morphological adaptations to periodic immersion, fluctuating salinity, anoxic conditions and high temperatures (Hogarth 2007). Waterlogged soil are virtually anoxic, especially where fine sediments prevail, with formation of toxic compounds such as sulphides. For this reason, mangroves do not penetrate deep into the soil, and taproots are absent. Therefore, to support the body in the soft, unstable, and tidally inundated substrates, mangroves evolved long cable roots radiating from the stem, which can run 20-30 cm below the substrate (e.g. *Avicennia*, *Sonneratia* and *Xylocarpus* spp.), or originate from the stem above ground as robust, looping adventitious roots (stilt roots; e.g. *Rhizophora* spp.; Fig. 10, e-h). The anchoring roots grow from the cable roots, and are below ground. The absorbing roots originate from the anchoring roots and penetrate the superficial layer of the substrate. Mangroves are periodically submerged by tides, and oxygen is absorbed from the air when they are exposed and retained below water by several types of specialised aerial roots (pneumatophores; Fig. 10, f, g; Tomlinson 1986).

Frequent and rapid salinity fluctuations pose serious physiological problems to vascular terrestrial plants, both for the salts' toxicity, and the difficult maintenance of a functional water potential gradient between leaves and sea, or hypersaline water. Mangroves cope with these problems through a variety of highly convergent mechanisms, including salt exclusion by roots, salt secretion by specialised trichomes (salt glands), and tolerance and accumulation of excess salts in the leaves and bark (Hogarth 2007; Tomlinson 1986). In secreters, salts evaporate and crystallize on the leaf surface in a conspicuous manner.

All mangroves have early stages which are dispersed by water (propagules), and several species are viviparous. In these latter cases (Fig. 10 a,b), seedlings grow on the parent tree, and when they fall, they never become quiescent, being always ready to germinate and produce roots. In most mangrove species propagules can float for kilometres before sinking, stranding, and rooting during the establishment (Hogarth 2007).

The interactions between man and mangroves were previously described. Perhaps the most iconic symbol of mangroves are the antlered stilt roots of *Rhizophora* spp., which often appear in the logos of NGOs and institutions. As the motto of the Mangrove Action Project goes, quoting a Thai fisher: "... mangroves are the roots of the sea".

Potential Flagship Species for Freshwater and Peat Swamps

Freshwater Fishes

Freshwater and peat swamps are the natural habitats of hundreds of freshwater fish species. Several species are currently Endangered or already extinct in nature, such as *Epalzeorhynchos bicolor* Smith, 1931 (Kottelat 1996a), which is bred in captivity and widely traded as aquarium fish. The main reasons for their decline are pollution, increased sediment load (e.g. after deforestation), flow alteration and water diversion, overfishing, and introduction of alien species (Kottelat and Whitten 1996).

The Asian Bonytongue, or Asian Arowana, *Scleropages formosus* (Müller and Schlegel, 1844) (Fig. 11) is a typical inhabitant of South-East Asian freshwater swamps, presently distributed from the Malay peninsula to New Guinea island (*Pouyaud et al. 2003*). This species belongs to an ancient order and family of teleost freshwater fishes (Osteoglossiphormes: Osteoglossidae) distributed in South America, Africa, Asia and Australasia. A recent molecular research (Kumazawa and Nishida 2000) showed that *S.*

formosus is closely related to the Australasian species *Scleropages jardinii* (Saville-Kent, 1892) and *Scleropages leichardti* Günther, 1864. Surprisingly, the estimated age of the most recent common ancestor of these taxa, present on both sides of the Wallace's Line, is more than 120 million years ago (Early Cretaceous). In this case, the separation would have occurred during the splitting of the eastern Gondwanaland and the continental drift of India or other blocks towards the Eurasian continent. The presence of fossils in the Paleocene of Europe also suggests the presence of extinct species in Africa during the earliest Cretaceous (Taverne et al. 2007). These studies would imply a remarkably conservative morphology, which granted these fish the attribute of "living fossils". Four colour morphs of *S. formosus* (Green, Red Tailed Golden, Super Red and Silver Asian Arowanas) are present in different regions (e.g. Borneo, Sumatra, Indochina), and probably originated in allopatry after the last Pleistocene glaciations; their taxonomic status is debated (Kottelat and Widjanarti 2005; Pouyaud et al. 2003).

S. *formosus* lives in whitewater rivers with abundant riparian vegetation, lakes and periodically flooded plains; some varieties (or species: *S. aureus* and *S. legendrei*: Pouyaud et al. 2003) also occur in more acidic blackwaters (pH < 5.5) nearby peat swamps (see also MacKinnon et al. 1996). *S. formosus* is a relatively large fish, reaching almost 1 m in total length, with large and ornamented scales, and a typically large, oblique mouth with a pair of sensory barbels on its chin. Its peculiar bite, from which its common name derives, involves several bones of the mouth and palate. It is a visual predator which mostly hunts arthropods, fishes and other small vertebrates (Kottelat and Widjanarti 2005); it has large eyes and is capable of powerful bursts and jumps out of water to grab its preys. The Asian Arowana is a mouthbreeder: the eggs are collected by the male and protected inside its mouth: parental care is protracted after hatching.

Figure 11. *Above*: the Asian Arowana, *Scleropages formosus* (variety Red Tailed Golden) in a private tank, Kuantan, Malaysia (photo courtesy of Jamalludin Ab Rahman). *Below*: the Mekong giant catfish, *Pangasianodon gigas*, photographed in a public aquarium (Gifu World Fresh Water Aquarium, Kakamihara, Gifu prefecture, Japan; photo courtesy of Teppei Ishida).

Currently, *S. formosus* is in the Appendix I of the CITES (UNEP-WCMC 2009) and is listed as Endangered in the IUCN Red List (Kottelat 1996b), as a consequence of both habitat loss and overfishing. In fact, the Asian Arowana was intensively fished both for its meat and for the aquarium trade.

This species is extremely popular: its resemblance with the mythical "Chinese Ancient Dragon" and Feng Shui beliefs that the "Dragon Fish" brings luck and wealth, promoted a wild aquarium trade since the late 1970s, which together with extensive habitat loss brought the species to the verge of extinction. At present, Asian Arowanas are legally traded under CITES regulations only if bred in captivity for at least two generations, and a microchip is implanted inside each traded individual to identify it.

The Mekong Giant Catfish (*Pangasianodon gigas* Chevey, 1931, Fig. 11) is a South-East Asian shark catfish (Siluriformes: Pangasiidae). Adults of *P. gigas* characteristically have neither teeth, nor barbels, eyes positioned below the jaws' rictus, rudimentary or absent gill rakers (*Pangasius gigas* sensu Roberts and Vidthayanon 1991) and attain gigantic size, as suggested by the name. The Mekong Giant Catfish can reach almost 3 m in total length and a weight of over 300 Kg, being one of the largest freshwater fishes on Earth. It mainly feeds on algae, occasionally swallowing stones covered by periphyton, and presents one of the highest recorded growth rates (150-200 kg in 6 years; Rainboth 1996). It is endemic of the Mekong basin and inhabits highly productive lakes and rivers; it is a migratory species, although its exact migration patterns are scarcely known. Based on catch reports (Roberts 1993) and tag studies (Hogan et al. 2004), *P. gigas* migrates from the Tonle Sap Lake (Cambodia) during the dry season into the deeper waters of the Mekong river, then migrating upstream to aggregate and breed, triggered by the onset of the rainy season, not unlike many pangasiid catfishes. The spawning grounds of *P. gigas* are probably located in north-eastern Cambodia, Upper Laos, and northern Thailand (Hogan 2003; Hogan et al. 2001; Kottelat and Whitten 1996). Young are then transported downstream during the rainy season and use freshwater swamps and flooded forests (e.g. Tonle Sap) as nurseries (Hogan et al. 2004). The Mekong freshwater capture fishery is one of the largest of the world, and catfish are often the most important catches of community-based fisheries, representing more than 90% of the aquaculture and 20% of inland fisheries in Cambodia. Fish farming presents a potential risk for fry overfishing and decline of wild populations. Nonetheless, the most important threat for the Mekong catfish apparently are damming and navigation projects, which destroy its habitats and prevent the migration to the spawning sites (Mitchell and Braun 2003). An estimated decline of about 90% of *P. gigas* occurred over the last two decades (Hogan et al. 2004), and this species is presently listed in the IUCN Red List as "critically endangered" (Hogan 2003) and in the Appendix I of the CITES (UNEP-WCMC 2009). In 1983 the Thai Department of Fisheries started an artificial breeding program to reintroduce this species into the Mekong. Since 2000, about 10,000 captive-bred fishes have been released. Nonetheless, genetic introgression within cultured stock is a considerable risk, and the species is being hybridized with the closely related congener *P. hypophthalmus*. *P. gigas* is protected in Cambodia, Laos and Thailand, although this does not efficiently prevent fishing, also because of tourists attracted by this peculiar and enormous fish (Hogan 2003). This fish is highly priced in Thailand, where eating it is believed to bring good luck, while Chinese people believe its meat has medicinal properties. Recently, the idea of conservation concessions in the Mekong area, purchasing fishing rights without exercising them, could reduce large-scale commercial unsustainable fisheries of this species in critical areas. Concessions may be established with the revenues of ecotourism (Hogan et al. 2004).

The Mekong Giant Catfish is integral part of the culture of South-East Asian peoples. In North-East Thailand this species (locally known as Pla Beuk) is illustrated in cave paintings at least 3,000 years old at Pha Taem (Owen 2005; Lonely Planet 2009).

Several freshwater fishes are endemic of peat swamps and blackwater slow-flowing streams, including one of the smallest vertebrates on Earth, *Paedocypris progenetica* Kottelat, Britz, Tan and Witte, 2006 (Fig. 12). Sexually mature individuals are less than 1 cm long (Cyprinidae: Rasborinae; Kottelat et al. 2006). Other small cyprinids living in these habitats are the congeneric *P. micromegethes* Britz, Tan and Witte, 2006; *P. carbunculus* Britz and Kottelat, 2008 (approximately the same size of *P. progenetica*); the closely related (Rüber et al. 2007) *Sundadanio axelrodi* (Brittan, 1976), which underwent similar miniaturization evolutionary processes; *Boraras maculatus* (Duncker, 1904); and *B. urophthalmoides* (Kottelat, 1991). A miniaturised cyprinid was recently found also in Africa, in a freshwater swamp in Benin: *Barboides britzi* Conway and Moritz 2006.

The conservational status of these recently discovered species had still not been assessed, but they will probably follow the fate of peat swamps and associated marginal habitats. The ecotourism potential of such small species is unknown, but their extremely small size and endangered habitats could capture the imagination of people, promoting them as excellent flag species.

Figure 12. *Paedocypris progenetica* is one of the smallest vertebrates on Earth, reaching only 7.9 mm in length. This cyprinid was described in 2005 after discovery in an Indonesian peat swamp in Sumatra. In the figure, a female photographed by Ralf Britz (© The Natural History Museum, London).

Crocodiles

10 of the 23 extant species of crocodiles (Sauropsida: Crocodylidae) are listed in the IUCN Red List as Vulnerable, Endangered, or Critically Endangered, and 17 are listed in the Appendix I of the CITES (UNEP-WCMC 2009). The main reason for crocodiles' decline is habitat destruction and poaching for their valuable skins.

Out of these species, the Asian *Crocodylus siamensis* Schneider, 1801 and *Crocodylus mindorensis* Schmidt, 1935; and the Neotropical *Crocodylus rhombifer* Cuvier, 1807, occur in freshwater swamps and are presently classified as Critically Endangered (Targarona et al. 2008; Crocodile Specialist Group, 1996); they are all included in Appendix I of the CITES (UNEP-WCMC 2009). *C. siamensis* and *C. mindorensis* are morphologically very similar, and closely related to the Asian species *Crocodylus porosus* Schneider, 1801 and *Crocodylus novaeguineae* Schmidt, 1928 (Britton 2009).

The Siamese Crocodile (*C. siamensis*) was once widely distributed throughout South-East Asia; now only small remnant populations survive in the wild (e.g. in Cambodia). Its ecology is poorly known: it lives in slow-moving fresh waters (rivers, lakes, swamps), may tolerate brackish water, and feeds on a variety of vertebrate and invertebrate preys. Recently, farming and reintroduction could reduce the risk of extinction; nonetheless, this species hybridizes in captivity with the much larger *C. porosus* (Britton 2009), and DNA tests are necessary not to introduce hybrids in nature.

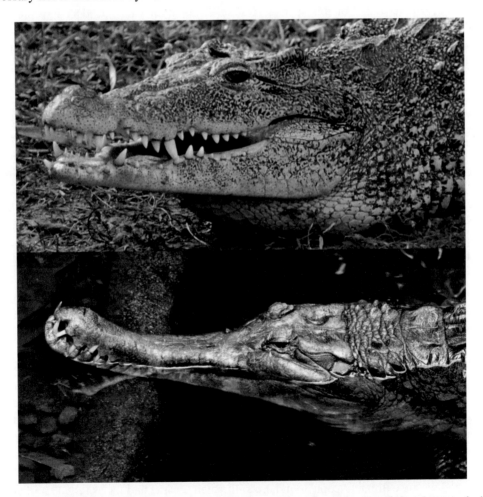

Figure 13. endangered crocodiles. *Above*: the Cuban Crocodile, *Crocodylus rhombifer*, photographed in the Miami Metro Zoo, US (photo courtesy of Zakery Pendleton). *Below*: the False Gharial, *Tomistoma schlegelii*, photographed in the Singapore Zoo (photo courtesy of Shirley Ng).

The Philippine Crocodile (*C. mindorensis*), previously considered as a subspecies of *C. porosus*, is a relatively small crocodile (< 3 m) with a heavy dorsal armour. This species is endemic of the Philippines, where it lives in small rivers, lakes and freshwater swamps, feeding on aquatic invertebrates and small vertebrates. Also in this case, its ecology is very poorly known. Recently, this species disappeared from several islands, and only one protected population remains (Britton 2009).

The endemic Cuban Crocodile (*C. rhombifer*, Fig. 13) is a medium-sized crocodilian, rarely exceeding 3.5 m, and characterised by a peculiar yellow and black colouration pattern. Also this species may tolerate brackish water. Once distributed also in the Bahamas and Caiman Islands, it is now only occurring in the freshwater Zapata and Lanier swamps (Cuba and Isla de Juventud, respectively), possibly being the crocodilian with the smallest natural distribution. It is capable of powerful jumps out of water, catching preys from the overhanging vegetation, such as small mammals. It is also well adapted to terrestrial locomotion. The rear teeth are particularly robust and turtles are a major component of its diet. Conservational risks for this species include competition with introduced species and hybridization in nature with *Crocodylus acutus* Cuvier, 1807 (Britton 2009).

The poorly known False Gharial, or False Gavial *Tomistoma schlegelii* (Müller, 1838) (Fig. 13) is possibly more closely related to gavials (Gavialidae) than to crocodiles, as some biochemical studies would suggest (Densmore and Owen 1989). This species is listed as Endangered (Crocodile Specialist Group 2000) and is included in Appendix I of the CITES (UNEP-WCMC 2009). It is distributed in Malaysia and Indonesia (Malay peninsula, Java, Sumatra and Borneo), with unconfirmed reports from Vietnam and Sulawesi (Stuebing et al. 2006; Crocodile Specialist Group 2000). Although it was found in several habitats including freshwater swamps, lowland forests and flood plains, it was described as a peat swamp specialist (e.g. Bezuijen et al. 1998). It exhibits a typical banded colouration pattern, which is highly cryptic in dark forested habitats. Its elongated snout would suggest a highly specialised fish diet, nonetheless, it has been reported to eat also insects, crustaceans, and even monkeys. It does not perform parental care, and the mortality of the hatchlings is high (Britton 2009). This large crocodile (up to 4-5 m) is probably the largest vertebrate occurring in the oligotrophic South-East Asian peat swamps, and naturally occurs at low densities. Although the historical distributional range of the False Gharial has apparently not changed, populations became increasingly isolated and fragmented since the 1940s, mainly due to habitat destruction (Stuebing et al. 2006).

The future of endangered crocodilian species is apparently linked to management and reintroduction practices being funded by the skin trade. Nonetheless, some species do not have a valuable skin (e.g. *Osteolaemus tetraspis* Cope, 1861) and captive breeding programs must take into account the risks of high inbreeding rates inside farms and of releasing fertile hybrids in nature. Another important issue is the lack of available areas for reintroduction, also due to the lack of understanding by local people (e.g. in India for *Crocodylus palustris* Lesson, 1831; Britton 2009). Last but not least, more baseline ecological data and new census techniques are urgently needed to understand and manage these species in the wild.

Crocodiles are extremely popular and crocodile theme parks and farms (e.g. Gatorland in Central Florida, US; and the Darwin Crocodile Farm, Darwin, Australia), or crocodile tours by boat (e.g. the "jumping crocodiles" tours of the Adelaide river, Australia) are effective touristic attractions. The ecotourism potential of crocodiles is still underdeveloped and could be a promising field for future management and conservational efforts.

ECOTOURISM AND PARKS' EQUIPMENT: THE CASE OF MANGROVE AND MUDFLAT PARKS

Boardwalks are widespread facilities in mangrove parks (e.g. Kuala Selangor Marine Nature Park, Malaysia; Triboa Bay Mangrove Park, Subic, Philippines; Edmund Kennedy National Park, Cardwell, Australia; Hong Kong Wetland Park, China; Kesaji mangroves, Okinawa, Japan; Everglades National Park, Florida; Isla de Salamanca National Park, Colombia; Kisite Marine Park, Wasini Island, Kenya). They allow access inside the extremely dense mangrove forests, which also typically occur on very soft and wet sediments. In some cases, they also extend onto open mudflats (e.g. Tanjung Piai National Park, Malaysia). Nonetheless, since in these systems tidal excursions can often be more than 2-3 m above ground level, they are often at considerable height above ground. As a consequence, visitors are usually not able to observe the interesting macrofauna living on the dark forest floor (e.g. fiddler crabs, mudskippers, skinks), and can only observe plants, or spot arboreal fauna, such as arboreal crabs and monkeys. Also on open mudflats, high boardwalks hamper the observation of the dense associations of smaller animals thriving on the mud surface.

The best option would be to bring the forest or the mudflat floor approximately at eye level. In these conditions, smaller animals are also not threatened by the human presence and can be observed at a much closer distance (GP pers. obs.). Unfortunately, it is particularly difficult to find sound and cost-effective solutions, since any open-pit cavity (e.g. a trench dug into the mud) would be partially or completely filled by water and mud, depending on the local tidal conditions. A possible solution could be concrete observation-bunkers inserted into the mud and provided with flat waterproof portholes, that would be closed during raining or high tide, and opened during low tide to allow a better visibility (Fig. 14). Larger structures would not only have elevated costs (building, maintenance, cleaning after each tidal cycle), but would probably have a large hydrologic and sedimentological impact on the mudflat. Indeed, depending on local rheologic and physiographic conditions, even boardwalks' concrete bases can heavily impact on the mudflat's sedimentary structures for hundreds of metres away from the boardwalk, due to their physical interaction with waves and tidal currents (GP, pers. obs.: Tanjung Piai, Malaysia).

Trade-off and less expensive solutions could be 1) low plankboards at the ground level parallel to boardwalks, to allow access during low tide; 2) binocular viewers positioned on the boardwalks (Fig. 15); and 3) waterproof webcams anchored on the mud surface, that could be viewed from the observatories or from the park's resorts. Such improvements could lead to a new naturalistic trend, that may be called "mud-watching".

A different problem is posed by larger animals (general size approximately ≥ 0.5 m) that keep themselves at distances of hundreds of metres from the observer (e.g. birds, deer). In this case, classical bird-watchers' observation towers and hides immersed in the vegetation are usually the best option (e.g. Kuala Selangor Marine Park).

Figure 14. *Left*: symplified drawing of a concrete bunker for the observation of the benthic macrofauna. The bunker is accessible from the boardwalk by a ladder (L) which is inside a sealed pipe (sectioned in the drawing to show the ladder), which allows access also during high tide. The longer side of the bunker is parallel to the prevalent direction of tidal currents (T), to minimize substrate erosion and formation of pools (p) due to turbulence during flood and ebb tides. A movable and sealable flat porthole (F) allows observation both during low tide, and during high tide, when turbidity does not prevent underwater visibility. *Right*: structures that facilitate the observation of the benthic macrofauna. Binocular viewers (A) can be placed at intervals on the boardwalk. A plankboard of 5-10 m (B) can be built at intervals parallel to the boardwalk to allow access for the visitors to the forest floor or to the mudflat. Drawings by GP.

Finally, other animals are best observed from the water, since they are often visible nearby the water's edge (e.g. crocodiles, monitor lizards, and some snakes). In this case, it is possible to guide tourists by boat on rivers or through the intricate creek networks (e.g. the world-famous "jumping crocodiles" tours in Australia). Also in this case, smaller animals can be observed by binoculars.

As already pointed out, all these facilities do impact the environment and the plant and animal communities, and their construction must be carefully considered in a Least Acceptable Change perspective.

CONCLUSION

In our time, one of the most globally debated issues is the need to achieve the twin goals of sustainable human development and the maintenance of biodiversity (UN Earth summit, Rio; Agenda 21, 1992), and the recognition of the tight connections between the so called "natural environment" and human economic and cultural activity (Doody 2005). A new pragmatic ecological synthesis of "natural processes" and human activities is urgently needed, envisioning man's activities as an organic part of the whole biosphere. This reconciling perspective is the paradigm of ecosystem-based management.

Coastal ecosystems offer a unique scenario to attempt such goal, promoting a multidisciplinary "alliance between the ecologist, geomorphologist, and coastal engineer in re-creating new coastal habitats" (Doody 2005). The pivotal socio-economic role of coastal ecosystems prompted the concept of Integrated Coastal Management (ICM), accepted, yet almost invariably not implemented, by most developing countries since the 1990s (e.g. Chua 1996). Subsequently, more attention was paid to the connections created by water between previously separately perceived systems, in a more holistic perspective (e.g. PEMSEA 2002; 2007a;b). The present contribution goes in this latter direction, proposing to utilize the same approach when planning to define a protected or managed area. In fact, we think that the proposed unitary vision of tropical coastal transitional systems should also include both more marine systems (e.g. seagrass beds and coral reefs) and the whole catchment area.

Tropical ecosystems are an explosive economic and ecological mixture. In fact, tropical developing countries are facing exponential and wild demographic and economic growth. At the same time, they are the repositories of the highest levels of biodiversity on Earth, hosting extraordinarily rich communities which evolved in relatively stable conditions over long evolutionary time (Tokeshi 1999). Nonetheless, developing countries have the unique opportunity to convert and manage their territory with much more rigorous and powerful scientific tools than past cultures, that irreversibly altered their much less rich and diverse ecosystems.

Even if more research is needed, valuable scientific tools are available. In fact, the most important obstacles come from political, financial and administrative problems.

The idea of urban ecosystems designed and managed to harmonically fuse with biotic and abiotic conditions is based on a concept of man as an important part of the "natural" system, and not as a counterpart. In this respect, we think that the key is to find sustainable ways to manage and protect the connections between systems previously perceived and managed as separate. In particular, future studies should focus on the holistic properties of transitional ecosystems as ideal models, and the services offered by interacting and interconnected rather than isolated systems. We foresee that the socio-economic and ecological advantages of the former scenarios would be much higher than the latter.

On the socio-economic side, environmentalism and animalism are growing political forces worldwide, whose role can be decisive for the achievement of the described goals at a global level. In this perspective, scientific concepts should become more accessible both to institutions and the population, to provide educational values, scientific methods, notions and tools to these political trends, thus improving the knowledge of the intimate ecological and evolutionary connections present on Earth. In this respect, the crucial role of media and environmentalist NGOs has been widely recognized (e.g. PEMSEA 2002) and the traditional conflict between science and media should be continuously challenged.

Ecotourism can be a precious resource. Nonetheless, careful optimism is needed, since the risks of a shortcut for easy profits with net detrimental effects on the environment is always present. Flagship species can be powerful promoters of ecotourism and environmentalist action, but care should be made in the attempt to utilize them as useful means to obtain effective results on whole and interconnected ecosystems in different geographical regions.

ACKNOWLEDGMENTS

We wish to thank Dr. Elizabeth Farnsworth (New England Wild Flower Society, Framingham, US) for her comments, and figure 2. Prof. Ulrich Saint-Paul (Leibniz Center for

Tropical Marine Ecology, Bremen, Germany), Mr. Harban Singh (Johor National Park Corporation, Malaysia) and Mr. Ben Brown (Mangrove Action Project) for their comments and encouragement. Dr. Jin Eong Ong, Dr. Wan Hong Jean Yong (National Institute of Education, Singapore) and Dr. Peter J. Hogarth (University of York, York, UK) critically revised and improved the manuscript. Several photographers contributed with their artworks: Ben Cook, Teppei Ishida, Marcus Ng, Shirley Ng, Zakery Pendleton, Jamalludin Ab Rahman, Tim South, Chia-Yang Tsai, Daniel Vaulot and Dr. Wan Hong Jean Yong.

REFERENCES

Agenda 21 (1992) UN Department of Economic and Social Affairs, Division for Sustainable Development. Agenda 21, section II, chapter 15: conservation of biological diversity. Available online at *http://www.un.org/esa/dsd/agenda21/res_agenda21_15.shtml*. Visited in August 2009.

Alongi D.M. (2002) Present state and future of the world's mangrove forests. *Environmental Conservation*, 29: 331-349.

Ashton E.C., Macintosh D.J. and Hogarth P.J. (2003) A baseline study of the diversity and community ecology of crab and molluscan macrofauna in the Sematan mangrove forest, Sarawak, Malaysia. *Journal of Tropical Ecology*, 19: 127-142.

Barber P.H., Palumbi S.R., Erdmann M.V. and Moosa M.K. (2000) A marine Wallace's line? *Nature*, 406: 406-407.

Barbier E.B., Koch E.W., Silliman B.R., Hacker S.D., Wolanski E., Primavera J., Granek E. F., Polasky S., Aswani S., Cramer L.A., Stoms D.M., Kennedy C.J., Bael D., Kappel C.V., Perillo G.M.E., Reed D.J. (2008) Coastal ecosystem-based management with nonlinear ecological functions and values. *Science*, 319(5861): 321-323.

Bezuijen M.R., Webb G.J.W., Hartoyo P., Samedi, Ramono W.S. and Manolis S.C. (1998) *The false gharial (Tomistoma schlegelii) in Sumatra*. In: Crocodiles. Proceedings of the 14th working meeting of the Crocodile Specialist Group, IUCN-The World Conservation Union: 10-31.IUCN/SSC Crocodile Specialist Group, Gland.

Bird E.C.F. (2008) *Coastal geomorphology: an introduction*. 2nd edition. John Wiley and Sons.

BirdLife International (2008) In: IUCN 2009. IUCN Red List of Threatened Species. Version 2009.1. Available online at *www.iucnredlist.org*. Visited in June 2009

Blaber S.J.M. (2007). Mangroves and fishes: issues of diversity, dependence, and dogma. *Bulletin of Marine Science*, 80: 457-472.

Botto F., Valiela I., Iribarne O.O., Martinetto P. and Alberti J. (2005) Impact of burrowing crabs on C and N sources, control, and transformations in sediments and food webs of SW Atlantic estuaries. *Marine Ecology Progress Series*, 293: 155-164.

Britton A. (2009) Crocodylians. Natural history and conservation. Available online at *http://www.flmnh.ufl.edu/cnhc/cnhc.html*. Visited in June 2009.

Broom M.J. (1985) *The biology and culture of marine bivalve mollusks of the genus Anadara*. International Centre for Living Aquatic Resource Management, Manila.

Cannicci S., Burrows D., Fratini S., Smith III T.J., Offenberg J. and Dahdouh-Guebas F. (2008) Faunal impact on vegetation structure and ecosystem function in mangrove forests: a review. *Aquatic Botany*, 89: 186-200.

Cha M.W., Young L. and Wong K.M. (1997) The fate of traditional extensive (gei wai) shrimp farming at the Mai Po Marshes Nature Reserve, Hong Kong. *Hydrobiologia*, 352(1-3): 295-303.

Chaw L.H., Teas H.J., Pannier F. and Baker J.M. (1993) *Biological impacts of oil pollution: mangroves*. IPIECA report series, Vol. 4. International Petroleum Industry Environmental Conservation Association.

Chua L.S.L. (1998) *Avicennia lanata*. In: International Union for Conservation of Nature (IUCN). Red List of Threatened Species. Version 2009.1. Available at: *www.iucnredlist.org*. Accessed on July 2009.

Chua T.-E. (1996) *Integrated Coastal Management in tropical developing countries. Lessons learned from successes and failures*. In: Summary proceedings of the international workshop on Integrated Coastal Management in tropical developing countries: Lessons learned from successes and failures. Xiamen, PRC, 2-28 May 1996.

Clayton D.A. (1993) Mudskippers. *Oceanography and Marine Biology, An Annual Review*, 31: 507-577.

Clough B.F., Boto K.G. and Attiwill P.M. (1983) Mangroves and sewage: a re-evaluation. In: Teas H.J. (ed.) *Tasks for vegetation science,* vol. 8, W. Junk, The Hague, p. 151-161.

Cochard R., Ranamukhaarachchi S.L., Shivakoti G.P., Shipin O.V., Edwards P.J., Seeland K.T. (2008) The 2004 tsunami in Aceh and Southern Thailand: a review on coastal ecosystems, wave hazards and vulnerability. *Perspectives in Plant Ecology, Evolution and Systematics*, 10: 3-40.

Coleman J.M., Gagliano S.M., Smith W.G. (1970) Sedimentation in a Malaysian high tide tropical delta. In: Morgan JP (ed) *Deltaic sedimentation, modern and ancient*. Special Publ. No 15, S.E.P.M., pp 185–197.

Cordell H.K. and Herbert N.G. (2002) The popularity of birding is still growing. *Birding,* 34: 54-61.

Corner E.J.H. (1978) *The freshwater swamp forest of South Johore and Singapore*. Gardens' Bulletin of Singapore, Suppl. 1.

Costanza R., d'Arge R., de Groot R., Faber S., Grasso M., Hannon B. et al. (1997) The value of world's ecosystem services and natural capital. *Nature*, 387: 253-260.

Crane J. (1975) *Fiddler crabs of the world: Ocypodidae: genus Uca.* Princeton University Press, Princeton, New Jersey.

Crocodile Specialist Group (1996) *Crocodylus siamensis*. In: International Union for Conservation of Nature (IUCN). Red List of Threatened Species. Version 2009.1. Available at: *www.iucnredlist.org*. Accessed on July 2009.

Crocodile Specialist Group (2000) *Tomistoma schlegelii*. In: International Union for Conservation of Nature (IUCN). Red List of Threatened Species. Version 2009.1. Available at: *www.iucnredlist.org*. Accessed on July 2009.

Dahdouh-Guebas (2001) Mangrove vegetation structure dynamics and regeneration. Ph.D. thesis, Vrije Universitet, Brussel.

Densmore L.D. III and Owen R.D. (1998) Molecular systematics of the order Crocodylia. *American Zoologist*, 29: 831-841.

Deppe F. (2000) *Intertidal mudflats worldwide*. Practical course at the Common Wadden Sea Secretariat (CWSS) in Wilhelmshaven 1st June - 30th September 1999.

Dittmann S. (2002) Benthic fauna in tropical tidal flats – a comparative perspective. *Wetlands Ecology and Management*, 10: 189-195.

Dodd R.S. and Ong J.E. (2008) Future of mangrove ecosystems to 2025. In: Polunin N.V.C. (ed) *Aquatic ecosystems. Trends and global perspectives*. Cambridge University Press, p. 172-187.

Doody P.J. (2005) History, coastal ecology. In: Schwartz M.L. (ed.) *Encyclopedia of Coastal Science*. Springer, The Netherlands, p. 515-519.

Duke N.C. (2001) Gap creation and regenerative process driving diversity and structure of mangrove ecosystems. *Wetlands Ecology and Management*, 9: 257-269.

Duke N.C. and Wolanski E. (2001) Muddy coastal waters and depleted mangrove coastlines – Depleted seagrass and coral reefs. In: Wolanski E. (ed.) *Oceanographic processes of coral reefs. Physical and biological links in the Great Barrier Reef*. CRC Press LLC, USA.

Duke N.C., Meynecke J.-O., Dittmann S., Ellison A.M., Anger K., Berger U., Cannicci S., Diele K., Ewel K.C., Field C.D., Koedam N., Lee S.Y., Marchand C., Nordhaus I., and Dahdouh-Guebas F. (2007) A world without mangroves? *Science*, 317: 41-42.

Dyer K.R., Christie M.C., Wright E.W. (2000) The classification of intertidal mudflats. *Continental Shelf Research*, 20: 1039-1060.

Ellison A.M. (2000) Mangrove restoration: do we know enough? *Restoration Ecology*, 8: 219-229.

Ellison A.M. and Farnsworth E.J. (2001) Mangrove communities. In: Bertness M.D., Gaines S., Hay M.E. (eds.) *Marine Community Ecology*. Sinauer Press, Sunderland, Massachusetts.

Ellison. A.M. (2008) Managing mangroves with benthic biodiversity in mind: moving beyond roving banditry. *Journal of Sea Research*, 59: 2-15.

Ellison J.C. (1993) Mangrove retreat with rising sea level in Bermuda. *Estuarine Coastal and Shelf Science*, 37: 75-87.

EMA (2009) Nariva swamp restoration. Project appraisal document; Environmental Assessment; May 29, 2009. Environmental Management Authority. Available online at *http://www.ema.co.tt*. Visited in June 2009.

Engelmann W.E. (2005) *Zootier Haltung. Tiere in Menschlicher Obhut (Fische)*. Verlag Harri Deutsch, Frankfurt, p. 686-689.

Evans P.R. (1988) *Predation of intertidal fauna by shorebirds in relation to time of the day, tide and year*. In: Chelazzi G. and Vannini M. (eds) Behavioral adaptation to intertidal life. North Atlantic Treaty Organization. Scientific Affairs Division. Proceedings of a NATO Advanced research workshop on behavioral adaptation to intertidal life, May 19-24, 1987. Castiglioncello, Italy.

Ewel K.C., Twilley R.R. and Ong J.E. (1998) Different kinds of mangrove forests provide different goods and services. *Global Ecology and Biogeography Letters*, 7: 83-94.

FAO (1998) Integrated coastal area management and agriculture, forestry and fisheries. Food and Agriculture Organization of the United Nations, Natural Resources Management and Environment Department. Available online at *http://www.fao.org*. Visited in June 2009.

Farnsworth E.J. and Ellison A.M. (1997) The global conservation status of mangroves. *Ambio*, 26: 328-334.

Furukawa K., Wolanski E. and Mueller H. (1997) Currents and sediment transport in mangrove forests. *Estuarine Coastal and Shelf Science*, 44: 301-310.

Gibson RN (1999) Movement and homing in intertidal fishes. In: Horn M.H., Martin K.L.M., Chotkowski M.A. (eds) *Intertidal fishes: life in two worlds*. Academic Press, San Diego, pp. 97-125.

Gill R.E. Jr, Tibbits T.L., Douglas D.C., Handel C.M., Mulcay D.M., Gottschalck J.C., Warnock N., McCaffery B.J., Battley P.F. and Piersma T. (2008) Extreme endurance flight by landbirds crossing the Pacific Ocean: ecological corridor rather than barrier? *Proceedings of the Royal Society, Series B*. doi: 10.1098/rspb.2008.1142.

Given D.R. and Harris W. (1994) *Techniques and methods of ethnobotany: as an aid to the study, evaluation, conservation and sustainable use of biodiversity*. Commonwealth Secretariat Publications.

Gong W.K. and Ong J.E. (1995) The use of demographic studies in mangrove silviculture. *Hydrobiologia*, 295: 255-261.

Hamilton L.S. and Snedaker S.C. (1984) *Handbook for mangrove area management*. East/West Center, Hawaii, UNESCO & IUCN.

Hancock J., Kushlan J. and Kahl M. (1992) *Storks, Ibises and Spoonbills of the World*. San Diego, CA: Harcourt Brace Jovanovich.

Harcourt C.S. and Sayer J.A. (eds) (1996) IUCN. *The conservation atlas of tropical forests: the Americas*. Simon and Schuster, New York.

Harris V.A. (1961) On the locomotion of the mudskipper *Periophthalmus koelreuteri* (Pallas): Gobiidae. *Proceedings of the Zoological Society of London*, 134: 107-135.

Hartnoll R.G. (1987) Eco-ethology of mangroves. In: Chelazzi G. and Vannini M. (eds) *Behavioural adaptations to intertidal life*. NATO ASI Series A: Life Sciences, 151: 477-489.

Hayman P., Marchant J. and Prater T. (1986). *Shorebirds*. Croom Helm.

Healy T.R. (2005) Muddy coasts. In: Schwartz M.L. (ed.) *Encyclopedia of coastal science*. Springer, The Netherlands, p. 674-675.

Hogan Z.S. (2003) *Pangasianodon gigas*. In: International Union for Conservation of Nature (IUCN). Red List of Threatened Species. Version 2009.1. Available at: *www.iucnredlist.org*. Accessed on July 2009.

Hogan Z.S., Moyle P.B., May B., Vander Zander M.J. and Baird I.G. (2004) The imperiled giants of the Mekong. *American Scientist*, 92: 228-237.

Hogan Z.S., Pengbun N. and van Zalinge N. (2001) Status and conservation of two endangered fish species, the Mekong giant catfish *Pangasianodon gigas* and the giant carp *Catlocarpio siamensis*, in Cambodia's Tonle Sap River. *Natural History Bulletin of the Siam Society*, 49: 26-282.

Hogarth P.J. (2007) *The biology of mangroves and seagrasses*, 2nd edition. Oxford University Press, Oxford.

Hoscilo A., Page S.E. and Tansey K. (2009) *Repeated and extensive fire as the main driver of land cover change in block C of the former Mega Rice Project area*. In: Rieley J.O., Banks C.J. and Page S.E. (eds.) Future of tropical peatlands in Southeast Asia as carbon pools and sinks. Papers presented at the special session on tropical peatlands at the 13th international peat congress. Tullamore, Ireland, 10th June 2008. Published by Carbopeat, University of Leicester, Leicester. Available online at *http://www.geog.le.ac.uk*. Visited in May 2009.

Hughes A.R. and Stachowicz J.J. (2004) Genetic diversity enhances the resistance of a seagrass ecosystem to disturbance. *PNAS*, 101: 8998-9002.

Ismail A., Badri M.A., and Ramlan M.N. (1991). Heavy metal contamination in fiddler crabs (*Uca annulipes*) and hermit crabs (*Clibanarius* sp.) in a coastal area of northern peninsular Malaysia. *Environmental Technology*, 12: 923-926.

Joosten H. (2004) The IMCG Global Peatland Database. Available online at *www.imcg.net/gpd/gpd.htm*. Visited in July 2009).

Karvonen A., Savolainen M., Seppälä O. and Valtonen E.T. (2006) Dynamics of *Diplostomum spathaceum* infection in snail hosts at a fish farm. *Parasitology Research*, doi 10.1007/s00436-006-0137-8.

Kelaher B.P., Underwood A.J. and Chapman M.G. (1998) Effects of boardwalks on the semaphore crab *Heloecius cordiformis* in temperate urban mangrove forests. *Journal of Experimental Marine Biology and Ecology*, 227: 281-300.

Kemp M. (2005) Dying for a drink. Evolution goes backwards in the latest Guinness advertisement. *Nature*, 438: 564.

Kizhakudan and Shoba (2005) *Role of fishermen in conservation and management of marine fishery resources in Gujarat, India - some case studies*. Centre for Maritime Research (MARE), July 7-9 2005 Conference Amsterdam, The Netherlands. Available online at: *http://www.marecentre.nl*. Visited in June 2009.

Kottelat M. (1996a) *Epalzeorhynchos bicolor*. In: International Union for Conservation of Nature (IUCN). Red List of Threatened Species. Version 2009.1. Available online at: *www.iucnredlist.org*. Accessed on July 2009.

Kottelat M. (1996b) *Scleropages formosus*. In: International Union for Conservation of Nature (IUCN). Red List of Threatened Species. Version 2009.1. Available online at: *www.iucnredlist.org*. Accessed on July 2009.

Kottelat M. and Whitten T. (1996). *Freshwater biodiversity in Asia: with special reference to fish*. World Bank Publications.

Kottelat M. and Widjanarti E. (2005) The fishes of Danau Sentarum National Park and the Kapuas Lakes area, Kalimantan Barat, Indonesia. In: Kottelat M. and Yeo D.C.J. (eds). Southeast Asian freshwater fish diversity. *The Raffles Bulletin of Zoology*, Suppl. 13, 208 pp.

Kottelat M., Britz R., Tan H.H. and Witte K.-E. (2006) *Paedocypris*, a new genus of Southeast Asian cyprinid fish with a remarkable sexual dimorphism, comprises the world's smallest vertebrate. *Proceedings of the Royal Society, Biological Sciences*, 273: 895-899.

Kristensen E. and Alongi D.M. (2006). Control by fiddler crabs (*Uca vocans*) and plant roots (*Avicennia marina*) on carbon, iron, and sulfur biogeochemistry in mangrove sediment. *Limnology and Oceanography*, 51: 1557-1571.

Kristensen E., Boullon S., Dittmar T. and Marshand C. (2008). Organic carbon dynamics in mangrove ecosystems: A review. *Aquatic Botany*, 89: 201-219.

Kumazawa Y. and Nishida M. (2000) Molecular phylogeny of osteoglossoids: a new model for Gondwanian origin and plate tectonic transportation of the Asian arowana. *Molecular Biology and Evolution*, 17: 1869-1878.

Lacerda (de) L.D. (2002) *Mangrove ecosystems: function and management.* Springer.

Lacerda (de) L.D., Carvalho C.E., Tanizaki K.F., Ovalle A.R. and Rezende C.E. (1993) The biogeochemistry and trace metals distribution of mangrove rhizospheres. *Biotropica*, 25: 252-257.

Lacerda (de) L.D., Kremer H.H., Kjerfve B., Salomons W. and Maeshall Crossland J.I. (2001) *South American basins: SamBas-LOICZ, Global assessment and synthesis of river catchment/coastal sea interaction and human dimensions*. LOICZ Reports & Studies No. 21, LOICZ, Texel, The Netherlands.

Lee S.Y. (2008) Mangrove macrobenthos: assemblages, services, and linkages. *Journal of Sea Research*, 59: 16-29.

Lewis R.R. III (2005) Ecological engineering for successful management and restoration of mangrove forests. *Ecological Engineering*, 24: 403-418.

Linnaeus C. (1758) *Systema naturae per regna tria naturae, secundum classes, ordines, genera, species, cum characteribus, differentiis, synonymis, locis* (Pisces) – Laurentii Salvii, Holmiae (edn 10): 824 pp.

Logan G. & Longmore A. (2003) Sediment organic matter and nutrients. Available online at *http://www.ozcoasts.org.au/indicators/sediment_org_matter.jsp*. Visited in May 2009.

Lonely Planet (2009) Available online at *http://www.lonelyplanet.com/thailand/ubon-ratchathani-province/pha-taem-national-park*. Visited in June 2009.

Lugo A.E. (1980) Mangrove ecosystems: successional or steady state? *Biotropica*, 12(2): 65-72.

Macintosh D.J., Ashton E.C. and Havanon S. (2002) Mangrove rehabilitation and intertidal biodiversity: a study of the Ranong mangrove ecosystem: Thailand. *Eastuarine Coastal and Shelf Science*, 55: 331-345.

MacKinnon K., Hatta G., Halim H. and Mangalik A. (1996) *The ecology of Kalimantan*. Oxford University Press.

Malaysian Wetland Directory (1987) Published by Department of Wildlife and National Parks, Peninsular Malaysia. Kuala Lumpur, 316 p.

Mancini A. (1991) Mudskippers in nature and captivity. *Tropical Fish Hobbyist*, 6/91: 10-23.

Manoj K. and Ragothaman G. (1999). Mercury, copper and cadmium induced changes in the total proteins level in muscle tissue of an edible estuarine fish, *Boleophthalmus dussumieri* (CUV). *Journal of Environmental Biology*, 20: 231-234.

Martini I.P., Martínez Cortizas A., and Chesworth W. (2006) *Peatlands: evolution and records of environmental and climate changes*. Elsevier Science Publishers. p. 606.

Mazda Y., Kanazawa N. and Wolanski E. (1995) Tidal asimmetry in mangrove creeks. *Hydrobiologia*, 295: 51-58.

Mazda Y., Magi M., Kogo M. and Hong P.N. (1997) Mangroves as a coastal protection from waves in the Tong King delta, Vietnam. *Mangroves and Salt Marshes*, 1: 127-135.

Mazda Y., Magi M., Nanao H., Kogo M., Miyagi T., Kanazawa N. and Kobashi D. (2002) Coastal erosion due to long term human impact on mangrove forests. *Wetlands Ecology and Management*, 10: 1-9.

Mazda Y., Yokochi H. and Sato Y. (1990) The behaviour of groundwater in a mangrove area and the influence on the properties of water and bottom mud. *Estuarine Coastal and Shelf Science*, 21: 687-699.

McCool S.F. (1996) *limits of acceptable change: a framework for managing national protected areas: experiences from the United States*. Workshop on impact management in marine parks, sponsored by Maritime Institute of Malaysia, August 13-14, Kuala Lumpur, Malaysia.

Menasveta P. (1996) Mangrove destruction and shrimp culture systems. *Thai Journal of Aquatic Science*, 2: 72-82.

Mitchell R. and Braun D. (2003) Giant catfish critically endangered, group says. *National Geographic News.* Available online at *http://news.nationalgeographic.com/news/2003/11/1118_031118_giantcatfish.html.* Visited in June 2009.

Mumby P., Edwards A., Arias-Gonzalez J., Lindeman K., Blackwell P., Gall A., Gorczynska M., Harborne A., Pescod C., Renken H., Wabnitz C. and Llewellyn G. (2004). Mangroves enhance the biomass of coral reef fish communities in the Caribbean. *Nature,* 427: 533-536.

Murdiyarso D., Suryadiputra N., Dewi S. and Agus F. (2009) *How can REDD scheme support the management of vulnerable carbon pools of Indonesian peatlands?* In: Rieley J.O., Banks C.J. and Page S.E. (eds.) Future of tropical peatlands in Southeast Asia as carbon pools and sinks. Papers presented at the special session on tropical peatlands at the 13th international peat congress. Tullamore, Ireland, 10th June 2008. Published by Carbopeat, University of Leicester, Leicester. Available online at *http://www.geog.le.ac.uk.* Visited in May 2009.

Murdy E.O. (1989) A taxonomic revision and cladistic analysis of the oxudercine gobies (Gobiidae: Oxudercinae). *Records of the Australian Museum*, Suppl. No. 11: 1-93.

Myers R. and Jewel J. (1990) *Ecosystems of Florida.* University Press of Florida.

Nagelkerken I., Blaber S.J.M., Bouillon S., Green P., Haywood M., Kirton L.G., Meynecke J.-O., Pawlik J., Penrose H.M., Sasekumar A. and Somerfield P.J. (2008) The habitat function of mangroves for terrestrial and marine fauna: a review. *Aquatic Botany*, 89: 155-185.

Nakata H., Sakai Y. and Miyawaki T. (2002) Growth-dependent and species-specific accumulation of polychlorinated biphenyls (PCBs) in tidal flat organisms collected from the Ariake Sea, Japan. *Archives of environmental contamination and toxicology*, 42: 222-228.

Ng P.K.L., Tay J.B. and Lim K.K.P. (1994) Diversity and conservation of blackwater fishes in Peninsular Malaysia, particularly in the North Selangor peat swamp forest. *Hydrobiologia*, 285: 203-218.

Ng P.K.L., Wang L.K. and Lim K.P. (eds) (2008). *Private lives. An exposé of Singapore's mangroves.* Raffles Museum of Biodiversity Research. National Univ. Singapore.

Nisbet I.C.T. (1968) The utilization of mangroves by Malayan birds. *Ibis*, 110: 348-352.

Noske R.A. (1995) The ecology of mangrove forest birds in Peninsular Malaysia. *Ibis*, 137: 250-263.

Okudo H., Toma T., Sasaki H., Higa Y., Fujikawa M. et al. (2004) A crab-hole mosquito, *Ochlerotatus baisasi*, feeding on mudskipper (Gobiidae: Oxudercinae) in the Ryukyu Islands, Japan. *Journal of the American Mosquito Control Association*, 20: 134-137.

Ong J.E. and Tan K.H. (2008) *Mangroves and sea-level change.* In: Chan H.T. and Ong J.E. (eds) Proceedings of the meeting and workshop on guidelines for the rehabilitation of mangroves and other coastal forests damaged by tsunamis and other natural hazard in the Asia-Pacific region. International society for mangrove ecosystems mangrove ecosystems proceedings, 5. pp. 89-96.

Ong J.E., Gong W.K. and Chan H.C. (2001). *Governments of developing countries grossly undervalue their mangroves?* In: Proceedings of the international symposium on protection and management of coastal marine ecosystems. Bangkok, Thailand, 12-13 December, 2000. EAS/RCU, UNEP, Bangkok, Thailand, pp. 179-184.

Othman J., Bennett J.and Blamey R. (2004) Environmental values and resource management options: a choice modelling experience in Malaysia. *Environment and Development Economics*, 9: 803-824.

Owen J. (2005) Grizzly bear-size catfish caught in Thailand. *National Geographic News.* Available online at *http://news.nationalgeographic.com/news/2005/06/0629_050629_giantcatfish.html.* Visited in July 2009.

Page S.E., Banks C.J. and Wust R. (2008) *Extent, significance and vulnerability of the tropical peatland carbon pool: past, present and future prospects*. In: Rieley J.O., Banks C.J. and Page S.E. (eds.) Future of tropical peatlands in Southeast Asia as carbon pools and sinks. Papers presented at the special session on tropical peatlands at the 13th international peat congress. Tullamore, Ireland, 10th June 2008. Published by Carbopeat, University of Leicester, Leicester. Available online at *http://www.geog.le.ac.uk*. Visited in May 2009.

Papadopoulos I., Wooldridge T.H. and Newman B.K. (2002) Larval life history strategies of sub-tropical southern African estuarine brachyuran crabs and implications for tidal inlet management. *Wetlands Ecology and Management,* 10: 249-256.

PEMSEA (1999) *Total economic valuation: coastal and marine resources in the Straits of Malacca.* Technical Report No. 24. Quezon City, Philippines.

PEMSEA (2002) *Proceedings of the national conference on media as key partners in environmental sustainability.* Manila, Philippines, 23 October 2002.

PEMSEA (2007a) *Coastal land- and sea-use. Zoning plan of the province of Bataan.* Bataan Coastal Care Foundation, Inc. wih technical assistance from GEF/UNDP/IMO Regional Programme on Partnerships in Environmental Management for the Seas of East Asia (PEMSEA).

PEMSEA (2007b) *Concept paper on collaboration in the ecosystem-based management of coastal areas and river basins in East Asia*. In: Third twinning workshop on ecosystem-based management of interrelated river basins, estuaries and coastal seas: Policy reform, sustainable financing and investment for pollution reduction in the East Asian Seas. Partnerships in Environmental Management for the Seas of East Asia. Tianjin, PR China, 17-19 October, 2007.

Pepping M., Piersma T., Pearson G. and Lavaleye M. (eds) (1997). *Intertidal sediments and benthic animals of Roebuck Bay, Western Australia*. Netherlands Institute for Sea Research (NIOZ). 212 p.

Polgar G. (2006*) Impact of mangrove deforestation on the diversity of Malaysian oxudercine gobies (Gobiidae: Oxudercinae). Preliminary observations and future research*. International Conference and Exhibition on Mangroves of Indian and Western Pacific Oceans (ICEMAN), 21-24 August 2006, Kuala Lumpur, Malaysia.

Polgar G. (2008) Species–area relationship and potential role as a biomonitor of mangrove communities of Malayan mudskippers. *Wetland Ecology and Management,* 17: 157-164.

Polgar G. and Crosa G. (2009) Multivariate characterisation of the habitats of seven species of Malayan mudskippers (Gobiidae: Oxudercinae) *Marine Biology*, 156: 1475-1486.

Polidoro B., Carpenter K., Collins L., Duke N., Ellison A., Ellison J., Eong O.J., Farnsworth E., Fernando E., Kathiresan K., Koedam N.E., Livingstone S., Miyagi T., Moore G., Nam V.N., Primavera J., Salmo S.G. III, Sanciangco J., Spalding M., Sukardjo S., Yong J.W.-H. and Wang Y. (*PLOS Biology*, under revision) The loss of species: mangrove extinction risk and failure of critical ecosystem services.

Polunin I.W. (1972) Who says fish cant' climb trees? *National Geographic*, 141: 85-91.

Por F.D., Dor I. (1984) *Hydrobiology of the mangal.* Dr Junk W. Publ., The Hague, pp. 1-14.

Pouyaud L., Sudarto and Teugels G. (2003) The different colour varieties of the Asian arowana *Scleropages formosus* (Osteoglossidae) are distinct species: morphologic and genetic evidences. *Cybium*, 27: 287-305.

Pratt A.E. and McLain D.K. (2006) How dear is my enemy: Intruder-resident and resident-resident encounters in male sand fiddler crabs (*Uca pugilator*). *Behaviour*, 143: 597-617.

Primack R. (2004) *A primer of conservation biology. 3rd edition.* Sinauer Associates.

Pugh D.T. (1997) Sea-level change: meeting the challenge. *Nature and Resources*, 33: 26-32.

Rainboth W.J. (1996) *Fishes of the Cambodian Mekong.* Food and Agriculture Organization (FAO), Rome.

Ramsar Convention on Wetlands (2009) official website: *http://www.ramsar.org/.* Visited in June 2009.

Ridd P.V. (1996) Flow through animal burrows in mangrove creeks. *Estuarine, Coastal and Shelf Science*, 43: 617-625.

Rieley J.O. and Page S.E. (2005) *Wise use of tropical peatlands: focus on Southeast Asia.* Alterra, Netherlands.

Risch S.J. (1981) Insect herbivore abundance in tropical monocultures and polycultures: an experimental test of two hypotheses. *Ecology*, 62: 1325-1340.

Roberts T.R. (1993) Artisanal fisheries and fish ecology below the great waterfalls of the Mekong River in southern Laos. *Natural History Bulletin of the Siam Society*, 41: 31-62.

Roberts T.R. and Vidthayanon C. (1991) Systematic revision of the Asian catfish family Pangasiidae, with biological observations and descriptions of three new species. *Proceedings of the Academy of Natural Sciences of Philadelphia*, 143: 97-144.

Rocha L.A. and Bowen B.W. (2008) Speciation in coral-reef fishes. *Journal of Fish Biology*, 72: 1101-1121.

Rosenberg M.S. (2001) The systematics and taxonomy of fiddler crabs: a phylogeny of the genus *Uca. Journal of Crustacean Biology*, 21: 839-869.

Rüber L., Kottelat M., Tan H.H., Ng P.K.L. and Britz R. (2007) Evolution of miniaturization and the phylogenetic position of *Paedocypris*, comprising the world's smallest vertebrate. *BMC Evolutionary Biology*, 7: 38. doi: 10.1186/1471-2148-7-38. Available online at *http://www.biomedcentral.com/1471-2148/7/38.* Visited in June 2009.

Sasekumar A. (1974) Distribution of macrofauna on a Malayan mangrove shore. *Journal of Animal Ecology*, 43: 51-69.

Sasekumar A. (1980) *The present state of mangrove ecosystems in Southeast Asia and the impact of pollution.* FAO/UNEP project: impact of pollution on the mangrove ecosystem and its productivity in Southeast Asia; (SCS/80/WP/94b). Publication of the South China Sea Fisheries Development and Coordinating Programme, 4–8 February 1980, Manila.

Sayer J.A., Harcourt C.S. and Collins N.M. (1992) *The conservation atlas of tropical forests: Africa.* IUCN and Simon & Schuster, Cambridge.

Siegert F. and Jaenicke J. (2009) *Estimation of carbon storage in Indonesian peatlands*. In: Rieley J.O., Banks C.J. and Page S.E. (eds.) Future of tropical peatlands in Southeast Asia as carbon pools and sinks. Papers presented at the special session on tropical peatlands at the 13th international peat congress. Tullamore, Ireland, 10th June 2008. Published by Carbopeat, University of Leicester, Leicester. Available online at *http://www.geog.le.ac.uk*. Visited in May 2009.

Skilleter G.A. and Warren S. (2000) Effects of habitat modification in mangroves on the structure of mollusc and crab assemblages. *Journal of Experimental Marine Biology and Ecology*, 244: 107-129.

Smith T.J., Boto K.G., Frusher S.D. and Giddings R.L. (1991) Keystone species and mangrove forest dynamics: the influence of burrowing by crabs on soil nutrient status and forest productivity. *Estuarine, Coastal and Shelf Science*, 33: 19-32.

Srinivasan, M. and Mahajan B.A. (1989) Mercury pollution in an estuarine region and its effect on a coastal population. *International Journal of Environmental Studies*, 35: 63-69.

Storr G.M., Smith L.A., Johnstone R.E. (1986) *Snakes of Western Australia*. Western Australian Museum, Perth.

Stuebing R.B., Bezuijen A.R., Auliya M. and Voris H.K. (2006) The current and historic distribution of *Tomistoma schlegelii* (the false gharial) (Müller, 1838) (Crocodylia, Reptilia). *The Raffles Bulletin of Zoology*, 54: 181-197.

Swennen C., Duiven P. and Spaans A.C. (1982). Numerical density and biomass of macrobenthic animals living in the intertidal zone of Surinam, South America. *Journal of Sea Research*, 15: 406-418.

Takegaki T. (2008) Threatened fishes of the world: *Boleophthalmus pectinirostris* (Linnaeus 1758) (Gobiidae). *Environmental Biology of Fishes*, 81: 373-374.

Takita T., Agusnimar, Ali A.B. (1999) Distribution and habitat requirements of oxudercine gobies (Gobiidae: Oxudercinae) along the Straits of Malacca. *Ichthyological Research*, 46: 131-138.

Tan K.H. and Ong J.E. (2008) *Coastal vegetation rehabilitation for the mitigation of coastal hazards. The Malaysian experience*. In: Chan H.T. and Ong J.E. (eds) Proceedings of the meeting and workshop on guidelines for the rehabilitation of mangroves and other coastal forests damaged by tsunamis and other natural hazard in the Asia-Pacific region. International society for mangrove ecosystems. *Mangrove Ecosystems Proceedings*, 5. p. 57-63.

Targarona R.R., Soberón R.R., Cotayo L., Tabet M.A. and Thorbjarnarson J. (2008) *Crocodylus rhombifer*. In: International Union for Conservation of Nature (IUCN). Red List of Threatened Species. Version 2009.1. Available online at: *www.iucnredlist.org*. Accessed on July 2009.

Taverne L., Nolfe D. and Folie A. (2007) On the presence of the osteoglossid fish genus *Scleropages* (Teleostei, Osteoglossiformes) in the continental Paleocene of Hainin (Mons Basin, Belgium). *Belgian Journal of Zoology*, 137: 89-97.

Tokeshi M. (1999) *Species coexistence. Ecological and evolutionary perspectives*. Blackwell Science.

Tomlinson P.B. (1986) *The botany of mangroves*. Cambridge University Press, London.

Townsend P.K. and Townsend W.H. (2004) Assessing an assessment: The Ok Tedi Mine. In: 758 *Bridging scales and epistemologies: linking local knowledge and global science in multi759 scale assessments*, Alexandria, 17-20 March.

Turay I., Vakily J.M., Palomares M.L.D. and Pauly D. (2006) Growth, reproduction and food of the mudskipper, *Periophthalmus barbarus* on mudflats of Freetown, Sierra Leone. In: Palomares M.L.D., Stergiou K.I. and Pauly D. (eds) *Fishes in databases and ecosystems. Fisheries Centre Research Reports*, 14: 49-54. Fisheries Centre, University of British Columbia.

UNEP (2006) *Protecting coastal and marine environments from land-based activities: a guide for national action.* UNEP/Earthprint, pp. 96

UNEP-DHI (2007) The benefits and the challenges of linked coastal and river basin management. 15 case studies. Draft report 22/06/07. Available online at: *http://www.ucc-water.org/.* Visited in June 2007.

UNEP-WCMC (2009). UNEP-WCMC Species Database: CITES-Listed Species. Available online at: *http://sea.unep-wcmc.org/isdb/CITES/Taxonomy/?displaylanguage=eng.* Visited in June 2009.

Walker H.J. and McGraw M. (2005) History, coastal geomorphology. In: Schwartz M.L. (ed.) *Encyclopedia of coastal science* Springer, The Netherlands, p. 519-525.

Wall G. (1997) Is ecotourism sustainable? *Environmental Management,* 21: 483-491.

Wikramanayake E., Dinerstein E., Loucks C. (2001) *Terrestrial ecoregions of the Indo-Pacific: A conservation assessment.* Island Press, World Wildlife Fund Ecoregion Assessments Vol. 3. 824 p.

Wilkie M.L. and Fortuna S. (2003) Part 1: global overview. In: *Status and trends in mangrove area extent worldwide.* Forest Resources Assessment Working Paper No. 63. Forest Resources Division. FAO, Rome. Available online at *http://www.fao.org/docrep/007/j1533e/J1533E02.htm#P199_6397.* Visited in June 2009.

Wolanski E. (1992) Hydrodynamics of mangrove swamps and their coastal waters. *Hydrobiologia,* 247: 141-161.

Wolanski E. (1995) Transport of sediment in mangrove swamps. *Hydrobiologia,* 295: 31-42.

Woodroffe (1992) Mangrove sediments and geomorphology. In: Robertson A.I., Alongi D.M. (eds) *Tropical mangrove ecosystems.* Coastal estuarine studies 41. American Geophysical Union, Washington DC, pp. 7-42.

World Conservation Monitoring Centre (1998) In: International Union for Conservation of Nature (IUCN). *Red List of Threatened Species.* Version 2009.1. Available at: *www.iucnredlist.org.* Visited in July 2009.

World Land Trust (2003) Annual report. Available online at *http://www.worldlandtrust.org.* Visited in July 2009.

World Wildlife Fund (Content Partner), Caley K.J. (Topic Editor) (2008a) Borneo peat swamp forests. In: Cleveland C.J. (ed.) *Encyclopedia of Earth.* Available online at *http://www.eoearth.org.* Visited in June 2009.

World Wildlife Fund (Content Partner), McGinley M. (Topic Editor) (2008b) Sumatran peat swamp forests. In: Cleveland C.J. (ed.) *Encyclopedia of Earth.* Available online at *http://www.eoearth.org.* Visited in June 2009.

World Wildlife Fund (Content Partner), McGinley M. (Topic Editor) (2008c) Southwest Borneo freshwater swamp forests. In: Cleveland C.J. (ed.) *Encyclopedia of Earth.* Available online at *http://www.eoearth.org.* Visited in June 2009.

Wösten J.H.M. (2009) *Risk assessment of tropical peatland carbon pools under different land uses and impacts.* In: Rieley J.O., Banks C.J. and Page S.E. (eds.) Future of tropical peatlands in Southeast Asia as carbon pools and sinks. Papers presented at the special session on tropical peatlands at the 13th international peat congress. Tullamore, Ireland, 10th June 2008. Published by Carbopeat, University of Leicester, Leicester. Available online at http://www.geog.le.ac.uk. Visited in May 2009.

Yeager C.P. and Russon A. (1998) Trial by fire. *International Primatological Society Newsletter*, 25: 8-9.

Young B.M. and Harvey L.E. (1996) A spatial analysis of the relationship between mangrove (*Avicennia marina* var. *australoasica*) physiognomy and sediment accretion in the Hauraki plains, New Zealand. *Estuarine Coastal and Shelf Science,* 42: 231-246.

Yu H. (2005) *PEMSEA's initiative in ecosystem-based management for interrelated river basins, estuaries and coastal seas.* In: Proceedings of the workshop on ecosystem-based management of interrelated river basins, estuaries and coastal seas. Masan, Republic of Korea, 1-3 June 2005.

Zhang Q.-Y., Hong W.-S., Dai Q.-N., Zhang J., Cai Y.-Y. and Huang J.-L. (1989) Studies on induced ovulation, embryonic development and larval rearing of the mudskipper (*Boleophthalmus pectinirostris*). *Aquaculture*, 83: 375-385.

In: Ecotourism: Management, Development and Impact
Editors: A. Krause, E. Weir, pp. 89-111
ISBN: 978-1-60876-724-3
© 2010 Nova Science Publishers, Inc.

Chapter 3

Environmental Education as a Crucial Component of the Environmentalist Dimension of Ecotourism: Inducing Short-Term Effects on Environmental Literacy with Long-Term Implications for Protected Area Management

Tasos Hovardas[1], Anatoli Togridou[2] and John D. Pantis[2]
[1]University of Thessaly
[2]Aristotle University of Thessaloniki.

Abstract

Ecotourism can be conceptualized as a reconciliation of tourism and environmentalism. The environmentalist dimension of ecotourism involves environmental education and financial support of nature conservation. In this regard, environmental education has the potential to enhance visitor environmental knowledge and prompt change of visitor environmental behaviour. For instance, one of the main challenges for ecotourism is to move visitors from a passive state to an active contribution to the sustainability of protected areas. Indeed, previous research showed that there is a significant potential of ecotourists financing environmental conservation and providing voluntary work in the frame of the protected area management. However, a considerable number of studies highlighted a significant inefficiency of educational programs to support nature conservation. Most ecotourism activity seems to foster a frivolous understanding of particular megafauna and does not aspire to transform visitor behaviour. The prevalent circumstances at most ecotourism destinations, including non-captive audiences and a limited time frame, challenge even the goal of effective interpretation. Superficial learning opportunities are usually concentrated on flagship species, which may be easier to provide and guarantee visitor satisfaction. The objective of this paper is to show how environmental education can support a comprehensive approach in ecotourism development, which wishes to foster a deep understanding of natural and social characteristics of ecotourism destinations and endeavors to transform visitors' and locals' behaviour. We recorded baseline information of visitors and local people in the National Marine Park of Zakynthos, Greece, including demographic information, self-reported environmental behaviour, pro-environmental behaviour intention, consensus estimates for pro-environmental behaviour intention, environmental knowledge, and environmental concern. The crucial questions to be addressed are (1) how can baseline information derived by the present study inform the development of aims and specifications of environmental education interventions targeting ecotourists who visit protected areas as well as local people residing in ecotourism destinations (2) how can the potential effects of environmental education programs contribute in protected area management.

INTRODUCTION

Environmental Education in Ecotourism Destinations

Ecotourism can be conceptualized as a reconciliation of tourism and environmentalism. The environmentalist dimension of ecotourism involves environmental education and financial support of nature conservation (Hovardas & Poirazidis, 2006). Indeed, environmental education is considered among the core constituents of ecotourism (Donohoe & Needham, 2006; Kimmel, 1999; Rodger et al., 2007). In this regard, environmental education has the potential to enhance visitor environmental knowledge and prompt change of visitor environmental behaviour. For instance, one of the main challenges for ecotourism is to move visitors from a passive state to an active contribution to the sustainability of protected areas. In an overview of ecotourism definitions formulated within academia and the ecotourism industry during the last twenty years, Donohoe and Needham (2006) underlined that ecotourism is theoretically rooted in educational experiences. Generally, it seems that the supply-side tries to be reflective of theoretical principles of ecotourism as far as environmental education is concerned (Rodger et al., 2007).

Increasing environmental knowledge levels and fostering motivation for pro-environmental behaviour are considered among the primary goals of environmental education in establishing environmental literacy (Pĕer et al., 2007). However, a considerable number of studies highlighted a significant inefficiency of educational programs to support nature conservation. First, simply taking visitors to unique sites does not guarantee learning (Kimmel, 1999). Second, most ecotourism activity seems to foster a frivolous understanding of particular megafauna and does not aspire to transform visitor behaviour (Mühlhäusler & Peace, 2001). The prevalent circumstances at most ecotourism destinations, including non-captive audiences and a limited time frame, challenge even the goal of effective interpretation. Superficial learning opportunities are usually concentrated on flagship species, which may be easier to provide and guarantee visitor satisfaction. Next to the above-mentioned results, there has been little measurement of the effects of environmental education interventions in ecotourism destinations (Tisdell & Wilson, 2005). These particularities call into question simplistic conceptualizations of environmental education frequently endorsed by international policy documents and adopted in ecotourism destinations, according to which the mere provision of information suffices to bring about changes to knowledge, attitudes, and behaviours and lead to the creation of a sustainable society (Blum, 2008).

The inefficiency of the theoretical background on which environmental education interventions are grounded is also manifested in the second cornerstone of environmental literacy, namely, the promotion of pro-environmental behaviour. For example, environmental educators in ecotourism destinations have mostly focused on informing visitors about any possible negative impact of their behaviour on the natural environment instead of promoting pro-social behaviours that necessitate the investment of considerable resources, cooperation and joint action. This has frequently led to a representation of visitors' own responsibilities and potential contribution in ecotourism destinations in terms of self-interested behaviours aimed at reducing personal impacts on the environment. In contradistinction, environmental activism is defined as engagement in pro-social activities focusing on preserving or improving the quality of the environment, and increasing public awareness of environmental issues (Seguin et al., 1998). However, environmental activism is not promoted by reference material and environmental education initiatives within ecotourism destinations, although previous research showed that there is a significant potential of recruiting visitors to finance environmental conservation and provide voluntary work for protected area management (Hovardas & Poirazidis, 2006; Machairas & Hovardas, 2005; McFarlane & Hunt, 2006; Tisdell & Wilson, 2005; Togridou et al., 2006a;).

A common practise in both formal and informal environmental education settings is to promote a simplistically conceptualized reinforcement of environmental awareness at the expense of knowledge acquisition (Hovardas, 2005). Quite a few environmental education interventions in ecotourism destinations have set as their foremost objective to raise the environmental awareness of visitors. However, ecotourists are by definition a quite aware group of people in environmental issues compared to other social groups. This apparent paradox, namely, the attempt to raise the environmental awareness of already aware visitors, reflects a crucial lack of adequate theoretical backing and assessment methodologies in the field of environmental education (Hovardas & Korfiatis, 2009). Indeed, a number of studies reported a 'ceiling' effect, where participants in environmental education programmes with high prior motivation presented only small gains after the intervention was completed (Beaumont 2001; Brossard et al., 2005; Hovardas & Poirazidis, 2006; Moody & Hartel, 2007). Since the general public demonstrates considerable pro-environmental intention (Tilikidou, 2007), most participants in environmental education projects come along with high inclination to act in a pro-environmental way already before any intervention has even started. In this case, educational objectives cannot any longer target at simply fostering pro-environmental intention. A crucial question to be addressed in this direction is how to reformulate the goals of educational interventions.

Moreover, literature on environmental literacy has not adequately addressed the socio-cultural context of both formal and informal educational interventions (Pooley & O'Connor, 2000). Endorsement of pro-environmental action depends on descriptive norms, that is, consensus estimates for a given behaviour or behaviour intention (Bamberg & Möser, 2007; Kallgren et al., 2000; Marion & Reid, 2007). Descriptive norms can have a crucial influence on pro-environmental intention (Thøgersen, 2008). This is especially valid for environmental activism (Kolstø, 2006), where the contribution of a single individual can only raise the probability of providing a behavioural outcome by a small amount (Diekmann & Preisendörfer, 1998; Lubell, 2002). A fact frequently neglected in empirical research is that people hold descriptive beliefs with some uncertainty. Namely, an individual is likely to decline a behaviour just because he/she has overestimated or underestimated the actual intention of similar others. The wide diffusion of the environmentalist discourse during the last decades increases the complexity of the potential mediation of social norms on behavioural outcomes (Michel-Guillou & Moser, 2006). At the time of its inception, environmental education may have been a rather confined field that attracted the attention of an academic and activist minority. However, environmental awareness is rising to a substantial degree all over the globe due to environmental problems such as the greenhouse effect, which leads the majority of people to acknowledge the urgency behind many environmental issues. Given this trend, pro-environmental dispositions should no longer to be addressed as of minorital status (Castro, 2006).

Unraveling the complexity of local communities: a hidden potential to support environmental conservation, ecotourism development and the structuring of environmental education interventions

Recent research has shown that local residents in ecotourism destinations are much more likely to adopt pro-environmental stances than expected (Bell et al., 2007; Hovardas & Stamou, 2006a). Indeed, this stands in sharp contrast with local residents' attitudes in the past, since they engaged in fierce park-people conflicts (Hovardas, 2005). This attitude shift could be mainly attributed to environmental non-governmental organizations leading initiatives for protected area designation in the first place (Carmin, 2003). These organizations use to launch numerous environmental education programmes that apparently contributed in the fading out of local reaction and the diffusion of environmentalist claims in rural areas (Hovardas & Korfiatis, 2008; Hovardas et al., 2009; Michel-Guillou & Moser, 2006; Papageorgiou et al., 2005; Pipinos & Fokiali, 2007). Further, locals themselves are engaged in ecotourism development, as well as environmental management and governance of protected areas (Bell et al., 2007; Papageorgiou & Kassioumis, 2004). However, the ecological discourse usually adopts a rather controversial and quite contradictory position towards local communities in protected areas. For instance, ecological discourse can cultivate negative stances toward extractive activities (e.g., fishing, hunting), mainly due to their impact on wildlife and the local environment (Bell et al., 2007). Indeed, this could be the case among even young children in protected areas (Korfiatis et al., 2009). At the same time, ecological discourse celebrates local environmental knowledge or traditional activities of local communities as best practice to face a series of current environmental problems.

A study on environmental policy beliefs of stakeholders in protected area management, including local people, revealed that stakeholders converged on the need for ecotourism development but this was accompanied by a divergence in their attitudes toward possible ways of establishing social consensus (Hovardas & Poirazidis, 2007). Ecotourism ideally integrates environmental conservation and economic development and drives land use change within protected areas toward sustainable development alternatives (Figure 1). This is enhanced by the fact that locals are urged to engage in ecotourism and gain supplementary income (Stem et al., 2003). However, visitors to protected areas inevitably leave an imprint even at low visitation levels. Ecotourism has to resolve a paradox tension: on the one hand, visitors arrive at ecotourism destinations to encounter endangered species of flora and fauna; on the other, increased visitor numbers posit a threat to biodiversity conservation (Russell, 2007). Sustaining pristine natural resource conditions while offering high quality recreational experiences are both primary goals for protected area managers. Further, it has been reported that environmental and economic motives hardly intercross under the ecotourism rhetoric, despite the fact that ecotourism is supposed to present a sustainable development option (Hovardas & Korfiatis, 2008). At the level of social representations, the incompatibility between the utilitarian and the nature conservation discourse can lead to the sealing of processes that apparently produced the ecotourism product, which may have crucial consequences in the way local communities are reconstructed. Through such a sealing, local communities may become just another exhibit of the ecotourism experience (Che, 2006; Hovardas, 2005).

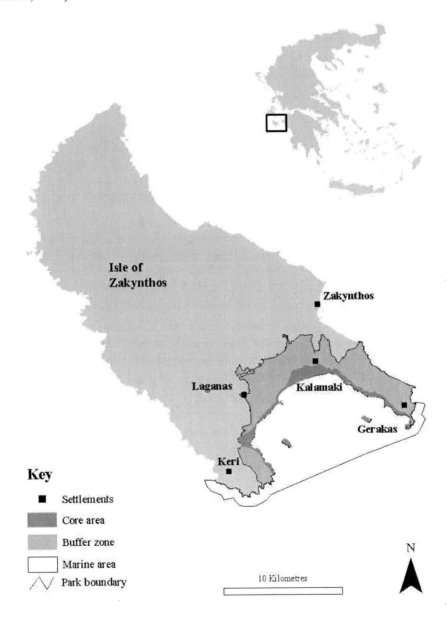

Figure 1. The National Marine Park of Zzakynthos.

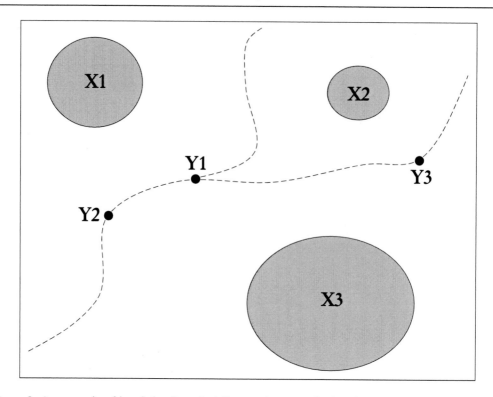

Figure 2. An example of heuristics for scheduling environmental education interventions in protected areas. The paths visitors will take should diverge from points of low natural carrying capacity (i.e. X1-X3; for instance, radius of increased concentration of sea turtles' nests) and converge to points of high educational potential (i.e. Y1-Y3, for instance, viewpoints where visitors can observe sand dune vegetation). In this design, environmental conservation and ecotourism development are integrated in a 'win-win' approach.

These findings point to a mixed-motive perspective in environmental policymaking (Hoffman et al., 1999) that is quite different from win–win and win–lose approaches in that it facilitates mutual gain solutions for both environmental and economic concerns while acknowledging their distributive aspects. Win-lose proponents argue that economic development and environmental protection are largely incompatible. Win-win proponents suggest that economic competitiveness can be improved through environmental protection. As solutions to environmental disputes require the balancing of interests among a complex array of participants, and because this can only be achieved through negotiations inevitably associated with a distributive aspect (frame of reference in win-lose models), Hoffman et al. (1999) suggested the mixed-motive model, which offers a theoretical and empirical reconciliation of the opposing perspectives. These authors argue that the range of players' interests does not bifurcate into simply economic and environmental camps, that there is an overlap of interests, and that this complexity tends to involve greater opportunities to expand the scope of the debate, finding solutions that will improve the potential outcome simultaneously for both parties (integrative principle of win-win models).

In this regard, the call to involve local people in environmental education interventions scheduled in ecotourism destinations (Wallace & Pierce, 1996) should not just be anchored in gaining their support for a pre-specified set of environmental management measures. Local people should be constructively involved as equal partners in two directions. On the one hand, they can take part as participants in programmes that aim to foster environmental awareness on modern issues at stake, such as climate change and efforts to decrease local ecological footprints. These programmes should ultimately facilitate public involvement in environmental governance (Blum, 2008). Further, local residents can enrich the content of interventions by offering local ways to handle environmental controversies and elucidating both traditional and modern alternatives. Given the heterogeneity that one can expect in local views under the diffusion of the environmentalist discourse in protected areas, an interesting question to pose is in what degree locals' environmental knowledge and pro-environmental behaviour intention differs from visitors' knowledge and intention, respectively.

Objectives of the Current Study

The objective of this paper is to show how environmental education can support a comprehensive approach in ecotourism development, which wishes to foster a deep understanding of natural and social characteristics of ecotourism destinations and endeavors to transform visitors' and locals' behaviour. In contrast to the homogeneity of participants that characterize structured educational settings, a factor that can limit setting objectives for environmental education interventions in ecotourism destinations is the variety of background of the participants (Kimmel, 1999). We recorded baseline information of visitors and local people in a Greek protected area, including demographic information, self-reported environmental behaviour, environmental knowledge, pro-environmental behaviour intention in the frame of environmental activism, consensus estimates for pro-environmental behaviour intention, and environmental concern. The crucial questions to be addressed are (1) how can baseline information derived by the present study inform the development of aims and specifications of environmental education interventions targeting ecotourists who visit protected areas as well as local people residing in ecotourism destinations (2) how can the potential effects of environmental education programs contribute in protected area management.

METHODS

Study Area

The Isle of Zakynthos is located at the southern part of the Ionian Island Complex (Figure 2). The 3.5 km sandy beach of Laganas Bay, located on the south coast of the island (Margaritoulis & Rees, 2003), is considered among the most important nesting biotopes for the loggerhead sea turtle (*Caretta caretta*) across the Mediterranean Basin. Depending on the year, 1000–2000 nests are recorded in this area. The National Marine Park of Zakynthos (NMPZ) was designated in 1999 at the south part of the island (Dimopoulos, 1999). In order to provide a legislative platform, which would allow for the satisfaction of NMPZ's goals, the Presidential Degree for the Establishment of the NMPZ followed the practice of defining zone–specific activities. The NMPZ consists of a marine area of 89.2 km^2, as well as a terrestrial area of 45.4 km^2. The latter is divided in to a core area, which covers 14.2 km^2 and includes the nesting beaches of *Caretta caretta*, and a buffer zone that covers 31.2 km^2.

Zakynthos is a prime tourist resort in the Mediterranean and has experienced rapid tourism growth over the past 20 years, which is believed to exert significant pressure on turtle nesting beaches. Park managers have to reconcile tourism and environmental conservation (Togridou et al., 2006b). However, a number of visitors that enter park borders could be characterized as ecotourists, since they present analogous characteristics (Togridou et al., 2006a). Even if the majority of these visitors should be assigned to the soft-type extreme along the ecotourism experience spectrum, there is a marked potential of financing environmental conservation and providing voluntary work in the frame of the protected area management (Togridou et al., 2006a).

The administrative body of NMPZ started implementing a voluntary program named 'Volunteers and environmental protection' in 2003 (LIFE, 2003). The aim of this program was to promote sustainable development within NMPZ. Monitoring and protection of the focal species *Caretta caretta*, raising environmental awareness of visitors and locals, as well as launching initiatives to clean the nesting beaches of *Caretta caretta* were the main actions taken during the program. At the time data collection for this study was under way, the administrative body of the NMPZ posted guards from May to October to protect nesting beaches to distribute environmental information and raise environmental awareness among visitors and locals within park borders. Ten gatehouses were constructed in the main entrances to the turtles' nesting beaches, where a guard and a volunteer were allocated. Their duties involved controlling people's movement on nesting beaches during day and night and informing people about the NMPZ and about the nesting behaviour of *Caretta caretta*. Furthermore, they distributed leaflets, which included information about *Caretta caretta* and the flora and fauna of Zakynthos. A total of 60 guards and volunteers were recruited for this initiative. Furthermore, six volunteers from the NMPZ in collaboration with volunteers from the environmental non governmental organization 'ARCHELON' were responsible for monitoring the nesting behaviour of *Caretta caretta*. Finally, nesting beaches were cleaned at frequent time intervals both before and during the nesting activity. In total, more than 120 volunteers were recruited for the successful implementation of this initiative.

Our research wishes to provide an assessment of these initiatives as far as visitors' and locals' environmental knowledge and pro-environmental behaviour intention is concerned. Further, our results can bring about changes in environmental education material and programmes already in use as well as to assist in scheduling new interventions in NMPZ.

Instrument

We investigated respondents' environmental knowledge on local biodiversity, i.e., species inhabiting Zakynthos, as well as knowledge on the flagship species of the protected area (*Caretta caretta*). Concerning local biodiversity, we asked participants to distinguish which of the following species, i.e. Black Pine, Posidonia Beds, Mediterranean Seal, and Black Vulture are found in Zakynthos. Posidonia Beds and Mediterranean Seal are the correct responses. Then, we estimated participants' aggregate knowledge on species by adding up the correct responses. We used a multiple-choice format to estimate knowledge on *Caretta caretta*. Participants were requested to record one out of three given replies, which they regarded as the correct one. Items referred to the focal species *Caretta caretta* and conservation measures implemented within the NMPZ, namely, zoning and restriction measures implemented on the nesting beaches. These environmental knowledge items were chosen, because they comprise, both qualitatively and quantitatively, the major piece of environmental information provided in NMPZ. The second, the third and the second reply were acknowledged as correct for the first, the second and the third conservation knowledge item respectively (see Appendix). Further, we estimated participants' aggregate knowledge on *Caretta caretta* by adding up correct replies across items. Participants' were also requested to provide a self-assessment of their overall environmental knowledge concerning the NMPZ on a 3-point Likert scale (1 = satisfactory, 0 = medium and -1 = not satisfactory).

Engagement in pro-environmental behaviours was assessed using a list of eight pre-given items. Respondents were asked if, during the previous year, they had engaged in any of the following behaviours: (1) attending public meetings on environmental issues; (2) providing financial support to non-governmental environmental organizations; (3) providing voluntary work for non-governmental environmental organizations; (4) participation in reforestation programmes; (5) sorting household waste for recycling; (6) purchasing organically grown foods; (7) participating in environmental education projects; and (8) attending rallies or protests about environmental issues. Such behaviours are thought to sufficiently capture one's pro-environmental behaviour profile (Korfiatis et al., 2004; Hovardas & Poirazidis, 2006). Participants recorded the annual frequency of the eight pre-given pro-environmental behaviours on a 4-point Likert scale (1 = never, 2 = seldom, 3 = sometimes, 4 = often).

Next, we focused on locals' and visitors' willingness to participate in voluntary initiatives concerning the cleaning of beaches of the NMPZ as well as the implementation of conservation measures within the NMPZ. Respondents were requested to declare whether they would be willing to participate in the above-mentioned activities. Locals and visitors were also asked to estimate the percentage of other members of their social groups, e.g. locals and visitors, respectively, who would be willing to participate in each activity. This second recording aimed to address the fact that environmental behaviour is often trapped in a specific dilemma situation: the problem is – from the perspective of an individual player who can personally make only a small contribution by his/her own behaviour – that an improvement of the environmental quality mainly depends on the behaviour of other people (Krueger & Clement 1997; Diekmann & Preisendörfer 1998; Krueger 1999). Based on both visitor and local resident intentions and estimations, we determined both the actual majority pertaining to each behaviour intention item, as well as the mean error in the estimation of the actual majority.

Locals and visitors were also requested to record the degree of their environmental concern on a 3-point Likert scale (1 = 'low' to 3 = 'high').

Respondents were finally asked to complete a section ascertaining gender, age, level of education, monthly income and whether they had children.

Sample and Data Selection

Local residents were selected among inhabitants and people working in the villages of Laganas, Kalamaki and Gerakas, which are situated within park boundaries, and the town of Zakynthos, where many park residents work. Questionnaires were collected in public places, such as cafeterias, shops and public buildings. Every fifth person entering survey locations was approached, briefly informed about the survey, and asked to participate. A total of 250 residents were requested to take part in the study from June to August 2004, to which 223 accepted (response rate = 89.2%). From these participants, 217 residents provided usable results.

Visitors were randomly selected from people accessing three main beaches of the NMPZ, namely Laganas, Kalamaki and Gerakas, where most recreational activity occurs; questionnaires were collected thrice per day, namely, at 12:00, 14:00, and 16:00 am, when visitor numbers are quite high. Every tenth visitor entering the survey locations was approached, briefly informed about the scope of the research, and requested to take part in the survey. A total of 550 visitors were contacted from June to August 2004, to which 495 consented (response rate=90%). From these participants, 484 visitors returned usable survey results. Questionnaires took about 10–15 min for each respondent to fill in. The sample included both Greek and foreign visitors (197 and 287 respondents, respectively).

For all respondents, participation in the study was voluntary and anonymous. It took between 5 to 8 minutes for respondents to fill in the questionnaire. Sample characteristics are presented in Table 1. Females prevailed in the Greek visitor subsample. Subsamples did not differ in terms of age classes. There were numerous University graduates among Greek visitors. About half of foreign visitors belonged to the highest income class, while a substantial percentage of them had children (76.9%).

Table 1. Sample characteristics

	Total sample (%)	Local residents (%)	Greek visitors (%)	Foreign visitors (%)	χ^2
Gender					8.27^*
Male (1)	50.5	54.4	44.4	56.4	
Female (0)	48.8	45.6	55.6	43.7	
Age					7.79^{ns}
<30 (1)	43.1	38.8	43.8	48.2	
30-40 (2)	28.8	33.0	33.0	24.5	
>40 (3)	25.8	28.2	23.2	27.3	
Education					11.20^*
Elementary/high school	2.6	3.3	1.5	2.8	
High school	36.8	42.1	28.9	39.5	
University	59.3	54.7	69.5	57.7	
Monthly income					17.43^{**}
<600 Euro	11.3	10.4	11.4	13.5	
600-1200 Euro	44.9	54.7	53.9	38.0	
>1200 Euro	37.9	34.8	34.7	48.5	
Children					27.26^{***}
Having children	67.6	54.9	69.0	76.9	
Not having children	32.0	45.1	31.0	23.1	

Note: The sample comprises 217 local residents, 197 Greek visitors, and 287 foreign visitors; ns = non significant, * $= p < 0.05$, ** $= p < 0.01$, *** $= p < 0.001$.

Table 2. Spearman's *r* correlations among knowledge indices

	Self-assessed knowledge	Knowledge on local biodiversity	Knowledge on *Caretta caretta*
Self-assessed knowledge	-	0.32	0.17
Knowledge on local biodiversity		-	0.32
Knowledge on *Caretta caretta*			-

Note: All coefficients are significant at $p < 0.01$.

Table 3. K-means clustering performed on self-reported environmental behaviour items

	Cluster 1 (45.9% of the sample)	Cluster 2 (54.1% of the sample)	F
Attending public meetings on environmental issues	2.72	1.45	510.49
Providing financial support to non-governmental environmental organizations	1.83	1.25	116.67
Providing voluntary work for non-governmental environmental organizations	1.62	1.10	134.22
Participation in reforestation programmes	1.65	1.14	115.99
Sorting household waste for recycling	3.09	1.40	837.24
Purchasing organically grown foods	3.01	1.61	519.86
Participating in environmental education projects	2.70	1.39	482.10
Attending rallies or protests about environmental issues	2.36	1.57	125.12

Note: Numbers presented refer to average annual frequency of self-reported behaviour along a four-point Likert scale (1 = never, 2 = seldom, 3 = sometimes, 4 = often); all F values were significant at $p < 0.001$.

Data Analysis

We conducted a k-means cluster analysis to distinguish respondent clusters according to their self-reported pro-environmental behaviour. We also conducted non-parametric analyses to examine interrelations among respondents' knowledge and behaviour intention indices as well as between these groups of variables and sample characteristics. All statistical analyses were done using SPSS (SPSS 2004).

Results

The majority of respondents (61.2%) were able to record at least one species present in Zakynthos; among these, 16.0% recorded both species included in the instrument. Concerning knowledge on *Caretta caretta*, about one-third of the sample (34.2%) were able to respond correctly to two out of three items, while another 13.0% replied adequately to all three items. Local people presented increased knowledge on local biodiversity ($\chi^2 = 67.68$; $p < 0.001$, *Cramer's V* = 0.22; $p < 0.001$) and the flagship species of the protected area ($\chi^2 = 49.57$; $p < 0.001$, *Cramer's V* = 0.19; $p < 0.001$) compared to Greek and foreign visitors. Self-assessed knowledge presented significant correlations with both knowledge on local biodiversity (Spearman's $r = 0.32$; $p < 0.01$) and knowledge on the flagship species of the protected area (Spearman's $r = 0.17$; $p < 0.01$) (Table 2). This implies that respondents can be reliable in assessing their own knowledge levels. However, the coefficient was much higher for self-assessment of knowledge on local biodiversity. Local people were much more confident while assessing their environmental knowledge compared to Greek and foreign visitors ($\chi^2 = 78.57$; $p < 0.001$, *Cramer's V* = 0.23; $p < 0.001$). Additionally, knowledge on local biodiversity was positively correlated to knowledge on the flagship species of the protected area (Spearman's $r = 0.32$; $p < 0.01$).

A k-means cluster analysis performed on self-reported environmental behaviour showed that respondents were distinguished in two groups, one of relatively higher frequency of pro-environmental behaviours (45.9% of the sample) and another of relatively lower frequency (54.1% of the sample) (Table 3). All behaviour items contributed significantly in classifying respondents in the two clusters. Foreign visitors were more likely to belong to the high-frequency cluster compared to Greek visitors and local residents ($\chi^2 = 33.53$; $p < 0.001$, *Phi* = 0.22; $p < 0.001$). Respondents in the high-frequency cluster were much more likely to be willing to engage in pro-environmental action within NMPZ, namely take part in the cleaning of beaches ($\chi^2 = 37.85$; $p < 0.001$) and implementation of conservation measures ($\chi^2 = 38.89$; $p < 0.001$). This finding indicates that environmental behaviour profiles of visitors are crucial in determining their willingness to engage in pro-environmental action within protected areas.

Respondents' majority were willing to engage in both behaviours (52.1% of the total sample for cleaning of beaches; 51.1% of the total sample for implementation of conservation measures). In both cases, local residents ($\chi^2 = 16.38$; $p < 0.001$, *Phi* = 0.15; $p < 0.001$ for cleaning of beaches and $\chi^2 = 8.93$; $p < 0.05$, *Phi* = 0.11; $p < 0.05$ for implementation of conservation measures) and males ($\chi^2 = 8.21$; $p < 0.01$, *Phi* = -0.11; $p < 0.01$ for cleaning of beaches and $\chi^2 = 6.59$; $p < 0.05$, *Phi* = -0.10; $p < 0.05$ for implementation of conservation measures) presented a marked willingness to contribute. Both contributors and non contributors underestimated actual consensus for both behaviour intention items (Table 4). However, there was a marked difference between contributors and non contributors in their estimate errors. Specifically, absolute values of errors were much higher among non contributors for both behaviour intention items. This result implies that intention to engage in pro-environmental action is accompanied by more accurate consensus estimation.

Behaviour intention items were interrelated, that is, respondents who were willing to take part in cleaning of beaches were also willing to provide voluntary work for the implementation of conservation measures ($\chi^2 = 469.80$; $p < 0.001$). Estimation errors were also correlated, namely, respondents who tended to either underestimate or overestimate consensus for the first behaviour intention item also tended to underestimate or overestimate, respectively, consensus for the second item (Spearman's $r = 0.80$; $p < 0.001$). Respondents with a profile of high frequency pro-environmental behaviour presented a significantly lower absolute value of error in their consensus estimates for both behaviour intention items (Mann-Whitney $Z = -4.76$; $p < 0.001$ for cleaning of beaches and Mann-Whitney $Z = -3.16$; $p < 0.001$ for implementation of conservation measures).

Table 4. Estimation errors for contributors and non contributors

	Contributors	Non contributors	Mann-Whitney Z
Cleaning of beaches	-37.22 (52.33)	-69.93 (70.73)	-10.58 (-9.14)
Conservation measures	-36.14 (51.29)	-69.65 (70.80)	-10.77 (-9.40)

Note: Absolute values of estimation errors are given in parentheses; all Mann-Whitney Z values are significant at $p < 0.001$.

Table 5. Binary logistic regression models of the behavioural intention item 'cleaning of beaches' on social group adherence, gender, age, education, income, having children, environmental behaviour frequency (cluster adherence derived by k-means clustering), absolute value of error in consensus estimates, self-assessed knowledge, knowledge on local biodiversity, knowledge on the flagship species of the protected area (*Caretta caretta*), and environmental concern

Variables in the equation	B	S.E.	Wald	df	Sig.	Exp(B)
Local residents (1 = locals; 0 = others)	0.47	0.22	4.53	1	$p < 0.05$	1.61
Gender (1 = female; 0 = male)	-0.32	0.18	3.03	1	$p < 0.05$	0.73
Environmental behaviour frequency	0.43	0.20	4.53	1	$p < 0.05$	1.54
Error in consensus estimates	-0.02	0.00	44.31	1	$p < 0.001$	0.98
Self-assessed knowledge	0.36	0.14	6.40	1	$p < 0.05$	1.44
Knowledge on local biodiversity	0.49	0.14	11.24	1	$p < 0.001$	1.63
Environmental concern	0.60	0.13	21.97	1	$p < 0.001$	1.82
Constant of the model	-0.10	0.34	0.08	1	ns	0.91

Note: The backward conditional method was used; ns = non significant.

About one-third of the sample recorded an intermediate degree of environmental concern (34.0%), while slightly more than one-fifth stated a high degree of environmental concern (22.4%). Environmental concern was positively correlated with knowledge indices (Spearman's $r = 0.25$; $p < 0.01$ for self-assessed knowledge, Spearman's $r = 0.24$; $p < 0.01$ for knowledge on local biodiversity, Spearman's $r = 0.20$; $p < 0.01$ for knowledge on the flagship species of the area). Respondents with a profile of high frequency pro-environmental behaviour showed increased levels of environmental concern ($\chi^2 = 117.67$; $p < 0.001$). Environmental concern was positively correlated with behaviour intention items ($\chi^2 = 77.35$; $p < 0.001$ for cleaning of beaches and $\chi^2 = 88.44$; $p < 0.001$ for implementation of conservation measures). Increased concern was also accompanied by lower errors in consensus estimates for both behaviour intention items (Kruskal Wallis $\chi^2 = 28.22$; $p < 0.001$ for cleaning of beaches and Kruskal Wallis $\chi^2 = 28.73$; $p < 0.001$ for implementation of conservation measures). Regarding this trend, there was a significant difference between respondents who adhered to a low degree of environmental concern and those who reported either an intermediate (Mann-Whitney $Z = -4.68$; $p < 0.001$ for cleaning of beaches and Mann-Whitney $Z = -5.28$; $p < 0.001$ for implementation of conservation measures) or a high degree of environmental concern (Mann-Whitney $Z = -4.11$; $p < 0.001$ for cleaning of beaches and Mann-Whitney $Z = -2.89$; $p < 0.001$ for implementation of conservation measures).

Binary logistic regressions were performed with behavioural intention as the outcome variable and social group adherence, gender, age, education, income, having children, environmental behaviour frequency (cluster adherence derived by k-means clustering), absolute value of error in consensus estimates, self-assessed knowledge, knowledge on local biodiversity, knowledge on the flagship species of the protected area (*Caretta caretta*), and environmental concern as predictors. Correlation coefficients among independent variables excluded any adverse effect of multicollinearity (Field, 2000; Wall et al., 2007). A backward conditional method was followed, where the predictor with the lowest p value was removed from the model at each subsequent step until all remaining predictors had significant coefficients. Willingness to engage in 'cleaning of beaches' (Table 5) was more likely for local residents, males, respondents in the high-frequency environmental behaviour cluster, those who committed relatively low error in their consensus estimates, those who assessed their environmental knowledge as satisfactory, participants who were aware of local biodiversity, and those with increased environmental concern (Hosmer and Lemeshov $\chi^2 = 9.98$, $p > 0.05$; Nagelkerke R *square* = 0.31; -2 Log Likelihood = 714.44; percentage correct = 70.2).

Table 6. Binary logistic regression models of the behavioural intention item 'implementation of conservation measures' on social group adherence, gender, age, education, income, having children, environmental behaviour frequency (cluster adherence derived by k-means clustering), absolute value of error in consensus estimates, self-assessed knowledge, knowledge on local biodiversity, knowledge on the flagship species of the protected area (*Caretta caretta*), and environmental concern

Variables in the equation	B	S.E.	Wald	df	Sig.	Exp(B)
Age (1 = <30; 2 = 31-40; 3 = >40)	-0.41	0.11	12.82	1	$p < 0.001$	0.66
Error in consensus estimates	-0.02	0.00	54.37	1	$p < 0.001$	0.98
Self-assessed knowledge	0.27	0.14	3.84	1	$p < 0.05$	1.31
Knowledge on local biodiversity	0.55	0.14	14.87	1	$p < 0.001$	1.73
Environmental concern	0.93	0.13	54.93	1	$p < 0.001$	2.53
Constant of the model	0.21	0.35	0.34	1	ns	1.23

Note: The backward conditional method was used; ns = non significant.

For 'implementation of conservation measures' (Table 6), the only sample characteristic that proved significant was age. Younger respondents were more likely to intent to engage in this behaviour. Unlike 'cleaning of beaches', frequency of self-reported environmental behaviour was not a significant determinant in this case. All other significant independent variables were also present in the first model, namely, error in consensus estimates, self-assessed environmental knowledge, knowledge on local biodiversity, and environmental concern (Hosmer and Lemeshov $\chi^2 = 15.33$, $p > 0.05$; Nagelkerke R square $= 0.33$; -2 Log Likelihood $= 707.39$; percentage correct $= 71.6$). It should be mentioned that regression coefficients for absolute value of error in consensus estimates were negative in both models, which indicates that respondents were less likely to be willing to engage in given behaviours as errors increased. Concerning models' fit, the Hosmer-Lemeshow goodness-of-fit statistic was not significant in both cases, which indicates a good fit. Hence, the models adequately fitted the data. Changes in -2 log likelihood were significant for all equations, which implies that there was in each case a marked improvement over the constant-only model. All models correctly predicted behavioural intention for more than 70% of participants. Nagelkerke's R square values showed that binary logistic regression models for 'cleaning of beaches' and 'implementation of conservation measures' explained equal variance in the data.

Discussion

Levels of environmental knowledge and environmental concern found in this study are comparable to the ones reported by previous research with Greek samples in ecotourism destinations (Hovardas & Poirazidis, 2006; Togridou et al., 2006a). Also in line with previous research, knowledge indices presented an increased interrelation with parameters such as environmental concern (Dimopoulos et. al, 2008). Indeed, it proved that it is knowledge on local biodiversity and not knowledge on just the flagship species of a protected area which can be a significant determinant of activism behaviour intention. We should mention that demographic variables presented a rather confined influence on parameters studied. This finding, together with locals' lead in environmental knowledge and pro-environmental behaviour intention prove that, indeed, the environmentalist discourse has diffused in the sample and the study area, respectively.

As far as consensus estimates are concerned, our findings confirm previous research, where contributors are reported to slightly underestimate the size of their own group, whereas non-contributors strongly underestimate the size of the actual majority, namely, contributors (Hovardas & Poirazidis, 2006; Krueger & Clement, 1997; Monin & Norton, 2003; Suls et al., 2006; Togridou et al., 2006a). The higher the estimation errors, the lesser the probability of behaviour intentions to correlate with actual behaviour: individual actors tend to underestimate the cooperation of others, which is considered as a crucial barrier in the enactment of pro-environmental behaviour (Diekmann & Preisendörfer, 1998). According to Alicke and Largo (1995), estimation errors decrease, when subjects receive information that explicitly negates the uniqueness of people's own positions. For instance, the homogenization process that characterizes educational settings could render both the majority and the minority concerning an issue salient; experience gained through interacting with non-similar others could in this case decrease estimation errors substantially.

Orams (1997) claimed that without a structured education program, nature-based tourism is unlikely to produce long lasting changes in tourists' behaviour. NMPZ managers are suggested to design collaborative learning environments in order to motivate and encourage group problem solving; such programs could provide the social context necessary to augment behaviour intentions (Kaplan, 2000; Olli et al., 2001), modify expectations one has for oneself and for others (Hormuth, 1999), and enhance efficacy of one's actions, which proved to be a determining factor in decisions regarding environmental conservation (Martinez & McMullin, 2004; Summit & Sommer, 1998; Trumbo & O'Keefe, 2001). Environmental education programmes in ecotourism destinations should be scheduled so as to account for the 'ceiling' effect, where knowledge, attitude, and behaviour gains are expected to be rather restricted after an environmental education intervention (Beaumont 2001; Hovardas & Poirazidis, 2006). Bogner (1998) and Dimopoulos et al. (2008) reported that people enrolled in environmental education programmes revealed relatively high pro-environmental orientations before the intervention has even started. This is expected to be especially pronounced among ecotourists, who are highly probable to have selected the destination due to its ecological significance.

Implications for developing objectives for environmental education interventions in ecotourism destinations

Fundamental disagreements over the content and goals of environmental education are familiar within both academic and practitioner discussion (Palmer, 1998). These tensions are not only about theoretical considerations but reflect complex relationships between the state, environmental non-governmental organizations and business interests (Blum, 2008). As social and economic support for environmental education increased considerably during the last years, environmental education can become an important point of intersection between state and non-governmental actors, both domestic and international. In this vein, the aims of environmental education and the content of environmental education interventions are expected to be the result of social interaction and negotiation among the various social groups engaged in the field. Such a negotiation on the development of environmental education goals is crucial in shaping but also being shaped by local environmental histories.

Some environmental educators tend to advocate science-oriented interventions and argue for an emphasis on teaching about biological and ecological issues. These educators claim that when students are taught about these topics they will come to appreciate nature. Supporters of programmes with a stronger social-values orientation, on the contrary, claim that environmental issues cannot be studied in isolation but should instead be taught in relation to human activities (Marion & Reid, 2007; Wals, 1996). Our approach for the purposes of the present paper will be one that attempts to integrate both above-mentioned views in an effort to promote the dialectical interplay of society and nature. Environmental education in the frame of ecotourism should involve a balanced provision of bio-cultural education for all stakeholders, namely both guests and the local community (Donohoe & Needham, 2006). Additionally, there is an important question to be addressed by future research: what is the efficiency of small-scale environmental education interventions in ecotourism destinations to promote knowledge on local societies and their interplay with nature?

Specific objectives for environmental education interventions in ecotourism destinations can center around two broad aims, namely, recruiting voluntary work for protected area management and outlining learning outcomes in the case of the 'ceiling' effect (Table 7). In the first case, protected area managers and educators should screen visitors and locals in order to examine their intention to participate in voluntary work. By means of measuring respondents' self-reported environmental behaviour and environmental concern, one would be able to distinguish between different levels of pro-environmental behaviour intention among visitors and locals before the intervention has even started. During the educational interventions, collaboration learning opportunities could lead to a decrease in errors in consensus estimation concerning participants' willingness to engage in voluntary work and, thereby, increase the potential of actual consensus. Collaborative learning environments can provide the social context needed to verify expectations from peers and render consensus estimates more accurate. Collaborative learning arrangements are frequently implemented in environmental education projects (Korfiatis & Paraskevopoulos, 2003). Previous studies have reported that feedback about performance of peers may be decisive for behavioural choices (Staats et al., 2004) because they promote descriptive norms (Abrahamse et al., 2007; Ohtomo & Hirose, 2007). Further, group discussion can obviously mediate behavioural intentions. Even for small-scale environmental education interventions, social interaction among peers can support participants in acknowledging majorities' and minorities' views more comprehensively (Werner et al., 2008). After the educational interventions, brochures on voluntary work opportunities could be administered to inform specific segments of visitors and locals about short-term and mid-term initiatives in the frame of environmental management. Potential contributors within target groups can be determined by means of measuring errors in consensus estimation, self-assessment of respondents' environmental knowledge and environmental concern.

The 'ceiling' effect describes cases, where learners with high prior knowledge or attitude present small knowledge or attitude gains, respectively (Beaumont 2001; Hovardas & Poirazidis, 2006). For visitors who fall under the category of the 'ceiling' effect, there still remain a number of issues to be examined. For instance, in a situation where the 'ceiling' effect has been detected, one should take into account not only percentages of knowledge and attitude items, but also the issue of their coherence as well as the interrelation between knowledge and behaviour intention. Regarding the establishment of learning outcomes in the case of the 'ceiling' effect, protected area managers and educators can distinguish between different levels of environmental knowledge among visitors and locals before the intervention has started on the basis of respondents' knowledge self-assessment to select appropriate reference material to structure environmental education interventions. During interventions, educators should strive to interrelate knowledge indices, intention items as well as knowledge indices with intention items. This can be achieved by modifying existing reference material accordingly and assessing knowledge and pro-environmental behaviour intention items in a pre-post test format. An objective that refers to the time after the interventions is the facilitation of social interaction between social groups engaged in ecotourism development to foster 'social' learning. This can be catalyzed by letting locals get informed about visitors' knowledge and intentions and letting visitors get informed about local environmental history. In this direction, messages promoted through education and outreach programs in the frame of ecotourism should concentrate on the interplay between society and nature, namely, on conservation aims, monitoring, and the coexistence and interdependence of local communities and the natural environment (Hovardas & Stamou, 2006b). The content of these messages should not be confined to mere descriptions of biodiversity and conservation measures applied within protected areas; instead, it should address the fact that human interventions are integral to any kind of environmental conservation initiative.

Table 7. Developing specific objectives for environmental education interventions in ecotourism destinations

Overall aim	Timing	Specific objective	Parameters assessed	Specifications
Recruit voluntary work for protected area management	Before the intervention has started	Distinguish between different levels of pro-environmental behaviour intention among visitors and locals	Environmental behaviour; environmental concern	Screen visitors and locals by means of their environmental behaviour profile and their environmental concern
	During the intervention	Decrease errors in consensus estimation	Errors in consensus estimation	Collaborative learning opportunities
	After the intervention	Inform specific segments of visitors and locals about short-term and mid-term initiatives in the frame of protected area management	Errors in consensus estimation; self-assessment of environmental knowledge; environmental concern	Administrate brochures on voluntary work opportunities; ask for visitors' and locals' participation in these programmes
Outline learning outcomes in the case of the 'ceiling' effect	Before the intervention has started	Distinguish between different levels of environmental knowledge among visitors and locals	Self-assessment of environmental knowledge	Select appropriate reference material to structure environmental education interventions
	During the intervention	Interrelate knowledge indices, intention items as well as knowledge indices with intention items	Knowledge indices; pro-environmental behaviour intention items	Modify existing reference material so as to interrelate environmental knowledge and pro-environmental intention items
	After the intervention	Facilitate social interaction between social groups engaged in ecotourism development to foster social learning	Visitors' knowledge and intentions; local environmental history	Inform locals on visitors' knowledge and intentions; inform visitors on local environmental history

ACKNOWLEDGMENTS

We are grateful to Aggeliki Leukaditou who helped during data collection. We also thank Stelios Heristanides, who prepared the map of the study area (Figure 2). The research was funded by EPEAEK II within the frame of 'HERAKLEITOS' (Greek Ministry of National Education and Religious Affairs).

REFERENCES

Abrahamse, W., Steg, L., Vlek, C. & Rothengatter, T. (2007). The effect of tailored information, goal setting, and tailored feedback on household energy use, energy-related behaviours, and behavioural antecedents. *Journal of Environmental Psychology*, 27, 265-276.

Alicke, M. D. & Largo, E. (1995). The role of the self in the false consensus effect. *Journal of Experimental Social Psychology*, 31, 28-47.

Bamberg, S. & Möser, G. (2007). Twenty years after Hines, Hungerford, and Tomera: A new meta-analysis of psycho-social determinants of pro-environmental behaviour. *Journal of Environmental Psychology*, 27, 14-25.

Beaumont, N. (2001). Ecotourism and the conservation ethic: recruiting the uninitiated or preaching to the converted? *Journal of Sustainable Tourism*, 9, 317-341.

Bell, S., Hampshire, K. & Topalidou, S. (2007). The political culture of poaching: a case study from northern Greece. *Biodiversity and Conservation*, 16, 399-418.

Blum, N. (2008). Environmental Education in Costa Rica: building a framework for sustainable development? *International Journal of Educational Development*, 28, 348-358.

Bogner, F. X. (1998). The influence of short-term outdoor ecology education on long-term variables of environmental perspective. *The Journal of Environmental Education*, 29, 17-29.

Brossard, D., Lewenstein, B. & Bonney, R. (2005). Scientific knowledge and attitude change: The impact of a citizen science project. *International Journal of Science Education*, 27, 1099-1121.

Carmin, J. (2003). Non-governmental organizations and public participation in local environmental decision-making in the Czech Republic. *Local Environment*, 8, 541-552.

Castro, P. (2006). Applying social psychology to the study of environmental concern and environmental worldviews: contributions from the social representations approach. *Journal of Community and Applied Social Psychology*, 16, 247-266.

Che, D. (2006). Developing ecotourism in First World, resource-dependent areas. *Geoforum*, 37, 212-226.

Diekmann, A. & Preisendörfer, P. (1998). Environmental behaviour: discrepancies between aspirations and reality. *Rationality and Society* 10, 79-102.

Dimopoulos, D., Paraskevopoulos, S. & Pantis, J. D. (2008). The cognitive and attitudinal effects of a conservation educational module on elementary school students. *The Journal of Environmental Education*, 39, 47-61.

Donohoe, H. M. & Needham, R. D. (2006). Ecotourism: the evolving contemporary definition. *Journal of Ecotourism*, 5, 192-210.

Field, A. (2000). *Discovering statistics: using SPSS for Windows*. London: Sage.

Hoffman, A. J., Gillespie, J. J., Moore, D. A., Wade-BenzoniK. A., Thompson, L. L. & Bazerman, M. H. (1999). A mixed-motive perspective on the economics versus environment debate. *American Behavioural Scientist*, 42, 1254-1276.

Hormuth, S. E. (1999). Social meaning and social context of environmentally-relevant behaviour: shopping, wrapping, and disposing. *Journal of Environmental Psychology*, 19, 277-286.

Hovardas, T. (2005). *Social representations on ecotourism – Scheduling interventions in Protected areas*. Thessaloniki, Greece: PhD-Thesis, Aristotle University, School of Biology (in Greek with an English summary).

Hovardas, T. & Korfiatis, K. J. (2008). Framing environmental policy by the local press: case study from the Dadia Forest Reserve, Greece. *Forest Policy and Economics, 10*, 316-325.

Hovardas, T. & Korfiatis, K. J. (2009). Applying social representations theory in educational evaluation: a methodological framework. In: M. Ortiz & C. Rubio (Eds.), *Educational Evaluation: 21st Century Issues and Challenges*, (pp. 1-29). New York: Nova Science Publishers, Inc.

Hovardas, T. & Poirazidis, K. (2006). Evaluation of the environmentalist dimension of ecotourism at the Dadia Forest Reserve (Greece) *Environmental Management, 38*, 810-822.

Hovardas, T. & Poirazidis, K. (2007). Environmental policy beliefs of stakeholders in protected area management. *Environmental Management, 39*, 515-525.

Hovardas, T. & Stamou, G. P. (2006a). Structural and narrative reconstruction of rural residents' representations of 'nature', 'wildlife', and 'landscape'. *Biodiversity and Conservation, 15*, 1745-1770.

Hovardas, T. & Stamou, G. P. (2006b). Structural and narrative reconstruction of representations on 'nature', 'environment', and 'ecotourism'. *Society and Natural Resources, 19*, 225-237.

Hovardas, T., Korfiatis, K. J. & Pantis, D. J. (2009). Environmental representations of local communities' spokespersons in protected areas. *Journal of Community and Applied Social Psychology*, in press.

Kallgren, C. A., Reno, R. R. & Cialdini, R. B. (2000). A focus theory of normative conduct: When norms do and do not affect behaviour. *Personality and Social Psychology Bulletin, 26*, 328-338.

Kaplan, S. (2000). Human nature and environmentally responsible behaviour. *Journal of Social Issues, 56*, 491-508.

Kimmel, J. R. (1999). Ecotourism as environmental learning. *The Journal of Environmental Education, 30*, 40-44.

Kolstø, S. D. (2006). Patterns in students' argumentation confronted with a risk-focused socio-scientific issue. *International Journal of Science Education, 28*, 1689-1716.

Korfiatis, K. J. & Paraskevopoulos, S. (2003). *Environmental education - theory and method*. Thessaloniki: Christodoulidis.

Korfiatis, K. J., Hovardas, T. & Pantis, J. D. (2004). Determinants of environmental behaviour in societies in transition: Evidence from five European Countries. *Population and Environment, 25*, 563-584.

Korfiatis, K. J., Hovardas, T., Tsaliki, E. & Palmer, J. A. (2009). Rural children's views on human activities and changes in a Greek wetland. *Society and Natural Resources, 22*, 339-352.

Krueger, J. (1999). On the perception of social consensus. *Advances in Experimental Social Psychology, 30*, 163-240.

Krueger, J. & Clement, R. W. (1997). Estimates of social consensus by majorities and minorities: The case for social projection. *Personality and Social Psychology Review, 1*, 299-313.

LIFE (2003). GR-000751: Volunteers and environmental protection in the National Marine Park of Zakynthos, Greece. Zakynthos, Greece: National Marine Park of Zakynthos.

Lubell, M. (2002). Environmental activism as collective action. *Environment and Behaviour*, *34*, 431-454.

Machairas, I. & Hovardas, T. (2005). Determining visitors' dispositions towards the designation of a Greek National Park. *Environmental Management*, *36*, 73-88.

Margaritoulis, D. & Rees, A. F. (2003). Loggerhead nesting effort and conservation initiatives at the monitored beaches of Greece during, 2002. *Marine Turtle Newsletter*, *102*, 11-13.

Marion, J. L. & Reid, S. E. (2007). Minimizing visitor impacts to protected areas: the efficacy of low impact education programmes. *Journal of Sustainable Tourism*, *15*, 5-27.

Martinez, T. A. & McMullin, S. L. (2004). Factors affecting decisions to volunteer in Nongovernmental Organizations. *Environment and Behaviour*, *36*, 112-126.

McFarlane, B. L. & Hunt, L. M. (2006). Environmental activism in the forest sector: Social psychological, social-cultural, and contextual effects. *Environment and Behaviour*, *38*, 266-285.

Michel-Guillou, E. & Moser, G. (2006). Commitment of farmers to environmental protection: From social pressure to environmental conscience. *Journal of Environmental Psychology*, *26*, 227-235.

Monin, B. & Norton, M. (2003). Perceptions of a fluid consensus: uniqueness bias, false consensus, false polarization, and pluralistic ignorance in a water conservation crisis. *Personality and Social Psychology Bulletin*, *29*, 559-567.

Moody, G. L. & Hartel, P. G. (2007). Evaluating an environmental literacy requirement chosen as a method to produce environmentally literate university students. *International Journal of Sustainability in Higher Education*, *8*, 355- 370.

Mühlhäusler, P. & Peace, A. (2001). Discourses of ecotourism: The case of Fraser Island, Queensland. *Language and Communication*, *21*, 359-380.

Ohtomo, S. & Hirose, Y. (2007). The dual-process of reactive and intentional decision-making involved in eco-friendly behaviour. *Journal of Environmental Psychology*, *27*, 117-125.

Olli, E., Grendstad, G. & Wollebaek, D. (2001). Correlates of environmental behaviours: bringing back social context. *Environment and Behaviour*, *33*, 181-208.

Orams, M. B. (1997). The effectiveness of environmental education: can we turn tourists into 'greenies'? *Progress in Tourism Hospitality and Research*, *3*, 295-306

Palmer, J. (1998). *Environmental education in the 21st century: theory, practice, progress, and promise.* London: Routledge.

Papageorgiou, K. & Kassioumis, K. (2004). The national park policy context in Greece: park users' perspectives of issues in park administration. *Journal for Nature Conservation*, *13*, 231-246.

Papageorgiou, K., Kassioumis, K., Blioumis, V. & Christodoulou, A. (2005). Linking quality of life and forest values in rural areas: an exploratory study of stakeholder perspectives in the rural community of Konitsa, Greece. *Forestry*, *78*, 485-499.

Pèer, S., Goldman, D. & Yavetz, B. (2007). Environmental literacy in teacher training: attitudes, knowledge, and environmental behaviour of beginning students. The *Journal of Environmental Education*, *39*, 45-59.

Pipinos, G. & Fokiali, P. (2007). An assessment of the attitudes of the inhabitants of Northern Karpathos, Greece: towards a framework for ecotourism development in environmentally sensitive areas. *Environment, Development and Sustainability*, DOI 10.1007/s10668-007-9135-y.

Pooley, J. A. & O'Connor, M. (2000). Environmental education and attitudes: emotions and beliefs are what is needed. *Environment and Behaviour, 32*, 711-723.

Rodger, K., Moore, S. A. & Newsome, D. (2007). Wildlife tours in Australia: characteristics, the place of science and sustainable futures. *Journal of Sustainable Tourism, 15*, 160-179.

Russell, A. (2007). Anthropology and ecotourism in European wetlands: bubbles, babies and bathwater. *Tourist Studies, 7*, 225-244.

Seguin, C., Pelletier, L. G. & Hunsley, J. (1998). Toward a model of environmental activism. *Environment and Behaviour, 30*, 319-331.

SPSS, Inc. 2004. SPSS base system's user's guide, release 12.0 edition. SPSS Inc, *Chicago, Illinois*.

Staats, H., Harland, P. & Wilke, H. A. M. (2004). Effecting durable change: A team approach to improve environmental behaviour in the household. *Environment and Behaviour, 36*, 341-367.

Stem, C. J., Lassoie, J. P., Lee, D. R., Deshler, D. D. & Schelhas, J. W. (2003). Community participation in ecotourism benefits: the link to conservation practices and perspectives. *Society and Natural Resources, 16*, 387-413.

Suls, J., Wan, C. K. & Sanders, G. S. (2006). False Consensus and False Uniqueness in Estimating the Prevalence of Health-Protective Behaviours. *Journal of Applied Social Psychology, 18*, 66-79.

Summit, J. & Sommer, R. (1998). Urban tree-planting programs—a model for encouraging environmentally protective behaviour. *Atmospheric Environment, 32*, 1-5.

Thøgersen, J. (2008). Social norms and cooperation in real-life social dilemmas. *Journal of Economic Psychology, 29*, 458-472.

Tilikidou, I. (2007). The effects of knowledge and attitudes upon Greeks' pro-environmental purchasing behaviour. *Corporate Social Responsibility and Environmental Management, 14*, 121-134.

Tisdell, C. & Wilson, C. (2005). Perceived impacts of ecotourism on environmental learning and conservation: turtle watching as a case study. *Environment, Development and Sustainability, 7*, 291-302.

Togridou, A., Hovardas, T. & Pantis, D.J. (2006a). Determinants of visitors' willingness to pay for the National Marine Park of Zakynthos, Greece. *Ecological Economics, 60*, 308-319.

Togridou, A., Hovardas, T. & Pantis, D.J. (2006b). Factors shaping implementation of protected area management decisions: a case study of the Zakynthos National Marine Park. *Environmental Conservation, 33*, 233-243.

Trumbo, C. W. & O'Keefe G. J. (2001). Intention to conserve water: environmental values, planned behaviour, and information effects. A comparison of three communities sharing a watershed. *Society and Natural Resources, 14*, 889-899.

Wall, R., Devine-Wright, P. & Mill, G. A. (2007). Comparing and combining theories to explain proenvironmental intentions. *Environment and Behaviour, 39*, 731-753.

Wallace, G. N. & Pierce, S. M. (1996). An evaluation of ecotourism in Amazonas, Brazil. *Annals of Tourism Research, 23*, 843-873.

Wals, A. E. J. (1996). Back-alley sustainability and the role of environmental education. *Local Environment, 1*, 299-316.

Werner, C. M., Sansone, C. & Brown, B. B. (2008). Guided group discussion asnd attitude change: The roles of normative and informational influence. *Journal of Environmental Psychology*, *28*, 27-41.

APPENDIX

Multiple-choice items used to elicit respondents' knowledge on the flagship species of the protected area.

Please, choose the correct reply (choose only one among the given replies in each case)

Sea turtles *Caretta caretta*

can be found in the marine belt of the park all year round	
come to Zakynthos every year at the beginning of spring, in order to mate	
come to Zakynthos several times per year, in order to mate	

Conservation measures implemented in the National Marine Park of Zakynthos

are equally strict through the park, in order to guarantee the effective protection of the sea turtle *Caretta caretta*	
refer primarily to the reproduction beaches of the sea turtle *Caretta caretta*	
are differentiated according to the zone of land they refer to	

When visitors stand on the beaches of the National Marine Park of Zakynthos, they

should not reach closer than five meters from the sea	
should not place their sun shields in a distance greater than five meters from the sea	
should not place their sun shields in a distance greater than 15 meters from the sea	

In: Ecotourism: Management, Development and Impact   ISBN: 978-1-60876-724-3
Editors: A. Krause, E. Weir, pp. 113-133   © 2010 Nova Science Publishers, Inc.

Chapter 4

ECOLOGICAL TOURISM AND CAMEROON-OPPORTUNITIES AND CONSTRAINTS

T. E. Ambe[a], E. A. Tsi[b], G. T. Chi[c], B. N. Siri[d] and D. F. Tita[e]
[a]MINRESI Douala
[b]University of Dschang
[c]De Montfort University, Leicester UK
[d]IRAD Ekona
[e]ICRAF Yaounde

ABSTRACT

In the tourism industry, Cameroon has often sold itself as "Africa in miniature" because of its rich biocenoses representing almost all ecotones found in Africa including a very wide variety of landscape patterns. About 75 percent of the flora is still virgin. The fauna diversity includes rare carnivores, herbivores, primates and a diversity of birds. On gaining independence, the government of Cameroon realised the strong socio-economic potential of the tourism and of course the ecotourism industry as a source of revenue and therefore tried to geared efforts towards its promotion. However, the discovery of oil in the late 70s as a cheap source of revenue led to the neglect of this sector as well as some other important ones thereby provoking the well documented Dutch disease in the country. Of late, there has been a resurgent in the ecotourism business and government policy in this domain are aimed at fostering the sustainable development and co-management of the ecotourism potentials, involving local communities as well as some international and local NGOs. Some ecotourism potentials in Cameroon include; national parks, reserves and world heritage sites. However, these efforts have bore little fruits in terms of attracting tourist to the country and thereby boasting its foreign exchange earnings. This paper analyses the current state of the art of ecotourism in Cameroon, its challenges and prospects to serve the dual purpose of conservation as well as income generation to the local communities. Some comparison has been made with Kenya, which is one of the most popular ecotourism destinations in Sub-Saharan Africa.

Keywords: Ecotourism, competitiveness, Landscape patterns, sustainable development, Co-management and management plan

A recess at the foot of Mount Cameroon just a few meters from the alantic ocean

1. Cameroon, "Africa in Miniature" or "All of Africa in One Country"

The unique location and orientation, tantalizing landscape patterns, richness in biodiversity and energizing socio-cultural diversity endowed Cameroon with one of the best ecological tourism potentials in Africa. Cameroon is found almost at the centre of Africa with a north-south orientation stretching from the gulf of Guinea to Lake Chad over passing five agro-ecological zones (marine, mangrove, rain forest, savannah sub-divided into guinea, sudan and sahel savannah, and the semi desert). It is therefore on the cross link between north and south; east and west of Africa. She is bounded by Nigeria on the West, Chad on the North-East, the Central African Republic on the East, Congo on the South-East, Gabon and Equatorial Guinea on the South. Figure 1 presents the map of Cameroon including some protected areas. These protected areas provide for; numerous camping sites, wildlife sanctuaries, biosphere reserves, world heritage sites, forest and game reserves, zoological and botanical gardens, lakes, waterfalls and mountains. All these offer the much needed attraction and satisfaction to eco-tourists. The combination of five agro-ecological zones, its strategic location and the unique combination of diverse vegetation and its associated fauna has endowed Cameroon with most of the available animal and plant species in Africa.

Cameroon also has a remarkable landscape patterns with rich sceneries from the mountain range that stretches from the gulf of guinea in the South West Region, moving Northwards through the Western highlands, to the Adamaoua plateau in the North and including numerous plains. Some of the prominent mountains in Cameroon include; the Mount Cameroon (highest mountain in West Africa with a height of 4095m above sea level), the Oku Mountain in the North West region with it rich collection of endemic species, especially its mountane forest and the Mandara Mountains in the North region. Most of the mountains in this range are inactive except mount Cameroon that lastly erupted in 2001 and vestige of the last lava flow can still be viewed at the coaster village of Bakigili. Interspacing these mountains are scenic volcanic lakes, such as the very beautiful twin Mwaan lakes of Muanenguba, or the active lake Nyos that spewed out volcanic gases in 1986, killing over 1500 humans and thousands of animals. Volcanic plugs such as the Rhumsiki in the north and other land forms such as the eye pleasing and scenic Sabga hills dotted this landscape.

Cameroon's position in the Congo basin, offers a natural, rich, virgin and complex biodiversity that makes her occupy the 4th position in terms of rich biodiversity in Africa after the Democratic Republic of Congo, Tanzania and Madagascar (Auzel, 1999).). There are also the biodiversity rich coaster mangroves and other wet lands, the virgin equatorial rain forest with rolling topography in the south that gradually makes way to the alluvial plains in the north. The country also has high natural habitat diversity with a rich and abundant biodiversity as well as many threatened, rare and near extinct species. According to Auzel, (1999) there are about 300 species of mammals, 850 birds, 190 amphibians and 9000 angiosperm species within the Central African sub-region. This region is home to many flagship endangered species such as the elephant (Loxodonta Africana), the buffalo (Syncerus cafer), the gorilla (Gorila gorilla), the chimpanzee (Pan troglodytes), the mandrill (Mandrillus sphinx), the leopard (Panthera pardus), the giant pangolin (Manis gigantean), the lion (Pantheria leo), the giraffe (Giraffa giraffe), the derby eland (Taurotragus derbianus). Of the 4,170 species of mammals censored the world over, 409 species are Cameroonian; constituting 9.8% and 26% of the world and Africa potential respectively with 11 endemic species and 27 threatened species (UNEP/SDNP, 1996).

Finally, Cameroon is richly blessed with a highly diversified and dynamic human population with its bewildering array of African ethnic groups and languages. There exist over 250 ethnic groups in Cameroon. The 5 major ethnic groups include: Bamiléké and Bamoun in the west, Fulani and Kirdi in the north, and Ewondo in the centre and south. The country has almost all the realm of people of African origin ranging from the pigmies of the equatorial rain forest through the Bantu in the savanna, and to the Arabs in the northern arid part of the country. These diverse populations express themselves with about 420 languages even though officially Cameroon is a bilingual country, speaking English and French (the foot prints of her colonial masters). In most cases, these highly diversified groups of people still live in close proximity to their natural environment thereby bringing forth a complex socio-cultural, and linguistic diversity that is unique to Cameroon.

It is therefore evident from the above points that Cameroon has a tantalizing uniqueness, in that she almost embodies all the socio-economic, cultural and geographical diversity of Africa. No wonder, the country sells itself in the tourism and ecotourism industry as "Africa in miniature" or recently, "all of Africa in one country".

The Importance of Ecotourism in Cameroon

According to the International Association of Scientific Experts in Tourism (AIEST), ecotourism also termed "ecological tourism" or eco-labeled nature tourism is regarded as the sum total of the phenomena and relationships arising from the travel and stay of non-residents in so far as they do not lead to permanent residence and are not connected with any earning activity (Tsi & Ayodele, 2004). However, this definition has an implicit limitation because it fails to clearly define the activities of eco-tourists at that destination. Other definitions focus on 'environmentally responsible' tourism (Ceballos-Lascurain, 1991) that provides 'direct benefits' to the nature conservation area and to 'the economic welfare of local residents' (Ziffer, 1989), or a 'nature tourism that promotes conservation and sustainable development' (Boo, 1992). The three main criteria for ecotourism include: minimal and social impact on the visited area, notable economic participation by local residents, and ecological education of the tourists at the natural site

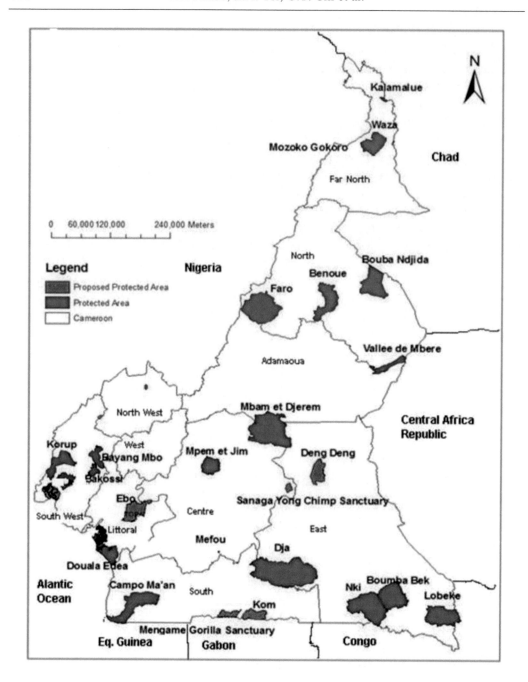

Figure 1. Map of Cameroon showing some protected areas

In this paper, ecotourism is hereby defined as "a recreational, temporary and short termed activity involving the movement of people from their normal place of residence to various ecological and natural destinations within or without their national borders and may sometimes earned minimal compensation for their activities. For example free boarding in exchange for volunteer labor or "tourism with a conscience" or "conservation holidays". In this way, tourism is attracting financial and human capital for conservation research (Wearing, 2001, 2004; Stebbins, 2004, Brightsmith et al, 2008).

In a world that is going green, ecotourism is therefore one of the fastest growing segment of the significantly growing tourism industry (World Tourism Organization, 1999). The economic and financial gains from ecotourism are manifold; In Cameroon, the growth in ecotourism encourages domestic investment both by the public and private sectors. It also attracts foreign direct investment as well as other forms of developmental aid and grants for the creation and maintenance of parks and other forms of reserves. In this light, the fusion of these various sources of investments expands the domestic markets by encouraging entrepreneurship and other spillover effects. This does not only increase foreign exchange earnings, it also expands the local labor markets in Cameroon by creating jobs and attracting foreign knowhow and talents. According to Ko (2005) all economic activities are necessary for sustainable development to enhance the quality of life both for the local community and for the natural environment. Therefore, ecotourism has a big role to play in achieving sustainable development

Ecotourism is also promoting good governance and better economic policy in Cameroon. It goes without saying that development aid comes with "pre-conditions", the now famous conditionality that is aimed at encouraging better governance. In a bit to attract these aids and grants, the government of Cameroon has been compelled to enact good policies such as the national forestry management plan. In addition, investors would only invest in economies where there is a guarantee or potential to make some profit. This assurance could be provided by the existence of favorable and appropriate investment climate in terms of policies and also appropriate institutional frameworks that could support such policies, for example effective judiciary and regulatory framework. As a result, the Cameroon government has been forced to overhaul the judicial system and put together a new investment code. However, these improvements in the governance structure of the country are still only on paper because its implementation leaves much to be desired.

Unlike earnings from some natural resources such as oil that accrue directly into the coffers of the government and high net worth individuals, the earnings form ecotourism accrue directly to all strata of the society. This is due to the fact that tourists and thus eco-tourists spend money as they interact with the society from the port of entry to their destination. Most of these destinations and sites are located in the interior of the country, where most of the poor lives. Local entrepreneurs therefore engage in economic activities by creating rural enterprises to provide for the needs of eco-tourists. Hence the earnings from ecotourism have a direct redistribution effect compared to other sources of foreign receipt. The poor and marginalized in the society can directly rip their benefit and do not have to wait for the trickle-down effect or for the government to reallocate at will; their own share of the national cake (e.g. proceeds from oil). Ecotourism therefore intrinsically encourages balance development. The ability of the local population to generate income through entrepreneurial activities helps reduce the reliance on natural resources, thereby reducing the pressure on endangered species and hence conserve the natural environment.

Ecotourism has the potential to empower the poor by making them independent. If the poor could be self reliant, they would be able to critically question government policies without being afraid of any form of retribution. As such, the government would be more accountable to its people and thus work for their interest. Hence, there might be a positive feedback loop between ecotourism and government policies. In comparison, Kenya seems to be performing better than Cameroon in every measure of governance, be it in the World Bank or the Mol Ibrahim governance index. This is probably due to this beneficial effect of ecotourism. According to the Ibrahim index of African governance, Cameroon was ranked 25th in 2008 whereas Kenya was ranked 17th out of 48 African countries (Mol Ibrahim foundation, 2009). Similarly, according to the World Bank governance index, the government of Kenya is more than twice as accountable as that of Cameroon (World Bank, 2009)

In a globalizing world, ecotourism encourages cultural exchange between Cameroon and the rest of the world at the international level. At the local level, it encourages rural and urban integration. Ecotourism involves the movement of people, material as well as ideas and way of life. Because of these movements, ideas and knowhow are sometimes interchanged thereby integrating people from different parts of the world.

Most importantly, ecotourism encourage the conservation efforts both by the government and private individuals. To the government, it is a source of hard currency and therefore good for the macroeconomic stability and to most private individuals it is a source of livelihood. Therefore, understanding the magnitude of the interactions and overlap of poverty, macroeconomic processes and conservation would be crucial in identifying illusive but a possible win-win solution (Fisher and Treg, 2007; Wunder, 2001)

Some writers especially Ambe et al (2008) posited that ecotourism might be a good source of revenue that could not only compensate the local population for the missed opportunity of consuming their local resources such as those available in some ecotourism sites but also could provide revenue in maintaining or increasing the appealing factors of such sites. Gössling (1999) is of the opinion that ecotourism has a role to play in safeguarding biodiversity and the ecosystem functions in developing countries. He feels that making a cost-benefit analysis of a tropical rainforests, leads to the conclusion that non-use values often outweigh the values of conventional uses such as clear-cutting, pasture, etc. Therefore, tourism and of course ecotourism with its high direct use value can play an important role as an incentive for conservation. This premise therefore leads to several questions. Can the use of ecotourism in the continuous fight against poverty alleviation be convergent with the fight to conserve some of the natural beauty and wonders of the country? To what extend can ecotourism be relied on to support poverty alleviation in Cameroon? Can ecotourism generate enough revenue for the government to replace the earnings from logging that does not only destroy the forest but also destroy and fragment the habitats of wildlife?

Hunting safari or sport hunting, although so despicable as an ecotourism activity is very profitable in the short term, offering poor families much needed income. Most big game are hunted for trophies and as live animals. In Cameroon, this is a highly lucrative trade. However, most of these trophies do not appear in official statistics. Hunting trophies particularly the horns (see Figure 2) are exported to Germany, the United States and Mexico. There is no effective control over the collection of these species and very little control over export. It is a highly corrupt trade with very high level of waste. The footprints of the developed world are therefore very clear on Cameroon's export of its biodiversity. Many managers of ecotourism sites have been forced by budgetary constraints to look increasingly to consumptive uses of natural resources such as trophy or sport hunting because they have more revenue producing potentials per visitor when compared to non-consumptive use such as photographic tourism. (Baker, 1997).

The principal species affected in sport hunting are Elephants, Lion, Bongo and Derby Eland. Sport hunting is socially disruptive because it antagonizes and marginalizes local communities. It is hard for local communities to understand why their own hunting needs, primarily for subsistence and economic survival is illegal, while sport hunting, a pastime in which only the horns or tusks are taken, is legal. From such activities foreign companies such as Four Star Adventures, African Trophy hunting, Fauna Safari Club etc. make lot of money from the industry and negligible amounts trickle-down to the local inhabitants. As a remedy of such a problem, Smith and Scherr (2003) proposed that regulations such as minimum standard for stakeholder consultation and mandatory social impact studies should be enforced by the governments to reduce risks for local communities. Figure 3 shows a list of sample price for the purchase of sport hunting licenses in Cameroon.

It can be observed from Figure 3 that the bulk of persons who indulge in sport hunting are foreign tourists, followed by resident tourists and then a few nationals in that decreasing order. The tourists are more interested in the big game for trophies while nationals go for small game probably because they lack the sophisticated weapons needed to bring down big game and they may not be able to afford the cost of the license to hunt big game.

Figure 2. Trophy of Derby Eland prepared in Mr. Carlo Rizzotti's Hunting zone No 2 Benoué National Park. Source: Tsi (2006)

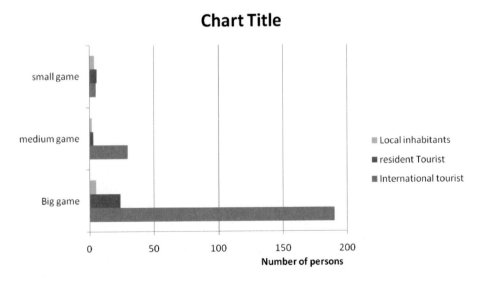

Figure 3. Categorization of Sport hunting permits in Faro and Benoue National Parks 2002- 2003

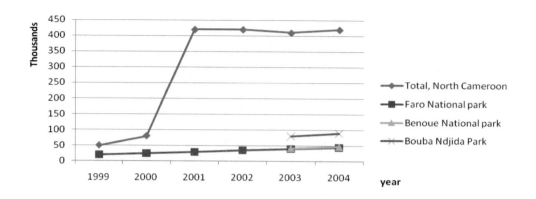

Figure 4. Evolution of hunting taxes from 1999- 2004 in US dollar Adapted from Kirda (2000) & Tsi (2006)

Tsi (2006) has shown that some of the income generated from park activities (ecotourism) in the north region of Cameroon are very substantial and accrue to the local inhabitants directly. For example, four hundred thousand US dollars were earned from official leisure hunting activities in the Northern Region of Cameroon. The government of Cameroon by law N° 98/006 of 14th April 1998 relating to tourist activities and Decree N° 99/443 of 25th March 1999 introduced co-management in which the local community participates in the decision making and benefits directly from tourism and ecotourism. Figure 4 shows benefits from tax quotas by rural communities in the north region of Cameroon. The local inhabitants in this area have also organized themselves into various groups and associations and provide backup services to leisure hunters. Part of the taxes earned is directly given to local community which could be used for developmental purposes. To buttress this point, Damania and John (2005) are of the opinion that the public sector has a very bad record in protecting protected or endangered species and prompted calls for the use of economic incentives and other market based instruments to promote more effective environmental outcome. It is worth noting that the so called endangered or protected species are a main attractive factor in ecotourism. Therefore, encouraging ecotourism would be one way of promoting the private sector participation in conservation.

It can be observed from Figure 4 that from 2001, the sum total of revenue generated from the three parks is less than the total revenue generated from the North Region, suggesting that there are other sources of income not linked to hunting taxes. However, wildlife resources contribute a significant portion through sport hunting with beautiful trophies like the trophy of Derby Eland (Figure 2). For comparison, the South African Hunting Industry, with an annual turnover of about R700 million (about 85.4 million USD, using the exchange rate of 28/5/2009) employs approximately 60,000 mostly illiterate rural people and supports approximately 250,000-300,000 dependents through those employed (Tsi, 2006).

Most tourists would visit Cameroon or another country or destination to consume touristic resources that are mostly not available in their area of origin. There is therefore an incentive for local people to forgo the consumption of some of their natural resources, and conserve them, in their natural state so that others could compensate them in terms of access rights. This in itself resolves the paradox of the necessity to destroy some natural resources as a mean to earn a living. This is a paradox because eco-tourists in general prefer prime sites that are in good form, in terms of its naturalness and wildness. On the other hand, harnessing some of these resources for commercial consumption or as a means to earn a living entails the destruction of the wildness or naturalness of such sites. It is therefore important to find a balance between the ever increasing need for conservation and poverty alleviation especially with regards to the exploitation of forestry resources in particular and ecotourism in general.

Brief Overview of Ecotourism and Economic Development in Cameroon

The uniqueness of Cameroon was noted in the colonial era and the then colonial masters created some national parks and reserves in the country mostly to serve as hunting reserves e.g. the flora rich Dja Biosphere Reserve and the big fauna rich Waza National Park that were created in 1950 and 1934 respectively. In a bid to conserve and preserve the natural beauty and wonders of these sites, the Cameroonian government upgraded them into conservation sites after the country became independent. Ever since, the government of Cameroon has continued to maintain these sites in addition to creating new ones. For example, the Deng Deng National park was created in 2002, following surveys on western lowland gorilla populations made by the Wildlife Conservation Society (Delaney, 2009).

On seizing its independence from France in the early sixties, the government of Cameroon realized that it could generate sustainable benefits from its natural endowed attractiveness by growing a sustainable tourism industry. Inventories of the tourism including ecotourism potentials of the country were made and a plan was put in place to sell them both locally and internationally. In the Seventies, the country made some commendable strives towards achieving this objective. Posters were printed and distributed throughout the national territory and abroad. The national radio stations sang praises to the country's natural endowments.

In the late seventies, oil was discovered in Cameroon and it fast became the main source of foreign exchange earnings, representing about 41 % of all export earnings (Khan and Gbetnkom, 2003). The government subsequently failed to build up on the impetus that has been generated by the earlier investment in the tourism sector. Over dependence on crude oil as the main source of foreign exchange earnings resulted in the neglect of other key revenue generating sectors of the economy such as the industrial sector as well as the tourism and ecotourism business thereby provoking the Dutch disease in the country (Khan and Gbetnkom, 2003). In the mid eighties, this problem was further exacerbated by a sharp declined in the prices of primary commodity including that of oil, coffee and cocoa, (the principal foreign exchange earners for Cameroon) in the world market, thereby seriously eroding the governments' foreign exchange earnings. The end effect was a crippling economic and financial crisis that nearly bankrupts the state of Cameroon. One of the consequences of the crises was a serious macroeconomic imbalance that even financial aid from the Britton Wood institutions and other donor governments were not able to remedy leading to heavy indebtedness (World Bank 1995)

To reduce the impact of macroeconomic imbalance and high indebtedness imposed by the economic crisis and the structural adjustment thereof, the government embarked on a massive sale of its forestry resources, which in itself could be profitable (Snook, 2000) to sustain the nation's economy. A prove of this is a drop in the forest cover from 48% of total land cover in 2000 to 46% in 2005 (UNDP, 2008). If this rate should continue, by the year 2030, Cameroon would no more have any natural forest which is vital in attracting foreign tourists and is also a good sink for carbon in this era of global warming. At this period, receipt from the logging industry became the biggest source of foreign earning to the government. The wanton destruction of the forest has a direct detrimental effect on the ecotourism sector as it is the base of the industry. Diversification of the sources of foreign exchange earnings including ecotourism is a possible way forward, and a priority for economic revival and survival.

It is also important to note that, over the years in Cameroon, there have been shifts in the use of the forest and other ecotourism sites. First of all the local population or communities looked at the forest or the savanna as a source of food for their well being, however, with population increase and the growth in urbanization, the use of these resources have shifted to acting as a source of income – cut-off and sell the trees as logs, firewood, planks etc. or poach, butcher and sell off the wild animals as bush meat, hide etc. The loss in the natural resources base became so dramatic that it alarmed the international community. In an attempt to stem the wanton destruction of these natural wonders, the government was compel to carry out a far reaching reform of not just the timber logging industry but that of all the natural resources in the country.

In the end, instead of destroying these resources to generate income through as described above, there has been a shift towards using the nature given environment as a source of income through the promotion of ecotourism. In spite of the efforts made by the inhabitants, the government and some local and international NGOs, the transition has not been very smooth and it is at the verge of unraveling all the efforts and gains that have so far been made. The analysis in this study shows that market failure, policy failure, institutional failure, and regulatory failure are the main reasons that could have hampered the effective transition to ecotourism. To understand this failure, the Boston Consultative Group (BCG) framework has been used to illuminate the sorry state of the ecotourism business in Cameroon.

Conceptual Framework

Before analyzing the intrinsic trajectory of the ecotourism business in Cameroon using the BCG framework, it would be important to first of all define the various terms in the framework;

1. **A Question Mark** refers to businesses that are in a fast growing industry but the business has a relatively low market share. Therefore, the business is a net consumer of cash or investment, in other words the business is not generating enough profit to compensate for the investment. In such a situation, succinct analyses needs to be done to determine whether it is worth investing more in a bit to increase market share and thus generate more profit that would one day cover up for the investment. On the other hand, the analyses would also made it evident if additional investment would not make the business profitable in the long run and therefore, the investment would have rather been made on some other business;

2. **A Dog** refers to a business that is in a slow growth but mature industry with a low market share. In this situation, the business is generally able to sustain itself or it can break even. Thereby the investment is able to generate enough profit to make the business worthwhile. The business can thus provide jobs and most importantly create both horizontal and vertical linkages to other industries. If synergies could be made at this stage, then from an economic stand point, it is profitable in spite of its low market share;

3. **A Cash cow** refers to a business in low growth industries but with a very high market share, thereby gaining more than substantiated profit or in this situation a rent. In other word the business is more or less a monopoly and therefore detects the market price. Very little economic value if any at all is created but rent is being enjoyed at a very high rate. Most business would like to be in this situation. Finally;

4. **A Star** refers to a business with a high market share in a fast growing industry. In this situation, there are very high returns for the invested funds. Both economic and financial values are created and the market is very dynamic. Management of a business in such a situation has to be on constant alert and very creative to defend and maintained their market shares. Investment would be needed to gain extra market shares.

In the case of Cameroon, following the high investment that was done in the industry in the sixties as described above by the government, the tourism business more or less attained the stage of a "dog", docile and calm with enough market share and thus earnings to sustain itself without additional investment from the government. However, just like a dog, to maximize benefit from it, a firm control has to be made in the sector with the right regulatory framework and institutions. Did the Cameroonian government show leadership in this situation? The answer to this question is no. In this light, it is clear that the ecotourism industry in Cameroon instead of migrating from the "Dog" quadrant as illustrated in figure 5 to the "good quadrants (Star or cash cow) instead went to the wrong one (Question Mark) and all its implications. At this point, it important for us to look at some of the factors that are contributing in maintaining the status quo (question mark) of the ecotourism industry in Cameroon as well as some of the regulatory policies that may help the country in moving out of the quagmire that it now find itself into the good direction and ultimately into the "right quadrant"

Comparatively, if we try to apply this framework to the situation in Kenya, it presents a completely different picture. The ecotourism business in Kenya shows the right trajectory, after a period of no growth and even a decline in 1997, the government succeeded in putting together the right combination of investments and policies to an extend that the business started growing at an exponential rate (UNDP, 2009) as evidenced by growth in the number of foreign tourists to the country (Figure 6). In this light, the business succeeded in migrating from a dog to a star on the BCG framework.

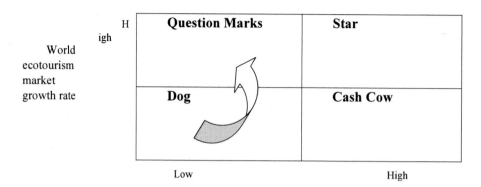

Cameroon's relative market share in the world tourism

Figure 5. A modified BCG (Boston Consultative Group) framework to analyze the ecotourism market position of Cameroon over time

A Brief Comparison of Cameroon and Kenya in Attracting Foreign Tourists

The number of tourist arriving a given destination or country is used by the international community as a measure of the popularity of that destination or country. However, it is important to note that this measure does not differentiate the various reasons for tourism, be it cultural, religious, mountain biking, sport hunting etc. In the context of this work, it has been assumed that ecotourism is the principal pulling factor for tourism in Cameroon and Africa in general. Therefore, in the graphs and analyses that follow, we have not adjusted the data to reflect ecotourism alone rather it represents the tourism business as a whole. It should however be noted that our assumption is in sharp contrast to that of the World Wide Fund for Nature (1995) that states "Ecotourism represents a small segment of nature- tourism. Nature-tourism is understood as travel to relatively undisturbed or uncontaminated natural areas and constitutes about 15% of all tourism" In this scenario, WWF was probably referring to the world as a whole and not just to tourism in Africa and in Cameroon in particular.

Figure 6 makes it clear that Kenya has always been a favored destination for ecotourism compared to Cameroon, attracting five times as many tourists from 1995 right up to 2003. Beyond 2003, the number of tourist favoring Kenya simply skyrocketed, whereas that of Cameroon stagnated and started declining. It can also be noticed that after 2007, there was a sharp decline in the number of tourists to Kenya because of the Post electoral violence in the country couple to the world recession of 2008. However, the number of tourists arriving Cameroon shows some resilience although the trend is still declining, albeit at a decreasing rate.

In terms of earning, Kenya earns about three times as much foreign exchange earnings as Cameroon right up to 2003 and after this period, the earning increased at an exponential rate (see Figure 7), while that of Cameroon stagnated and started declining after 2003. However, it seems Cameroon attracts the high end tourists because in 2004 an average tourist spends $1,116 US in Cameroon compared to $670 US in Kenya. On one hand this may imply that tourists consider the services provided by the Cameroonian tourism industry to be of superior quality and are therefore willing to pay a premium. On the other hand, it might mean the services are just plain expensive, in which case many tourists cannot afford it. There are strong indications that the latter seems to be the situation that exists in the country. Whereas, Kenya has succeeded in bringing down the cost of the industry to an extent that it is its unique selling point. Sundbo et al (2007) has illustrated that the competitiveness of a tourism firm depends on their innovativeness in achieving lower cost, higher quality outputs and introducing new products that meets the demand requirement of potential customers. In this regards, the firms in Kenya seems to have gotten the right recipe in attractive more customers by being innovative in providing higher quality products at a lower cost.

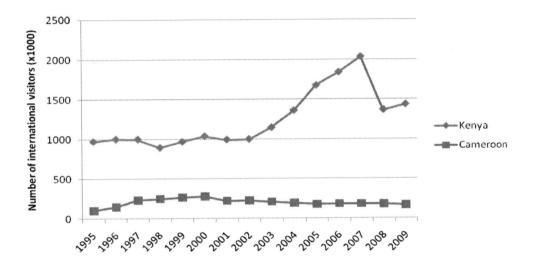

Figure 6. Number of international tourists arrivals in Cameroon and Kenya from 1995-2008

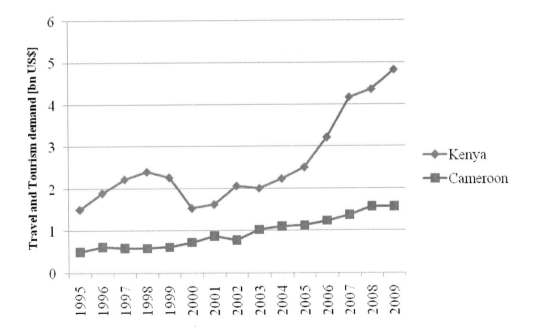

Figure 7. International tourism receipts for Cameroon compared to that of Kenya from 1995-2008

Table 1. Benefits to some rural communities in Garoua from exchange earnings through ecotourism in US dollar (exchange rate used 1USD=500FCFA):

	Rural Community	Amount	Exchange premium	Net Amount received
1	Tchollire	38151	576	37575
2	Touboro	21561	288	21273
3	Poli	16728	288	16440
4	Madingring	9573	288	9285
5	Lagdo	5729	288	5441
6	Ray Bouba	4596	288	4308
7	Tcheboa	3994	2880	3706
8	Beka	1714		1714
	Total			99743

Source: Delegation MINEF Garoua, (2005) & Tsi, (2006)

Furthermore, Kenya's earning from tourism in 2005, is better than Cameroon's earning from its principal source of government receipt (oil). In addition, oil is a non sustainable (non-renewable) source of revenue because it is depletable. On the other hand, earning from ecotourism is sustainable as long as the country can maintain its competitive advantage. Between 2003 and 2006, the tourism industry in Kenya grew by a whopping 91%. In 2002, Cameroon started showing the same growth potential as Kenya, but somehow, failed to live up to expectations. From the above analyses, it is therefore clear that the ecotourism industry in Cameroon is not living up to expectation in spite of its huge potentials.

At the micro level, it has been shown by Tsi (2006) that the local community could also earn directly from foreign exchange earnings through exchange rate premium charged for exchanging foreign currency for the FCFA (francs of the cooperation Frence-Africa) at the local level. In addition, the cash so exchanged are direct spent in the local communities. Table 1 represents an example of these benefits to some rural communities.

From the various sources of income that are linked to ecotourism, it is therefore clear to the local inhabitants that, there is a strong link between conservation and their source of income (Fisher and Treg, 2007; Sanderson, 2005). As a matter of fact, Lee and Barrett (2001) has illustrated that in Cameroon, Brazil and Indonesia, forest gardens are responsible for 50-80% of the cash incomes of farm households. Therefore there is a strong link between conservation, income to rural communities and poverty alleviation. This link is not loss to the local communities and therefore it is of their interest to conserve their natural environment in a bid to attract tourists who in turn would provide them with the means to fight poverty.

In spite of the above causality, very little gains have been made because the government has failed in its catalytic role of integrating local communities and private individuals as the main actors in the ecotourism business. In this paper, it would be shown that market failure, policy failure, institutional failure and regulatory failures are the main reasons that could account for the failure of the transition to viable ecotourism. To this list of failures, Mbatu (2009) added debt crisis, population growth as some of the factors that intricately work together resulting in a complex socio-economic and political failure on the part of the government and private individuals to produce the negative outcome witnessed in the forest sector in Cameroon.

Constraints to the Emergence of Cameroon As an Attractive Ecotourism Destination

In the ecotourism business, the ministry of tourism together with related services has a sketchy plan or strategy on the management of natural resources not to talk of the promotion of ecotourism. The legal framework of this plan are define in law N° 98/006 of 14th April 1998 relating to tourist activities and Decrees N° 99/443 of 25th March 1999 and N° 047/PM of 26th September 2001. Countries with well defined strategic plans such as Rwanda and Kenya, sell themselves with the mountain gorillas and the safari respectively. This completely differentiates these countries from other ecotourism destinations. Reading through the plan, it is difficult to find key words such as; "competition", "potential customers", etc in the whole documents. It is clear that understanding the competitive forces and their drivers are very important in elucidating the economic and financial gains and thus the competiveness of the industry. The head of the tourism board is the prime minister of the country and if you visit the website of the PM office, a page has been dedicated to the tourism industry. Unfortunately, it was last updated five years ago that is in 2004. In this webpage, there is a plan of some investment in the sector but one would wonder is this is not just a window screen because there is little if any change in the tourism infrastructure in the country.

It is therefore not surprising that on the webpage of the prime minister's office, one would find the most shocking banner that completely summarizes the tourism and ecotourism business in Cameroon. "Standing as a haven of peace and political stability in Africa, Cameroon is a good business risk for potential investors of the tourist sector" (Prime Minister's office website, 2009) is there any business strategic plan that would make such a fatal error? How can Cameroon be a haven of peace and security and yet a "good business risk"? Is this a strategy of attracting potential foreign investors by telling them how bad a place Cameroon would be for their investment? If in reality Cameroon is a potential business risk, should this be brandish in the face of investors without clarifying the situation? This is pure and clear bad marketing. Ayaba hotel that used to be one of the flagships of the tourism business in the North West Region of Cameroon is at this point in time is just a shadow of its former self. Completely dilapidated and under maintained.

Very little information could be found online on ecotourism in Cameroon. Some industrious Cameroonians are promoting just their area of origin such as "ecos of the twin lakes" by Melle (2009) and others are promoting tourism in general such as the platform of Sarah Limunga Enow or that of Jerry W. Bird "Africa in One Country". These stand alone sites are not sufficient because a potential tourist would like to have a mix of as much ecotourism offerings as possible to make a choice. It would be beneficial to maintain a website that carries all such information, e.g. the website of the authority in charge of tourism in Kenya. The website of the ministry of tourism in Cameroon is not fit for this purpose and so in dire need of improvement. It provides very limited information about ecotourism or even tourism in general but rather focuses on the politics of the ministry. It is therefore clear that the marketing of the ecotourism potential of Cameroon is still very lagging.

There is also the problem of the valorization and valuation of the ecotourism potentials in the country. In terms of valorization, much have been done by national park authorities such as the Korup National Park, Campo Mann, etc; Non Governmental Organizations such as "Ecosystème Forestière d'Afrique Central", World Wide Fund for Nature, etc; Educational Institutions such as the Universities of Dschang, Ngoundere, Buea, the National Herbarium, etc; Research Bodies such as the World Agroforetry Centre, Institute of Agricultural Research for Development, International Institute of Tropical Agriculture etc. in compiling the fauna and flora resources of the country in their respective area of interest. However, these resources are still to be evaluated and valuated in such a way that ecotourism synergies could be found amongst the various offerings.

The poor transport network and related infrastructure in Cameroon greatly hinders the development of ecotourism. Most of the parks are located very far away from the airports in very remote areas. The communication links to this area are often very poor especially in the rainy seasons. This tends to increase the cost (time and money) of visiting touristic sites

Another important point that might hinder the development of the ecotourism industry is the conflict between resources in protected land and their human neighbors; Ravaging elephants and evading lions that kill domestic animals and even humans etc could lead to conflicts between the interest of inhabitants and the interest of conservation. In anticipation of such conflicts, the government of Cameroon resettled most of the local inhabitants of protected land out of the protected zone. Peluso (1992) and Skonhoft (1998) also noted similar practices in Asia and in East Africa, where such practices led to conflicts because rights to forest resources are unclear and subject to multiple claim by different social actors and sanctioned by different institutions. The exception to this rule in Cameroon are in the biosphere reserves, where humans have been left to interact with the conserved resources such as the in the Dja Biosphere reserve (Ambe et al 2008). The creation of national parks have often created conflicts as the local people look onto the resources of the parks or reserve as theirs by right. Therefore, they demand compensations for the missed income of exploiting these resources or in the case of biospheres to exploit the resources without any constraints. In addition, population increase, both in-situ and ex-situ of protected areas and in some wild animal species, have led to increase competition over the available resources. Oyono et al (2005) posited that both inter and intra generational access to forestry resources and the resulting financial benefit is also a big problem in Cameroon.

Generally, insecurity in Cameroon is making matters worse. The country used to pride itself as a haven of security in a very insecure Central Africa Region, but of late, this has not been the case with the constant rise in urban banditry. Tourists are afraid of their security within the borders of the country.

There is also the problem of over hunting or over exploitation of the natural resources. This has been spurred by the fact that most of the reserves have been abandoned by the government. In some cases, the management of the reserves and parks etc do not have enough resources to completely keep out poachers who in most cases are better armed than the so called "ecoguards". In fact, in some of the reserves, the moral authorities of the authorities as custodians of the protected resources have been broken because of poor pay and lack of motivation. All these problems do exist mostly due to the fact that the reserves or national parks are not able to generate enough resources to maintain some of their vital services.

In the specific case of the Santchou reserve, Ndongo (2009) postulated that the reserve has been program for a slow death by the power that be, because of the lack of a management plan. Everything is being done haphazardly and therefore, poachers and gatherers have taken advantage of the situation, and are over exploiting the resources especially the fauna to almost near extinction. In this light, most of the game that were meant for conservation have either seek secure pasture elsewhere such as the elephants or have simply been over poached to the extent that it is very difficult to locate them in the reserve. In addition, the local population derives very little benefit from the reserve and therefore considers it as a hindrance to the access of badly needed land for cultivation. It should be also be noted that the reserve is located in an area with one of the highest population density in the country.

Perspective

From the above analyses, it is very clear that the government has failed to an extent in playing its role as the facilitator for the development of a viable local ecotourism industry. The future expectations of a well managed ecotourism industry include increased foreign exchange earnings, leading to more employment opportunities both at the national and local levels that could make an impact in the fight against poverty on one hand and on the other help in the conservation efforts. This is due to the fact that there is a positive reinforcement between earnings from ecotourism and conservation. In the long run, this would promote ecological diversity and stability through the preservation of gene pool, natural heritage, and better utilization of food and recreation resources. To take advantage of the above situation, both the government of Cameroon and local entrepreneurs have to act now by focusing on the following points;

Have a well define strategy for the sector in addition to a management plan. Such plans should be dynamic in order to cope up with the rapidly globalizing world marked by constant changes in technology. A unique selling points should be defined or elaborated that would differentiate Cameroon from other ecotourism destinations, and hence be the source of competitive advantage.

A good strategic plan would also strive to sustain (where they exist) and built new (where they don't exist) networks right across the value chain not only within the local industry but also internationally. It has been shown by Erkuş-Öztürk, (2008) that viable networks increase the potential attractiveness of an ecotourism destination. The larger the firms in the ecotourism industry the more it would benefit from the global network. Some elements in the network would include; tourist information offices, attractions and travel agencies, restaurants and accommodation (hotels, pensions, youth hostels, camping sites) etc

Establish an effective organ for the planning, development, promotion and marketing of tourism in and outside Cameroon including well defined roles for the stakeholders. Make available information about the eco touristic potential of the country. The internet age has facilitated and eased the distribution of information; hence this tool could be exploited to the benefit of the ecotourism industry in Cameroon. Other available free websites and web pages such as, MySpace, LinkedIn, or blog should be exploited by the employees of this ministry and other stakeholders to sell the country to the rest of the world. Examples could be drawn from other countries that are currently performing well in the industry. The promotion of the local consumption of the ecotourism potentials of the country should be pursued by al a sundry. Most local tourists are attracted just to the coaster cities, where there is a wealth of infinite attractions and diversions. However, the hinterlands also have adequate ecotourism attractions that need to be effectively valorized to be appealing to local inhabitants. It should not be surprising to note that most Cameroonians have never visited the parks or zoos or reserves. To them it is the domain of foreign tourist alone. This perception has to change.

Co-management or support from local people is crucial for the success of any ecotourism business not to talk of the effort at conservation. Mbaiwa (2005) has illustrated that for community based tourism projects to be successful, local empowerment in the management of natural resources and tourism development are crucial. The local inhabitants engaged in the tourism business should be encouraged to be entrepreneurial and come up with innovative products (Schumpeter, 1961) that are market driven The products should not only able to meet up with the present needs of tourist but must be able to anticipate their future needs and be ready to provide these services even before they demand them. In this regards, there is the need to increase visitor's experiences through the offering of a diverse product mix such as forest walk away, easy wild animal sightings, buggy jumping. The ecotourism offering should be targeted to the right market; most young visitors are sensation seekers and therefore offering such as buggy jumping, or close encounter with wild animals such as lions, buffaloes would be highly valued. Whereas aged visitors would prefer scenic environment such as the Twin Lakes of Muanenguba in Mwaan, or a hike up mount Cameroon, etc.

The government should focus on seriously promoting the Fako area of Cameroon as a dream ecotourism destination. The area boasts one of the most attractive packages of any touristic destination in the country. First of all, the Fako region is just few miles away from the nearest port of entry, be it the Douala seaport or airports and it is linked by well paved and maintained roads. This area also has not just the supporting infrastructures such as hotels, hospitals, etc. but also has a collection of dream ecotourism sites. Starting with the mount Fako or Cameroon, where visitors may have the option of making the tedious and exhilarating clime to the summit or visit its abundant wildlife such as the elephants. There is also the Limbe botanical garden with its world collection of endemic flora species that could be visited. Nearby, there is the Limbe wildlife centre with a rich collection of wildlife especially the cross river baboons, monkeys, lion etc. After making such an exhaustive tour in an area few kilometers of radius, visitors are now on a spoil of a collection of good tropical beaches, such as the Seme, Mile six etc, where they could swim away their frustrations, exhaustions or excitements. After this tour, those who are still in need of more could then catch the next bush taxi to the Korup national park and environ, where more scintillating ecotourism sites awaits them.

To boast the attractiveness of this area as a dream ecotourism destination especially for low budget pack parkers, the Fako ecotourism haven needs to be further developed to cater for the needs of all realms of eco-tourists. Be it sensation seekers, wildlife lovers, mountaineers, bird watchers, etc. For example, a daredevil mountain biking trails could be built along the foot of mount Cameroon, a kayaking trail along one of the main stream in the area, the institution of an annual national cultural carnival in the area. The attractiveness of the Limbe wildlife centre could be increase by providing it with some of the rich fauna that could found at the Waza national park such as the giraffe, hippopotamus, etc. To optimizing the various offering it is important that a management board such as the existing Mount Cameroon inter communal ecotourism board, made up of both the private and governmental institution should be empowered in the area. Such a board would control the various activities of the site to achieve maximum efficiency and effectiveness. The board should also put in place the necessary support services such as adequate and up to date health care facilities and accommodating facilities, adequate personal security, etc. If this could be achieved then the mount Cameroon can become the unique selling point of Cameroon in the ecotourism industry and therefore a way of differentiating Cameroon from the rest of the African countries in the tourism industry.

In this paper, it has been established that there is a strong dependency link between ecotourism and conservation on one hand and foreign exchange earnings on the other. Therefore the promotion of ecotourism is like killing two birds with a stone – poverty alleviation and conservation. Is this then not a lofty policy to follow?

REFERENCES

Ambe, T. E., Nji, A., Tita, D. F., Ntonga, M. L. & Bongsiysi, I. B. (2008). Demographic pressure and natural resources conservation. *Ecological Economics., vol. 64, issue* 3, pages, 475-483.

Auzel, P. (1999). Site forestier industriels et durabilite de l'exploitation de la faune dans le Sud-Est du Cameroun. DEA en Science Agronomique et ingenierie biologique. *Faculte Universitaire des Sciences Agronomiques, Gembloux, Belgique, 117.*

Baker, J. E., (1997). Development of a model system for touristic hunting revenue collection and allocation. *Tourism Management., 18/ 5,* 273-286.

Brightsmith, D. J., Amanda, S. & Kurt, H.(2008). Ecotourism, conservation biology, and volunteer tourism: A mutually beneficial triumvirate. *Biological conservation, 141,* 2832 - 2842.

Boo, E. (1992). The ecotourism boom, planning for development and management, WHN Technical Papers Series, paper 2, *World Wildlife Fund, July, Washington, DC.*

Ceballos-Lascurain, H. (1991) Tourism, ecotourism and protected areas. In J.A. Kusler, Ecotourism and resource conservation (54-61). *Ecotourism and Resource Conservation Project, Washington D.C.*

Damania, R. & John, H., (2005). Protecting Eden: markets or government? *Ecological Economics., 53/3;* 339-351.

Delaney, J. (2009). Wildlife Conservation Society helps Cameroon create new national park. Article by wcs (see www.wcs.org; *last consulted,* 25/02/2009).

Fisher, B., & Treg, C. (2007). Poverty and biodiversity: Measuring the overlap of human poverty and the biodiversity hotspots. *Ecological Economics., 62/1,* 93-101.

Gössling, S. (1999). Ecotourism: a means to safeguard biodiversity and ecosystem functions?. *Ecological Economics, 29,* 303–320.

Khan, S. & Gbetnkom, D. (2003) Agricultural exports supply determinants in Cameroon's economy. In Developing a sustainable economy in Cameroon. Ed. *A. Ajab Amin.* 29-48.

Kirda, P. (2000). Les activites cynegetiques dans la province du Nord Cameroun entre 1983 et 1997. *Ecole de la faune Garoua.*

Ko, T. G. (2005). Development of a tourism sustainability assessment procedure: a conceptual approach. *Tourism Management, 26,* 431-445.

Lee, D. R. & Barrett, C. B. (2001). (Editors) *Tradeoffs or synergies? Agricultural intensification, economic development and the environment,* CABI Publishing, Wallingford, UK.

Limunga, S. E. (2009). Tourism in Cameroon. (http://www.africanews.com/site/page/ tourism_in_cameroon) last consulted 25/04/2009.

Mbaiwa, J. E. (2005). Wildlife resource utilisation at Moremi Game Reserve and Khwai community area in the Okavango Delta, Botswana. *Journal of Environmental Management.*, *77*, 144-156.

Mbatu, R. S. (2009). Forest policy analysis praxis: Modelling the problem of forest loss in Cameroon. *Forest Policy and Economics*, *11*, 26-33.

Mbile, P., Vabi, M., Meboka, M., Okon, D., Arrey-Mbo, J., Nkongho, F. & Ebong, E. (2005). Linking management and livelihood in environmental conservation: case of the Korup National Park Cameroon. *Journal of Environmental Management, 76*, 1-13.

Melle, I. (2009). 'Ecos' of the Twin Lakes: Ecotourism Development in Mwaam (Muanenguba), Cameroon. (http://www.ecoclub.com/library/epapers/080905.html) last consulted, 25/04/2009.

Mol Ibrahim Foundation, (2009). Ibrahim index of African governance 2008. (http://www.moibrahimfoundation.org/index-2008/pdf/press_release/kenya.pdf)   last consulted, 25/04/2009.

Ndongo, A. (2009). Réserve de Santchou: Mort programmée d'une réserve. Le messager.

Oyono, P. R., Charlotte K. & William, M. (2005). Benefits of forests in Cameroon. Global structure, issues involving access and decision-making hiccoughs. *Forest Policy and Economics, 7/3*, 357-368.

Peluso, N. L. (1992) Rich forests, poor people: resource control and resistance in Java., *University of California Press, Berkeley, USA.*

Prime Minister's Office, (2009). Tourism. (http://www.spm.gov.cm/showdoc.php?rubr= 6000&srubr=6109&lang=en&tpl=2) last consulted, 25/04/2009.

Sanderson, S. (2005). Poverty and Conservation: The New Century's "Peasant Question"?, *World Development, 33/2*, 323-332.

Schumpeter, J. A. (1961). The Theory of Economic Development, Oxford University Press, New York, *USA.*

Skonhoft, A. (1998). Resource utilization, property rights and welfare—Wildlife and the local people. *Ecological Economics, 26/1*, 67-80.

Smith, J. & Scherr, S. J. (2003). Capturing the Value of Forest Carbon for Local Livelihoods. *World Development., 31/12*, 2143-2160.

Snook, L. K. (2000). Utilization and management of timber and non-timber forest resources in the forest Ejidos of Quintana Roo Mexico. FAO case studies on combined Timber-*Non-timber Management, FAO*, 6-15, Rome,.

Stebbins, R. ed. (2004). Volunteering as Leisure/Leisure as Volunteering: *An International Assessment.* CABI, Wallingford.

Sundbo, J., Francina, O. S. & Flemming, S. (2007). The innovative behaviour of tourism firms—Comparative studies of Denmark and Spain. Research Policy. *Volume 36, Issue 1, Pages*, 88-106.

Tsi, E. A. & Ayodele, I. A. (2004). Birds: a strong potential in Eco-tourism development of Kilum-Ijim community forest. Faculty of Science, *University of Port Harcourt, Nigeria Sientia Africana, Vol. 3(1)*, 45-50.

Tsi, E. A. (2006). Statuts of wildlife and its utilization in Faro and Benoue national Parks North Cameroon. Case study of theDerby Eland (*Taurotragus derbianus* gigas 1849) and the African Wild Dog (*Lycaon pictus* Temminck 1947). PhD thesis Faculty of Environmental Sciences and Process Engineering, Brandenburg University of Technology, Cottbus Germany., 149 P.

UNDP (2009). World Development Indicators 2008.

UNEP/SDNP. (1996). Cameroon Project Document: Sustainable development Networking Program. No INT/91/716 MINEF (http://sdnhq.unedp.org/countries/af/cm/cmpdoc.html) Last date of access, 27/12/2005.

Wearing, S. (2004) Examining best practice in volunteer tourism. In: Stebbins, R. (Ed.), Volunteering as Leisure/Leisure as Volunteering.

Wearing, S. (2001). Volunteer Tourism: Experiences that Make a Difference. CABI, Wallingford.

World Bank, (2009). World Governance indicator 2008. (http://info.worldbank.org/ governance/wgi/mc_chart.asp) *last consulted*, 25/04/2009.

World Bank, (1995). Cameroon: Diversity, Growth, and Poverty Reduction. Report No. 13167-CM, World Bank, Washington, D C.

World Tourism Organization. (1999). Tourism 2020 Vision. World Tourism Organization, Madrid.

WWF (World Wildlife Fund), (1995). Ecotourism: conservation tool or threat? *Conserv. Iss.*, *2 (3)*, 1-10.

Wunder, S. (2001). Poverty alleviation and tropical forest-what scope for synergies?. *World development*, *29/11*, 1811-1833.

Ziffer, K. A. (1989). Ecotourism: the uneasy alliance, Conservation International Working Papers on Ecotourism, Ernst and Young, Washington, DC.

In: Ecotourism: Management, Development and Impact   ISBN: 978-1-60876-724-3
Editors: A. Krause, E. Weir, pp. 135-157   © 2010 Nova Science Publishers, Inc.

Chapter 5

ENVIRONMENTAL IMPACTS OF RECREATIONAL ACTIVITIES ON THE MEDITERRANEAN COASTAL ENVIRONMENT: THE URGENT NEED TO IMPLEMENT MARINE SUSTAINABLE PRACTICES AND ECOTOURISM

Josep Lloret[*]

University of Girona, Faculty of Sciences, Department of Environmental Sciences,
Campus Montilivi s/n, 17071 Girona, Catalonia, Spain

ABSTRACT

This chapter summarizes the documented impacts of recreational uses on the coastal marine environment of the Mediterranean. These range from the impact of recreational boating on seagrass meadows, the influence of recreational fishing on littoral species (particularly the vulnerable ones), the effects of scuba-diving on hard-sessile benthic invertebrates, the human trampling's effects on rocky shallow areas or the possible disturbance of marine mammals by whale and dolphin watching activities. Considering all these effects, a shift from the actual mass tourism model to an ecologically responsible marine tourism model involving sustainable practices is urgently needed in all Mediterranean border countries. This model implies the management of physical stresses produced by tourist activities on the marine environment including energy and waste minimization and wider environmental impacts cited before.

To implement this responsible model, coastal integrated management plans should consider specific policy tools (described in this chapter) to safeguard the vulnerable (threatened) Mediterranean species and habitats. It is also concluded that recreational fisheries could be reconverted into sustainable practices if a list of new regulations and management actions are implemented to avoid the environmental problems associated with this type of fishing

If responsible tourist practices should be implemented all along the Mediterranean coast, the learning orientation concept should be considered as well, at least in marine

---

[*] Corresponding author: Email: josep.lloret@udg.edu

protected areas to allow the development of marine ecotourism there. This chapter proposes a list of practices that create awareness on the impacts of human uses on the marine environment. In particular, the long-term consensus building with all stakeholders is necessary to establish marine ecotourism.

Overall, this chapter concludes that the sustainability of the tourism industry and the marine environment in the Mediterranean are closely linked to each other and depend upon the urgent adoption of sustainable environmental practices all along the Mediterranean coast as well as the establishment of a marine ecotourism model, at least in marine protected areas.

1. INTRODUCTION

The Mediterranean (Photo 1) is currently the main tourist destination in the world. Every year over 175 million tourists move to the Mediterranean coasts with the number likely to reach around 300 million people per year by 2025 (Bluen Plan, 2007). The increasing desire to conduct maritime leisure activities during the summer is behind these huge numbers. About 60% of European holiday-goers prefer the coast, particularly the Mediterranean (European Commission, 1998). During 2000–2006, the number of tourists in the countries around the Mediterranean increased 8.4% (Eurostat, 2008). However, the growth in tourist arrivals stopped in 2007 and has slowed drastically in 2008 and 2009 under the influence of an extremely unfavorable global economy (WTO, 2009).

During the last decades, many Mediterranean border countries have invested heavily in mass coastal tourism development following the increasing global demand for sand, sea and sun. Mass tourism is thus a reality in the north-western Mediterranean, and it is developing on certain sites in the southern and eastern basin. Only some regions of the south and eastern Mediterranean have little or no tourism. As a consequence of all these facts, the tourism sector makes a considerable contribution to the economy of Mediterranean countries. Thus, for example, about 17% of Spain's Gross Domestic Product (GDP) is accounted for by tourism compared to about 10% of the European GDP (Deutsche Bank Research, 2008).

The excessive tourism, along with other human activities such as construction, shipping and resource exploitation, has put enormous pressures on the coasts and represent a major threat to the environment and long-term socioeconomic development. Today many tourism sites are receiving a huge influx of visitors, especially in peak periods—when the number of inhabitants doubles in the coastal zone—which causes a deterioration of the environmental conditions as well as severe management difficulties and deterioration of the visitor experience. The human impact has altered original Mediterranean landscapes and local cultural traditions resulting in many marine species and habitats being vulnerable, ecologically valuable and protected. Much of the damage already done to some coastal areas of the northern parts of the Mediterranean is essentially irreversible. Repeating this approach in yet more areas of the southern parts of the Mediterranean will simply degrade the coastal zone.

The human impacts on coastal areas have also evolved according to the socioeconomic changes that happened over the years. The evolution of the human uses in many coastal areas over the last decades has been characterized by the increasing socioeconomic importance of recreational activities in detriment to the small-scale commercial fisheries such as artisanal fishing and red coral exploitation (Lloret and Riera, 2008a). These small-scale fisheries had principally an impact on species, whereas the rise of recreational activities is affecting both species and habitats. Then, these areas have evolved from a species-based impact model due to small-scale professional fisheries to an ecosystem-based impact model due to recreational uses, which could be in the long term even more harmful for the whole marine environment.

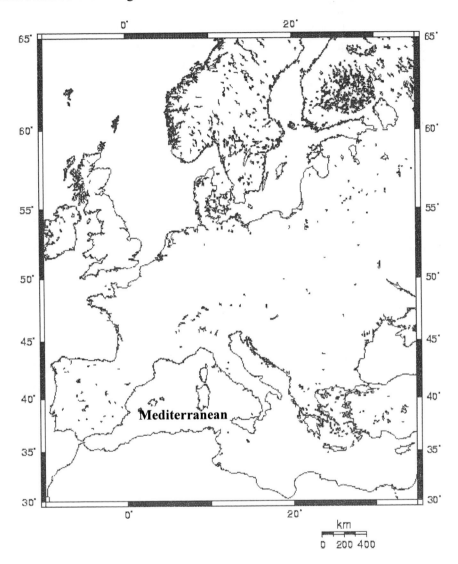

Photo 1. Map of the Mediterranean, a leading world tourist destination where the leisure uses severely impinge on the coastal marine environment.

Apart from the direct impacts of tourist activities, there are numerous, large indirect impacts of tourism on the environment such as the removal of sands near shore to regenerate beaches, eutrophication or pollution in some southern Mediterranean countries due to the absence of a wastewater treatment system or the excessive building of houses, apartments, harbours, marinas, etc. in many coastal areas of the northern Mediterranean (Blue Plan, 2007). The trend-based scenario assumes an additional 200 km of built-up coasts per year, leading to a loss of about 5,000 kilometers of natural areas by 2025 (Blue Plan, 2007). If these scenarios materialize, half of the Mediterranean coast may end up built-on by then. The huge number of residents inhabiting the Mediterranean coastal zone (approximately 46,000km long), which in 2000 accommodated 143 million inhabitants (i.e., 33% of the Mediterranean population; Blue Plan, 2007) adds to the tourism pressures on the environment. This chapter will not develop these indirect impacts from overdevelopment (concentration of people and activities on the coastal zone) but will concentrate on the direct impacts of leisure activities on the marine environment (the following section). These are the only ones that can be properly managed with innovative actions. The impacts from overdevelopment could be "easily" solved by stopping urban development (houses, hotels, harbors, etc.) in overdeveloped Mediterranean countries and fixing maximum capacities compatible with environmental and social issues in undeveloped countries.

2. IMPACTS OF RECREATIONAL ACTIVITIES ON THE COASTAL MARINE ENVIRONMENT OF THE MEDITERRANEAN

The most frequent leisure activities in many parts of the Mediterranean coast are recreational fishing, boating, scuba diving, snorkeling and human trampling. These activities have negative impacts on the coastal marine environment.

2.1. Recreational Fishing

Recreational fishing (boat fishing, spearfishing, shellfish collection on the rocks and fishing from the shore; Photo 2) in the Mediterranean involves large numbers of people and consequently high levels of fishing effort (see e.g. Lloret et al. 2008 b,c; Gordoa, 2008; Morales-Nin et al., 2004, 2005; Coll et al., 1999, 2004). Each fishing method exerts a pressure on different fish communities. Angling (from a boat or from the shore) mainly catches small, short-lived, fast growing benthic species like *Serranus cabrilla* and *Coris julis* (Lloret et al 2008b; Morales-Nin et al., 2005).

Photo 2. Anglers fishing from a beach in Roses, a major tourist village in the Costa Brava (Catalonia, Spain). Photo: J. Lloret

On the other hand, spearfishing exerts a pressure on long lived, slow growing species with low reproductive potential inhabiting the rocky shores (Lloret et al., 2008c, Coll et al., 2004). These species are ecologically vulnerable, usually have a high trophic level and are endangered (i.e. included in the annexes of international conventions for the protection of wild flora and fauna such as the Barcelona, Bern and Bonn conventions). Thus for example, dusky grouper (*Epinephelus marginatus;* Photo 3), which is one of the most usual target species of spearfishing in the NW Mediterranean, is included in Annex III of the Barcelona and Bern Conventions and listed on the Red List of the IUCN. Despite of this, the ban on spearfishing for *E. marginatus* only exists in particular Mediterranean areas such as the French coast. Other vulnerable species such as *Sciaena umbra*, *Diplodus cervinus* or *Dentex dentex* have not a fishing ban anywhere. Furthermore, there is not a minimum legal landing size for most of these species. The removal of large individuals by spearfishing can adversely affect the reproductive potential of these vulnerable fish populations. This is because larger females are proportionally more fecund, reproduce over an extended period and spawn bigger eggs and larvae with better survival rates (reviewed by Birkeland and Dayton, 2005). Finally, for sequential hermaphrodites such as *Diplodus sargus sargus* (Mouine et al., 2007) and *E. marginatus* (Bouain and Siau, 1983), where all the larger individuals may be of the same sex, significant removal of large fish may prejudice the spawning success of the population. The differences in the species targeted by each fishing method make the average intrinsic vulnerability in the spearfishing catch higher than the average intrinsic vulnerability in the angling catch (Lloret et al., 2008c). These differences also make also the spearfishing catch per unit effort higher than that obtained with a fishing rod. Apart from these environmental problems, recreational fishers often compete with space and resources with traditional (artisanal) fishers and scuba divers, rising conflicts between these different user's types (Gomez et al. 2006).

Photo 3. Dusky grouper (*Epinephelus marginatus*), a vulnerable coastal fish species, caught by a spear fisher in the marine protected area of Cap de Creus (NW Mediterranean). Photo: D. Caballero

2.2. Scuba Diving

Over the last twenty years, a narrow strip of Mediterranean coastal waters varying between around 10 and 30 m deep, particularly in marine protected areas with coralligenous assemblages (Photo 4) has attracted an increasing number of scuba divers. Despite that scuba diving is generally considered a nondestructive activity and diving centers guarantee some control of this activity, the increment of scuba divers over the last decades has given rise to widespread concern that they cause negative environmental impacts. Thus, some popular diving sites have become over frequented. In these sites, the coralligenous community suffers from unintentional contact from divers, particularly hard sessile, slow-growing invertebrates such as gorgonians and bryozoans (see e.g. Sala et al., 1996; Garrabou et al., 1998; Badalamenti et al., 2000; Di Franco et al., 2009). Most of these negative impacts arise from contact of divers with the seabed. A recent study conducted in a Mediterranean marine reserve revealed that 97% of the divers made at least one contact with the seabed, causing potentially serious damage to the benthic community, particularly the coralligenous community composed of many sessile, filter-feeding, long-lived organisms with fragile skeletons and slow rates of growth (Luna et al., 2009).

Photo 4. The coralligenous assemblage, an ecologically valuable habitat of the Mediterranean where fragile species such the gorgonian *Paramuricea clavata* inhabit, attracts large numbers of divers. (Photo: Bernd Mörker, Poseidon Diving Center)

Regarding snorkelling, there are yet not documented impacts of this activity on marine environment as it have been reported in other world oceans, e.g. Indian Ocean and Red Sea, where snorkelling has negative effects of reef condition (Allison, 1996, Hawkings and Roberts, 1993)

2.3. Recreational Boating

Recreational boating has a large effect on the marine environment. The rapid growth in the number of boats during the second half of the last century brought a high demand for moorings sites in the Mediterranean area. During the summer, many pleasure boats sail from the facilities nearby which the vast majority in many places are motor craft (see e.g. Lloret et al. 2008d). Small cruise operators have also developed in the last decades in many Mediterranean tourist maritime villages. The large numbers of boats that can be found affect the marine environment. In particular, *Posidonia oceanica* meadows (which are ecologically very important) are suffering from mechanical damage caused by anchors since half of the boats are anchoring on these seagrass beds (Boudouresque et al., 1995, Francou, 1994, Milazzo et al 2004a; Montefalcone et al, 2006; Lloret et al. 2008d). Other marine phanerogams, such as *Zostera noltii, Z. marina* and *Cymodocea nodosa*, have also suffered from anchoring (Lloret et al 2008a). By fragmenting seagrass beds, anchors from boats can also impact the diverse faunal assemblages associated with this habitat. Thus, in areas with frequent and or intense boating activity, nursery functions of seagrass beds may be severely compromised (Bishop, 2008). Anchors also damage the community of the *Cystoseira* algae inhabiting the infralittoral zone, contributing to the disappearance of a number of species of this genus (Thibaut et al., 2005).

Although anchoring on the seabed appears to be the most severe environmental impact of recreational boating, there are other potential impacts such as speed excess associated with motor craft, which can disturb breeding, resting or feeding of birds in coastal waters (see e.g. Bellefleur et al., 2009; Madroño et al., 2004), the discharge of bilge waters, which commonly contain oil, fuel, antifreeze, and other contaminants (see e.g. Wilson, 1996); the increasing levels of turbidity due to the resuspension of bed sediments by motor craft (see e.g. Garrat and Hey, 1987), the use of toxic antifouling products to paint the vessel's hull (see e.g. Eriksson, 2008), and the dispersion of alien invasive species, e.g. dispersion of fragments of the invasive algae *Caulerpa taxifolia*, which remain attached to boat anchors till they are released and settle into a new place (see e.g. Sant et al., 1996)

2.4. Human Trampling

Human trampling's effects on rocky shallow Mediterranean coastal areas are of growing interest. Rocky shore areas have become popular recreational sites for a range of activities including, for instance, general exploration and recreational fishing. Rocky shore communities are sensitive to the effects of anthropogenic disturbance, which may play an important role in the shaping of fauna and flora. Human trampling may have a negative impact on biological diversity of rocky shores in the Mediterranean (Milazzo et al., 2002; Milazzo et al., 2004b; Casu et al., 2006; Ballesteros et al 2007) and in other world oceans (Brown and Taylor, 1999; Brosnan and Crumrine, 1994). In particular, there is growing evidence that areas subject to trampling experience declines in both density and number of species. Algal community provides habitat for extremely diverse assemblages of small and cryptic invertebrates. These organisms deserve attention owing to their abundance, species richness, high productivity, trophic diversity, and importance as food for higher trophic levels (Brown and Taylor, 1999). Trampling can have effects on the reduction of the thickness of the algae and may lead to the loss of the holdfast, so that the associated fauna and flora can be crushed and the available habitat reduced. Vulnerability to human trampling mainly depends on the nature and morphology of local communities and on the level of human use. In particular, **shellfish collectors** trampling on the midlittoral and infralittoral rocky areas, besides contributing to the decline of the rock sea urchin (*Paracentrotus lividus*) communities in some parts of the Mediterranean coast (Pais et al, 2007; Guidetti et al., 2004), are responsible in part of the disappearance of a number of species of the genus *Cystoseira* from some places. Tourist disturbance is the proximate cause of loss of *Cystoseira* in many parts of the Mediterranean, where the disappearance of these algae causes an increase in cover of turf-forming species in disturbed habitats (Benedetti-Cecchi et al., 2001).

2.5. Whale and Dolphin Watching

Whale and dolphin watching activities by boats and swimmers offer a nonlethal commercial use of whales. However, several studies conducted elsewhere have proved that these activities can disturb marine mammal behaviour and acoustic activity in the sort term (e.g. Constantine, 2001; Constantine et al 2004; Constantine and Bejder 2008; Corkeron, 1995; Magalhaes et al, 2002; Bjeder and Samuels, 2003). Whether these short-term behavioural changes are accompanied by longer term effects remains to be determined (Bjeder and Samuels, 2003). Despite whale and dolphin watching activities are on the rise in many parts of the Mediterranean, to date there have been not documented such negative effects.

3. THE UNDERDEVELOPMENT OF MARINE ECOTOURISM IN THE MEDITERRANEAN

The concept of marine ecotourism in the Mediterranean is usually misunderstood and in practice is often used as a marine-based tourism or as a marketing tool to promote tourism related to nature. Marine ecotourism should be regarded as a subset of marine nature-based tourism, learning-based tourism and of sustainable marine tourism (Garrod and Wilson, 2003). According to this definition, marine ecotourism (i) should have a learning orientation, achieved through the process of learning and interpretation and (ii) should be fundamentally underpinned by sustainability, involving the management of physical stresses on the environment, including energy and waste minimization, and wider environmental impacts. This basic definition of marine ecotourism can be further expanded to include characteristics such as the provision of direct financial benefits for conservation and for local people, the respect of local culture and the support of human rights and demographic movements (Honey, 2008)

Following the basic definition of ecotourism provided by Garrod and Wilson (2003), marine ecotourism in the Mediterranean potentially includes activities such as wildlife viewing (e.g. whale, dolphin and bird watching), scuba diving, snorkeling or sightseeing trips by boat or submarine (including glass-bottom ones for the observation of underwater fauna). It's not clear that other activities such as sunbathing from a boat can be considered potential ecotourism activities. Marine ecotourism has also the potential to utilize a wide variety of non-wildlife resources as well. Tours based on the appreciation of geological coastal features are good examples. Furthermore, many coastal communities also have a rich maritime heritage (e.g. submarine archaeology such as Roman, Greek and World War vessels lying on the seabed) and unique cultural characteristics (e.g. traditional artisanal fisheries, which have a socio-cultural value; Gómez et al, 2006) that are of interest to tourists.

However, it is contentious as to whether or not all these marine-based activities can be always considered ecotourism operations regarding the basic definition of marine ecotourism given before. This is because, despite all these activities are marine-based, they have not everywhere a learning basis (no educational programs offered) and they have often many environmental impacts (e.g. the environmental impacts of scuba diving and recreational boating that have been described before). Regarding the learning basis, emphasis has been given in only a few sites (usually MPAs) to promote public awareness of the environmental concerns (Badalamenti et al, 2000; www.medpan.org). If we further consider the provision of direct financial benefits for conservation and for local people, the respect of local culture and the support of human rights and demographic movements of all these marine activities (according to the expanded definition of ecotourism made by Honey, 2008), we can conclude that marine ecotourism is currently nearly absent in the Mediterranean considering both the basic or expanded definition of marine ecotourism.

However, some few projects of marine ecotourism or sustainable tourism have been able to demonstrate that sensible policies can lead to well-balanced and durable tourism development with positive long-term economic, environmental and social gains in the Mediterranean. Thus for example, the European SMAP III TA project (www.smap.eu) has shown that coastside development in the Mediterranean can be achieved through the use of new environmental construction technologies with low to no environmental impacts, that pressure can be reduced on the coastal areas through development and promotion of countryside sustainable tourism; that acquiring eco-friendly labels has helped increase demand for destinations; and that sustainable tourism in its different forms has led to positive impacts on the three pillars of sustainable development: economic, social and environmental. In particular, discussions on the development of sustainable tourism in marine protected areas have been a hot topic during the last years.

The SUBMED project (www.submed.org), which developed underwater tourism in the Mediterranean, has stimulated awareness amongst tourism operators of all the issues pertaining to this field of activity and in particular to define a European-wide recognized eco-label. It also raised the awareness of practitioners through the drafting of a diving charter that will take into account natural resources and seek to ensure their respect. The promotion of concrete actions, such as the setting up of a minimum impact buoy system, the creation of underwater trails, the establishment of specific environmental and socio-economic indicators, has been shown to be crucial to enabling the Mediterranean to occupy a choice place amongst quality destinations for sub-aquatic tourism. SUBMED's is structuring a high environmental quality offer for diving, steering the activity towards an eco-tourism approach. To this end, the project has mobilized local authorities, tourism stakeholders in coastline areas and the diving community towards the sustainable development of this practice in the Mediterranean. The CoastNet's (http://www.coastnet.org.uk) and the "Mediterranean Ecotourism" projects (http://www.ecoturismomediterraneo.net/), the MedPAN network of managers of marine protected areas in the Mediterranean (www.medpan.org), the Blue Plan program (www.planbleu.org), and DESTINET (http://destinet.ew.eea.europa.eu/) system are experiences dealing with sustainable tourism too. There are also some ecotourism experiences in relation to marine mammal's watching such as the whale and dolphin watching project NINAM in Catalonia (Spain) (www.projecteninam.org) or a Turkish project that experimented with controlled visits to observe the Mediterranean monk seal (Gucu and Cemal, 2003)

4. THE URGENT NEED TO IMPLEMENT SUSTAINABLE TOURISM PRACTICES ALL ALONG THE MEDITERRANEAN COAST

From all the examples described above it is clear that, although there has been an increased awareness about marine ecotourism and sustainable tourism practices, these are still very scarce in the Mediterranean. The recently approved European Marine Environment

Strategy Directive will generate new opportunities in the field eco-ecotourism. This law aims to ensure that all European Union (EU) marine waters are environmentally healthy by 2021 so that people are able to benefit from seas and oceans that are safe, clean and rich in nature. For this, it gives guidelines and deadlines towards the development of marine strategies by the EU member states.

The protection of the marine environment is the only strategy that can guarantee the sustainable development of tourism in the Mediterranean countries. There is a huge necessity of managing tourist activities in a manner that is reasonable and compatible with the conservation of natural richness. Thus, a shift from the actual mass tourism model to an ecologically responsible marine tourism model involving sustainable practices is urgently needed in all Mediterranean border countries. This model implies the management of physical stresses produced by tourist activities on the marine environment including energy and waste minimization and wider environmental impacts (e.g., impacts of anchoring or scuba divers on benthic flora and fauna communities). To achieve this goal, coastal integrated management plans should be established (at a local, regional and/or national level) to safeguard the most frequent vulnerable (threatened) Mediterranean species and habitats considered in laws or included in the annexes of international conventions for the protection of flora and fauna such as Bonn, Barcelona, Bern or CITES conventions or the red list of the IUCN (Table 1). These plans would make also possible to fulfill the criteria of sustainable tourism given by the World Tourism Organization, the specialized agency of the United Nations and the leading international organization in the field of tourism.

These management plans should consider specific policy tools listed in Table 2 aiming at better manage all tourist activities (scuba diving, recreational fishing, trampling on the rocks, whale and dolphin watching and recreational boating). Other strategies such as trying and spreading tourism throughout the year in an attempt to alleviate the summer peak is not the right solution because it will probably result in an increase of the annual visits and in a reduced period of time in which ecosystems can recover from the stress they have endured.

5. CAN FISHING BE RECONVERTED INTO SUSTAINABLE TOURISM PRACTICES?

As it is currently practiced in many parts of the northern Mediterranean, recreational fishing (angling from the shore, boat angling, shellfish collection on the rocks and spearfishing) totally falls outside the marine ecotourism and sustainable practices realm because it implies huge, increasing fishing efforts, affecting negatively on a wide spectrum of coastal fishes and inducing changes in both the trophic structure and the intrinsic vulnerability of taxa (see section 2). Nevertheless, recreational fisheries could be reconverted into sustainable practices if new regulations and management actions are implemented to avoid the environmental problems raised before. New regulations should limit the fishing effort and the total catch per fisher and consider banning the catch of highly vulnerable fishes targeted by fishers through permanent or seasonal closures during the spawning season, the establishment of a minimum legal length for all species (based on the species' size at maturity) and/or the enlargement of no-take areas.

Recreational fishers should only be allowed to catch bony fishes (Osteichthyans), except those included at international conventions for the protection of fauna (Table 1). All cartilaginous fishes (Chondrichthyans) and invertebrate species should be forbidden.

Furthermore, additional bony fish species whose populations have declined severely in some parts of the Mediterranean and which in general show slow growth, late maturation and long life span (e.g. *Dentex dentex, Argyrosoma regius, Labrus bimaculatus, Labrus viridis, Labrus merula, Mycteroperca rubra, Diplodus cervinus, Scorpaena scrofa,* Photo 5) should be considered in the future to be included at the international conventions for the protection of flora and fauna, and therefore their catch by recreational fishers should be forbidden in the future. Also, stronger enforcement of regulatory measures is needed in view of the low compliance of sport fishers with current regulations (Lloret et al. 2008b). It would be desirable to engage them in a partnership with scientists and fishery and MPA managers (through, for example, workshops and survey advisory groups), since this could help foster their participation in fisheries management and would raise their awareness of the vulnerability of some species they target.

Photo 5. The scorpionfish (*Scorpaena scrofa*), an example of vulnerable fish species that has slow growth, late maturation and long life span, that should be included among a number of other coastal species at the international conventions for the protection of flora and fauna. (Photo: J. Lloret)

There have also been a few attempts in the Mediterranean to provide alternative income to the local artisanal (commercial small-scale) fishers (Photo 6) through ecotourism following the decline of small scale fisheries in many parts of the coast. Some projects have shown positive economic consequences of the development of ecotourism on fishing communities of poor countries (see e.g. Travers and Cormier-Salem, 2008). However, it is contentious as to whether or not the experiences conducted so far in the Mediterranean can be considered ecotourism operations regarding the basic definition of marine ecotourism. This is because usually they had not a learning basis (no educational programs offered) and the environmental impacts still persisted (because a reduction of the fishing effort was not on the plan). In the future, artisanal fisheries could be in part reconverted to sustainable tourism practices if projects consider measures to reduce fishing effort and to educate tourists on fishing, cultural and environmental aspects when they are on board the fishers' vessels.

Photo 6. Artisanal fishers from the Mediterranean could participate in sustainable tourist projects if these projects consider measures to reduce fishing effort and to develop educational programs when tourists are on board. (Photo: J. Lloret)

Table 1. List of the most frequent Mediterranean species that are included at international conventions for the protection of fauna and flora.

Group	Species	Normative base
Mollusks	*Litophaga litophaga*	Habitats Directive[1] (European Union, EU), Barcelona Convention, Bern Convention, Washington Convention (CITES)
	Charonia lampas lampas	Barcelona Convention ,Bern Convention, Red List International Union for Conservation of Nature (IUCN)
	Zonaria pyrum	Bern Convention, Barcelona Convention
	Cypraea lurida (=Luria lurida)	Bern Convention, Barcelona Convention
	Ostrea edulis	OSPAR convention initial list
	Pinna nobilis	Habitats Directive (EU), Barcelona Convention
Crustaceans	*Scyllarides latus*	Habitats Directive, Barcelona Convention, Bern Convention
	Scyllarus pigmaeus	Barcelona Convention, Bern Convention
	Scyllarus arctus	Barcelona Convention, Bern Convention
	Homarus gammarus	Barcelona Convention, Bern Convention
	Palinurus elephas	Barcelona Convention, Bern Convention
	Maja squinado	Barcelona Convention, Bern Convention
Sponges	*Spongia agaricina*	Barcelona Convention
	Spongia officinalis	Barcelona Convention, Bern Convention
	Aplysina cavernicola	Barcelona Convention, Bern Convention,
	Axinella polypoides	Barcelona Convention, Bern Convention
	Tehya aurantium	Barcelona Convention, Bern Convention
	Geodia cydonium	Barcelona Convention ,Bern Convention
Sea stars	*Asterina pancerii*	Barcelona Convention, Bern Convention
	Ophidiaster ophidianus	Barcelona Convention, Bern Convention
Sea urchins	*Centrostephanus longispinus*	Habitats Directive (EU), Barcelona Convention, Bern Convention
	Paracentrotus lividus	Barcelona Convention
Briozoans	*Hornera lichenoides*	Barcelona Convention, Bern Convention
Gorgonians	*Gerardia savaglia*	Barcelona Convention, Bern Convention)
	Corallium rubrum	Habitats Directive (EU), Bern Convention, Barcelona Convention
	Lophelia pertusa	OSPAR convention initial list
Sea lampreys	*Petromyzon marinus*	Habitats Directive (EU), Barcelona Convention, Bern Convention, OSPAR convention initial list

---

[1] Council Directive 92/43/EEC on the Conservation of natural habitats and of wild fauna and flora, European Union

Group	Species	Normative base
Cartilaginous fishes (Chondrichthyans)	*Cetorhinus maximus*	Washington Convention (CITES), Barcelona Convention, Bern Convention, Red List IUCN, OSPAR Convention, Bonn Convention (CMS)
	Isurus oxyrinchus	Barcelona Convention, Bern Convention, Bonn Convention (CMS)
	Lamna nasus	Barcelona Convention, Bern Convention, Bonn Convention (CMS)
	Prionace glauca	Barcelona Convention, Bern Convention
	Galeorhinus galeus	Red List IUCN
	Pristis pristis	Red List IUCN
	Raja alba	Barcelona Convention, Bern Convention
	Squatina squatina	Barcelona Convention, Bern Convention, Red List IUCN
	Mobula mobular	Barcelona Convention, Bern Convention, Red List IUCN
	Squalus acanthias	Bonn Convention (CMS)
Bony fishes (Osteychthians)	*Hippocampus hippocampus* and *H. guttulatus=H. ramulosus*	Washington Convention (CITES), Barcelona Convention, Bern Convention, Red List IUCN, OSPAR
	Alosa spp	Habitats Directive (EU), Barcelona Convention, Bern Convention, Red List IUCN, OSPAR
	Syngnathus spp	Bern Convention
	Sciaena umbra	Barcelona Convention, Bern Convention
	Umbrina cirrosa	Barcelona Convention, Bern Convention
	Anguilla anguilla	Barcelona Convention, Bern Convention
	Xiphias gladius	Barcelona Convention, Bern Convention, Red List IUCN
	Thunnus thynnus	Barcelona Convention, Bern Convention, OSPAR, Red List IUCN
	Epinephelus marginatus	Barcelona Convention, Bern Convention, Red List IUCN
	Pagrus pagrus	Red List IUCN
Marine mammals	All species	Habitats Directive (EU), Bern Convention, Bonn Convention (CMS), Washington Convention or CITES, Red List IUCN, OSPAR, ACCOBAMS Agreement
Marine turtles	All species	Habitats Directive (EU), Bern Convention, Bonn Convention (CMS), Washington Convention (CITES), Red List IUCN, OSPAR
Marine seagrasses	*Posidonia oceanica*	Habitats Directive (EU; priority habitat), Barcelona Convention, Bern Convention
	Zostera noltii	Barcelona Convention

Table 1. (Continued)

Group	Species	Normative base
Algae	*Cystoseira mediterranea*	Barcelona Convention, Bern Convention
	Lithophyllum lichenoides (= L. tortuosum)	Barcelona Convention, Bern Convention
	Maërl species: *Lithothamnium coralloides* and *Phymatholithon calcareum*	Habitats Directive (EU), OSPAR convention initial list

6. THE NECESSITY TO IMPLEMENT MARINE ECOTOURISM IN MARINE PROTECTED AREAS (MPAS)

In a context where the impacts of excessive and uncontrolled recreational activities are increasing along the Mediterranean coast, marine protected areas (MPAs) have gained recognition as effective tools to protect the marine environment. MPAs are currently much in favor in the Mediterranean, where about a hundred of them have been declared during the recent decades to grant special protection to sites perceived to contain the most valuable marine habitats and species (Adbulla et al., 2008). If MPAs protect sensitive environments and threatened species, they also contribute to increasing the productivity of fishing areas, regulating the different uses of the sea, fostering sustainable tourism and creating new job-generating activities. However, mass tourism exercises considerable pressure on MPAs located near large tourist resorts and villages.

If responsible tourist practices should be implemented all along the Mediterranean coast, in MPAs the learning orientation concept should be added to the criteria of the sustainable tourism. This will ensure that marine ecotourism is at least implemented in MPAs and that it becomes the only type of tourism allowed in these protected areas. Ecotourism provides one of the most important justifications for protecting biological diversity in the framework of sustainable development.

The learning orientation concept should be achieved through the process of learning, interpretation and consensus building. By doing so, the sustainable practices listed on Table 2 would be accompanied by practices that create awareness on the impacts of human uses on the marine environment, the biological, geological and sociocultural richness of the coastal area and the possible solutions to environmental challenges (including climate change). The most important proposed practices are listed on Table 3. In particular, the long term consensus building with all stakeholders is necessary to establish marine ecotourism in MPAs. The development of consensus building tools (convention and contract type approaches that take into account a code of conduct for users) would be an effective tool to achieve this consensus. Existent experiences (e.g. scuba diving convention/eco-label in French MPAs such as Banyuls-Cerbere and Port Cros) show that this approach is very useful (Medpan, 2008).

Table 2. Specific policy tools to minimize / avoid the impacts of tourist activities on marine species and habitats along the entire Mediterranean coast

Human activity	Proposed policy tools
Recreational fishing	Only bony fishes (Osteichthyans) should be allowed to be catch, except those included at international conventions for the protection of fauna (Table 1). All cartilaginous fishes (Chondrichthyans) and invertebrate species should be forbidden. Limit total fish catch (kg or numbers per fisher and outing) and effort (number of gears used simultaneously by a fisher and hours per outing) Interdiction to use professional fishers fishing gears (e.g. nets, longlines, traps). Interdiction to fish (particularly spear fishing) in no-take MPAs Establish seasonal closures during the spawning season of particular species Establishment of a minimum landing size for all species (based on the species' size at maturity) Limit the number of recreational fishers in a particular area through the establishment of fishing licenses.
Human trampling	Interdiction to trample in certain areas of high ecological value (e.g. Cystoseira beds) Establish specific trails/paths along the coast to avoid environmental damage
Recreational boating	Installation of ecological mooring boys for recreational boats. Interdict anchoring in sensitive habitats (e.g. Posidonia oceanica beds and coraligenous and Cystoseira assemblages), particularly in MPAs Limit the number of moored boats per creek / beach Interdiction of toxic anti-foulings to paint the recreational vessel's hulls Interdiction to discharge bilge and grey waters and all type of waste Limit speed in shallow and open waters where marine mammals and sea turtles are found and where breeding or resting areas for birds are recorded. Allow the use of nautical sports needing high speed motor craft (e.g jet-skis, parasailing, sky-bus, etc) only in particular areas of the coast. Interdict in MPAs. Promotion of environmental-friendly boats (e.g. those with tanks for the retention of bilge ad grey waters), particularly non-engine powered (e.g. kayaks, sail boats, etc) and small, traditional Mediterranean boats. Promotion of anchor types that minimise their impact on the bottom (e.g. Hull type) Exclude navigation of recreational boats in breeding or resting places for birds. Establish a minimum boating distance to these places.
Scuba-diving	Install and maintain mooring boys for scuba diving vessels Limit the number of divers per site, particularly in submarine caves Establish a minimum number of guides by group of divers who will also assure correct briefing of divers before diving takes place Interdiction to feed fish Interdiction to touch any species Exclude training courses and inexperienced divers from sensitive areas, e.g. areas with high densities of gorgonians and in certain zones within MPAs. Training courses should be restricted to appropriate and less vulnerable habitats.
Whale and dolphin watching	Limit number and proximity of whale watching vessels to the animals Limit the number of tourists by vessel and vessel's noise and size Promote the use of sail boats instead of motor boats

Table 3. Practices that should be followed in marine protected areas (MPAs) to create environmental awareness.

Proposed practice	Objectives
Creation of marine interpretation centers equipped with different communication instruments	To help tourists to learn about the marine environment
Presence of a minimum number of professional guides in all commercial recreational activities (such as scuba diving)	To create awareness on visitors in connection with the activities they develop and control the environmental impacts
Edition of dissemination materials (videos, leaflets, brochures, books, etc)	To raise awareness of visitors about specific environmental issues, e.g. the environmental threats caused by discharging wastewater and sewage and anchoring on seagrass beds To educate tourists on specific issues, e.g. the necessity to keep motor engines of boats properly maintained, to clean anchors to avoid dispersion of alien invasive species, etc. To help training visitors on specific issues, e.g. training boaters about the anchoring process (to minimize the impact on the seabed)
Establishment of underwater trails (snorkeling and diving)	To help tourists to learn about the subaquatic flora and fauna
Establishment of voluntary agreements with commercial operators (diving centres, whale watching vessels, etc). Creation of eco-labels	To promote awareness among commercial operators and distinguish (support) those that contribute the most to the environmental protection.

In a second step, the basic definition of marine ecotourism implemented in MPAs could be further expanded to include characteristics such as the provision of direct financial benefits for conservation and for local people, the respect for local culture and the support of human rights and demographic movements (following the expanded definition of marine ecotourism given by Honey, 2008).

However, attention should be paid to avoid that marine ecotourism in a given location, which starts by appealing to small numbers of tourists who require minimal infrastructure and have little ecological or social effect, is replaced later by general wildlife tourists who demand enhanced infrastructure that has measurable impacts on the local ecology and society (Davenport and Davenport, 2006).

7. CONCLUSION

The sustainability of both the tourism industry and the marine environment in the Mediterranean are closely linked to each other and depend upon the urgent adoption of sustainable environmental practices all along the coast. Considering the numerous impacts from leisure activities on the coastal marine environment of the Mediterranean, there is a huge necessity of managing tourist activities in a manner that is reasonable and compatible with the conservation of marine resources and habitats.

A shift from the mass tourism model which is implemented at present in many Mediterranean border countries to an ecologically responsible marine tourism model involving sustainable practices is urgently needed all along the Mediterranean coast. To achieve this responsible model, coastal integrated management plans should be established that consider explicitly the conservation of the vulnerable (threatened) Mediterranean species and habitats. If there is not scientific information on the status of a particular species in a particular area, the vulnerable species could be determined by considering those included in the annexes of international conventions for the protection of flora and fauna such as Bonn, Barcelona, Bern or CITES conventions or the red list of the IUCN, as well as those protected by European or national laws.

Furthermore, marine ecotourism, in which sustainable practices are complemented by practices that create awareness on the impacts of human uses on the marine environment (learning concept orientation), should be at least implemented in marine protected areas, thus becoming the only type of tourism allowed in these areas.

ACKNOWLEDGMENTS

This chapter is a result of my collaboration with the marine reserve of Cap de Creus over the last years and my participation at the MedPAN project (supported by the European Union porgram Interreg IIIc). I wish to thank Mss. Victoria Riera, Director of the Natural Park of Cap de Creus (Dep. of Environment and Housing, Autonomous Government of Catalonia, Spain) for her valuable support and to all MedPAN members.

REFERENCES

Abdulla, A., Gomei, M., Maison, E. & Piante, C. (2008). Status of Marine Protected Areas in the Mediterranean Sea. *IUCN, Malaga and WWF, France. 152.*

Allison, W. R. (1996) Snorkeler damage of reef corals in the Maldive Islands. *Coral reefs. Volume, 15(4),* 215-218.

Badalamenti, F., Ramos, A., Voultsiadou, E., Sanchez-Lizaso, J. L., D'Anna. G., Pipitone, C., Mas, J., Ruiz, J. A., Whithmarsh, D. & Riggio, S. (2000). Cultural and socio-economic impacts of Mediterranean protected areas. *Environmental Conservation,* 27, 1-16.

Bejder, L. & Samuels, A. (2003). Evaluating the effects of nature-based tourism on cetaceans. In: Gales, N., Gales, N., Hindell, M., Kirkwood, R (eds). Marine Mammals: *Fisheries, Tourism and Management Issues,* 229-256.

Bellefleur, D., Lee, P. & Ronconithe, R. A. (2009). The impact of recreational boat traffic on Marbled Murrelets (*Brachyramphus marmoratus*) *Journal of Environmental Management, 90(1),* 531-538.

Benedetti-Cecchi, L., Pannacciulli, F., Bulleri, F., Moschella, P. S., Airoldi, L., Relini, G. & Cinelli, F. (2001). Predicting the consequences of anthropogenic disturbance: large-scale effects of loss of canopy algae on rocky shores. *Marine Ecology Progress Series*, 214, 137-150.

Birkeland, C. & Dayton, P. K. (2005). The importance in fishery management of leaving the big ones. *Trends in Ecology and Evolution*, *20*, 356-358.

Bishop, M. J. (2008). Displacement of epifauna from seagrass blades by boat wake *Journal of Experimental Marine Biology and Ecology*, *354(1)*, 111-118.

Blue Plan, (2007). Environment and Development in the Mediterranean. Blue Plan (United Nations Environmental Programme) Notes nr. 6 May 2007. http://www.planbleu.org/red/pdf/4pages_littoral_uk.pdf.

Bouain, A. & Siau, Y. (1983). Observations on the female reproduction cycle and fecundity of the species of groupers (*Epinephelus*) from the southeast Tunisian seashores. *Marine Biology*, *73 (21)*, 1-220.

Boudouresque, C. F., Arrighi, F., Finelli, F. & Lefevre, J. R. (1995). Arrachage des faisceaux de *Posidonia oceanica* par les ancres: un protocole d'etude. *Rapports de la Comission internationale d'Exploration de la Mer Mediterranee*, *34*, 21 (In French).

Brosnan, D. M. & Crumrine, L. L. (1994). Effects of human trampling on marine rocky shore communities, *Journal of Experimental Marine Biology and Ecology*, *177*, 79-97.

Brown, P. J., Taylor, R. B., (1999). Effects of trampling by humans on animals inhabiting coralline algal turf in the rocky intertidal. *Journal of Experimental Marine Biology and Ecology*, *235*, 45-53.

Casu, D., Ceccherelli, G., Curini-Galletti, M. & Castelli, A. (2006) Human exclusion from rocky shores in a mediterranean marine protected area (MPA): An opportunity to investigate the effects of trampling. *Marine Environmental Research*, *62*, 15-32.

Coll, J., Garcıa-Rubies, A., Moranta, J., Stefanni, S. & Morales-Nin, B. (1999). Sport-fishing prohibition effects on the population structure of *Epinephelus marginatus* (Lowe, 1834) (Pisces, Serranidae) in the Cabrera Archipelago National Park (Majorca,W. Mediterranean). *Bulletı de la Societat d'Historia Natural de les Illes Balears*, *42*, 125-138.

Coll, J., Linde, M., García-Rubies, J., Riera, F. & Grau, A. M. (2004). Spearfishing in the Balearic Islands (west central Mediterranean): species affected and catch evolution during the period 1975–2001. *Fisheries Research*, *70*, 97-111.

Constantine, R. & Bejder, L. (2008). Managing the whale-and dolphin watch industry: Time for a paradigm shift. In: J. E. S. Higham, M. Lück (Eds). Marine Wildlife and Tourism Management: Insights from the Natural and Social Sciences. Oxford, CABI *International Publishing*, 321-333.

Constantine, R. (2001). Increased avoidance of swimmers by wild bottlenose dolphins (Tursiops truncatus) due to long-term exposure to swim-with-dolphin tourism. *Marine Mammal Science*, *17(4)*, 689-702.

Constantine, R., Brunton, D. H. & Dennis, T. (2004). Dolphin-watching tour boats change bottlenose dolphin (*Tursiops truncatus*) behaviour. *Biological Conservation*, *117(3)*, 299-307.

Corkeron, P. J. (1995). Humpback whales (*Megaptera novaeangliae*) in Hervey Bay, Queensland: behaviour and responses to whale-watching vessels. *Canadian Journal of Zoology*, *73(7)*, 1290-1299.

Davenport, J. & Davenport, J. L (2006). The impact of tourism and personal leisure transport on coastal environments: A review. *Estuarine, Coastal and Shelf Science*, *67*, 280-292.

Deutsche Bank Research (2008) Climate change and tourism. Where will the journey lead? Technical report Issue 11 April 2008, 28 pp. http://www.dbresearch.com.

Di Franco, A., Milazzo, M., Baiata, P., Tomasello, A. & Chemello, R. (2009). Scuba diver behaviour and its effects on the biota of a Mediterranean marine protected area. *Environmental Conservation, 36 (1)*, 32-40.

Eriksson, M. (2008). Impact of Antifouling Compounds on Photosynthesis, Community Tolerance and psbA Genes in Marine Periphyton. Ph. D. Thesis University of Gothenburg.http://gupea.ub.gu.se/dspace/bitstream/2077/18714/2/gupea_2077_18714_2. pdf.

European Commission (1998) Fact and Photos on the *Europeans on holiday*, 1997-98. Eurobarometer 48, Brussels.

Eurostat (2008). Statistiques en bref nr. 95/2008. http://ec.europa.eu/eurostat/.

Francour, P. (1994). Impact du mouillage sur l'herbier a *Posidonia oceanica* dans le baie de Port-Cros (Mediterranee nord-occidentale, France). *Marseille: GIS Posidonie*.

Garrabou, J., Sala, E., Arcas, A. & Zabala, M. (1998). The impact of diving on rocky sublittoral communities: a case study of a bryozoan population. *Conservation Biology, 12*, 302-312.

Garrad, P. N. & Hey, R. D. (1987). Boat traffic, sediment resuspension and turbidity in a Broadland river. *Journal of Hydrology, 95(3-4)*, 289-297.

Garrod, B. & Wilson, J. C (2003). Marine ecotourism: issues and experiences. *Channel View Publications, 266*.

Gómez, S, Lloret, J, Riera, V. & Demestre, M. (2006). The decline of the artisanal fisheries in Mediterranean coastal areas: the case of Cap de Creus (Cape Creus). *Coastal Management, 34(2)*, 217-232.

Gordoa, A. (2008). Characterization of the infralittoral system along the north-east Spanish coast based on sport shore-based fishing tournament catches. *Estuarine Coastal and Shelf Science, 82 (1)*, 1-49.

Gucu, G. & Cemal, A. (2003). Is ecotourism an appropriate tool to ensure sustainable Mediterranean monk seal conservation in the Cilician Basin, Turkey? Evaluation report of the experimental Eco-tourism application in Bozyazi . Middle East Technical University Institute of Marine Sciences. Report 33pp. http://www.monachus-guardian.org/library/gucu03a.pdf.

Guidetti, P., Terlizzi, A. & Boero, F. (2004). Effects of the edible sea urchin, Paracentrotus lividus, fishery along the Apulian rocky coast (SE Italy, Mediterranean Sea). *Fisheries Research, 66 (2-3)*, 287-297.

Hawkins, J., Roberts, C. M. (1993). Effects of Recreational Scuba Diving on Coral Reefs: Trampling on Reef-Flat Communities . *Journal of Applied Ecology, 30(1)*, 25-30.

Honey, M. (2008). Ecotourism and Sustainable Development: Who Owns Paradise? (Second edion). Washington, DC: *Island Press*. 29 - 31.

Lloret, J. & Riera, V. (2008a). Evolution of a Mediterranean Coastal Zone: Human Impacts on the Marine Environment of Cape Creus. *Environmental Management, 42*, 977-988.

Lloret, J., Zaragoza, N., Caballero, D. & Riera, V. (2008b) Biological and socioeconomic implications of recreational boat fishing for the management of fishery resources in the marine reserve of Cap de Creus (NW Mediterranean). *Fisheries Research*, 91, 252-259.

Lloret, J., Zaragoza, N., Caballero, D. & Riera, V. (2008d) Impacts of recreational boating on the marine environment of Cap de Creus (Mediterranean Sea). *Ocean & Coastal Management, 51*, 749-754.

Lloret, J., Zaragoza, N., Caballero, D., Font, T., Casadevall, M. & Riera, V. (2008c). Spearfishing pressure on fish communities in rocky coastal habitats in a Mediterranean Marine Protected Area. *Fisheries Research*, *94*, 84-91.

Luna, B., Valle Pérez, C. & Sánchez-Lizaso, J. L. (2009) Benthic impacts of recreational divers in a Mediterranean Marine Protected Area. *ICES Journal of Marine Science. 66(3)*, 517.

Madroño, A., González, C. & Atienza, J. C. (2004). Libro Rojo de las Aves en España. Ministry of Spain & Seo/BirdLife. 452 pp. In Spanish http://www.seovanellus.org/ 06archivohistorico/Libro%20Rojo/Libro-Rojo.pdf.

Magalhaes, S., Prieto, R. Silva, M. A. Goncalves, J. Afonso, D. M. Santos, R. S. (2002). Short-term reactions of sperm whales (Physeter macrocephalus) to whale-watching vessels in the Azores. *Aquatic Mammals*, *28(3)*, 267-274.

Milazzo, M., Badalamenti, F., Ceccherelli, G. & Chemello, R. (2004a). Boat anchoring on *Posidonia oceanica* beds in a marine protected area (Italy, western Mediterranean): effect of anchor types in different anchoring stages. *Journal of Experimental Marine Biology and Ecology*, *299*, 51-62.

Milazzo, M., Chemello, R., Badalamenti, F. & Riggio, S. (2002). Short-term effect of human trampling on the upper infralittoral macroalgae of Ustica Island MPA (western Mediterranean, Italy). *Journal of the Marine Biological Association UK*, 82, 745-748.

Milazzo, M., Riggio, S., Badalamenti, F. & Chemello, R. (2004b). Patterns of algal recovery and small-scale effects of canopy removal as a result of human trampling on a Mediterranean rocky shallow community. *Biological Conservation*, *117*, 191-202.

Montefalcone, M., Lasagna, R., Bianchi, C. N., Morri, C. & Albertelli, G. (2006). Anchoring damage on *Posidonia oceanica* meadow cover: a case study in Prelo cove (Ligurian sea, NW Mediterranean). *Chemistry and Ecology*, *22(1)*, S207-17.

Morales-Nin, B., Moranta, J., Garc´ıa, C., Tugores, M. P. & Grau, A. M. (2004). Evaluation of the importance of recreational fisheries in a Mediterranean Island. In: Proceedings of the Fourth World Fisheries Congress. Reconciling with Conservation: *The Challenge of Managing Aquatic Ecosystems, Vancouver, British Columbia, Canada*, 2-6.

Morales-Nin, B., Moranta, J., García, C., Tugores, M. P., Grau, A. M., Riera, F. & Cerdà, M. (2005). The recreational fishery off Majorca Island (western Mediterranean): some implications for coastal resource management. *ICES Journal of Marine Science*, *62*, 727-739.

Mouine, N., Francour, F., Ktari, M. H. & Chakroun-Marzouk, N. (2007). The reproductive biology of *Diplodus sargus sargus* in the Gulf of Tunis (central Mediterranean). *Scientia Marina*, *71 (3)*, 46-469.

Pais, A., Chessa, L. A., Serra, S., Ruiu, A., Meloni, G. & Donno, Y. (2007). The impact of commercial and recreational harvesting for *Paracentrotus lividus* on shallow rocky reef sea urchin communities in North-western Sardinia, Italy. *Estuarine, coastal and shelf science*, *73 (3-4)*, 589-597.

Publications, (1994). 51 pp.

Sala, E., Garrabou, J. & Zabala, M. (1996). -Effects of divers frequentation on Mediterranean sublittoral populations of the bryozoan *Pentapora fascialis*. *Marine Biology*, *126(3)*, 451-459

Sant, N., Delgado, O., Rodríguez-Prieto, C. & Ballesteros, E. (1996). The spreading of the introduced seaweed *Caulerpa taxifolia* (Vahl) C. Agardh in the Mediterranean sea: testing the boat transportation hypothesis. *Botanica Marina, 39,* 427-430.

Thibaut, T., Pinedo, S., Torras, X. & Ballesteros, E. (2005) Long-term decline of the populations of Fucales (*Cystoseira* spp. and *Sargassum* spp.) in the Alberes coast (France, North-western Mediterranean). *Marine Pollution Bulletin, 50,* 1472-1489.

Travers, M. & Cormier-Salem, M. C. (2008). Can Ecotourism Be An Alternative To Traditional Fishing? An analysis with reference to the case of the Saloum Delta (Senegal) In: Sarr, O., Boncoeur, J. (eds). Economics Of Poverty, Environment And Natural-Resource Use. Publisher Springer Netherlands. R. Dellink and A. Ruijs. 2008 *Wageningen UR Frontis Series Volume, 25.*

Wilson, C. (1991). An Assessment of the Environmental Impacts from the Discharge of Bilge Water in the Norfolk Naval Station Harbor. Master Thesis. *Pennsylavania State University Park.*

WTO, World Tourism Organization (2009). UNWTO barometer. Volume 7.

In: Ecotourism: Management, Development and Impact   ISBN: 978-1-60876-724-3
Editors: A. Krause, E. Weir, pp. 159-179   © 2010 Nova Science Publishers, Inc.

Chapter 6

IS ECOTOURISM IN MARINE PROTECTED AREAS A RELEVANT WAY FOR SHARING BENEFITS FROM BIODIVERSITY CONSERVATION? A CASE STUDY IN WEST AFRICA

Omar Sarr[1a], Marie-Christine Cormier-Salem[2a], Claire Bernatets[3a] and Sébastien Boulay[4b]
[a] UMR208, Local Patrimonies, (IRD-MNHN, Paris, France)
[b] UMR208, Local heritages, (IRD-MNHN, Paris, France)

ABSTRACT

Establishing marine protected areas (MPAs) comes along with restrictions on biological resources extraction in the concerned zones. It is one of the conditions for reaching biodiversity conservation objective. These restrictions can engender high costs for the local communities. It can be particularly true when these communities are strongly dependent on the uses affected by the MPAs. However, MPAs by achieving biodiversity conservation objectives can also generate monetary and non monetary, social and economic benefits. This paper analyses the relevance of ecotourism as a way to share these benefits with local populations in order to establish a sustainable trade-off between conservation and social, economic and cultural development. Using the recent results of a

[1] Omar SARR is an economist, associated researcher at UMR208 « Local Patrimonies» (IRD-MNHN, Paris, France) and in charge of the scientific secretariat and coordination of the Western African Littoral Team of Biodivalloc program (omar.sarr@gmail.com).

[2] Marie-Christine CORMIER-SALEM is Director of Research in social sciences, Director of UMR208 «Local Patrimonies» (IRD-MNHN, Paris, France) and coordinator of the Biodivalloc program (ANR Biodiversité/IFB, France,) (cormier@mnhn.fr. www.paloc.ird.fr).

[3] Claire BERNATETS is doctorante in geography at UMR208 « Local Patrimonies» (IRD-MNHN, Paris, France) and in charge of studies in Guinea-Bissau for the research program Biodivalloc (claire.bernatets@wanadoo.fr).

[4] Sébastien BOULAY is an anthropologist, currently working at the Mauritanian Institute for Oceanographic Research and Fisheries (IMROP), associate researcher at the UMR 208 "Local heritages" (IRD-MNHN, Paris, France); boulay@univ-nkc.mr.

research program (Biodivalloc[5]) related to biodiversity conservation in Southern countries, we study the case of three MPAs in Western Africa: the Banc d'Arguin National Park (Mauritania), the Saloum Delta Biosphere Reserve (Senegal) and the Bolama-Bijagos Biosphere Reserve (Guinea Bissau). These MPAs shelter high diversities as well from a biologic point of view as sociocultural. In these three countries, many projects intend to develop ecotourism in MPAs. However, the concept of ecotourism is very often merged with the other forms of nature-based tourism like fishing and hunting. Are these last ones really ecotourism or could be ecotourism if practiced according to a sustainable way? How communities living inside the concerned MPAs benefit or could benefit from tourist activities in their livelihood? Our casework tries to assess all these questions. It suggests that if the local communities are well involved in the management of ecotourism development programs and projects in MPAs which affect them, they can benefit from their social and economic effects and would better accept the MPAs conservation strategies. In that case, ecotourism can be perceived as a means to share benefits from biodiversity conservation.

Keywords: Marine Protected Area, Biodiversity conservation, Ecotourism, Nature-based tourism, Benefits Sharing, Saloum delta, Banc d'Arguin,, Bolama-Bilagos.

INTRODUCTION

In developed as well as in developing countries, the coastal zone is more and more perceived as a "collective and recreational garden", designation that goes along with the savage and authentic desire of the public (Legrain, 2001). This desire comes along with the need to find solutions at the overexploitation of renewable natural resources and accounts for the success of new travel and discovery means, thus enabling a tradeoff between environment and development.

At the international level, declarations and incentives in favor of ecotourism are gaining ground, for instance, as shown by the opening speech of the Costa-Rica president Mr Anguel A. Rodriguez during the International Conference on Wetlands (the 7th Conference of the Ramsar Convention at San Jose in February 1999), boasting about the specificity of his country in the field of protection and valorization of wetlands, through Green tourism. A world ethic code on tourism was adopted in 1999 in Santiago (Chili) and an ethical world committee on tourism is being drawn up. 2002 was declared 'Ecotourism International year" and in May 2002, in Quebec the first world summit on ecotourism was held.

At national levels, policies are also being set up. Some West African countries seem particularly interested to develop that field. In Senegal, the appointment of an ecotourism advisor next to the ministry of tourism and the workshop organized during the national meetings on tourism, on March 4th and 5th 2002 in Dakar put attention to a new kind of biodiversity valorization and the will of the government to develop " a tourism for and by Senegalese" (Cormier-Salem, 2006).

---

[5] Biodivalloc program « From localised products to geographical indications: which tools which tools to manage biodiversity in mega-biodiverse countries?" has been supported by the French National Agency (ANR) Biodiversity and by the French Research Foundation of Biodiversity (FRB).

Local strategies of ecotouristic development were drawn up in the framework of these national policies and in relation with local management plans for the biodiversity, mobilizing conservation tools such as protected areas. In West Africa, these areas notably the marine ones, constitute one of the main pillars of these strategies. Developing ecotourism in these areas would enable a fair share of the biodiversity conservation benefits with local communities; as the later often support high coast associated with the biodiversity conservation measures and should therefore profit from the advantages of this conservation.

Thus in Mauritania, the government defined since 1998 a development strategy of ecotourism in the Banc d'Arguin National Park (PNBA). In the same way, the Fatick regional council (Senegal) declined in 2000 its development objectives of a rural integrated tourism in Saloum Delta Biosphere Reserve (RBDS) (CRF, 2000). Guinea Bissau has not defined a policy to promote this sector especially, but some projects aim to promote ecotourism in the Boloma Bijagos Biosphere Reserve (RBABB).

This following analysis is about the relevance of the role that ecotourism plays or will play in sharing the actual or potential profit of the biodiversity conservation in the three protected areas we just cited. To answer that question we will at first present an analysis based on the costs and benefits in the framework of MPAs. Then, we will discuss about the definitions of "ecotourism" as well as its principles. Lastly, we will present ecotourism experiences in our area of research, and its role regarding to the valorization of the biological diversities, local cultures and the sharing of benefits issued from conservation.

COSTS AND BENEFITS OF MPAS

Coastal ecosystem has been undergoing various pressures among which, extraction activities of biological resources and tourism (OCDE, 1999; Cormier, 2008). These sectors contribute at different scales to national and local socioeconomic development but also constitute a source of negative effects on the environment (Pigou, 1932).

Several management tools are mobilized to cut these externalities, restore the damaged ecosystem as well as the overexploited resources. Some of these tools aim at the conservation of the productive and reproductive capacity of exploited biological stocks, still others at the distribution of its capacities among users, in other words, the regulation of individual access to resources (Troadec and Boncoeur, 2003).

MPAs are part of the tools that draw special attention to the international community, especially researchers on marine and coastal environment, marine resources managers, international institutions in charge of environmental questions, and nongovernmental organizations (NGOs) of environmental conservation. It both combines conservation and regulation of resource access. This double function results from an evolution, because until the 70s, MPAs were seen as conservation tools; economic activities were generally forbidden in these areas. Since the 80s, they have been rather used as management tools, of economic diversification, briefly, as a sustainable socioeconomic and cultural development tools (Weigel and Sarr, 2002).

However, the creation of a marine protected area generates costs. Emerton (1999) distinguishes the direct operational costs of the indirect ones. The former represent the direct expenditures for the establishment and the maintenance of MPAs (infrastructures, maintenance, staff, enforcement, research). The latter is linked to losses of use, or opportunities of uses, resulting from establishment of MPAs (Congestion, limitation or prohibition of resources access, investment for development of alternative activities...) . Other types of indirect costs concern the damages caused by an overpopulation of animals in the protected areas. For example in the RBDS, the populations of birds are increased, what lead to an increased punction on cereal cultures, entailing the abandonment of agricultural activities in some villages. The same phenomenon is observed in the RBABB where it is rather the population of hippopotamuses that creates damages in the ricefields of the Orangos Park. Even though in the area aimed at through this research, NGO (UICN, WWF...) generally provide the necessary financial resources to MPAs creation, local communities support an important part of the direct costs (Philips, 1998) through their participation to the consultation process, to infrastructure building, and supervision activities etc. Local populations also support almost all the indirect costs linked to area closure that they exploit traditionally or access restrictions to area resources. These costs are in employment opportunity loss, income, of feeding sources, and the disorganization of the social and cultural milieu, contributing to the vulnerability and pauperization of the local populations. According to Emerton (1999), these indirect costs are generally much higher than direct costs and have a strong impact on the status of an MPA (Emerton 2003). So, the acceptation of an MPA would partially depend on the possibility of compensating these indirect costs.

However, MPAs, can also generate various types of benefits linked to different ecosystem services. On the one hand, benefits are drawn from present and/or potential direct and indirect resources and ecosystems uses. On the other hand, benefits comes from the existence of resources, rather than the desire to conserve them for future generations (Philips 1998; Emerton 1999; Centre d'Analyse Stratégique, 2008). All these benefits constitute the total economic value of an ecosystem including its biological resources (Figure 1). The figure 2 indicates how the costs and advantages of a MPA are distributed within the society.

In a nutshell, let's note that the existence of costs generated by MPAs seems obvious and these costs that are expressed in terms of expenditures or immediate economic opportunity losses (Emerton 2003) are, in the case of our study area, supported by local populations and NGOs. Nevertheless, it is much less obvious to state that MPAs, generate benefits on direct uses, particularly, extractive uses, from which local communities are strongly dependent. In the best of the cases, MPAs could only generate benefits in a long term, which benefits are more advantageous to external groups (Sanchirico & al, 2002). This disparity between supported costs and received benefits in the framework of MPAs establishment and management, constitute an important issue. The question is how to reduce the costs and increase the benefits for local populations, so that they better accept and integrate MPAs, as conservation tools for their cultural and natural heritage and as social and economic development tools. The economic diversification is often seen as an answer to that question.

In the framework of the West-African MPAs, developing none extractive resources activities is considered as an alternative and /or complements to extractive activities. Ecotourism is at the heart of objectives diversification. The concept is defined below.

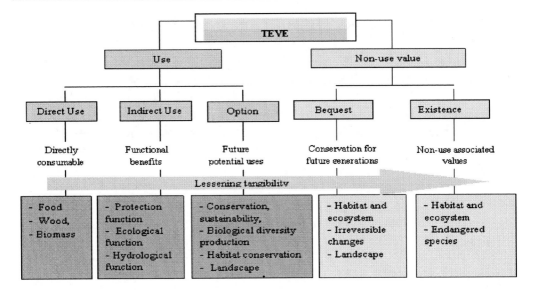

Source: Modified from Centre d'Analyse Stratégique (2008).

Figure 1. Total economic value of ecosystem (TEVE).

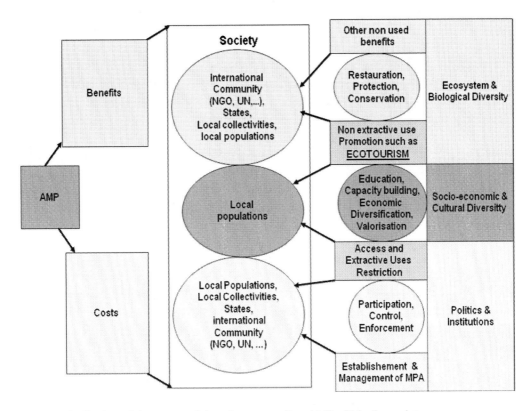

Figure 2. Distribution of the costs and the advantages of an AMP within the society.

ECOTOURISM: DEFINITION AND PRINCIPLES

The explosion of terms (alternative, mild, sustainable tourism, tourism from nature to nature, green and rural tourism, etc.) highlights the creativity of touristic promoters and the expansion of the market where several recent works are trying hard to precise the framework and consequences. The notion of "ecotourism" or "tourism of nature" covers large activities of discovery and observation of nature, which is different from tourism in nature, based on outdoor sport (Baron-Yelles,1997). As an alternative to mass tourism, it defines itself as "a responsible tourism which preserves the natural framework and the welfare of the local populations" (official definition of the Institution of Ecotourism Society). The ecotouristic procedure has been structured in the US in the 80s, with the support of powerful institutions such as Smithsonian and the Natural History Museum of New York and is first about naturalist journeys with ethnography tunes, towers, south hemisphere. The term that might have been created by Boo (1990) has been spread by NGO's such as WWF and has gained increasing success following the Rio convention (1992), leading to an environmental ethic.

So, bird watchers or birders, have for proverb "take only photograph, do not let any footmarks". According to the schedules of the WTO for 2000-2002, after the adventure tourism, nature based tourism would rank fourth of recreative journeys, before cultural tourism.

Ecotourism favorite destinations are poor countries because of the wealth of their biodiversity, but also because there is behind the concept of "ecotourism", a whole ideology (philosophy) of solidarity and equity, so ecotourism often rhymes with fair tourism.

Costa Rica and Kenya are the two countries, where this type of tourism is very developed. Implementing tourism protected areas, and the observation of wild species, is often associated with another kind of tourism which links environment and development: "community tourism". More and more people that journey "integrate" in their catalogues "local communities" and give tourists the possibility to integrate in the field to discover the natural but also the cultural diversity of visited areas, most often situated in inter tropical areas (Blangy, 1999).

In the framework of the survey, the ecotourism concept refers to all types of tourism which contribute to the restoration and conservation of natural and cultural frameworks as well as the betterment of local populations' well-being.

The idea to promote such tourism within MPAs as an alternative to extractive resource activities among which fishing, lies on the principle of negative external resources and their ecosystem in that field are not important rather inexistent. So the users could diversify their economic activities by relocating their productivity efforts between extractive activities and ecotourism which should contribute elsewhere to reduce resources pressure while generating additional resource possibilities (Sarr & al, 2008). Ecotourism is also seen among others as a kind of valorization of cultural and biological diversities, an employment and income source. It would also favor the promotion of local micro enterprises and would contribute to local population education and capacity building (Watkin, 2003). In a word, it would make financial and socioeconomic sustainable advantages (Kelleher & al, 1995) that are likely to strongly compensate the conservation cost. However, is the sharing of these advantages always done in a fair way? That's what we are going to see below in the West African context

THE WEST AFRICAN REGIONAL CONTEXT

PNBA, RBDS, & RBABB which constitute our study area are part of a regional network of marine protected areas in West Africa (RAMPAO) that extends from Mauritania to Sierra Leone (Figure 3). This network shows the importance given to the conservation of resources by the states and also the protections of marine species and ecosystems. In fact, the local socio-economic systems are very much dependent on marine resources. This dependence is strengthened by the crisis of the agricultural sector which is linked to three main factors (Sarr & al, 2005):

- An "exponential" demographic increase that lead to land pressure and therefore degradation and rarity of arable land.
- Climate change that takes place through drought cycles since the 70s with a consequence of soil acidification and decrease of productivity. A dearth of necessary water to irrigation and breeding activities,
- The liberalization of world trade that lead to a fall of prices of raw materials from poor agricultural countries increasing the vulnerability of peasants and cattle breeders.

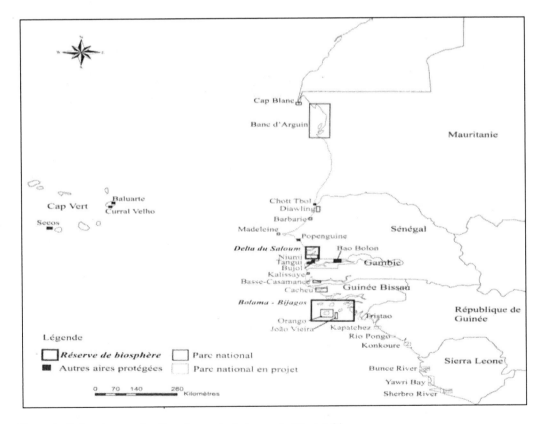

Figure 3. Rgional network of marine protected areas in West Africa.

Thus, the later rushed towards the coast economy, where a free access was almost existent, bringing about the over exploitation of halieutic resources which constitutes a serious threat of the social economic stability of the countries in question. Let's note for instance that the halieutic crisis explains partially the West African migrants who tried to cross oceans in canoes to go to Europe.

The survey that we made in the Saloum Delta shows that 48 per cent of people who migrated from the Saloum Delta were active in fishing against 43, 8 per cent of women who have migrated were active in shell collecting and non industrial transformation of sea products. Moreover, 25 per cent of these women were feeding on the sales of mangrove wood, used as a main source of energy in the Saloum delta households. The same survey also reveals that every family of the Saloum delta has at least three male immigrants aged between 22-35 against five females aged between 12-35 yet the migration of the women of the Saloum delta is mainly seasonal and mainly oriented towards the Gambia whereas the males aim at reaching Europe, Spain particularly. To that type of migration, one can add rural exodus. Without laying the emphasis on the negative socio cultural consequences of these two migratory movements (Migration and Rural Exodus), however we underline that, they constitute the main causes of destruction of the local socio cultural milieus. Conserving maritime resources in West Africa, while giving favor to the local economy development, is probably the only means to restrain local populations from migrating, youngsters in particular. It is that objective that is aimed at in the framework of development policies of ecotourism within MPAs in West Africa. Ecological and cultural heritage of these MPAs constitute potential ecotouristic products.

CULTURAL AND ECOLOGICAL HERITAGE OF WEST AFRICAN MPAS: A CASE STUDY OF PNBA, RBDS, AND RBABB

These three MPAs shelter rich cultural and ecological heritages, which constitute an important potential for the development of ecotourism (Table 1).

In fact, PNBA, which is vast of 12,000 km2 (Figure 4) has two approximate equal areas, a maritime one and a terrestrial one. It represents a third of the Mauritanian littoral and possesses the biggest herbarium concentration of the African continent. It is as such a spawning ground for a big number of fish and migrating birds. PNBA was classified on the list of UNESCO World Heritage in 1989. The first one is made of traditional fishermen called Imragen. They are mainly composed of statutory groups situated at the bottom of Moorish social hierarchy. Formerly, Imragen were nothing else that "shepherds partially affected to the collect of abundant game" (Cheikh, 2002). As the time elapses, these fishing pastors know how and techniques perfectly adapted to that difficult field and gave birth to a unique cultural heritage. Since the 1970s, this small group has become famous thanks to certain documentary films showing the assistance of dolphins in the fishing of yellow mule. These films have also contributed to the popularity of Banc d'Arguin. The second community is composed of pastors moving in the terrestrial part of the Banc d'Arguin, characterized by a weather a fauna, and flora of Saharan type. This community lives permanently or in a seasonal way in the PNBA and also claims a strong territorial anchoring. They have however remained for a long time the forgotten actors of the park institution, whose all attention were on fishing and Imragen.

Having being isolated for a long time, PNBA is today of easy access thanks to the building of a road linking the Western Sahara to Senegal, Nouadhibou, and Nouakchott. This opening up exposes it more to the different external anthropic risks, but at the same time constitutes an opportunity of economic development activities such as ecotourism.

Unlike the PNBA, the RBDS is constituted of a mangrove system (Figure 5). It covers an area of 3300 km2, almost the quarter of the PNBA, with 760 km2 erected in a national park: Saloum Delta National Park (PNDS). It is formed of three major ecosystems, among which, one is continental, another estuarine and another maritime.

The continental one is constituted in its low part of mangrove forests and "tannes", in its high part of forests and savannahs, alternatively with cultural areas and villages (LERG, 2004). The fauna continental resources are composed of great and average savage fauna, among which, several mammal species.

The estuarine ecosystem has an area of 1800 km^2 and has important mudflat as well as several inhabited islands. Biological resources are mainly composed of fish, shellfish, mollusks, turtles, and aquatic birds. This is a reproduction area and nurseries for several species (Diouf, 2003). RBDS is classified first world site of tern royal reproduction (Dia 2003), so listed in Ramsar Convention as a wetland for international importance.

The maritime ecosystem expands on a two kilometer length in the Atlantic Ocean (LERG, 2004). The maritime ecosystem expands on a two kilometer length in the Atlantic Ocean (LERG, 2004). It counts islands with important ecological functions, especially for the nesting of birds and marine turtles. These resources are also composed of several fish species, shellfish, mollusks, (EPEEC, 1998). Species of marine mammals are also signaled in particular whales, dolphins, manatees, porpoises, and seal monks (EPEEC, 1998). Peasant fishermen are composed of two main communities: the Serer Niominka and the Soce. Besides these local populations, there are more and more migratory users (fishermen, woodcutters, shellfish collectors, etc.), who contribute to natural resources extraction. This increasing pressure, along with disfunctionnement of traditional territorial use rights in the context of modern state, leads to biodiversity erosion and actors competitions (Cormier-Salem, 2008). On the cultural level, RBDS has several sacred sites and hundreds of shell tumulus among which, some are very old graves. These sacred sites and those shell tumuli are part of the main ecotouristic attraction of the area.

RBABB, as well as RBDS, have mangrove ecosystems. It is an archipelago of 88 islands among which, 21 are inhabited, with a total area of 10,500 km2 (Figure 6). The inventory and the survey of the line landscape (Vidigal & Baston, 1993), map making after (Cuq, 2001), has shown the division of soil occupation by different vegetal shape : first of all we find palm groves (41 per cent) then the concentrated and semi concentrated (25 per cent), the dry savannah (15 per cent), crops or cultures of impoverished landscape (7 per cent), humid savannah, (5 per cent), damaged forests (5 per cent), and at last tans that are salt soils (2 per cent). The marine fauna is composed of fish, shellfish, mollusks, marine mammals (manatees, big dolphins, humped dolphin, hippopotamus,) and reptiles (five species of marine turtles and two crocodile species). The terrestrial fauna is also mainly composed of mammals and birds, but also reptiles. (Limoges and Robillard, 1991; Paris, 1994; Altenburg, Wymenga, Zwarts, 1992; Asbirk and Peterson, 1998). RBABB is the main place of turtles clutch in the whole West African coast and the second wintering site of paleartic birds species of the region after the PNBA. These important mudflats enable more than a million birds to feed themselves and to spend each year the wintering season in the area. It shelters also the most important manatee population of whole West Africa. This specie is a whole part of the bijagos mythology. This community represents ninety per cent of the RBABB population estimated in 2000 about 30,000 inhabitants.

Table 1. characteristics three studied AMPs

MPA	Saloum Delta	Bolama Bijagos Islands	Banc d'Arguin National Park
Surface area (km²)	3 300	10 500	12 000
Category, date of creation	National Park (76 000 ha), 1976 Biosphere Reserve, 1981 Ramsar site	Orango National Park, 1997 Cacheu National Park, 1997 João Vieira et Poilào National Park, 2001 Bolama-Bijagos Biosphere Reserve, 1996 Comunity Reserve of Urok's Islands, 2005	National Park, 1976, World Heritage (UNESCO), Ramsar site
Population living in the Park	120 000	29 000	< 2000
Population density (individuals/ha)	122	13	
Number of villages	114	189	9 villages + nomadic camps
Major groups	Serer-Niominka and Soce	Bijagos	Moors (fishermen and herders)
Other minorities	Many migrant groups from other areas of Senegal and other countries (Guinea, Mali, etc.)	Some groups from Guinea Bissau (Pepel, Manjak) and Senegal	
Main activities	Fishery and mangrove resources exploitation	Agriculture (rice cultivation)	Fishing and cattle breeding
Other cash-earning activities	Tourism, fruit and vegetable garden	Gathering of various products from mangrove (shellfish, fish, honey) and terrestrial forest (cashew nuts, palm oil, palm wine, cola nuts, etc.)	Tourism, trading
Main conservation projects	A lot of projects supported by international and local NGOs (FIBA, IUCN, WWF, and WAAME) and by international cooperation (France, Japan, Belgium, etc.):	Very few projects supported by FIBA, IUCN, WWF, and Tiniguena	RARES program (FIBA)

This community has several other peoples, among which balants, pepels, manjacks... as well as migrants from Senegal Saloum Delta specially and other countries from the sub region. The Bijagos practice rice agriculture mainly, fruit farming (palm oil and wine) and small agriculture. Culture, clan, age group and accommodation unit are the basic of this community identity (Fernandes & Kardoso 1989, Henry 1991) who evolve in a matrilineary system on the one hand, in a naturally managed environment as being part of a cosmogony on the other. Traditionally, every sampling or use of high importance of a natural resource must be preceded by a ritual towards species or sacrilege natural resources. The three MPAs introduced below shelter rich cultural and biological diversities which represent important ecotouristic potential products. The valorization of these products in the framework of ecotourism project development could be an opportunity for local populations to better their leaving conditions. This implies that socioeconomic and financial advantages generated by the sector of ecotourism be fairly shared between the stakeholders among which local populations and the domain contribute to the conservation of cultural and biological diversities within aimed MPAs. All the ecotouristic initiatives undertaken within these MPAs are based on these principles. It is going to be verified below whether the latter has been well followed.

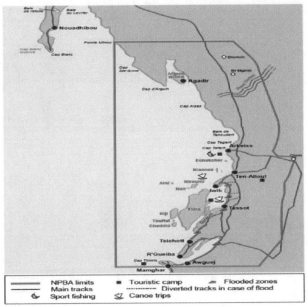

Source: from PNBA (realized by M.C. Cormier-Salem, 2009).

Figure 4. Map of the PNBA.

Source: from DPN[6] (realised by M.C. Cormier-Salem, 2009).

Figure 5. Map of the RBDS.

---

[6] National Parks Head Office (Senegal)

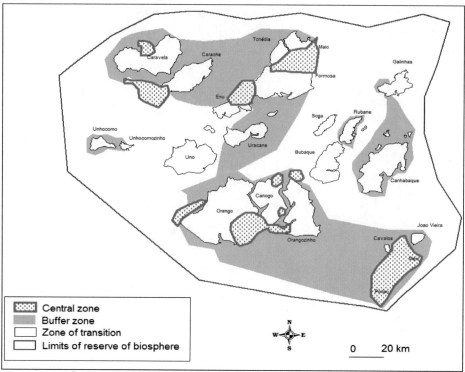

Source: from IBAP[7] (realized by C. Bernatets, 2009).

Figure 6. Map of the RBABB.

SHARING THE BENEFITS OF ECOTOURISM IN WEST AFRICAN MPA: THE PART OF LOCAL COMMUNITIES

Ecotourism development in the West African MPAs involve many stakeholders, amongst which, the concerned States, the environment protection NGOs such as FIBA, UICN and the WWF, the touristic promoters and tourists. However, the goals and aspirations of the ones and the others are very different and may even be divergent sometimes. This raises the whole issue of sharing in a "just and fair" way the advantages generated by that activity (OCDE 1999), in regard with the Convention's third goal on biological diversity ("just and fair sharing of advantages generated by genetic resources exploitation").

In Mauritania, the PNBA managers and their partners (NGO) first considered tourism as a threat for the natural habitat. Afterwards, the activity progressively emerged as a potential tool of socioeconomic development for Imragen community living in the park. This change took place in the context of the desert tourism birth and development in the Mauritanian Adrar (Boulay, 2006), starting from 1996, which targeted European customers who are "well-educated" and respectful of the local natural and cultural heritage. Little by little mixed tours came to be proposed connecting trip to Adrar and to Banc d'Aguin national Park. This ended

---

[7] Institute of Biodiversity and Protected Areas (Guinea-Bissau)

in the first ecotourism development strategy in the park and the construction in 2000 of two touristic campsites. Today, eight out of the nine villages of the PNBA have each a community campsite and Imragen women are trained on management and on tourist reception.Sixteen other persons are currently being trained in ecoguiding, in the field of ornithological tourism programme. The ecotouristic activities main deal with sail tours organisation departing from Iwik village for the visitors who wish to have a view of the PNBA ornithological trumps. Exchange visits are also organized in partnership with other Senegalese national parks. About 2,500 tourists would have visited the park during the 2007-2008 campaign which generated UM 8,000,000 (about 24 000 €) income registered with 700 bed-nights and 75 sails (Sakho, 2008). On average, ecotourism activities generate 12 € of expense per visitor corresponding to the trifling ratio of 12 € of receipts per inhabitant for a year. Besides, only two of the eight campsites operate correctly and these campsites' management involves some families more than others. This raises the issue of profit sharing within the community. Thus, ecotourism cannot at the present state of things compensate the losses which would be associated to the restriction measures against access to fishing in the PNBA.

At the moment, ecotourism in the PNBA can be considered as being at the inception. All has to be done in this protected area with exceptional landscapes, interesting historical touristic sites, rare species and an authentic cultural environment. The Nouadhibou-Nouakchott road construction in 2004 would greatly facilitate access to Park villages and so the possible rush of visitors because the population that has been in touch with Europeans for many centuries seems to look very favourably at tourism. However, tourism development in Mauritania in general is facing cyclical constraints amongst which the collapse of the desert tourism in Mauritania due to national political instability since 2005 and four French tourists murdered in 2007 by "Islamic fundamentalists". As for the PNBA in particular, one notice the total lack of visit "products" which usually generates frustration among visitors. Moreover, contradictions appear between the official discourse stating that a tourism respectful of the nature would be the aimed goal and the fact that, for example, groups of "rally men" usually ride through the MPA under Park managers' permission. It's clear that motorcycled sport and the conditions it is performed do not favour neither ecosystem nor resources preservation.

The ecotourism development level in the PNBA is very different from that in the RBDS characterised by a mangrove ecosystem. In fact in several countries the mangrove offers many touristic potentialities from trip by canoe, walk along ecological waymarked paths belvedere, fishing in the bolons[8], visit of shell heaps, declared "ancestor heritage" in the Saloum, to mangrove oyster and crab tasting. The limicol birds, numerous when the tide is low as they feed themselves with microfauna vases, remain the main view touristic attraction. We can also talk about marine mammals like turtles, dolphins and alligators (in Guiana) to be seen in the nature or in farms. Those of crocodiles (*C. niloticus*) are growing, from Guinea to Malagasy, for eye pleasure as well as for supply in leather and skin etc. The sharks, more unpredictable, are with the sailers and swordfish, the sport fishing privileged target. Accommodation is often in light structures like the carbets in Guiana (with beds or hammock such as floating carbet on Kaw river), the forests' huts and lodges. On the model of integrated rural tourism initiated in Low Casamance in the late 1970s, the village encampments are increasing, so do the lodges and hotel channels. In the Saloum Delta there is a real explosion

---

[8] Network of tidal channels

of touristic offers to discover the delta. At Ndangane Sambou, on the Northern bank, the two ancient hotels (Le Pelican and Le Cordon bleu) have been enlarged and modernised (swimming pool), whereas encampments and hunt or fishing inns mushroom (Figure 7): from 9 in 2000, amongst which only three were registered as belonging to Senegalese, they were more than 15 two years later. It should be noted that in Senegal, tourism is nowadays the basic source of currency. A long time ago, it was all about mass tourism based on the "4 S" – sand, sea, sun, sex and concentrated on the Petite Cote light sand beaches. The Senegalese littoral from Cap Vert down Joal-Fadiouth is urbanised, even concreted, almost without interruption. To the first clubs of the 1970s (Aldiana Club) vast multi-leisure seaside complexes have been adjoined around Saly-Portudal station. The land hold is much that other activities hardly extend: at Joal, the fish transformation sector has been "driven away" and re-lodged on an immense tanbark, far of 5km from the wharf. Some people consider this progress of the "touristic front" towards Saloum as a real economic manna. Yet for the local users, the tourism fallouts are not evident: touristic structures certainly create jobs, directly or indirectly and the turnover at the local level, represented in 2002, next 75% of the fishing landings' estimated value in the RBDS, evaluated at 7.6 million € for 25,000 tourists (60,000 bed-nights) (Sarr & al., 2008). The hotel business expenses are estimated at 70 % of that turnover against 4 % of expenses for ecotouristic outings, leisure fishing or hunting (hiring canoe, paying an ecoguide...) and 26 % of miscellaneous expenses (beverages, souvenirs, presents).

Figure 7. Tourist camp at Ndangane Sambou (RBDS).

About 15 % of fishermen owning canoes occasionally rent their crafts to touristic structures managers or directly to tourists, as a way to diversifying their sources of income. There are other types of indirect jobs tourism creates in fields such as arts and crafts, service crafts and tailoring. The subordinate personnel (maids, cooks, tourist guides or ecoguides, etc.) directly hired in the touristic structures is also recruited on the spot at the rate of 8 full-time and 5 seasonal per structure (Sarr & al., 2008) However, the majority of executives come from Dakar, sometimes even from abroad and most manufactured and food supplies come from Dakar, apart from fresh products like fish. Most of reception structures belong to foreigners, even though there are a few community encampments in some of the RBDS villages. Risks of local communities' competition, marginalization and acculturation are also obvious. In the RBDS, village communities are forbidden to exploit the mangrove resources while hunting and fishing permits are delivered to tourists. Besides, traditional fishing and landing places which are close to the littoral are privatised and so out of access for the local populations. Despite all these sources of conflict, an inquiry conducted in 2003 before the fishermen and women collecting shells reveals that 44 % of the former and 46 % of the latter think that tourism in general can cohabit with their respective activities against 17 % and 4 % thinking differently. The same inquiry indicates that 16 % of the RBDS hotel managers have once been in conflict with the inhabitants (blocked sailing ways to prevent tourists from passing, fishing landing in front of hotels preventing 'jet-skyers" from enjoying their activity, managers' opposition to mangrove wood cutting and to birds eggs' collection by the inhabitants, etc.).

Similarly to what happens in RBDS, tourism is more and more developing in the RBABB especially since 1996, date when it was erected into biosphere reserve. There are 16 structures amongst which hunting clubs (08), hotels (06) and inns (02) (Figure 8).

Figure 8. Tourist camp at Bubaque (RBABB).

The fishing clubs create more direct jobs than other structures. However, their impact on other segments of the local economy is weak, for they dispose autonomy in terms of transport and food. Their activities are based on leisure fishing outings organizing. As for the hotels, they only propose accommodation services and do not have any leisure activity for their customers mainly composed of expatriates living in Bissau. The very few inns usually receive ecotourists (visit of the local natural and cultural environment). Though having limited purchase capacity, these ecotourists generally buy their consumption products before modest small structures held by local people (food, pension, spice, cafes). The surveys conducted from 2005 to 2007 in the Boubaque Island which hosts 10 from the 16 touristic structures of RBABB (Figure 9), reveal that local tourism creates about 150 direct jobs half of which is occupied by Bijagos living in the island. They are especially subordinate (housewives, gardeners, chef assistants, etc.), and remunerated between 15,000 and 20,000 Fcfa (20 and 30 €) per month compared to 40.000 and 70.000 cfa (60 and 106 €) for qualified positions (marine/skipper, mechanic, barmen and managers). Most of these qualified employees are Senegalese who can speak French fluently (3/4 of tourists are French) and are trained in their countries in various fields of hotel industry. There are on average 2 to 33 employees per touristic structure. All these structures belong to foreigners (60 % of French; 20 % portugese and 20 % Senegalese). Tourism creates jobs in the island as well, direct jobs like coalers, canoemen, guides, translators, craftsmen tailors, etc.

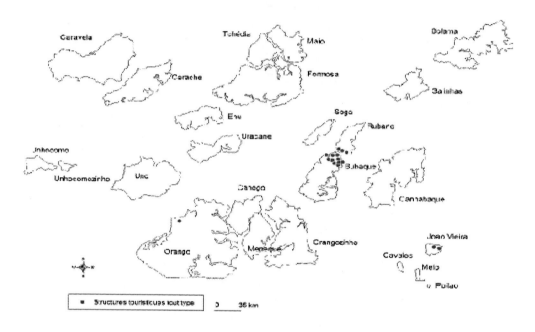

Figure 9. Distribution of the touristic structures in the RBABB (from Bernatets, 2009).

The number of tourists received seasonally at Boubaque is estimated at 868, about 23 and 300 tourists per structure. The turnover for 9 of the 10 the island touristic establishments is evaluated at more than 19.6 and 25.2 million Fcfa (30.000 and 38.500 €) per season.

To sum up, it can be said that tourism practiced in our field of study is essentially based on the nature but also discovering the local cultures. At the PNBA, the main touristic activities consist of sail outings. In the RBDS, tourists' activities consist of fishing, hunting, sea or forest trips to contemplate nature (flora, birds, other animals), village and cockles piles visit,...(Table 2). In the RBABB, survey conducted in 2006 and 2007, shows that the particularity of archipelago (landscape, high quality of water, typicity and authenticity of Bijagos culture) stands as the main reason for the presence of hotels and tourists (Table 3). The area protection status has favoured touristic visits. In the RBDS and in the RBABB, that status of MPA explains respectively the stay of 34 % (Sarr, 2005) and 31 % (survey 2006/2007) of tourists. It's difficult to consider all the area touristic activities as related to ecotourism. As much as we know, no assessment of those activities' effective impacts, namely in terms of resources collection, has been realised. However, the local communities gain very little or almost nothing from the touristic activities economic fallouts (direct and indirect jobs, financial fallouts), on the one hand because those fallouts are trivial (PNBA) or unfairly shared when they likely important (RBDS, RBABB). A survey conducted before the RBABB populations, informs about the perception the latter has on tourism. Indeed 46.6 % of them believe that has no effect on their living conditions and above all it does not contribute to its well-being. On the other hand, 26 % state the contrary whereas 27.3 % have no response. Ecotourism or simply tourism is thus far from ranking as alternative activity for resource extraction activities such as fishing. That is potentially possible, but supposes, on the one hand, local communities entrepreneurship and management ship capacity building and, on the other hand incitement measures' implementation favouring them to integrate ecotourism sector (Sarr & al., 2008) a "fair and equitable" benefits sharing system.

Table 2. Tourists activities[9] in the RBDS

Activity	% tourists
Leisure fishing	54
Trips on sea	54
Trips in the forest	60
Cultural Visits	32

Source: Sarr, 2005.

Table 3. Tourism interest in the RBABB

Motivation	% Hotel owners	% Tourists
Landscape (fauna, flora, beach, climate, islands)	100	100%
Water/fishing richness	62.5	56
Typicalness/authecity/ local culture	49	75
Quietness / isolation	93.7	56

CONCLUSION

A growing number of works ponder over the repercussion of the new forms to preserve and enhance the biodiversity and decry threats of a two-pace nature and tourism: the local communities are marginalised whereas the littoral biodiversity which is supposed to be protected through measures forbidding access to it is impoverished because of the touristic flows, leading to treading and disturbing the wild life. Ecotourism success supposes an entrance limitation, fixing the maximum number of visitors, imposing circulation permits, all these measures clearly show that ecotourism is not an alternative to mass tourism but a formula reserved to some elite. We tend towards setting up over protected "natural"[10] balloon for the benefit of a few privileged consumers, surrounded with ordinary spaces, exposed to concrete or many pressures. The same tendency is noticed in West Africa, especially in

---

[9] This table indicates that one tourist performs many activities at the same time

[10] In this respect, the park center, "nature-leisure" balloons' extreme cases, may be the less bad solution because those American-like attraction zoos, designed like tropical heaven for great numbers pleasure, save from disturbing the "nature-environment" (Baron-Yelles, 1997).

mangroves ecosystems, where developing ecotourism is considered within MPAs as a panacea, even if in facts, the results are far from the local communities' aspirations. These latter still wait in vain for the jobs and incomes promised as substitutes to their traditional activities, forbidden in the name of preservation, even though converting turtle hunters or shark fishermen into ecoguides[11] suffers from internal contradictions. In fact, the landscape, particularly the mangrove, is under risk highly of not being entertained and the ecological as well as cultural heritage of disappearing. That mangrove assigned to tourists visit is far from the muddy fields full of mosquitoes. It is preferred to peaceful waters of tide channels where herd of animals come and feed themselves, red ibis' flight above a forest of palm trees immortalised by Yann Arthur-Bertrand..

Contrasting with mangrove ecosystems, desert zones appeared also as an ecotouristic destination (UNEP, 2006), but the expectations of the populations in desert areas with regard to the ecotourism, are identical to those of the populations in mangrove ecosystems.

Selecting remarkable and media elements leads to staging nature, in where the local actors hardly find themselves, so much that this artificial staging often goes with putting their practices and knowledge into folklore. The relations between cultural and natural heritage, ecotourism and ethnotourism are very close as the ecomuseums, environment houses and other events and collections' exhibitions prove it in protected surfaces for instance. The renewed interest for the sacred sites is another illustration. In Guinea Bissau, the choice of Poilao islands as marine national zoo was determined by the bio-ecological value as green turtle laying areas, as well as cultural as "traditional sacred site for the bijago culture". These initiatives highlight the links between regarding biodiversity as sacred and its protection and knowledge and traditions putting into inheritance.

In front of the mangrove idealised and somehow stereotyped image and given the changes and manifold crisis context in the Southern countries for the late decades, the "mangrove people" are very often in quest of identity. Isn't it paradoxical to call them the "global sea garden's" guards whereas they tend to lose their job and their space control? Moreover, the situation is the same for the populations of the desert.

Most of inheritance, exogenous processes undertaken at the national or international scale come up against the local or "endogenous"[12] nature exploitation, management and appropriation dynamic. The disagreements lie in the valorised objects selection as heritage, in the implemented improvements and regulation tools, and also in the targeted goals. In this abundance of public as well as private initiatives that bespeak of the diversity of values and enhancements attached to mangrove and desert, it is worth underlining the way the local

---

[11] In Senegal, a reflexion is being carried on to harmonise and organise volunteers' movements and explain "ecoguards" and "ecoguides" status: ecoguards (or "eco-amazons" for girls) are more or less voluntary workers from the villages and they self-finance through remunerations they get from services and activities they do. Ecoguides receive training and are responsible for protected areas ecological monitoring. They are officially recognised by the Ministry of Tourism. The main problem is these agents' remuneration and so the system's sustainability, this explains the protocols under elaboration between the National Parks Office and Parks and Reserves Voluntaries Organisations National network: reserves managed by the National Parks Office.

[12] This opposition between exogenous and endogenous, though manifest in the Southern countries (Cormier-Salem et al, 2002), needs to be qualified, so much as processes are imbricate, the stages intricate and the stakeholders of mixed origins. Very often the big international NGOs are relayed on the field by local ones; more and more nationals, enlightened elected representative, retired notables, young qualified, set up their own NGOs.

communities, with their uses, knowledge and rights, are taken into account and their territory, inheritance and identity strategies.

REFERENCES

Altenburg, W., Wymenga, E., Zwarts, L. (1992). Ornithological importance of the coastal wetlands of Guinea-Bissau. *WIWO Report.* 26. Zeist.

Asbirk, S. & Petersen, I. K. (1998). Waterbirds in Guinea Bissau. Partnership between Guinea-Bissau and the Trilateral Wadden Sea Cooperation on the Protection of the Wadden Sea. *Report on the Activities of the Work Program.* 1995-96.

Baron-Yelles, N. (1997). Espaces protégés et tourisme de nature sur le littoral atlantique français:stratégies et enjeux. Paris, Université Paris-1, *doctorat de géographie,* 380 p.

Blangy, S. (1999). Tourisme autochtone et communautaire, Paris, *Courrier de l'UNESCO, juillet-août* 1999 : 32-33.

Boo, E. (1990). *Ecotourism: the potentials and pitfalls.* Vol 1. Washington, DC: World Wildlife Fund.

Boulay, S. (2006). Le tourisme de désert en Adrar mauritanien : réseaux « translocaux », économie solidaire et changements sociaux, in A. Doquet and S. Le Menestrel (ed.), Tourisme culturel, réseaux et recompositions sociales, *Autrepart, Revue des Sciences Sociales au Sud,* 40 : 67-83

Cardoso, L. (1989). *Ponto de vista historico. Criaçao e evoluçao da RBABB, povoamento e fluxo migratorio, entidades geopoliticas e gestao do espaço.* INEP.

Centre d'analyse stratégique. (2008). La valeur tutélaire du carbone. Rapport de la commission présidée par A. Quinet, Rapports et documents, juin.

Cheikh, A.W.O. (2002). Création, évolution, peuplement et identité imraguen, gestion de l'espace. Le Parc National du Banc d'Arguin, CONSDEV Working Document/WP1/02, Nouakchott, 35 p.

Cormier-Salem, M.-C. (2006). Entre exploitation et sanctuarisation des écosystèmes côtiers ouest-africains, l'écotourisme, une option durable ? In : J.J. Symoens, ed, Les écosystèmes côtiers de l'Afrique de l'Ouest.. *Bruxelles, Fondation pour favoriser les recherches scientifiques en Afrique* : 249-268.

— (2007). Etude de cas – Quelle durabilité pour quelles mangroves ? Chap. 3 : 91-97, In : Y. Veyret, dir, Le développement durable. Paris, SEDES, Capes-Agrégation Géographie, 432 p.

— (2008). Les zones humides : la vitrine mangrove. In :Y. Veyret et P. Arnould, dir, Atlas des développements durables. Un monde inégalitaire, des expériences novatrices, des outils pour l'avenir. Paris, Autrement, collection Atlas/Monde, planche 58-59.

Cormier-Salem, M.-C. (ed), Juhé-Beaulaton, D. (ed), Boutrais, J. (ed), Roussel, B. (ed). (2002). Patrimonialiser la nature tropicale : Dynamiques locales, enjeux internationaux. Paris (FRA) ; Paris : IRD ; MNHN, 2002, p. 125-166. (Colloques et Séminaires).

CRF-Conseil Régional de Fatick. (2000). "Schéma Régional d'Aménagement du Territoire de Fatick. Version Finale". *République du Sénégal.* 193 p.

Cuq, F. (2001). Un système d'information géographique pour l'aide à la gestion intégrée de l'archipel des Bijagos (Guinée-Bissau) - 1). Carte de l'environnement littoral de l'archipel des Bijagos, 10 feuilles à 1 : 50 000, Géosystèmes, Brest ; 2). Notice de la carte, constitution et exploitation du SIG, Géosystèmes, Brest, 88 p., 56 ill

Dia, I. M. M. (2003). "Elaboration et mise en oeuvre d'un plan de gestion intégrée - La Réserve de biosphère du delta du Saloum, Sénégal". UICN, Gland, Suisse et Cambridge, Royaume-Uni. xiv + 130 pp.

Diouf, P.S. (1996). "Les peuplements de poissons des milieux estuariens de l'Afrique de l'Ouest : l'exemple de l'estuaire hyperhalin du Sine-Saloum". Thèse de Doctorat, Uni. de Montpellier II, 267 p.

Emerton, L. (1999). Economic Tools for the Management of Marine Protected Areas in Eastern Africa.

— (2003). Covering the economic costs of Marine Protected Areas: extending the concept of financial diversity and sustainability, V[th] World Parks Congress: Sustainable Finance Stream, IUCN – The World Conservation Union, September 2003 •Durban, South Africa.

EPEEC - Equipe Pluridisciplinaire d'Etude des Ecosystèmes Côtiers du Sénégal. (1998). "Aménagement Participatif des pêcheries artisanales du Sine-Saloum (Sénégal) ". Rapport Final. UNESCO - Coastal and Small Islands Program (CSI).

Fernandes, M. R. (1989). *O espaco e o tempo na sistema politico bidjogo,* Soronda (Bissau), 8 : 5-23

Henry, C. (1994). *Les îles où dansent les enfants défunts. Age, sexe et pouvoir chez les Bijogo de Guinée-Bissau.* CNRS Edition, éd de la maison des sciences de l'Homme , Paris214. IUCN, The World Conservation Union Eastern Africa Office, Economics and Biodiversity Series, Nairobi.

Legrain, D. (dir). (2001). Jardins du littoral. Luçon, Actes Sud, *Conservatoire du Littoral,* 222 p.

LERG. (2004). Etude de base sur la biodiversité. Rapport Final". Programme GIRMAC. Sénégal.

Limoges, B., Robillard, M. J. (1991). Proposition d'un Plan d'Aménagement de la Réserve de Biosphère de l'Archipel de Bolama-Bijagos. Vol 1 : Les secteurs de développement : zonages et recommandations. *CECI/UICN.* Bissau. 271 p. OCDE, 1992.

Paris, (1994). La faune des îles Bolama-Bijagos : mise au point sur les connaissances. GPC/MDRA/UICN. Bubaque.

Phillips, A. (1998). Economic Values of Protected Areas. Guidelines for Protected Area Managers. IUCN The World Conservation Union.

Pigou, A. C. (1932). The Economics of Welfare. 4th edition. London: Macmillan.

Sakho, Z. 2008, Rapport d'évaluation de la campagne éco-touristique 2007-2008 au PNBA, rapport interne PNBA, 15 p.

Sanchirico, J.N., Cochran, K.A. and Emerson, P.M. (2002). Marine Protected Areas: Economic and Social Implications, Discussion Paper 02–26, Resources for the Future, Washington DC.

Sarr, O. (2005). Aire marine protégée, gestion halieutique, diversification et développement local : le cas de la Réserve de Biosphère du Delta du Saloum (Sénégal). Thèse de Doctorat en Sciences Économiques. École Doctorale des Sciences de la Mer, Université de Bretagne Occidentale. 245 p.

Sarr, O., Boncoeur, J., Travers, M., Cormier-Salem, M-C. (2008). Can ecotourism be an alternative to traditional fishing? An analysis with reference to the case of the Saloum

Delta (Senegal). Wageningen UR Frontis Series, Vol. 25, *Economics Of Poverty, Environment And Natural-Resource Use,* Rob B. Dellink and Arjan Ruijs editors, Springer Netherlands, 87-100.

Sarr, O., Travers, M., Boncoeur, J., Appéré, G. (2005). Modelling interactions between farming and fishing activities: the case of the Saloum Delta, Senegal. 54ème Congrès de l'Association Française de Science Economique 15-17 Septembre, Paris, France.

Troadec, J.-P. & Boncoeur, J. (2003). "La régulation de l'accès". In Exploitation et surexploitation des ressources marines vivantes. Rapport sur la science et la technologie n°17. Laubier L. animateur. *Académie des sciences,* 355-392.

UNEP. (2006). Tourism and Deserts A Practical Guide to Managing the Social and Environmental Impacts in the Desert Recreation Sector. 48 p.

Vidigal, M. P., & Basto, P. M. F. (1993). Missao de estudo realizado às Ilhas de Bubaque, Canhabaque, Joao Vieira, Orango Grandes e Cute do Arquipélago dos Bijagos. Lisboa: IICT/Centro Botânica.

Watkin, J. R. (2003). The Evolution of Ecotourism in East Africa: From an idea to an industry. *IIED Wildlife and Development Series N°* 15. 29p.

Weigel, J-Y., Sarr, O. (2002). Bibliographical analysis of marine protected areas. General and regional references for West Africa. IRD. Dakar. *Juillet* 2002. Ref.: CONSDEV Synthesis/WP1/02. 21 pages.

In: Ecotourism: Management, Development and Impact   ISBN: 978-1-60876-724-3
Editors: A. Krause, E. Weir, pp. 181-200   © 2010 Nova Science Publishers, Inc.

Chapter 7

THE ECO-INN AND ITS EVALUATION INDICATORS IN TAIWAN

Nae-Wen Kuo[a], Chiou-Lien Huang[b] and Ying-Jiun Chen[c]*

[a]Department of Geography, National Taiwan Normal University, Taiwan, R.O.C.
[b]Department of Bio-Industry Communication and Development, National Taiwan University, Taiwan, R.O.C.
[c]Graduate Institute of Tourism and Health Science, National Taipei College of Nursing, Taiwan, R.O.C.

ABSTRACT

Rural tourism is often considered an economic alternative for rural areas facing decreasing profits and requiring a second or third economic footing. However, like other tourism activities, rural tourism results in a full range of environmental impacts. In particular, accommodation, one important element of the tourism system, generates various environmental loadings. Some obvious impacts are the following: architectural pollution owing to the effect of inappropriate hotel development on the traditional landscape, and the resort infrastructure becoming overloaded and breaking down in periods of peak usage. An Eco-inn, the environmentally friendly accommodation, is proposed to reduce the negative impacts from tourism.

However, no evaluation indicators and related assessment criteria for the Eco-inn are investigated up to now. Hence, the purpose of this study is to explore the indicators that can be used for evaluating the Eco-inn in Taiwan. This evaluation indicator system is based on the findings from literature review, and then the Delphi Method is employed to collect experts' opinions. Finally, 50 of the 109 candidate indicators were selected after three rounds of the Delphi method. These indicators can be categorized into the following sectors: green building, sustainable landscape construction, organic agriculture, environmental education, local benefit and others. Hence, the five core principles of eco-inns are: (1) green building, (2) sustainable landscape construction, (3) organic agriculture, (4) environmental education, and (5) local benefit. Furthermore, the eco-inn

---

* Communicating author: P. O. Box 22-96, Taipei, Taipei City, 10699, Taiwan., E-mail: niven@ntnu.edu.tw or nivenkuo@ntu.edu.tw, Telephone: 886-2-23637874, Fax: 886-2-23691770.

can be linked with ecotourism development and may be the low-impact accommodation choices for ecotourists.

Keywords: Eco-inn, ecotourism, the Delphi method.

1. INTRODUCTION

The decline in agricultural and other forms of rural employment in many countries has created a need for a diversified range of rural businesses. In most cases, tourism and recreation have become important elements of the diverse activities in post-productivist rural areas of Taiwan. Although tourism continues to be viewed as a panacea for the economic ills in rural areas, some negative impacts in physical, socio-economic, and cultural environment must be considered (Roberts and Hall, 2001). In the physical environment, habitat destruction, littering, emissions and other forms of pollution, and congestion are the main negative impacts. In the socio-economic sector, economic leakages, local price inflation, labour in-migration, and distortion of local employment structure are often reviewed as impacts.

In particular, accommodation, one important element of the tourism system, generates various environmental loadings. Mathieson and Wall (1982) offer a number of insights into the environmental problems associated with accommodation. Some obvious impacts are the following: architectural pollution owing to the effect of inappropriate hotel development on the traditional landscape, and the resort infrastructure becoming overloaded and breaking down in periods of peak usage.

However, previous studies concerned about rural tourism and accommodation had been conducted mainly in the operational sector such as Oppermann (1996) and Weaver and Fennell (1997). Little of previous research is about the environmental issues of accommodation in rural areas (e.g., Lane, 2001). Hence, impacts from accommodation in rural areas should be investigated further and low-impact accommodation needs to be developed to decrease the potential impacts. Kuo (2008) has proposed the idea of the Eco-inn, a kind of low-impact accommodation that is optimal in Taiwan rural areas. However, no evaluation indicators and related assessment criteria for the Eco-inn are investigated up to now. Hence, the purpose of this study is to explore the indicators that can be used for evaluating the Eco-inn in Taiwan.

2. ENVIRONMENTAL ISSUES OF RURAL ACCOMMODATION IN TAIWAN

With the decline in agricultural (for example, only 1.8% of GDP in 2005), the Council Of Agriculture (COA) in Taiwan tried to develop recreational activities in rural areas since 1988. When the 'two-holiday one week' policy carried out from 2000, people have more leisure time for recreation and about 76% people prefer to enjoy their holidays in rural areas away from urban areas (COA, 2001). Hence, 369 country towns (100%) have created recreational activities related with agriculture and 1002 agricultural farms are established for tourism with the increasing demand of rural tourism (Agritourism association of Taiwan, 2004). For most rural communities in Taiwan, tourism is one of the important elements in their diversified economy. In addition, for some others, tourism has become the primary economic endeavour which dominates community life and upon which the local area is dependent such as Chi-Chi and Shwei-Li in Nantou County.

In Taiwan, inns and Bed and Breakfast (B&B) are the major types of rural accommodation and they have been formed since 1980's in order to provide lodging when too many tourists are visiting Ken-Ding at summer vacation. With increasing demand of rural tourism, the capacity of existing accommodation is far away from competent; consequently, hundreds of inns and B&B are built between 2000 and 2001. According to data of the Tourism Bureau of Taiwan, the number of rural inns and B&B in 2007 was 2,934 (Tourism Bureau of Taiwan, 2008).

The Rural Accommodation Management (RAM) Act was legislated in December 2001, in order to control the over-development problems and environmental issues of rural accommodation. However, up to 2008, there still 499 (17%) inns and B&B cannot achieve the criteria in RAM Act (Tourism Bureau of Taiwan, 2008). In addition, without comprehensive planning and careful construction, some accommodation has resulted in serious environmental impacts in rural areas. For example, over-development problems in Ching-Chin, a very beautiful landscape in central of Taiwan, have destroyed the natural landscape. Too many inns and B&B are established here (56 in 2004), and they are built inharmoniously with local environment (Tou, 2005). In particular, some buildings are of European-style, some are west of American-style, and others are of Japanese-style.

In addition, various negative impacts during accommodation construction result in the decreasing of environmental quality of Ching-Chin such as air pollution (emissions of PM10), together with noise and vibration. Moreover, rural tourists in Taiwan like to play 'karaoke', which is the Japanese custom of singing popular songs solo to an accompaniment in bars and similar public places, and make so much noise that local people cannot sleep at night. Conflict of water supply between innkeepers and local people, even between different owners is becoming more and more serious, because the amount of water resources in Ching-Chin is not sufficient to meet demand. In addition, wastewater and solid waste generated by a large number of tourists (about 1.2 millions per year) cannot be treated properly because it lacks a sanitary sewer system and adequate equipments (the original capacity was just designed for local people not including rural tourists).

3. THE ECO-INN

The idea of the Eco-inn that is optimal in Taiwan rural areas is proposed by Kuo (2008). The 'eco-inn' programme that aims to develop the 'green' accommodation to minimise the negative impacts in rural areas as mentioned above was initiated by Graduate Institute of Tourism and Health Science with the support of Chrshang Township Government. The 'eco-' in eco-inn has dual meanings. One is 'ecological' means that the inn has planned and managed on the basis of ecological principles. Another is 'e' and 'co' means that the eco-inn is not only beneficial for 'environment' but also beneficial for local 'community'. It specifies five core principles that, in their interplay, would distinguish an eco-inn from other inn: (1)

green building; (2) sustainable landscape construction; (3) organic agriculture; (4) environmental education; and (5) local benefit.

3.1. Green Building

Building construction operations significantly contribute to the degradation of the environment, through both the consumption of non-renewable natural resources and the generation of waste. Awareness is increasing; however, of design and construction strategies that can help reduce the environmental impact of the built environment, leading to rapid growth in the popularity of 'green building' technologies. Green building has its roots in the energy-conservation movement of the 1970s and 1980s, and has matured to embrace a wide set of design standards and building techniques. The techniques involved in green building are manifold, and are listed in several manuals and guides (Roodman and Lenssen, 1995; Rocky Mountain Institute, 1998).

Most buildings concerned about green issues are located in urban areas; in comparison, few are in rural areas. However, the physical environment of rural areas is more nature and more sensitive than that of urban areas, and then the building construction in rural areas should be planned more carefully to reduce the environmental impacts. Consequently, when developing accommodation in rural areas, the sustainable issues of green building need to be taken into consideration firstly.

In Taiwan, the Ministry of Interior (MOI) has been promoting the green building for a few years. The MOI established the nine criteria for green buildings and encourage the architects to design green buildings, the suppliers to provide green materials, and the researchers to develop relevant equipment, material and recycling systems for green buildings. The nine criteria for green building certification are: (1) greening index; (2) ability of rain storage; (3) water saving index; (4) energy saving index; (5) the decrement of carbon dioxide; (6) construction waste reduction; (7) sewage and waste management; (8) biodiversity index; and (9) indoor environmental quality. First, the public buildings such as government offices are required to follow the green building criteria since 2001, and then the MOI increases to educate the private builders to adopt green building technologies. According to data of the MOI, about one hundred private buildings win the certification (MOI, 2003). Since such green building technologies in Taiwan are well developed in practice, the application of these technologies into green accommodation in rural areas may become feasible. In addition, the idea of green building will be recognized and accepted by local people and put into practice in the future if the eco-inn successes.

3.2. Sustainable Landscape Construction

In general, writing and action about green building are often the work of architects and builders; although well-meaning toward the landscape. Including site, habitat, and ecosystem protection in green construction is essential. A perfectly resource-green house that replaces a healthy ecosystem is a poor substitute. Badly sited, such a building destroys the site and with it, the environmental services provided to the 'green' functioning of the building. Hence, sustainable landscape construction should be regarded as important concept of the eco-inn, together with green building.

Many constructed landscapes are deliberately constructed to recall the qualities of natural places and serve the practical and spiritual needs of humanity in ways similar to wild places. However, they remain constructed, even if less obviously so than buildings. Hence, concern for the heath of outdoor places is a central theme in sustainable landscape architecture, while most constructed landscapes are designed for the needs of humanity. It will be a concern shared by many members of related disciplines such as architecture, planning, public-lands administration, and horticulture, as well as by private gardeners. A small but growing number of landscape-makers in Taiwan are looking for that landscapes are built eco-friendly or environmentally friendly. From their experiences, the following five principles that may guild how to plan and design sustainable landscape construction around the eco-inn are suggested here.

Principle 1: Keep sites health. Every site resembles a living organism, and like organisms, sites vary in health. Healthy sites are recognized with the following characteristics: they support a diversity of plant and animal life; they are seldom dominated exclusively by one species; the community or ecosystem of the site is essentially self-maintaining; the living species of the site are self-reproducing; and the community will succession naturally. Protecting a healthy site requires care throughout the design and construction process. In addition, sustainable design anticipates and integrates appropriate construction methods.

To heal injured sites is also important when the sites damaged by prior use or during the process of construction. Restoration techniques may include: removing damaging structures; removing excess paving; replacing over-engineered drainage structures; restoring damaged soils on-site; removing invasive plants; and restoring native succession. However, these techniques should be evaluated appropriate to both community and site in practice.

In general, widespread paving is a very common phenomenon in rural areas of Taiwan and has made sites become unhealthy. For all its popularity and functionality, paving has been implicated in a wide range of ecological problems. Most paving materials create surface stability by excluding water from the soil, and this impermeability causes a number of difficulties. Soil absorbs rainfall and nurtures flora, fauna, and humans, but impervious surfaces increase runoff, causing erosion and flooding, depleting soil water, and contributing to siltation and water pollution. Pave less is a design options to decrease this unnatural area and its site impact and should be taken into account in sustainable landscape construction.

Principle 2: Consider origin and fate of materials. The materials used in landscapes have many environmental impacts. Extraction of raw materials for making landscape products has environmental and energy costs. Products that are themselves quite clean may originate in air- or water-polluting factories far from the landscape site.

Almost every construction material is extracted from somewhere. Some extraction processes are more destructive than others; some products are renewable or reusable. The hidden costs can be high, from the nonrenewable petroleum products used in asphalt to the destruction of rain forests for tropical hardwoods. Such hidden costs of landscape materials and the hazards they can pose for landowners, tourists and for landscape workers are also need to be considered, as well as for the micro and larger environment. The Life Cycle

Assessment technologies often used in Industrial Ecology (Graedel and Allenby, 2003) may be applied to evaluate the environmental costs of materials and to choose more environmentally friendly materials. Some realistic alternatives might be using on-site and local resources, reusing or recycling materials, and avoiding toxic materials.

Principle 3: Celebrate light, respect darkness. Landscape lighting is a source of great pleasure, extending the use of outdoor space into night-time hours and contributing to user safety; moreover, attracting tourists. Outdoor lighting, however, can be either well designed and constructed or excessive or inappropriate. Extravagant lighting can be wonderful for temporary effects, but as a permanent feature of a landscape it not only wastes energy resources but also causes direct damage to plant and animal species (Moyer, 1992).

Inns in rural areas, unlike hotels in urban areas, lighting needs to be considered based on the native environment and respects the requirement of sensitive species and the opinions of local people. Although the night held primitive dangers, and still holds modern ones, it also offers mystery and is in fact biologically necessary to most species. It is important not to forget the value of darkness when current lighting technology makes it so easy to exorcise ancient fears. Most animals and plants have seasonal or daily rhythms that are regulated by patterns of darkness and light. Excessive lighting, especially outdoors, can disrupt these patterns, causing serious harm to some species, including humans. All-night lighting can cause sleepless for people exposed to it and may contribute to the well-known stresses that affect shift-workers. Since most local people in rural areas go to bed earlier than tourists, lighting in the inns, especially outdoors, must be controlled to avoid the disturbance of local people lifestyles.

Principle 4: Quietly defend silence. Rural environment has traditionally been retreats where silence could be sought and savored. But this feature of traditional landscapes is being eroded by the rural tourism activities and the increase in tourists. Noise has physiological and psychological effects on living things, and the effects of constant noise are not healthy. If human lives are to be sustainable not only in basic physical needs, but psychologically sustainable, noise reduction becomes an important issue much like energy consumption or toxicity.

Like the darkness of nighttime skies, silence is something worth respecting. Ironically, despite technology, darkness and silence cannot be created; light and noise can only be masked or excluded, since to wall off the landscape is to make it something else than a landscape. It is worth to notice that don't rely on noise 'barriers' (such as walls, or berms) often used in most urban landscapes; by contrast, should to find the source of noise and protect soundscapes through well-planning.

Principle 5: Maintain to sustain. In fact, landscapes are living things. In one important sense, they are never finished. Growth, natural succession, weathering, and change of use all keep the landscape evolving and then it requires maintenance. Maintenance is the way an evolving landscape keeps pace with evolving human demands. Most landscape professionals, and many landowners, are well aware that sustainability and careful maintenance go hand in hand. However, the specialist structure of professional relationships often means that maintenance, construction, and design occur in totally separate compartments. Hence, the future maintenance work should be taken into account both in design and construction stages. For example, reducing pesticide and fertilizers use, conserving and using on-site resources, establishing and maintaining native plants, estimating the long-term costs and benefits of maintenance, and evaluating maintenance options are some useful strategies. Among these, coordinating design, construction, and maintenance will be the most important one. The most forward-thinking landscape designers prepare a site-specific maintenance plan for their clients (Kellum, 1999).

Energy saving is another important issue in the landscape maintenance. However, despite energy's increasing importance in building design and construction, it is still rare to find energy conservation principles systematically applied to landscape construction. It is necessary to know the costs of energy over time to maintain the landscape. One strategy is to reduce demand of energy such as mini-machinery design, and use high-efficiency equipments. Another approach is to use alternative power sources, such as solar and wind. For example, lighting system in the garden can be powered by solar-generated electricity, and irrigation equipment can be powered by wind-generated electricity.

3.3. Organic Agriculture

In contrast to the trend toward industrialized agriculture, some farmers are going back to a low-impact sustainable agriculture that their grandparents might have used a century ago. Organic agriculture is regarded as one of the low-impact sustainable agriculture with none pesticides and inorganic fertilizer use. These alternative farming methods are regarded by proponents as environmentally beneficial (Food and Agriculture Organization of the United Nations, FAO, 2003). Using fewer or none chemicals and manipulating the soil less reduces erosion and pollution and improves the long-range health of the land. Although this movement is too new to yet have good human health statistics, it seems likely that low-impact farming could be good for the farmers, and might be good for the tourists visiting rural areas, too. In addition, organic agriculture preserving small-scale, family farms also helps preserve rural culture.

In principle, an eco-inn is based on organic agriculture; hence, food and other agricultural products used in the accommodation must be cultivated with organic agriculture. These organic foods will be cultivated by the innkeeper or purchased from the local farmers' market. The product is fresh, and profits go directly to the person who grows the crop. Producers are guaranteed a local market for organic food. The tourist can be assured of quality and can even be involved in production. Consequently, it is beneficial for the local farmers and tourists. In addition, extra benefits will create in many ways such as rural air quality will become better because no pesticides use, reduce transportation pollution by using native foods, and save energy by using fresh vegetables and fruits without refrigeration.

An example of a hotel chain that has taken the initiative to encourage organic agriculture to produce foodstuffs for use in the hotels is proposed in the Grecotel program (Holden, 2000). In 1995, Grecotel funded an organic agriculture project. The use of environmental procedures, besides benefiting the environment, have also proved to be financially beneficial to Grecotel. For instance, the use of garden flowering plants produced under organic principles has resulted in less of a requirement for fertilizer and pesticides, achieving a cost saving of US$52,000 in 1996. The use of hotel garden and kitchen organic waste to produce compost in the four hotels has saved US$80,000.

3.4. Environmental Education

The educative characteristic of an eco-inn is a key element that distinguishes it from other forms of inns. If the eco-inn seeks to promote responsible tourism, then its foundation must be education, and it should aim to include both local community and the tourists. In general, a rural tourism experience is usually associated with learning and natural consciousness. The range of outputs that the public might want from agriculture and the rural sector in general have been outlined (Hall, McVittie, and Moran, 2004), and educational activities are the important one. Tourists will eventually acquire a consciousness and knowledge of the natural environment together with its cultural aspects. In the rural tourism context, interpretation and education can serve two distinct roles, that of satisfying visitor information needs and of visitor management. Tourists want to learn about the rural environments they visit and interpretation has become an important role in rural tourism. Through interpretation and environmental education, tourists can gain a better understanding, awareness, and appreciation of the rural landscape and local culture.

Environmental education and interpretation are important tools in creating an enjoyable and meaningful rural tourism experience. Interpretation is the art of helping people to learn and it might be a central tenet of an eco-inn. It is a complex activity that goes beyond making the communication of information enjoyable. Environmental education activities often involve active participation, such as organic agriculture activity, which allows the tourists to appreciate the importance of natural and cultural conservation.

Interpretation has become a widespread management tool in the natural resource management profession as it has the capacity to reduce inappropriate behavior on a voluntary basis through education. Since the role of interpretation as an effective management technique is now being acknowledged by managers, education and interpretation should no longer be seen as a frill or a luxury (Orams, 1996; Hall and McArthur, 1996). It can also be useful as a management tool for rural tourism and should be implemented by the innkeeper and the staff. Environmental education can influence tourist, community and industry behavior and assist in the longer-term sustainability of tourist activity in rural areas. Interpretation helps tourists see the whole picture regarding the environment. It acknowledges the natural and cultural values of the area visited as well as other issues such as resource management. In other words, the development of environmental education assisted in the creation of environmentally literate citizens of nation and then they will behave friendly to the environment.

3.5. Local Benefit

Benefits are defined here as an improved condition or lessening of a worse condition to individuals and communities. They can be categorized as personal (physical and psychological), sociocultural, economic, and environmental. There is an extensive literature on the benefits of recreation and tourism (Driver, 1996; Kraus, 1997), and local communities often view rural tourism as an accessible development alternative that can enable them to improve their living standards. Hence, an eco-inn, one element of rural tourism system, must achieve the goal of local benefit as soon as possible.

Direct benefit can be created in various forms, including: employment opportunity provided (occasional part-time or full-time staff for inns), and other services (owned by local people) suggested to tourists, such as special food, and bike renting. In addition, eco-inns and the local communities can develop dependent partnerships. For example, eco-inns can purchase and use materials from local market, advocate new community tourism programs to attract tourists, and establish a united brand of local products for marketing.

In addition to this direct or indirect economic benefit, an eco-inn can serve as a 'mirror' that make local people to see themselves, find self-confident, and feel proud of their traditional lifestyles. They are sociocultural benefits include learning, awareness, appreciation, family bonding, community pride, a firmer sense of ethnic identity, increased understanding and tolerance of others, and stronger cultural identity (Driver, Brown, and Peterson, 1991; Besculides, Lee, and McCormick, 2002).

Some previous research has found additional positive effects of tourism to be cultural exchange, revitalization of local traditions, increased quality of life, and an improved image for the community (Weikert and Kerts-tetter, 1996; Clements, Schultz, and Lime, 1993). Through proper planning and management, tourism has been found to improve the quality of life of the residents as well as to enhance the sense of place (Burr, 1996). With the growing recognition among communities that rural tourism may offer opportunities for sustainable development, there has been an increased awareness among researchers that active local participation in the planning process and in operations management of tourism is essential in order to achieve the goal of local benefit.

4. METHOD

In the past decades, Delphi has been considered a reliable qualitative research method with potential for use in problem solving, decision making, and group consensus reaching in a wide variety of areas (Cochran, 1983; Uhl, 1983). Delbecq, Ven and Gustafson (1975) has been defined Delphi as "a method for systematic solicitation and collection for judgments on a particular topic through a set of carefully designed sequential questionnaires interspersed with summarized information and feedback of opinions derived from earlier responses". In general, Delphi is primarily a communication device, which is applied when the consensus of experts on an uncertain issue, often intangible, is desired (Linstone and Turoff, 1975). The Delphi approach is an iterative forecasting procedure characterized by three important features which are including (Murry and Hammon, 1995; Dickey and Watts, 1978): (1) Anonymous group interaction and responses; (2) Multiple iteration or rounds of questionnaires or other means of data collection with research-controlled statistical group responses and feedback; (3) Presentation of statistical group responses. The Delphi approach offers an additional advantage in situations where it is important to define areas of uncertainty or disagreement among experts. In these instances, Delphi can highlight topics of concern and evaluate uncertainty in a quantitative manner. Group evaluation of belief statements made by panel members is an explicit part of Delphi. Goldstein (1975) points out that, although the group view has a higher probability of being correct than an individual, its success depends principally on the careful selection of the panel and the formulation of questions.

Three rounds of the Delphi questionnaire survey were implemented in this research. In the first round, the Modified Delphi Technique was used to develop the half-open-questionnaire to collect the opinions from experts openly. The half-open-questionnaire was designed according to the eco-inn fundamental principles that proposed by Kuo (2008). Figure 1 shows the candidate indicators system of Eco-inn evaluation in Taiwan and there are 109 candidate indicators in this system. Totally, 26 academic experts and government staff joined the three rounds of the Delphi questionnaire survey. The five Likert scale was used to measure the important of each candidate indicators and the SPSS software was employed to analysis the research results.

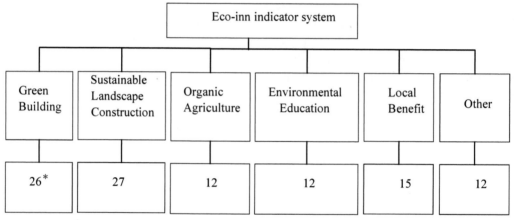

*The number of candidate indicators in different categories

Figure 1. The candidate indicators for the evaluation system of the Eco-inn in Taiwan

5. RESULTS AND DISSCUSSION

In this study, 109 candidate indicators were included in the questionnaire and the Delphi survey was carried out form December 2007 to May 2008. The opinions from the various experts including professors, including professors in tourism, hotel and B&B management, and environment, and the management staff of government. An interval scale is used here with a maximum score of 5 accounting for the indicator as a most important. After three rounds of the Delphi survey, the opinions from the experts have reached stability (less than 15%). The final expert questionnaire survey data are shown in Appendix A, and the mean of all indicators in the questionnaire was 4.3. Those indicators with scores higher than 4.3 and reach stability (less than 15%) were chosen as appropriate indicators for the Eco-inn evaluation according to the experts' suggestions. Finally, 50 of the 109 candidate indicators were selected, and the indicator system for Eco-inn was established, which contains 9 indicators of Green Building, 12 indicators of Sustainable Landscape Construction, 5 indicators of organic agriculture, 8 indicators of Environmental Education, 8 indicators of Local Benefit, and 8 indicators of other dimension. Figure 1 shows the whole indicator system for Eco-inn evaluation in Taiwan.

Six categories of indicators were identified and discussed here. First, the ratio of selected indicators to candidate indicators is 9:27 in "Green Building" category. According the final results, the experts considered the following nine indicators are important. They are indicators of "The innkeeper pulls out the plug of electrical products that the long-term doesn't use," "The innkeeper uses the low-flow and water-saving sanitary equipment," "The innkeeper designs the building that has enough natural light," "The inn uses natural ventilation," "The innkeeper offers the drinking water that meets the legal *standards,*" "The innkeeper implements classification of the solid waste and recycles," "The innkeeper reduces the amount of waste from its source," "The innkeeper recycles kitchen waste properly," and "The innkeeper uses the nonpoisonous natural painting."

Second, the ratio of selected indicators to candidate indicators is 12:26 in "Sustainable Landscape Construction" category. The experts emphasized the importance of the surrounding environment of the inn, and regarded that inadequate landscape construction will impact the environment. Hence, there are twelve indicators selected in this category. They are indicators of "The innkeeper safeguards the health and vitality of soil in plan and construction process," "The innkeeper reserves the land ability to conserve the humidity and storage rain water," "The innkeeper creates a diverse environment for symbiosis living," "The innkeeper increases the area of greening land," "The innkeeper reserves the vacant lot as the green land," "The innkeeper uses the local resources as construction materials," "The innkeeper reuses the recycled resources as construction materials," "The innkeeper avoids using the toxic materials," "The innkeeper doesn't use the chemical herbicides," "The innkeeper uses physics methods instead of chemical insecticides," "The innkeeper incorporates the local culture and landscape into the design of buildings," and "The innkeeper maintains the harmonious between the inn and local landscape."

Third, the ratio of selected indicators to candidate indicators is 5:12 in "Organic Agriculture" category. The development of the eco-inn is based on the organic agriculture. Hence, in this evaluation category, indicators of "The innkeeper purchases the organic food," "The innkeeper provides the food waste for compost to the farmers," "The innkeeper offers consumers the organic diet that is health and hygiene," "The innkeeper offers the market and chance to sale the local organic food," and "The innkeeper takes the LOHAS attitude toward the inn, and keeps respect to the environment and ecosystem" are regarded as important.

Fourth, the ratio of selected indicators to candidate indicators is 8:13 in "Environment Education" category. The important indicators in this category including the following: "The innkeeper participates in the program of environmental education regularly," "The innkeeper shares the notion and practice of the environmental protection with tourists," "The innkeeper provides the tourists full environment information in the public place, guest rooms and websites," "The innkeeper evaluates the attitudes of employees toward environmental protection," "The innkeeper promotes the importance of environmental protection toward the local residents," "The innkeeper provides environmental interpretation to the visitor," "The innkeeper educates visitors to use water resource wise," and "The innkeeper promotes the self-prepared hygiene equipments of tourists."

Fifth, the ratio of selected indicators to candidate indicators is 8:15 in "Local Benefit" category. "Local benefit" is the core principle of the ecotourism development and it is also the fundamental elements of the eco-inns. Hence, indicators of "The innkeeper uses local manufacture products," "The innkeeper employs local manpower," "The innkeeper develops the special local product according to materials that are in season," "The innkeeper provides economic benefits to local people," "The innkeeper holds the activities of environmental protection that with local community," "The innkeeper advocates the action of local resources protecting," "The innkeeper increases the visitor's understanding the local natural environment," and "The innkeeper increases the visitor's understanding the local culture" are regarded as important.

Finally, the ratio of selected indicators to candidate indicators is 8:16 in "Others" category. Some important indicators for eco-inn evaluation can not be categorized into the five major issues are shown in this category. They are the indicators of "The bathroom or other danger places are under full non-slip design," "The innkeeper prepares basic equipment of the medical treatment, for instance, first-aid kit," "The innkeeper pays attention to the sanitation and hygiene of the environment and facility," "The innkeeper uses the fresh food material and avoids the artificial foods," "The innkeeper purchases the reusable tableware," "The innkeeper increases the rate of the customer backflow," "The innkeeper surveys the recreational satisfaction of visitors," and "The innkeeper establishes the connection with the fire and first aid agency."

In addition, the issues of health and safety concerned about inns are also emphasized by the experts in this research; hence, thirteen indicators related to health and safety are selected here. They are "provide the drinking water that meets the legal *standards*", "use the nonpoisonous natural coating", "avoid using the toxic material", "replace the physics method with chemical insecticide", "purchase the organic food", "offer consumers the organic diet that is health, security and hygiene", "holds the activities of green, environmental, protection, security and hygiene that cooperate with community", "use the non-slip design in the bathroom or other easily wet slippery places", "prepares basic equipment of the medical treatment", "pay attention to the sanitation and hygiene of the environment and facility", "use the fresh food material and avoid the artificial foods", "establish the connection with the department of fire and first aid."

6. CONCLUSIONS

The idea of the Eco-inn that is optimal to be linked with ecotourism development is proposed by Kuo (2008). The 'eco-inn' is aimed to develop the 'green' accommodation to minimize the negative impacts from tourism activities in rural areas. The 'eco-' in eco-inn has dual meanings. One is 'ecological' means that the inn has planned and managed on the basis of ecological principles. Another is 'e' and 'co' means that the eco-inn is not only beneficial for 'environment' but also beneficial for local 'community'. It specifies five core principles that, in their interplay, would distinguish an eco-inn from other inn: (1) green building; (2) sustainable landscape construction; (3) organic agriculture; (4) environmental education; and (5) local benefit.

However, no evaluation indicators and related assessment criteria for the Eco-inn are investigated up to now. Hence, the purpose of this study is to explore the indicators that can be used for evaluating the Eco-inn in Taiwan. This evaluation indicator system is based on the findings from literature review, and then the Delphi Method is employed to collect experts' opinions. Finally, 50 of the 109 candidate indicators were selected after three rounds of the Delphi method. After the evaluation system established, it can help management staff to assess the sustainability of the inns in Taiwan and the innkeepers can also to improve their inns according to these indicators to minimize the accommodation impacts.

REFERENCES

Agritourism Association of Taiwan. (2004). The comprehensive survey of agritourism in Taiwan. Agritourism Association of Taiwan, ROC Taipei.

Cai, L. A. (2002). Cooperative branding for rural destinations. *Annals of Tourism Research, 29*, 720-742.

Cochran, S. W. (1983). The Delphi method: Formulating and refining group judgements. *Journal of Human Sciences, 2(2)*, 111-117.

Council of Agriculture (COA) (in Chinese). (2005). *Agritourism Policies in Taiwan,* Council of Agriculture, ROC Taipei.

Delbecq, A. L., Ven, A. H. V. & Gustafson, D. H. (1975). *Group Techniques for Program Planning: a Guide to Nominal Group and Delphi Processes.* Publisher: Glenview, IL.: Scott, Foresman & Company.

Dickey, J. & Watts, T. (1978). *Analytic techniques in urban and regional planning.* New York: McGraw-Hill.

Goldstein, N. (1975). *A Delphi on the future of the steel and ferroalloy industries.* The Delphi Techniques and Applications, 210-26.

Hall, C. M. & McArthur, S. (1996). *Heritage Management in Australia and New Zealand.* Oxford University Press, Melbourne.

Hall, C. M., McVittie, A. & Moran, D. (2004). What does the public want from agriculture and the countryside? A review of evidence and methods. *Journal of Rural Studies, 20*, 211-225.

Kuo, N. W. (2008). Sustainable Rural Tourism Development Based on Agricultural Resources: the Eco-inn initiative in Taiwan. *International Journal of Agricultural Resources, Governance and Ecology, 7(3)*, 229-242.

Lane, B. (2001). Accommodation: the key to rural tourism. in Majewski, J. and Lane, B. (Eds.): *Turystyka Wiejska I Rozwoj Lokalny (Rural Tourism and Local Development),* Fundacja Fundusz Wspólpracy, Poznań, 83-100.

Linstone, H. A. & Turoff, M. (1975). *The Delphi Method: Techniques and Applications.* Addison-Wesley, USA.

Mathieson, A. & Wall, G. (1982). *Tourism: Economic, Physical and Social Impacts,* Longman, Harlow.

Ministry of Interior (MOI). (2003). *Yearbook of the Ministry of Interior*, MOI, ROC Taipei.

Murry, J. W. & Hammons, J. O. (1995). Delphi: A versatile methodology for conducting qualitative research. *The Review of Higher Education, 18(4)*, 423- 436.

Oppermann, M. (1996). Rural tourism in Southern Germany. *Annals of Tourism Research, 23*, 86-102.

Orams, M. B. (1996). Using interpretation to manage nature-based tourism. *Journal of Sustainable Tourism, 4*, 81-95.

Roberts, L. & Hall, D. (2001). *Rural Tourism and Recreation: Principles to Practice*. CABI Publishing, Wallingford.

The International Federation of Organic Agriculture Movements (IFOAM). (2002). *Organic Agriculture and Biodiversity: Making the Links*. Germany, IFOAM.

Tou, W. S. (2005). *The Environmental Problems of Agritourism Development in Ching-Chin Village*. National Policy Foundation Commentary, ROC Taipei.

Tourism Bureau of Taiwan. (2008). *Yearbook of Tourism Information of the Republic of China*. Tourism Bureau of Taiwan, ROC Taipei.

Uhl, N. P. (1983). Using the Delphi technique in Institutional Planning. *New Directions for Institutional Research*, Issue, *37*, 81-94.

Weaver, B. & Fennell, D. (1997). The vacation farm sector in Saskatchewan: a profile of operations. *Tourism Management, 18*, 357-365.

Appendix A

A. Green Building	Score		Selected
	Mean	S.D.	
01. The innkeeper uses the green building materials as much as possible.	4.3	0.53	
02. The inner setting of the inn avoids excessive decoration.	4.2	0.67	
03. The innkeeper uses alternative energy; for instance, the *small* wind or solar energy.	4.0	0.45	
04. The innkeeper selects the air conditioner that wins the environmental label.	4.3	0.53	
05. The innkeeper uses the electric equipment with low noise.	4.2	0.69	
06. The innkeeper adopts the high-efficiency and energy-saving *lamp*.	4.7	0.69	
07. The innkeeper selects the refrigerator that wins the environmental label.	4.3	0.74	
08. The innkeeper pulls out the plug of electrical products that the long-term doesn't use.	4.4	0.81	O
09. The innkeeper uses the water-saving equipment; for instance, water-saving tap.	4.6	0.86	
10. The innkeeper uses the low-flow and water-saving sanitary equipment.	4.4	0.75	O
11. The innkeeper uses the monitoring system for water consumption	3.8	0.61	
12. The innkeeper uses the water recycling system.	4.2	0.49	
13. The innkeeper sets the monitoring system for water for *water* supply.	4.1	0.43	
14. The innkeeper provides shower to replace the bath in a tub.	4.0	0.53	
15. The innkeeper designs the building that has enough natural light.	4.7	0.47	O
16. The innkeeper reduces the usage of light in the night.	4.0	0.49	
17. The inn uses natural ventilation.	4.6	0.58	O
18. The innkeeper decreases using synthetic aromatic chemicals.	4.1	0.71	
19. The innkeeper offers the drinking water that meets the legal *standards.*	4.8	0.40	O
20. The innkeeper implements classification of the solid waste and recycles.	4.9	0.33	O
21. The innkeeper reduces the amount of waste from its source.	4.8	0.43	O
22. The innkeeper recycles kitchen waste properly.	4.7	0.47	O
23. The innkeeper uses the nonpoisonous natural painting.	4.8	0.40	O
24. The nose level of daytime doesn't exceed the control standards.	4.0	0.60	
25. The nose level of nighttime doesn't exceed the control standards.	4.3	0.55	
26. The innkeeper uses the sweep products that have the environmental label.	4.3	0.55	
27. The innkeeper provides the choice that doesn't change bed sheet and towel every day for the long-stay visitors.	4.3	0.55	

B. Sustainable Landscape Construction	Score		Selected
	Mean	S.D.	
01. The innkeeper considers the soil characteristics comprehensively.	4.3	0.45	
02. The innkeeper safeguards the health and vitality of soil in plan and construction process.	4.7	0.49	O
03. The innkeeper uses the appropriate technique to recovery the land fertility.	4.2	0.65	
04. The innkeeper reserves the land ability to conserve the humidity and storage rain water.	4.4	0.58	O
05. The innkeeper creates a small-scale ecological pond.	3.8	0.71	
06. The innkeeper decreases using the waterproof pavement.	4.2	0.51	
07. The innkeeper avoids using the *water*-consuming artificial greensward.	4.3	0.47	
08. The innkeeper creates a diverse environment for symbiosis living.	4.4	0.57	O
09. The innkeeper increases the area of greening land.	4.6	0.50	O
10. The innkeeper reserves the vacant lot as the green land.	4.6	0.50	O
11. The innkeeper increases the diversity of *plant*ing.	4.3	0.80	
12. The innkeeper assess the life cycle of construction materials.	4.1	0.43	
13. The innkeeper uses the local resources as construction materials.	4.4	0.50	O
14. The innkeeper reuses the recycled resources as construction materials.	4.4	0.50	O
15. The innkeeper avoids using the toxic materials.	4.8	0.51	O
16. The innkeeper doesn't use the chemical herbicides.	4.7	0.56	O
17. The innkeeper uses physics methods instead of chemical insecticides.	4.5	0.65	O
18. The innkeeper uses the organic fertilizer for horticultural work.	4.2	0.59	
19. The innkeeper uses the native plant species.	4.2	0.69	
20. The innkeeper pays attention to the efficiency of outdoor lamps.	4.2	0.63	
21. The innkeeper reduces outdoor lighting at night.	4.0	0.66	
22. The innkeeper incorporates the local culture and landscape into the design of buildings.	4.6	0.57	O
23. The innkeeper maintains the harmonious between the inn and local landscape.	4.7	0.45	O
24. The innkeeper reduces the artificial furniture.	4.2	0.65	
25. The innkeeper avoids the *electric* line to reduce the pollution of sky line.	3.9	0.82	
26. The innkeeper avoids burning in open space.	4.7	0.56	
C. Organic Agriculture	Score		Selected
	Mean	S.D.	
01. The innkeeper help local farmer to promote organic agriculture.	3.8	0.49	
02. The innkeeper help farmer to obtain an organic identification.	3.8	0.49	
03. The innkeeper implements the organic agriculture in the own farmland.	4.0	0.34	
04. The innkeeper offers the curriculum of the organic farming experience.	3.9	0.48	
05. The innkeeper contracts with farmer for the purchase of electronic instruments Sign with peasant and eat the cooperative agreement that the organic food.	4.0	0.53	
06. The innkeeper purchases the organic food.	4.2	0.40	O
07. The innkeeper provides the food waste compost for the farmers.	4.2	0.43	O
08. The innkeeper offers consumers the organic diet that is health, security and hygiene.	4.5	0.51	O
09. The innkeeper offers the market and chance to sale the local organic food.	4.3	0.45	O
10. The innkeeper sells the organic product in the B&B.	3.8	0.59	

Appendix A. Continued

C. Organic Agriculture	Score		Selected
	Mean	S.D.	
11. The innkeeper develops souvenirs related to organic agriculture.	4.3	0.68	
12. The innkeeper takes the LOHAS attitude toward the B&B, and keeps a respect to the environment and ecosystem.	4.7	0.56	O
D. Environmental education	Score		Selected
	Mean	S.D.	
01. The innkeeper participates in the program of environmental education regularly.	4.4	0.57	O
02. The innkeeper shares the notion and practice of the environmental protection with tourists.	4.3	0.45	O
03. The innkeeper provides the tourists with the green information in the public place, guest room and website.	4.2	0.43	O
04. The innkeeper evaluates the degree that the employee protects resource.	4.0	0.53	
05. The innkeeper evaluates the importance that the employees understood environmental protection.	4.2	0.51	O
06. The innkeeper promotes the importance of environmental protection toward the local residents.	4.2	0.46	O
07. The innkeeper provides the visitor with the narration of the local ecological environment.	4.4	0.50	O
08. The innkeeper educates visitors to use the water resource rationally.	4.2	0.49	O
09. The innkeeper helps the local to hold the activity of environmental education.	4.1	0.48	
10. The innkeeper helps the local school to hold the activity of environmental education for children.	3.9	0.65	
11. The innkeeper offers the discounts of room price to green tourists.	4.0	0.60	
12. The innkeeper rents the bicycles out to tourists.	4.1	0.56	
13. The innkeeper promotes the notion of self-provided hygiene and toiletries to tourists.	4.3	0.72	O
E. Local Benefit	Score		Selected
	Mean	S.D.	
01. The innkeeper uses local manufactures.	4.5	0.58	O
02. The innkeeper employs local manpower.	4.4	0.58	O
03. The innkeeper develops the special local product according to materials that are in season.	4.3	0.56	O
04. The innkeeper provides the residents with the substantial opportunity to benefit.	4.3	0.55	O
05. The innkeeper and local stores becomes the strategic partner.	4.3	0.49	
06. The innkeeper holds the activities of green, environmental, protection, security and hygiene that cooperate with community.	4.3	0.49	O
07. The innkeeper's participation degree of the community public affairs.	4.1	0.69	
08. The innkeeper's contribution degree of the quality of the life and community's environmental protection.	4.0	0.60	
09. The innkeeper provides the recreational experience activity that combines with local culture.	4.2	0.71	
10. The innkeeper adopts the action of protecting to local resources.	4.5	0.65	O
11. The innkeeper increases the visitor's understanding to the local natural environment.	4.3	0.75	O

E. Local Benefit	Score		Selected
	Mean	S.D.	
12. The innkeeper increases the visitor's understanding to local history.	4.2	0.94	
13. The innkeeper increases the visitor's understanding to local culture.	4.3	0.74	O
14. The innkeeper reminds the visitors to respects local residents and reduces the interference.	4.7	0.68	
15. The innkeeper takes the initiative in marketing community.	4.1	0.59	
F. Other	Score		Selected
	Mean	S.D.	
01. The innkeeper plans the action to improve the environmental problems.	4.0	0.53	
02. The bathroom or other easily wet slippery places are non-slip design.	4.6	0.64	O
03. The innkeeper prepares basic equipment of the medical treatment, for instance, first-aid kit.	4.8	0.51	O
04. The innkeeper pays attention to the sanitation and hygiene of the environment and facility.	4.8	0.40	O
05. The innkeeper uses the fresh food material and avoids the artificial foods.	4.6	0.50	O
06. The innkeeper purchases the reusable tableware.	4.7	0.55	O
07. The innkeeper purchases the recycled paper products.	4.3	0.55	
08. The innkeeper has priority to buy the products of the green packaging.	4.2	0.61	
09. The innkeeper increases the rate of the customer backflow.	4.7	0.45	O
10. The innkeeper establishes the database of each tourist characteristics.	4.6	0.64	
11. The innkeeper sets the website in order to obtain the customer's commons.	4.8	0.49	
12. The innkeeper surveys the recreational satisfaction.	4.8	0.37	O
13. The innkeeper increases the contact ways to communicate the nearby medical units.	4.3	0.63	
14. The innkeeper establishes the connection with the fire and first aid department.	4.6	0.50	O
15. The innkeeper and staff should participate in the first aid training.	4.8	0.43	
16. The innkeeper chooses the low environmental impact of furniture, for instance, the low volatility and organic material of sofa and mattress.	4.2	0.54	

In: Ecotourism: Management, Development and Impact   ISBN: 978-1-60876-724-3
Editors: A. Krause, E. Weir, pp. 199-211   © 2010 Nova Science Publishers, Inc.

Chapter 8

INFANT MORTALITY AND STRESS INDICATORS LINKED TO TOURISM MANAGEMENT OF TIBETAN MACAQUES

C.M. Berman[1] and M.D. Matheson[2]

[1]Department of Anthropology and Graduate Program in Evolution, Ecology and Behavior, University at Buffalo, Buffalo, NY 14261
[2]Department of Psychology, Central Washington University, Ellensburg, WA 98926

ABSTRACT

Here we summarize research on the impact of tourism management on a population of wild Tibetan macaques. We compared long term data on infant mortality and adult aggression rates before, during and after a single group was used for tourism, and investigated short term effects of tourist presence and behavior on the behavior of the monkeys in the same social group and in an additional group. Long term results strongly suggest causal links between infant loss and management for tourism, and raise the hypothesis that artificial range restriction jeopardized infants by raising levels of aggression in the provisioning area. Infant mortality was significantly higher in the 11 years of tourist management than in the 6 preceding years, but was similar before and after management. Although few infanticides were witnessed, many infant corpses were found with wounds, and serious attacks on infants by adults were observed following outbreaks of aggression among adults in the provisioning area. Yearly rates of infant mortality were positively correlated with adult aggression rates in the provisioning area, and both factors were strongly associated with the degree to which the group's range was artificially restricted. Analysis of immediate responses of monkeys suggested multiple ways in which tourist behavior may cause monkeys stress and aggression in the provisioning area. Threat rates increased when tourist noise levels were high and when tourists directed behavior towards the monkeys, especially when tourists pointed or slapped the rail. Increases in tourist density were associated with increases in self-directed behavior by the monkeys, a behavioral index of stress. Collectively these results suggest that tourism leads to high levels of stress, aggression and infant loss at this site. We offer several recommendations to minimize harmful effects and help ensure that natural behavioral patterns are fostered.

INTRODUCTION

Conservationists now generally recognize that wildlife tourism can pose serious risks of disease transmission [Adams et al., 2001; Köndgen et al., 2008; Wallis & Lee, 1999; Woodford et al., 2002]. However, many are less familiar with evidence that tourism can also pose serious risks to the behavioral health of targeted species. Recently, several reports have appeared about tourism-related changes in habitat use and activity patterns [De la Torre et al., 2000; Dellatorre in press; Goldsmith et al., 2006; Griffiths & van Schaik, 1993; Kauffman, in press; Kinnard & O'Brien, 1996; Koganezawa & Imaki, 1999; Leary & Fa, 1993: Treves & Brandon, 2005], communication [de la Torre et al., 1999; Johns, 1996] and social interaction [de la Torre et al., 2000]. These changes could potentially endanger health and decrease population fitness through their effects on foraging, hunting, predator avoidance and social stability. But so far there is little systematic research into the precise ways in which tourism translates into behavioral risk. This short communication attempts to begin to fill that gap by summarizing the results of two research groups both working on the same population of Tibetan macaque monkeys (*Macaca thibetana huangshanensis*) at Huangshan, China. One research team, composed of Carol Berman, Jinhua Li, Hideshi Ogawa, Consuel Ionica and Huabao Yin (Berman's Research Group), analyzed long term data on infant mortality from a single social group, comparing mortality rates 6 years before tourism, 11 years during tourism, and one year after tourism was temporarily suspended. Their results [Berman et al., 2007] strongly suggest that tourism placed infants at increased risk of wounding, and they implicate one aspect of management, range restriction, as particularly harmful. The second research team, composed of Megan Matheson, Lori Sheeran, Jinhua Li, Steve Wagner and students of the Joint Central Washington University-Anhui University Biodiversity and Primate Field Research Program (Matheson's Research Group), examined the immediate behavioral responses of monkeys to tourists and tourism practices. They found troubling links between particular tourist behaviors, monkey aggression and behavioral stress indicators [Jones et al., 2008; Mack et al., 2008; Matheson et al., 2006, 2007; McCarthy et al., 2007; Ruesto, 2007; Yenter et al., 2008].

SPECIES, STUDY SITE, GROUP AND MANAGEMENT HISTORY

Tibetan macaques live in small isolated populations in sub-tropical, montane forests consisting of mixed deciduous and broadleaf evergreen trees across central China and parts of India. The IUCN Red list classifies the species as being of lower risk/conservation dependent [IUCN, 2007]. Like most macaques, they live in permanent social groups with several adult males and females and their young. They show female philopatry, male dispersal and linear dominance hierarchies [Berman et al., 2004; Deng & Zhao, 1987; Li & Wang, 1996; Li et al., 1996b; Zhao, 1996]. Reproduction is seasonal with overlapping birth seasons (January to August [Yin et al., 2004]) and mating seasons (July to January [Li et al., 2005]). We studied the population living at Huangshan (118.2E, 30.2N, elevation 1841 m), a well-known scenic area in east-central China about 1045 km south of Beijing. Millions of tourists come each year primarily for the scenery and secondarily to view the monkeys. The monkeys live in the middle elevations of the mountain range where they are protected from hunting and trapping.

Researchers began to observe our main study group (YA1) in 1986, six years before tourist management began. To facilitate observations, they provisioned the group with corn in an open area (142 m^2) by a stream. They recorded behavior using all occurrences and focal-animal sampling methods [Altmann, 1974] in the provisioning area and in the surrounding forest [Li, 1999; Ogawa, 2006]. This continued until 1992, when the local government translocated the group to an area adjacent to their natural range in preparation for tourism [Berman et al., 2002]. Observation and provisioning continued as before in a new open area (144 m^2) that was also by a stream and was virtually the same size as the previous provisioning site. At first the group frequently attempted to return to its original range, but the staff prevented this by physically herding them back when they strayed. In so doing, they reduced the group's range from about 7.75 km^2 to less than 3 km^2.

Within 2 years, a viewing pavilion had been constructed and tourism began. Tourists climbed a stairway up a hill to the open pavilion and observed the monkeys in the provisioning area for 30-45 minutes at a time, usually at 3-4 set times of day. A mean of about 20 tourists and 2-6 staff were present at each feeding. Rules prohibited tourists from feeding, shouting and contacting the monkeys directly, but they were unevenly enforced. The monkeys often threatened tourists and staff, and adult males occasionally jumped into the pavilion to attack them. The staff sometimes responded by throwing stones at the adult males. To assure that the monkeys would show up at feeding time, the staff continued to restrict their range by herding, and in fact did so more consistently than they had before tourism began, but provisioning and data collection continued much as before. This pattern of management continued for 9 years, until 2002, when a new director further restricted the group's range to only 1 square km immediately surrounding the provisioning area in order to make the group continuously available to tourists. In early 2003 operations were suspended due to the SARS epidemic. They resumed later in the year, when they also began using a second monkey group for tourism. Thus between 1986 and 2004, range restriction occurred at 4 levels—none before 1991 and during the suspension of management in 2003, inconsistent during 1992, 1993 and 2004, consistent from 1994 to 2001, and severe in 2002. Between 1994 and 2004, the numbers of tourists varied from 8,915 to 43,881 per year (mean $\pm$ SD= 24,760 $\pm$ 10,861).

The second study group, named Yulingkeng A2 (YA2), resulted from a fissioning of YA1 in 1996. Active management of this group for tourism began in 2002. As with YA1, a wooden pavilion was built within YA2's range. Tourists climbed a stairway to the pavilion, where they observed park staff provision the monkeys with corn at four set times per day. Between feeding times, staff followed the group and herded it by yelling and throwing stones when it strayed too far from the provisioning site, and when it did not respond to loud calls given by staff in the provisioning area to announce the start of provisioning.

BERMAN'S RESEARCH GROUP

Soon after the main study group (YA1) was translocated in 1992, researchers noticed two major changes. First, they had the impression that rates of aggression increased. Also, for the first time, they observed severe attacks on infants by adults, and infant corpses with bite wounds. Based on these observations, Berman et al., [2007] examined the general hypothesis that management for tourism was associated with high rates of aggression among adults and infant mortality, and then tested several nonexclusive hypotheses aimed at identifying specific aspects of management that may have been most harmful to infants. See Berman et al. [2007] for details of group composition, management, data collection and analysis.

Figure 1 shows the percentage of infants that died before 1 year of age from 1986 to 2003. Infant mortality was very low in the six years before management began, except in 1988, when a disease killed many group members in a single week [Li, 1999; Wada & Xiong, 1996]. Infant mortality began to increase in 1992, the year the group came under tourism management. Although mortality varied considerably during the period of management from 1992 to 2002, there were two peaks—one in 1994 when tourism and consistent range restriction began and one in 2002 when the group's range was more severely restricted. Mortality fell in 2003 after tourism management was suspended. When we compared infant mortality for individual infants born before (1986-91), during (1992-2002, 2004) and after management (2003), the differences were statistically significant (logistic regression model χ^2 = 17.0, df=2, P < .001). Rates of mortality were significantly higher during management than before it (during: 53/97=54.6%; before: 4/27=14.8%; β =-1.9, Exp (β)=.14, Wald=11.2, df=1, p=0.001), but they were similar before and after (before: 4/27=14.8%; after: 1/6=16.7%).

Many of the infants that died during management were severely injured shortly before their deaths. Overall, there were 24 infant deaths of which 15 (or 62.5%) were due to wounding. This is in contrast to the pre-management period when no infant deaths were attributed to wounding. We directly observed only a few lethal attacks on infants, but we have no reason to believe that any of the wounds were caused by humans, predation or inter-group aggression. In most cases, infants appeared with wounds after an outbreak of aggression between adults in the provisioning area. Typically, the fight moved into the forest where visibility was limited. After the fight died down, the mother carried the injured or dead infant back into the provisioning area. Thus, we could not be sure about the details of all the fights, such as which individuals attacked or defended infants, or whether infants were targets vs. innocent bystanders. Nevertheless, there was a clear contextual link between adult aggression in the provisioning area and subsequent infant mortality.

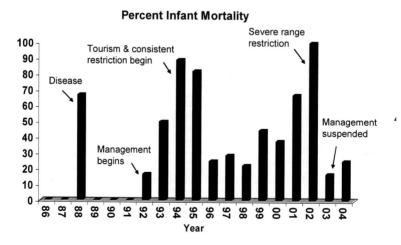

Figure 1. The percentage of infants that died before 1 year of age each year from 1986 to 2004 in the main study group (YA1) of Macaca thibetana. From Berman et al. (2007) with permission.

Rates of Aggression

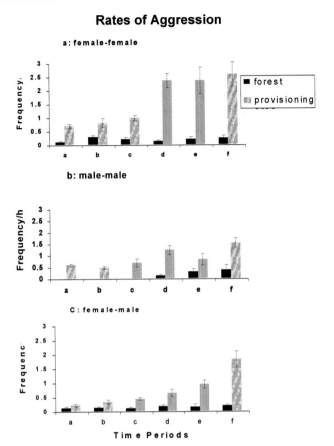

Figure 2. Mean +/- SE rates of aggressive interaction between different sex partner combinations of adults (female-female, male-male and female-male) in the forest and in the provisioning area during 6 time periods: a=immediately before translocation (no tourism or range restriction); b=immediately after translocation (no tourism, inconsistent range restriction); c=7 months after translocation (no tourism, inconsistent range restriction); d=8 years after translocation (tourism and range restriction well established); e=9 years after translocation (tourism and range restriction well established; f=10 years after translocation (tourism well established, range restriction severe). See Berman et al. (2007) for exact dates and other details. From Berman et al. (2007) with permission.

Quantitative data on aggression also pointed to a link between adult aggression in the provisioning area and infant mortality. We were able to examine aggression data for adults for 6 time periods: immediately preceding the group's relocation, immediately following the relocation, 7 months after relocation, during the fall and winter of 2000, the spring of 2001 and the spring and summer of 2002. Within each period, we used virtually identical data collection methods, and dominance relationships among adults were stable. Aggression rates in the provisioning area (mean $\pm$ SE=3.22/hour $\pm$ 0.73) varied significantly across the six time periods (F=7.20, df=5,119, $p<0.001$) (Figure 2) and correlated positively with yearly infant mortality rates (r_s=0.90, n=5 years, p=0.037) (Figure 3). They were significantly lower during the first three time periods (before translocation and in the early period of management when tourists were absent and range restriction was inconsistent) than during the second three time periods (when tourism and consistent range restriction were in full force), and significantly higher during 2002 (the year that the group's range was severely restricted) than in any other time period. In contrast, mean rates of aggression in the forest were generally low (mean $\pm$ SE=0.33/hour $\pm$ 0.03), similar across all six time periods (F=0.55, df=5, 56, ns) and unrelated to infant mortality rates (r_s=0.70, n=5 years, p=0.19).

Given the contextual and statistical links between infant mortality and adult aggression in the provisioning area, we next attempted to narrow down aspects of management that may have been responsible. We examined possible direct effects of management: numbers of tourists and the degree of range restriction. We did not directly examine provisioning, because provisioning was done consistently each year both before and during the management period. Thus it could not be the sole cause of increases in infant mortality. We also examined demographic variables (group size, numbers of adults, adult male:female sex ratios, and whether or not the group fissioned in a given year), reasoning that management might affect aggression and infant mortality indirectly through its effects on group composition. Finally, we tested a prediction based on the sexual selection theory of infanticide [Hausfater & Hrdy, 1984]. This theory posits that under certain circumstances, new alpha males might benefit reproductively from infanticide. To do this we asked whether infant mortality was greater in years in which there was a change in the alpha male position than in years in which there was no change.

The only strong relationship found for infant mortality was with degree of range restriction. Infant mortality rates were higher in years with higher degrees of range restriction (F=6.0, df=3,15, n= 19 years, p<0.007). Indeed range restriction accounted for 54.5% of the variance in infant mortality rates. Mean rates of total adult aggression in the provisioning area were also significantly and positively related to degree of range restriction (F=888.6, df=3,4, n= 5 years, R^2=100%, p<0.025) in spite of the small sample of years for which we had aggression data (Figure 4).

These results strongly suggest that range restriction jeopardized infants by raising levels of aggression in the provisioning area. We hypothesize that range restriction may have done this in at least two ways: First, range restriction may have increased dependence on and aggressive competition over clumped sources of provisioned food. Second, the way range restriction was done (by herding) may have been highly stressful, leading to increased aggression.

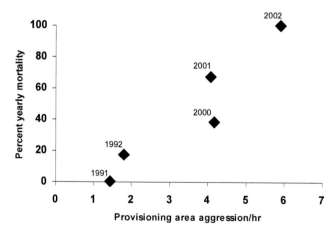

Figure 3. Total adult-adult aggression in the provisioning area: mean rates per year by percentage of infant mortality. From Berman et al. (2007) with permission.

Degree of range restriction

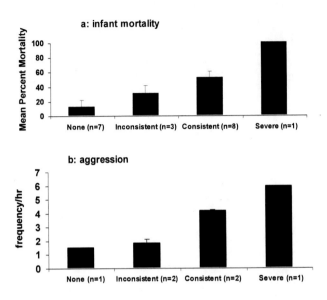

Figure 4. Mean +/- SE a) percentage of infant mortality and b) rate of adult-adult aggression by degree of range restriction. See text for definitions for each degree of range restriction. N= number of years. From Berman et al. (2007) with permission.

MATHESON'S RESEARCH GROUP

Matheson's research group examined both the original (YA1) and the second social group (YA2) of monkeys from 2004-2008, recording moment to moment behavioral responses of individual monkeys to tourists as a function of the levels of noise they made and of the tourists' behavior toward the monkeys [Jones et al., 2008; Mack et al., 2008; Matheson et al., 2006; McCarthy et al., 2007; Ruesto, 2007]. In addition to recording monkey aggression, they recorded how often the monkeys showed self-directed behaviors (SDBs), including self-scratching, self-grooming, body shaking and yawning Matheson et al., 2007; Yenter et al., 2008]. These SDBs have been shown to be reliable correlates of stress hormone levels in a variety of primates and contexts [Maestripieri et al., 1992]. Details about group composition, data collection and analysis are in Jones et al. [2008], Mack et al. [2008], Matheson et al. [2006, 2007], McCarthy et al. [2007], Ruesto [2007] and Yenter et al. [2008].

Several results support the hypothesis that tourism was associated with increased levels of stress in the monkeys. For example, self-grooming rates were positively related to tourist density across all subjects in YA1 ($r=0.353$, $df=33$, $p=.04$) (Figure 5) as well as among adult males specifically ($r=0.345$, $df=33$, $p=.04$) [Mack et al., 2008]. In addition, the rate of SDBs in general appeared to vary by the location of the monkeys relative to the tourists. There was no significant correlation between tourist densities and total frequencies of SDBs in YA1 subjects when location was not taken into consideration. However, there was a significant correlation specific to monkeys in the only quadrat (quadrat #1) of the provisioning area in which monkeys were surrounded on two sides rather than one side by human observers ($r=0.378$, $df = 69$,

$p<.01$) (Figure 6). There was also a significant correlation between tourist densities and SDB frequencies for monkeys in another quadrat of the provisioning area that was close to the pavilion, but only among those monkeys who spent above-median amounts of time in that quadrat ($r=.388$, $df=27$, $p<.05$). Taken together, these results, along with the finding that YA1 monkeys spend less time in both near quadrats 1 and 2 than in the three more distant quadrats (Wilcoxon $T=0$, $n=8$, $p=.01$) [Yenter et al., 2008], suggest that humans have the potential to induce stress in the monkeys, but that monkeys that are either more susceptible to stress or more stressed on a given day may simply avoid the human-proximate areas.

In general, threat behavior was not associated with tourist density per se. However, threat behavior was associated with particular human behaviors. Rates of threats directed to monkeys and to humans per observation period were significantly correlated with both total numbers of behaviors directed by humans towards monkeys ($r = .391$, $df= 38$, $p = .014$) (Figure 7) and with decibel levels on the observation platform ($r = .334$, $df = 38$, $p = .038$) (Figure 8) [Ruesto, 2007]. Thus, both the behavior of the humans and the noise generated by them may negatively affect monkeys. Human behavior directed at monkeys also seemed to prolong negative interaction, as behavioral sequences involving both human and macaque behaviors consisted of significantly more behaviors than tourist-only and macaque-only sequences (M=9.56 behaviors vs. 4.75 and 4.89, respectively; $F(2, 484)=13.24$, $p<.001$) [McCarthy et al., 2009]. Humans, and particularly keepers who sometimes threw rocks and other objects at the monkeys, were the most frequent targets of monkey threats in both groups [Jones et al., 2008]. The most common human behavior was pointing (44.97% of 1503 human behaviors recorded), followed by "mouth noise" (16.76%), waving (16.03%), and throwing food (10.18%). The monkeys responded with threats most consistently when humans pointed to them or slapped the rail to get their attention [McCarthy et al., 2007].

Self-grooming and Tourist Density

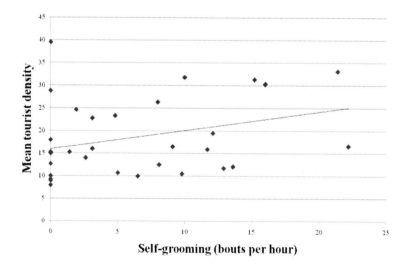

Figure 5. Rates of self-grooming in provisioning area as a function of the mean number of tourists on viewing platforms.

SDBs and Tourist Density in Quadrat 1

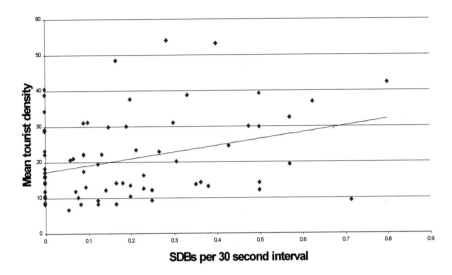

Figure 6. Rates of self-directed behavior by monkeys while in Quadrat 1 as a function of the mean number of tourists on the viewing platforms.

Macaque Threats vs. Tourist Behaviors Directed Toward Macaques

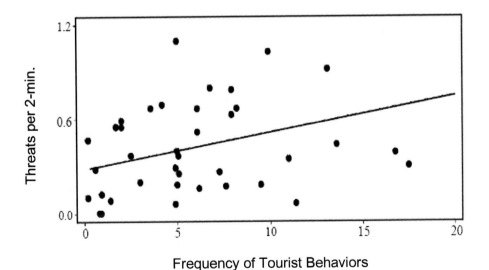

Figure 7. Frequency of threats given by monkeys as a function of the frequency of tourist behaviors directed at monkeys.

Macaque Threats vs. Decibel Levels

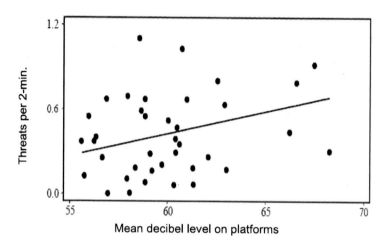

Figure 8. Frequency of threats given by monkeys as a function of mean decibel levels on the tourist viewing platform.

CONCLUSION

The approaches of our two research teams were complimentary and our results were largely congruent, providing a broad critique of the negative effects of tourism on the behavior and mortality of Tibetan macaques at Huangshan [Berman et al., in press]. First, tourism was strongly associated with high rates of infant mortality. Infant mortality was significantly higher during tourism management than either before or after. Second, most infant deaths were from wounds, and appeared to be byproducts of high levels of aggression among adults within the provisioning area. Third, range restriction was strongly associated with both high infant mortality and aggression by adults. We hypothesize that range restriction, which was done by herding, may lead to aggression by increasing competition for food or by raising levels of fear-induced stress. These effects may be particularly intense when tourists are allowed to throw highly palatable foods, such as candy, to the monkeys. Third, while aggression is not directly related to the density of humans present either immediately or over the long term, there is evidence that specific human behaviors do indeed provoke aggression in the monkeys. Monkeys frequently respond to herding, human noise, pointing, rail-slapping and rock-showing with threats directed to the offending humans, and sometimes with lunges and physical attacks. Notably, they direct the most threats at keepers some of whom behave antagonistically toward them. Finally, there is also evidence that human density alone is associated with increases in stress indicators such as self-scratching, self-grooming and body shaking.

Clearly, high infant mortality is unsustainable and counterproductive to the long term success of both tourism and the population. Given this risk and the negative effects of specific human behaviors on the monkeys, we suggest that management adopt stricter rules regarding human behavior and enforce them more consistently. In particular, herding and other interaction with the monkeys by tourists, staff and observers should be vigorously discouraged. Specifically, our recommendation are: 1) an immediate end to artificial range restriction; 2) the institution of a management policy that does not guarantee that tourists will see the monkeys on any given day; 3) a stronger emphasis on education of tourists about the value of wildlife conservation, the behavior and ecology of Tibetan macaques, and on the need for appropriate behavior on their parts before they enter the viewing pavilion; 4) a prohibition on the sale, showing or eating of food by humans on the staircases or in the viewing pavilions; 5) a requirement that keepers escort groups of tourists to the platforms, to avoid potentially aggressive interactions between monkeys and humans on the stairs leading to the platforms; 6) the construction of barriers (e.g., chain-link) between tourists and monkeys in the viewing pavilion to limit interaction and the transmission of disease (particularly given that monkeys are frequently seen with used tissue or water bottles that tourists have dropped in the monkey areas); 7) the use of monkey-proof trash containers along the staircases and in the pavilions; 8) education of keepers and observers about both appropriate methods to control monkey behavior and to prevent provoking stress as well as about behavior that humans should not use under any circumstances; 9) education of keepers about the problems associated with hostile behavior, particularly when it is unprovoked; 10) the institution of rewards for keepers who behave appropriately toward monkeys and enforce rules for appropriate behavior by tourists; 11) continued research and monitoring of both long term and immediate effects of tourist management practices on the behavior and ecology of macaques; and 12) the formation of an advisory committee, composed of experts in conservation, primate behavior, wildlife management and ecology as well as park managers and representatives of the local community, to review and approve management practices periodically. We are optimistic that with these measures, a valuable natural resource could be put back on track to achieve its original goals of conservation, education and recreation, while also providing a source of local income.

REFERENCES

Adams, H. R., Sleeman, J., Rwego, I. & New J. C. (2001). Self-reported medical history survey of humans as a measure of health risk to chimpanzees (Pan troglodytes schweinfurthii) of Kibale National Park, *Uganda. Oryx, 35*, 308-312.

Altmann, J. (1974). Observational study of behavior: Sampling methods. *Behaviour, 49,* 227-266.

Berman, C. M., Ionica, C. S. & Li, J. H. (2004). Dominance style among Macaca thibetana on Mt. Huangshan, China. *Int. J. Primatol., 25,* 1283-1312.

Berman, C. M. & Li, J. H. (2002). The impact of translocation, provisioning and range restriction on a group of Macaca thibetana. *Int. J. Primatol., 23,* 383-397.

Berman, C. M., Li, J. H., Ogawa, H., Ionica, C. & Yin, H. (2007). Primate tourism, range restriction and infant risk among Macaca thibetana at Mt. Huangshan, China. Int. *J. Primatol., 28,* 1123-1141.

C. M. Berman, C. M., Matheson, M. D., Li, J. H., Ogawa, H. & Ionica, C. S. (in press). Tourism, stress indicators and infant risk among Tibetan macaques at Huangshan, China.

In Russon, A. E. & Wallis, J. (eds.), Primate-Focused Tourism (pp. xx-xx). Norman, OK: American Society of Primatologists.

De la Torre, S., Snowdon, C. T. & Bejarano, M. (1999). Preliminary study of the effects of ecotourism and human traffic on the howling behavior of red howler monkeys, Alouatta seniculus, in Ecuadorian Amazonia. *Neotropical Primates, 7*, 84-86.

De la Torre, S., Snowdon, C. T. & Bejarano, M. (2000). Effects of human activities on wild pgymy marmosets in Ecuadorian Amazonia. *Biol. Conservation, 94*, 153-163.

Dellatore, D. (in press). Behavioural Health of Reintroduced Orangutans (Pongo abelii) in Bukit Lawang, North Sumatra, Indonesia. In Russon, A. E. & Wallis, J. (eds.), *Primate-Focused Tourism* (pp. xx-xx). Norman, OK: American Society of Primatologists.

Deng, Z. Y. & Zhao, Q. K. (1987). Social structure in a wild group of Macaca thibetana at Mount Emei, China. *Folia Primatol., 49*, 1-10.

Goldsmith, M. L., Glick, J. & Ngabirano, E. (2006). Gorillas living on the edge: literally and figuratively. In Newton-Fisher, N.E., Notman, H., Paterson, J. D. & Reynolds V. (eds.), *Primates of Western Uganda* (pp. 405-422). New York: Springer.

Griffiths, M. & van Schaik, C. P. (1993). The impact of human traffic on the abundance and activity periods of Sumatran rain forest wildlife. *Conservation Biol., 7*, 623-626.

IUCN (2007). 2007 IUCN Redlist of Threatened Species. http://www.redlist.org.

Johns, B. G. (1996). Responses of chimpanzees to habituation and tourism in the Kibale forest, Uganda. *Biol. Conservation, 78*, 257-262.

Jones, A. M., Matheson, M. D., Sheeran, L. K., Li, J. & Wagner, R. S. (2008). Aggression and habituation toward humans in two troops of Tibetan macaques (Macaca thibetana) at Mt. Huangshan, China. *Am .J. Primatol., 70 (Suppl. 1)*, 61.

Kauffman, L. (in press). Interactions between tourists and white-faced monkeys (*Cebus capucinus*) at Manuel Antonio National Park, Quepos, Costa Rica. In Russon, A. E. & Wallis, J. (eds.), *Primate-Focused Tourism* , (pp. xx-xx). Norman, OK: American Society of Primatologists.

Kinnaird, M. F. & O'Brien, T.G. (1996). Ecotourism in the Tangkoko DuaSudara Nature Reserve: opening Pandora's box? *Oryx, 30*, 65-73.

Koganezawa, M. & Imaki, H. (1999). The effects of food sources on Japanese monkey home range size and location, and population dynamics. *Primates, 40*, 177-185.

Köndgen, S., Kuhl, H., N'Goran, P. K., Walsh, P. D., Schenk, S., Ernst, N., Biek, R., Formenty, P., Matz-Rensing, K., Schweiger, B., Junglen, S., Ellerbrok, H., Nitsche, A., Briese, T., Lipkin, W. I., Pauli, G., Boesch, C. & Leendertz, F. H. (2008). Pandemic human viruses cause decline of endangered great apes. *Current Biology, 18*, 260-264.

Leary, H. O. & Fa, J. E. (1993). Effects of tourists on Barbary macaques at Gibraltar. *Folia Primatol., 61*, 77-91.

Li, J. (1999). The Tibetan Macaque Society: a Field Study. Hefei: Anhui University Press.

Li, J. & Wang Q. (1996). Dominance hierarchy and its chronic changes in adult male Tibetan macaques (Macaca thibetana). *Acta Zool. Sinica, 42*, 330-334.

Li, J., Wang, Q. & Li, M. (1996b). Migration of male Tibetan macaques (Macaca thibetana) at Mt. Huangshan, Anhui Province, China. *Acta Theriol. Sinica, 16*, 1-6.

Li, J., Yin, H. & Wang, Q. (2005). Seasonality of reproduction and sexual activity in female Tibetan macaques Macaca thibetana at Huangshan, China. *Acta Zool. Sinica, 51*, 365-375.

Mack, H., Matheson, M. D., Sheeran, L. K., Li, J. & Wagner, R. S. (2008). Grooming behavior of Tibetan macaques (Macaca thibetana) in the presence of tourists at Mt. Huangshan, China. *Am .J. Primatol., 70 (Suppl. 1)*, 59.

Maestripieri, D., Schino, G., Aureli, F. & Troisi, A. (1992). A modest proposal: Displacement activities as an indicator of emotions in primates. *Animal Behaviour, 44(5)*, 967-979.

Matheson, M. D., Hartel, J., Whitaker, C., Sheeran, L. K., Li, J. H. & Wagner, R. S. (2007). Self-directed behavior correlates with tourist density in free-living Tibetan macaques (Macaca thibetana) at the Valley of the Wild Monkeys, Mt. Huangshan, China. *Amer. J. Primatol., 69 (Suppl. 1)*, 41-42.

Matheson, M. D., Sheeran, L. K., Li, J. H. & Wagner, R. S. (2006). Tourist impact on Tibetan macaques. *Anthrozoos, 19*, 158-168.

McCarthy, M. S., Matheson, M. D., Lester, J. D., Sheeran, L. K., Li, J. H. & Wagner, R. S. (2007). Sequences of Tibetan macaque (Macaca thibetana) behaviors and tourist behaviors at Mt. Huangshan, China. *Amer. J. Primatol., 69 (Suppl.1)*, 42.

McCarthy, M. S., Matheson, M. D., Lester, J. D., Sheeran, L. K., Li, J. H. & Wagner, R. S. (2009). Sequences of Tibetan macaque (Macaca thibetana) behaviors and tourist behaviors at Mt. Huangshan, China. *Primate Conservation, 24*, online 1-7.

Ogawa, H. (2006). Wily Monkeys: Social Intelligence of Tibetan Macaques. Kyoto: Kyoto University Press.

Ruesto, L. A. (2007). Investigation of possible impacts of tourist density, decibel levels, and behavior on threats in Tibetan macaques (Macaca thibetana). Master's thesis, Central Washington University.

Treves, A. & Brandon, K. (2005). Tourist impacts on the behavior of black howling monkeys (Alouatta pigra) at Lamanai, Belize. In Paterson, J. & Wallis, J. (eds.), *Commensalism and Conflict: The Human-Primate Interface* (pp. 146-167). Norman, OK: American Society of Primatologists.

Wada, K. & Xiong, C. P. (1996). Population changes of Tibetan monkeys with special regard to birth interval. In Shotake, T. & Wada, K. (eds.), Variations in the Asian Macaques (pp. 133-145). Tokyo: Tokai University Press.

Wallis, J. & Lee, D. R. (1999). Primate conservation: the prevention of disease transmission. *Int. J. Primatol., 20*, 803-826.

Woodford, M. H., Butynski, T. & Karesh, W.B. (2002). Habituating the great apes: the disease risks. *Oryx, 36*, 153-160.

Yenter, T. A., Matheson, M. D., Sheeran, L. K., Li, J. & Wagner, R. S. (2008). Self-directed behaviors, tourist density and proximity in a free-living population of Tibetan macaques (Macaca thibetana) at an ecotourism destination in Anhui Province, China. *Am .J. Primatol., 70* (Suppl. 1), 52.

Yin, H., Li, J., Zhou, L., Ge, J., Ionica, C. & Berman, C. (2004). Birth of Tibetan monkey (Macaca thibetana) in winter. *Acta Theriologica Sinica, 24*, 19-22.

Zhao, Q. K. (1996). Etho-ecology of Tibetan macaques at Mount Emei, China. In Fa, J. & Lindburg, D.G. (eds.), *Evolution and Ecology of Macaque Societies* (pp. 263-289). Cambridge: Cambridge University Press.

In: Ecotourism: Management, Development and Impact   ISBN: 978-1-60876-724-3
Editors: A. Krause, E. Weir, pp. 213-225   © 2010 Nova Science Publishers, Inc.

Chapter 9

COASTAL ECOTOURISM AND WATER QUALITY IN YUCATÁN PENINSULA

Nancy ArandaCirerol[*]

Facultad de Química. Unidad de Química-Sisal. Universidad Nacional Autónoma de México (UNAM). Puerto de Abrigo S/N. 97356. Sisal, Yucatán, México.

ABSTRACT

Extensive and intense human activity has altered the balance of ecosystems to the detriment of the natural environment. Human migration has occurred throughout history. The movement of people, capital, goods, and services has caused different ecosystem changes, including deforestation. Coastal urbanization is a challenge for conservation, as people moving away from rural and protected areas has increased per capita demand for energy, goods, and services. Nowadays, most people migrate either temporarily or permanently to tropical coastal tourist areas. In the Yucatán Peninsula, migration has been taking place since the 1970s, with differing environmental impacts. The tourists are increasing every year, which demanding ecotourism facilities and industrial development increases to support population and business activities. Coastal water quality is also affected by increasing tourism development. Environmental awareness is lagging as efficient waste treatment systems are lacking. The water quality of the aquifer and the coast are threatened. This area has no rivers because of its karst geomorphology, the coastal freshwater comes from springs or seeps, and aquifers are the only freshwater source. Domestic garbage and wastewater are the main sources of pollution. The Yucatán Peninsula coast is undoubtedly an important economic resource for México, which requires the implementation of integrated coastal management, keeping in mind that continental human activities have a direct impact into coastal environment. It is unquestionable that successful coastal management of ecotourism must be implemented on the basis of efficient waste treatment, which requires more in-depth knowledge of the area. There should be permanent water quality monitoring programs, as well as long-term studies on the oceanographic and biogeochemical processes that control water quality

---

[*] Corresponding author: Phone: +52 988 9120147, FAX +52 988 931 1000; e-mail: acirerol@unam.mx, arandacirerol@gmail.com, (N. ArandaCirerol).

dynamics, which are probably driven by stochastic events and by probable climate change. These factors will also complicate both conservation and migration flows. Also, this will involve fostering agreements among people, industrialists, and government to execute preventive and corrective actions. Water quality conservation is important for two reasons: first, for the preservation of coastal water quality and the beautiful scenery for ecotourism; and second, for freshwater quality protection. Taking action will contribute to the sustainable development of this region of México.

1. INTRODUCTION

Water is a limited resource and its quality is threatened by human activities. Preserving water quality must be a priority for governments in all countries to keep groundwater and coastal waters safe for a wide range of uses, such as drinking water, recreation, food production, fish and aquatic life, and irrigation.

Ensuring that environmental sustainability goals given by the *Millennium Development Goals* are met is of particular importance for our survival. These goals include maintaining the health of our environment; integrating the principles of sustainable development into government policies and programs, reversing the loss of environmental resources, as well as supplying safe drinking water to the population (UN-MD, 2000).

The United Mexican States –México-, like other countries, faces problems with water availability and quality; water education and environment preservation must be emphasized, and because environmental protection programs have begun only recently, few efficient waste depuration systems are operational. The water quality of rivers, lakes, lagoons, estuaries and coastal zones is threatened by pollutants from several sources, such as domestic, urban and industrial sewage, solid waste, agriculture, livestock, aquaculture, acidification, mining and oil spills (Alonso-Rodríguez et al., 2000; ArandaCirerol, 2001, 2004, in press; Rivera-Arriaga & Villalobos, 2001; Beach et al., 2008), and probably also from atmospheric deposition (Paerl, 1997; Pryor & Barthelmie, 2000). There is also an accumulated effect due to poor water resources management decisions and the lack of a water quality database (ArandaCirerol, 2001, 2004, in press); despite the fact that water quality research is a top priority.

2. YUCATAN PENINSULA WATER RISK

The Yucatán Peninsula is a tropical ecosystem that is surrounded by the Caribbean Sea and the Gulf of México, enclosing the states of Campeche, Yucatán and Quintana Roo (Figure 1), covering 139 470 km^2 with a coastal littoral of about 1 000 km (INEGI, 2000). It is an extensive platform of limestone karst geology with complex underground rivers, or aquifers, which discharge either as springs or seeps in the coast. The peninsula has particular bodies of groundwater (sinkholes), locally known as "cenotes" (dzonot -ts'onot-, a Maya word meaning "hole") that are situated in caves or land breaks formed by the dissolution of limestone or by tectonic activity (Logan et al., 1969; Back & Lesser, 1981; Bryant et al., 1991).

The local population has multiplied during the last 50 years; the census taken in 2005 showed a population of 3 708 987 inhabitants (Table 1). The economy is growing along with agriculture, livestock breeding, aquaculture, tourism, oil, and ports, mainly, agriculture and swine and poultry, because the products of these industries are the constituents of the Yucatán gastronomy (ArandaCirerol, 2001, 2004). Besides, tourism is the third largest economic activity in México and represents eight percent of the gross internal product (GIP). The state-by-state contribution to this total is 7.5% by Campeche, 23.1% by Yucatán and, 46.8% by Quintana Roo (IMCO, 2008). Deforestation, remnants of pesticides and fertilizers, and non-depurated effluents are the consequences of this development. Domestic and industrial wastewaters are disposed of using inefficient systems, thus pollutants can leach into the subsoil without depuration. Solid waste recycling is incipient; garbage is thrown in landfills, and lixiviates percolate easily by the karst subsoil that has caused environmental and ecological problems similar to those in karst areas of other parts of the world. Thus, pollutants are leaching to groundwater, which is discharged into the coastal waters (e.g. Bell, 1991; Thorburn et al., 2003).

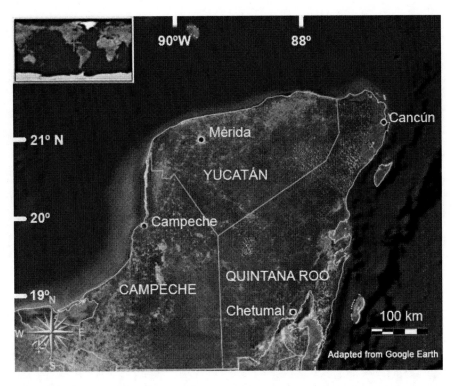

Figure 1. Yucatán Peninsula, México. Campeche, Mérida and Chetumal are the capital of states.

The Yucatán Peninsula shows pollution-warning signs that threaten environmental quality. In Campeche City, the state capital, swimming in the beaches is forbidden due to fecal coliforms contamination, because sewage is disposed directly into the sea

(ArandaCirerol, 2004). In Yucatán, the groundwater shows high concentrations of nitrates, so the aquifer at an average depth of 8 meters is not potable (ArandaCirerol, 2001; Pacheco & Cabrera, 1997; Graniel et al., 1999). Today, the freshwater source of Mérida, the state capital, is located at an average depth of 40 meters. Therefore, the aquifer is at a high risk of becoming unsuitable for human use if a management program for the protection and conservation of groundwater is not implemented (Back & Lesser, 1981; Pacheco & Cabrera, 1997; ArandaCirerol, 2004; ArandaCirerol et al., 2006). In Quintana Roo, particularly in Cancún and Riviera Maya, tourism is the major economic activity. For many years, sewage from hotels were discharged into cenotes and coastal lagoons, like Nichupté and Bojórquez lagoons, the principal lagoonal system of Cancún (Figure 2), that are eutrophicated, as a consequence of high nutrient inputs from inefficient wastewater treatment systems (Merino et al., 1992; ArandaCirerol, 2001). On the other hand, in the state capital of Chetumal, located in the southeast part of the territory (Figure 1), wastewater has been disposed of in the adjacent bay, which is contaminated by pesticides and fertilizers from nearby agricultural fields (ArandaCirerol, 2001; Schmook & Vance, 2009).

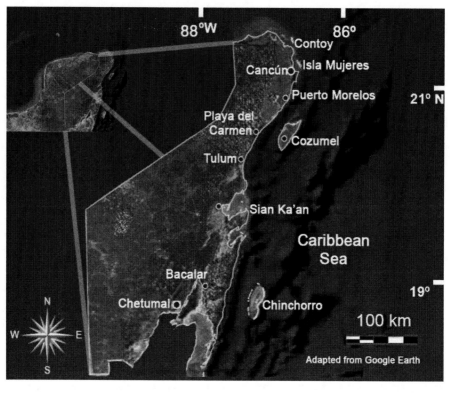

Figure 2. Quintana Roo state, México. Riviera Maya is the coast from Cancún to Playa del Carmen.

3. FURTHER WATER QUALITY DIAGNOSIS

Nitrate contamination of the Yucatán aquifer is well documented, but data from other pollutants, as heavy metals and pharmaceuticals have not reported (ArandaCirerol, 2004, in press); these also pose a risk to water quality and human health (Storelli et al., 2001; Mukherjee et al., 2004; Ashton et al., 2004; Zuccato et al., 2005). The atmospheric deposition of nutrients has not been documented either, and this also may be altering water quality (Paerl, 1997; Pryor & Barthelmie, 2000; Kangas & Syri, 2002, Pryor & Sorensen, 2002; ArandaCirerol, 2004). Only one preliminary study of wind has been documented (Soler-Bientz et al., 2009).

Table 1. Demography of United Mexican States and Yucatán Peninsula (INEGI, 2001, 2003a).

Region/ Year	1950	2000	2005
	Inhabitants		
United Mexican States (México)	25 791 017	97 361 711	103 263 388
Campeche	122 098	689 656	754 730
Yucatán	516 899	1 655 707	1 818 948
Quintana Roo	29 967	873 804	1 135 309
Yucatán Peninsula	668 964	3 219 167	3 708 987

Nutrient sources, water quality pressures, and coastal eutrophication have been studied since 1998 in the northwestern area of the Yucatán. Learning about the coastal water quality and ecosystem responses, started a coastal water quality monitoring program to establish a baseline for the implementation of an integrated coastal management for the Yucatán Peninsula (e.g. Hauxwell et al., 2001; ArandaCirerol, 2001, 2004; Herrera et al., 2004, 2007; ArandaCirerol et al., 2006). In Campeche and Quintana Roo, several water quality studies have been done; their results are presented like technical reports and theses, and a few have been published in national and international journals (Bravo et al., 2000; Rivera-Arriaga & Villalobos, 2001; Sánchez-Gil et al., 2004; Carruthers et al., 2005). It is necessary to implement a water quality-monitoring program among the three states to make a diagnosis of the groundwater and coastal water quality in the Yucatán peninsula.

4. CANCUN AND RIVIERA MAYA, QUINTANA ROO: CHALLENGES TO APPROACH SUSTAINABLE DEVELOPMENT?

Since 1974, when hotels began to operate in the then recently founded city of Cancún, the coastal zone of Quintana Roo has sustained development by governmental programs that aimed to promote tourism based on the Mayan archeological towns and Caribbean beaches. Today, the coast has been urbanized from Cancún to Tulum, which is known as Riviera Maya (Figure 2); consequently, the population has grown exponentially in last two decades. In

1990, the population was 493 277 inhabitants in seven municipalities. Cancún heads the Benito Juárez municipality, and in that year 35.83% of the population lived there. During 2005, the population was 1 135 309 inhabitants in eight municipalities, with the new Solidaridad municipality, which reduced the size of the Benito Juárez area, and 47.98% of population was concentrated in Cancún and the surrounding areas where tourist activities were developing, and this is approximately fifty percent of the total population (Table 1, Figure 3A). Tourism development in the last thirty years has caused national and foreign emigration; in 2000 only 42% of state population was native (Table 2). If the population growth rate of 4.7% (2000-2005) continues, the population will double in the next thirteen years (INEGI, 2003b, 2008). The next population census will be in the 2010.

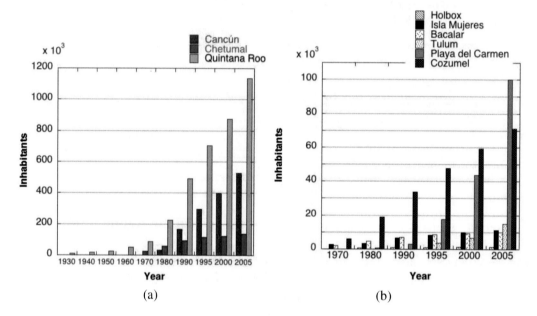

Figure 3. Demography (A) Quintana Roo and principal cities; (B) Islands (Holbox, Isla Mujeres and Cozumel) and main coastal localities (INEGI, 2003b).

Playa del Carmen and Tulum are the principal towns of Riviera Maya, and Cozumel is the main island, and their population has also grown exponentially (Figure 2 and 3B). The population increase is erratic between the towns of Quintana Roo, for example, Isla Mujeres is the second largest island in the state, while Bacalar and Chetumal, located in the south, have grown, but not at the same rate as the northern coast (Figure 3A and 3B). This is evidence of the economic development of Cancún and Riviera Maya.

Although Isla Mujeres is near to Cancún (Figure 2), its demography has been moderated, probably because the economy has been driven by the native people, or perhaps because it is only a small island with an area of ~4 km^2, in contrast to Cozumel, which is approximately 500 km^2, where the economy is also controlled by the native people, but having greater foreign trade, especially ports for tourist cruises.

Increases in tourism have remained constant; in fifteen years, hotel availability has tripled, with 57 612 rooms (Figure 4A); with the lowest number of vacancies in Cancún, Playa del Carmen, Cozumel, and Isla Mujeres (Table 3). Foreigners are the principal visitors to Quintana Roo; in 2003 more than four million people visited the region (Figure 4B). Consequently, tourist development causes a hazard to the water resources because in a short time, a greater rural area has been urbanized. Therefore, food demand and domestic and municipal sewage are increasing.

Nevertheless, in spite of the risks of the economic development of Quintana Roo and the legislative environmental protection concern, Non-Governmental Organizations (NGOs) have been established, and, together with academic institutions, have obtained important advances for the protection of the integrity of the ecosystem. Consequently, with state and federal government support, two Biosphere Reserves have been declared: the forest and coral reef of Sian Ka'an, and the Chinchorro Bank coral reefs. Also, the Cozumel and Puerto Morelos coral reefs, the western coast of Isla Mujeres, Punta Cancún and Punta Nizuc in Cancún, Contoy Island, and Tulum have been declared as National Parks (Figure 2), (INEGI, 2003b). On February 2nd, 2005, Cozumel National Marine Park was added to the Ramsar coral reef sites, so wetland, mangrove, and coral reef management can be improved. All of these are components of the Mesoamerican Reef protection program.

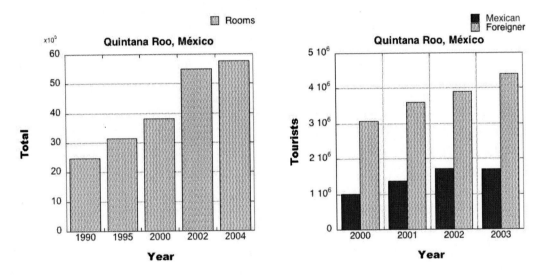

Figure 4. Tourism activity in Quintana Roo, México. (A) Rooms*; (B) National and foreign tourists (SECTUR, 2005). * villages, apartments, guest house, inns, bungalows, campings, cabins, suites, condominiums and hotels

Interdisciplinary studies must be done over 50 843 km^2 of state area and 380 km of shoreline, bearing in mind that continental human activities affect the coastal environment via groundwater discharges (ArandaCirerol, 2004; ArandaCirerol et al., 2006; Carruthers et al., 2005; Perry et al., 2009). All activities must be geared towards Mesoamerican Reef protection, as is the support of Quintana Roo coast. Native people have changed their lifestyles, adjusting to development by changing agriculture practices, and receiving education based on environmental and reef protection. These should improve their quality of life (Tundi Agardy, 1993, 1994; Rodríguez-Martínez & Ortíz, 1999; Morales-Vela et al., 2000; Hostettler, 2003; Torres, 2003; Cinner & Pollnac, 2004; Ellis & Porter-Bolland, 2008).

As part of the change, ecotourism activities have been reduced to a regional scale, as an approach to finding sustainable development.

Table 2. Demography of Quintana Roo (INEGI, 2001).

Population	2000 (inhabitants)	Percent
Quintana Roo	874 963	
Quintana Roo natives	367 591	42.0
Migrants from other Mexican state	485 255	55.5
Unknowing	14 026	1.6
Foreigners	8 091	0.9

This leads to a series of questions about water hazards: What is the groundwater and coastal water quality of Quintana Roo? What are the main sources of pollution? What is the response ecosystem to pollution? What is the best sustainable management program of the groundwater and coastal water resources? What is the environmental quality of Quintana Roo?

Historical water quality data is lacking, so a comparison between the past and present conditions is not possible without scientific research. The challenge is to be able to determine past and present water quality, pollutant sources and the impact of contaminant inputs that are generated by human activities in Quintana Roo State to learn about the environmental fragility.

Table 3. Percentage of hotel occupancy in Riviera Maya and islands, Quintana Roo, México, 2001-2004 (SECTUR, 2005).

Town / Year	2001	2002	2003	2004
Cancún	70.35	65.85	69.97	77.40
Isla Mujeres	39.70	40.01	43.52	53.98
Cozumel	57.71	49.42	51.69	60.03
Playa del Carmen	71.60	71.98	76.61	86.19

5. ACTIONS FOR THE FUTURE

Water resources and economic development of Yucatán Peninsula must be based on groundwater management goals; 1) to develop regional groundwater reserves for the increased demand from a growing population and a governmental program to promote tourism and ecotourism; and 2) to control groundwater pollution in a chemically sensitive system made critically vulnerable by climate change and geologic conditions.

Regionalization of the Yucatán Peninsula must be undertaken to identify continental and coastal ecoregions, and to classify them according to their fragility, environmental quality and water quality (Gallant et al., 1989).

Karst managers are priority for national protection of water resources through the highest quality of basic and applied research as demanded by local society, with a) qualifying and quantifying point and non-point pollution sources; b) designing, implementing, and operating a spatial and temporal monitoring network of the groundwater and coastal water of the Yucatán Peninsula, in order to build a time series of variables that is useful in measuring the health ecosystem as a baseline for management programs; c) contributing to national socioeconomic development through scientific support in the formation of qualified human resources with interdisciplinary criteria; d) establishing permissible maximum concentrations of substances in wastewater in order to update the Mexican Official Norms, specifically adapted to the conditions of Yucatán Peninsula, since the biodiversity and geohydrology of this region requires more rigorous parameters for waste disposal and treatment; e) applying this knowledge in the search for solutions to existing issues of the scope of water quality, integrating the economic and social sectors of the Yucatan Peninsula, coordinated with the regional and federal government, as well as with other private and public organizations; and f) educating a widespread awareness that due to the carbonated karst subsoil of the Yucatán Peninsula, land activities have a direct impact on the groundwater and coastal environment.

6. CONCLUSION

The groundwater and coastal water quality of the Yucatán Peninsula is at risk, if remedial practices of waste disposal are not implemented, the availability of potable groundwater will not depend on its quantity, but rather on its quality. Groundwater may be affecting the coastal environment and can cause damage to the biological diversity and aesthetic value of this peninsula, and consequently to the main economic source of tourism.

Cultural eutrophication, water quality and environmental quality are highly linked to these kinds of anthropogenic activities. These tripartite studies must be followed to guarantee usable water for diverse uses as potable water, irrigation, bathing, and as an aquatic habitat. Also, this can be a contribution of México to the environmental protection of Gulf of México and Caribbean Sea, because water preservation is both a national and international priority. With this action, México will be one of the participating countries in the United Nations Call on March 22, 2005, World Water Day, when the International Decade for Action, Water for Life, from 2005-2015, was declared (UN, 2005).

In the Yucatán Peninsula, as in any other region of the world, indiscriminate use of the natural resources exceeding the recovering capacity of environment to regulate this pressure cannot continue. Furthermore, coastal regionalization sustained by environmental and water quality should act as the baseline for natural resources management as an approach to sustainable development.

REFERENCES

Alonso-Rodríguez, R., Páez-Osuna, F. & Cortés-Altamirano, R. (2000). Trophic Conditions and Stoichiometric Nutrient Balance in Subtropical Waters Influenced by Municipal Sewage Effluents in Mazatlán Bay (SE Gulf of California). *Marine Pollution Bulletin, 40,* 331-339.

ArandaCirerol, N. (2001). Alimentando al mundo envenenando al planeta: eutrofización y calidad del agua. *Avance y Perspectiva, 20,* 293-303.

ArandaCirerol, N. (2004). Eutrofización y Calidad del Agua de una zona costera tropical. Ph.D. Thesis. Universitat de Barcelona, España (Spain) 230 pp. URL: http://www.tesisenxarxa.net/TDX-0709104-090122/index.html.

ArandaCirerol, N. (In press). *Eutrophication and water quality in a tropical coast: Yucatán, México.* VDM Verlag Dr. Müller Aktiengesellschaft & Co. KG Editor. ISBN 978-3-369-18870-7.

ArandaCirerol, N., Herrera-Silveira, J.A. & Comín, F.A. (2006). Nutrient water quality in a tropical coastal zone with groundwater discharge, northwest Yucatán, Mexico. *Estuarine, Coastal and Shelf Science, 68,* 445-454.

Ashton, D., Hilton, M. & Thomas, K. V. (2004). Investigating the environmental transport of human pharmaceuticals to streams in the United Kingdom. *Science of The Total Environment, 333,* 167-184.

Back, W. & Lesser, J. M. (1981). Chemical constraints of groundwater management in the Yucatán Peninsula, Mexico. *Journal of Hydrology, 10,* 330-368.

Beach, T., Luzzadder-Beach, S., Dunning, N. & Cook, D. (2008). Human and natural impacts on fluvial and karst depressions of the Maya Lowlands. *Geomorphology, 101,* 308-331.

Bell, P.R.F. (1991). Status of Eutrophication in the Great Barrier Reef Lagoon. Marine Pollution Bulletin, 23, 89-93. doi:10.1016/0025-326X(91)90655-C.

Bravo, H. A., Saavedra, M. I. R., Sánchez, P. A., Torres, R. J. & Granada, L. M. M. (2000). Chemical composition of precipitation in a Mexican Maya region. *Atmospheric Environment, 34,* 1197-1204.

Bryant, W. R., Lugo, J., Cordova, C. & Salvador, A. (1991). Physiography and bathymetry. In: Salvador A. (Ed.). The Gulf of Mexico Basin, Geological Society of America: Boulder, Colorado, *The Geology of North America,* 13-30.

Carruthers, T. J. B., van Tussenbroek, B. I. & Dennison, W. C. (2005). Influence of submarine springs and wastewater on nutrient dynamics of Caribbean seagrass meadows. *Estuarine, Coastal and Shelf Science, 64,* 191-199.

Cinner, J. E. & Pollnac, R. B. (2004). Poverty, perceptions and planning: why socioeconomics matter in the management of Mexican reefs. *Ocean & Coastal Management, 47,* 479-493.

Ellis, E. A. & Porter-Bolland, L. (2008). Is community-based forest management more effective than protected areas?: A comparison of land use/land cover change in two neighboring study areas of the Central Yucatan Peninsula, Mexico *Forest Ecology and Management, 256,* 1971-1983.

Gallant, A. L., Whittier, T. M., Larsen, D. P., Omernik, J. M. & Hughes, R. M. (Eds). (1989). Regionalization as a tool for managing environmental resources. Environmental Protection Agency (EPA). 1989, EPA/600/3-89/060, 182 pp.

Graniel, C. E., Morris, L. B. & Carrillo-Rivera, J. J. (1999). Effects of urbanization on groundwater resources of Mérida, Yucatán, México. *Environmental Geology*, *37*, 303-312.

Hauxwell, J. A, Cebrian, J., Herrera-Silveira, J. A., Ramírez, J., Zaldivar, A., Gomez, N. & ArandaCirerol, N. (2001). Measuring production of *Halodule wrightii*: additional evidence suggests clipping underestimates growth rate. *Aquatic Botany*, *69*, 41-54.

Herrera-Silveira, J. A., ArandaCirerol, N., Troccoli Ghinaglia, L., Comín, F. A., Madden, C. (2007). Coastal eutrophication in the Yucatán Peninsula. In Withers, K. & Nipper, M. (Eds.), *Environmental Analysis of the Gulf of México.* (Special Publication Series No. 1, 695 pp. 512-532). Instituto Nacional de Ecología (Mexico), Harte Research Institute for Gulf of Mexico Studies, Texas A & M University . Corpus Christi.

Herrera-Silveira, J. A., Comin, F. A., ArandaCirerol, N., Troccoli, L. & Capurro, L. (2004). Coastal water quality assessment in the Yucatan Peninsula: management implications. *Ocean & Coastal Management*, *47*, 625-639.

Hostettler, U. (2003). New inequalities: changing maya economy and social life in central Quintana Roo, Mexico. *Research in Economic Anthropology. Anthropological Perspectives on Economic Development and Integration*, *22*, 25-59.

IMCO (Instituto Mexicano para la Competitividad). 2008. Competitividad Estatal de México 2008. Aspiraciones y realidad: las agendas del futuro, 2008. Instituto de Planeación del Estado de Guanajuato (IPLANEG). URL: http://seip.guanajuato.gob.mx/observa/index.php?option=com_content&view=article&id=166:pib-servicios&catid=63:sectores-economicos-con-potencial&Itemid=56. In Spanish.

INEGI (Instituto Nacional de Ecología, Mexico). (2000). Anuario Estadístico Nacional. Estados Unidos Mexicanos. XII Censo General de Población y Vivienda, 1999. 120pp. In Spanish. INEGI (Instituto Nacional de Estadística, Geografía e Informática). (2000). INEGI IV al XII Censos de Población y Vivienda, 1930 a 2000. INEGI. Estados Unidos Mexicanos. Conteo de Población y Vivienda, 1995. Resultados Definitivos. Aguascalientes, Ags., México, 1996. Anuario de estadísticas por Entidad Federativa, 348 pp.

INEGI (Instituto Nacional de Estadística, Geografía e Informática). (2001). Anuario Estadístico Nacional. Estados Unidos Mexicanos. XII Censo General de Población y Vivienda, 2000. Instituto Nacional de Estadística, Geografía e Informática (INEGI) México, 120pp. In Spanish.

INEGI (Instituto Nacional de Estadística, Geografía e Informática). (2003a). Anuario de estadísticas por Entidad Federativa. Instituto Nacional de Estadística, Geografía e Informática (INEGI) México, 430 pp. In Spanish.

INEGI (Instituto Nacional de Estadística, Geografía e Informática). (2003b). Anuario Estadístico. Quintana Roo, 432 pp. in Spanish.

INEGI (Instituto Nacional de Estadística, Geografía e Informática). (2008). México y sus Municipios. INEGI, Mexico, 438 pp. URL: http://www.inegi.org.mx/prod_serv/contenidos/espanol/bvinegi/productos/integracion/municipios/mexympios/MexIICon_1.pdf.

Kangas, L. & Syri, S. (2002). Regional nitrogen deposition model for integrated assessment of acidification and eutrophication. *Atmospheric Environment*, 36, 1111-1122.

Logan, B. W., Harding, J. L., Ahr, W. M., Williams, J. D. & Snead, R. G. (1969). Late Quaternary carbonate sediments of Yucatan shelf, Mexico. Carbonate Sediments and

Reefs, Yucatan Shelf, Mexico; Memoir II. Ed. Brian W. Logan, 5-128. Tulsa, Okla.: American Association Petroleum Geologists.

Merino, M., González, A., Reyes, E., Gallegos, M. & Czitrom, S. (1992). Eutrophication in the lagoons of Cancún, México. *Science of the Total Environment,* Suplement, 861-870.

Morales-Vela, B., Olivera-Gómez, D., John, E. Reynolds III, J. E. & Rathbun, G. B. (2000). Distribution and habitat use by manatees (Trichechus manatus manatus) in Belize and Chetumal Bay, Mexico. *Biological Conservation, 95,* 67-75.

Mukherjee, A. B., Zevenhoven, R., Brodersen, J., Hylander, L. D. & Bhattacharya, P. (2004). Mercury in waste in the European Union: sources, disposal methods and risks. *Resources, Conservation and Recycling, 42,* 155-182.

Pacheco, J. & Cabrera, A. (1997). Groundwater Contamination by Nitrates in the Yucatan Peninsula, Mexico. *Hydrogeology Journal, 5,* 47-53.

Paerl, H. W. (1997). Coastal eutrophication and harmful algal blooms: Importance of atmospheric deposition and groundwater as "new" nitrogen and other nutrient sources. *Limnology and Oceanography, 42,* 1154-1165.

Perry, E., Paytan, A., Pedersen, B. & Velazquez-Oliman, G. (2009). Groundwater geochemistry of the Yucatan Peninsula, Mexico: Constraints on stratigraphy and hydrogeology. *Journal of Hydrology, 367,* 27-40.

Pryor, S. C. & Barthelmie, R. J. (2000). Particle Dry Deposition to Water Surfaces: Processes and Consequences. *Marine Pollution Bulletin, 41,* 220-231.

Pryor, S. C. & Sorensen, L. L. (2002). Dry Deposition of reactive nitrogen to marine environments: recent advances and remaining uncertainties. *Marine Pollution Bulletin, 44,* 1336-1340.

Rivera-Arriaga, E. & Villalobos, G. (2001). The coast of Mexico: approaches for its management. *Ocean and Coastal Management, 44,* 729-756.

Rodríguez-Martínez, R. & Ortíz, L. M. (1999). Coral reef education in schools of Quintana Roo, Mexico. *Ocean and Coastal Management, 42,* 1061-1068.

Sánchez-Gil, P., Yáñez-Arancibia, A., Ramírez-Gordillo, J., Day, J. W. & Templet P. H. (2004). Some socio-economic indicators in the Mexican states of the Gulf of Mexico. *Ocean and Coastal Management, 47,* 581-596.

Schmook, B. & Vance, C. (2009). Agricultural Policy, Market Barriers, and Deforestation: The Case of Mexico's Southern Yucatán. *World Development, 37,* 1015-1025.

SECTUR (Secretaría de Turismo). (2005). Sistema Nacional de Información Turística (NIT). Sistema de Información Turística Estatal (SITE). Secretaría de Turismo del Gobierno del Estado. Dirección de Planeación y Desarrollo Turístico. Anuario Estadístico del Estado de Quintana Roo, Edición 2004. Agenda estadística de los Estados Unidos Mexicanos. INEGI, 221pp.

Soler-Bientz, R., Watson, S. & Infield, D. (2009). Preliminary study of long-term wind characteristics of the Mexican Yucatán Peninsula. *Energy Conversion and Management, 50,* 1773-1780.

Storelli, M. M., Storelli, A. & Marcotrigiano, G. O. (2001). Heavy metals in the aquatic environment of the Southern Adriatic Sea, Italy: Macroalgae, sediments and benthic species. *Environment International, 26,* 505-509.

Thorburn, P.J., Biggs, J.S., Weier, K.L., Keating, B.A. (2003). Nitrate in groundwaters of intensive agricultural areas in coastal Northeastern Australia. Agriculture, Ecosystems and Environment 94, 49-58.

Torres, R. (2003). Linkages between tourism and agriculture in Mexico. *Annals of Tourism Research, 30*, 546-566.

Tundi Agardy, M. (1993). Accommodating ecotourism in multiple use planning of coastal and marine protected areas. *Ocean and Coastal Management, 20*, 219-239.

Tundi Agardy, M. (1994). Advances in marine conservation: the role of marine protected areas. *Trends in Ecology & Evolution, 9*, 267-270.

UN (United Nations). (2005). International Decade for Action. Water for Life, 2005-2015. URL: http://www.un.org/waterforlifedecade/faqs.html#11.

UN-MD (UNITED NATIONS MILLENNIUM DECLARATION). (2000). United Nations A/RES/55/2. General Assembly Distr.: General. Fifty-fifth session. Resolution adopted by the General Assembly [without reference to a Main Committee (A/55/L.2)] United Nations Development Programme and the United Nations Department of Public Information. Nations. New York, USA. Published by the UN Development Programme and the UN Department of Public Information 2000. URL: http://www.un.org/millenniumgoals/.

Zuccato, E., Castiglioni, S. & Fanelli, R. (2005). Identification of the pharmaceuticals for human use contaminating the Italian aquatic environment. *Journal of Hazardous Materials, 122*, 205-209.

In: Ecotourism: Management, Development and Impact   ISBN: 978-1-60876-724-3
Editors: A. Krause, E. Weir, pp. 227-240   © 2010 Nova Science Publishers, Inc.

Chapter 10

ECOTOURISM WITH UTILIZATION OF WILD ANIMALS — ITS IMPACT ON CONSERVATION MEDICINE AND RISK ASSESSMENT IN HOKKAIDO, JAPAN

Mitsuhiko Asakawa

Department of Pathobiology/Wild Animal Medical Center, School of Veterinary
Medicine, Rakuno Gakuen University Ebetsu, Hokkaido 069-8501, Japan

ABSTRACT

Regarding the natural and cultural backgrounds of Japan, ecotourism to gain access to wild animals will be developed more in the future, and so adequate utilization of the animals for tourism is needed because the wild animals are valuable tools and should continue to be sustainable resources. But, some wild animals are regarded as a public/captive animal/ecosystem health risk factor due to their carrying agents of infectious/parasitic diseases. Therefore, before or in performance of the ecotourism with utilization of the animals on the site, educational opportunities are needed. To start a discussion, a case of Rakuno Gakuen University in Hokkaido was given. There have been suspicious infectious and parasitic diseases in wild and zoo/exotic animals since the 1990s, and to provide facilities for conservation medicine research and education, the Wild Animal Medical Center was established. The facility has helped indirectly to accelerate the creation of solid relationships between zoological gardens and aquariums' directors/wildlife officers and researchers/exotic veterinarians, etc., and the facility. Such relationships provide not only clinical benefits with its positive diagnoses but also educational activities as byproducts of exchanging information between the organizations and university staffs. Also, to maintain ecotourism, some potential strategies including monitoring with consideration of ecology of the agents will be continued because the agents related to the diseases could infect not only humans but also captive animals. Finally, education related to wildlife or nature is one of the developing businesses in Japan, and we will discover a new business field between the ecotourism and wildlife education in the future.

INTRODUCTION

The aim of the present paper is to develop an adequate utilization of wild animals for ecotourism, and its contents, which include a model case related to intimately by the author, are divided into 3 parts. First of all, the author will present an overview of the current status quo of ecotourism and its educational activities, with its utilization of wild animals in Hokkaido, Japan, as a case matter, because the animals are one of the most charismatic resources for developing the tourism.

Next, the author will refer to several cases or future possibilities for conservation medicine, namely human medicine, veterinary medicine and ecological (Aguirre et al., 2002) health risks of infectious and/or parasitic diseases provoked by direct/indirect approach to the animals during tourism. Finally, some potential strategies performed by the author and his colleagues including monitoring with consideration of the sociology and ecology of relationships among human/captive and wild animals and infectious/parasitic agents (Asakawa & Taniyama, 2005) were given briefly as one of the prominent cases in the field in Japan.

Utilization of Charismatic Wild Animals for Ecotourism

Japan is located in the Japanese Sea and Pacific Ocean just next to the Far Eastern part of the Eurasian Continent, so you could meet many migrating avian species and marine mammals. Also, because most of the country contains forested and/or secondary woods, the Japanese people have enjoyed the natural landscape with wild animals as one of their own culture. Because of the natural and cultural backgrounds, tourism to gain access to wild animals is common there.

For example, bird or small mammal watching or feeding organized by non-profit organizations (NPO) is typically popular in not only mountainous regions but also the country side or even in small parks of busy towns (Figures 1–2). In sea coast towns or villages, people could take part in watching tours for finding sea eagles and turtles, whales, seals, etc.; they have paid expensive fees for hiring ships (Figure 3). Some tours have included so-called feeing attractions (Figures 4–6), but this activity is not good for the wildlife or for human health.

Figure 1. Volunteer guides of wildlife ecology in the Ueno Zoological Garden, Tokyo. The guides are highly popular and competitive for senior persons.

Figure 2. Flying show in a zoo in Sapporo, Japan, is very popular for visitors.

Figure 3. Wintering seals in Rausu-cho, Shiretoko Peninsula which is one of the UNESCO World Heritage Sites in Japan.

Figure 4. A visitor feeds a squirrel in Izu-Ohshima I. Natural Park, Tokyo. Visitors may feed seeds sold in the park to the semi-free ranging animals and they have to use a pair of gloves which is provided by the park as well.

Figure 5. A visitor feeds a free-ranging fox in Shiretoko Peninsula, Hokkaiodo. Because most foxes in Hokkaido may carry zoonotic taenid parasites (*Echinococcus multirocuralis*), the feeding is regarded as high risk for human health and this is illegal in some cities. The fox had a radio telemetry apparatus attached around its neck.

Figure 6. People feeding fowl on Utonai-ko Lake, one of the waterfowl feeding sites in Hokkaido (left), although feeding has been forbidden since March 2009 because of infectious diseases among people and the fowl (right).

Besides the watching tours mentioned above, wild animals are used in foods of traditional or exotic cuisine in the countryside, and because the cuisine is popular to tourists, farmers keep emergent livestock (e.g., ostrich, semi-wild duck, pigeon and so on) (Figures 7 & 8). Finally, some people love to keep wild animals or so-called exotic pet animals (Figures 9 &10) including illegal cases. Anyway, now, the wild animals are valuable tools for ecotourism, and people economically dependent on the tours have to try to keep the animals as sustainable resources.

So-called Wild Animal Issues in Japan

But, at mostly the same time and places with ecotourism, some wild animals (e.g., wild boars, deer, raccoons etc.) are regarded as pests who damage local agricultural products or ones relatated to fishing (e.g., herons, American mink, seals, etc.). Also, Japanese macaques, Japanese black bears, brown bears and wild boars have directly attacked humans or captive animals (e.g., chickens, cattle and horses) every year. After the 1970s, alien species have invaded and damaged Japanese natural ecosystems (Ecological Society of Japan, 2002). In 2004, the Alien Species Act had been established by the Japanese Government, but the law has not been sufficiently effective for the issues. Since the 1990s, infectious diseases (e.g., psittacosis, intestinal hemorrhagic colibacillosis, leptospirosis, salmonellosis) in humans due to agents transmitted by wild, zoo or semi-free ranging animals have occurred (Ministry of Health, Labour and Welfare of Japan, 2009).

Figure 7. Ostrich and duck farms in Hokkaido. Such farms are popular sites for tourism as well.

Figure 8. Roast pigeon of so-called exotic cuisines served for tourists in a natural park.

Figure 9. Man and squirrel monkey in a metropolitan subway station of Tokyo. Several Japanese people want to keep exotic animal as pets.

Figure 10. A man holds an injured kite in Ebetsu, Hokkaido. Most Japanese people have sympathy for such injured wild animals, and some persons want to keep the animals even though it is illegal.

Each issue mentioned above seems to be independent, but in general the issues are compounded. For example, a raccoon is regarded as not only an agricultural pest but also an ecosystem enemy, and the animal could carry zoonotic infectious agents. So, these complicated situations are called "wild animal (or wildlife) issues" in Japan (Hayama, 2001). Consequently, such animals have been controlled for the stated issues, and in activities including hunting, over 4,000,000 birds and 400,000 mammals killed in Japan a year (Figures 11-13).

Figure 11. Deer hunted at Kitami, next to Shiretoko Peninsula, in the winter season. Most of the deer are prepared for eatable meat (venison) at shooting sites (left), and the meat and head, for trophy, are carried to town. The meat is one of the important elements of ecotourism.

Figure 12. Seal issues in Hokkaido in the winter season. Cods eaten by seals (top), and the seals (top) hunted by a fisherman (bottom), at Rausu, Shiretoko Peninsula.

Necessity of Educational Opportunities for Utilization and Risk Management of Wild Animals

As mentioned above, wild animals have absolutely different aspects, namely the resources versus the issues, for human society. Some people try to conserve wild animals, other continue to kill them. Therefore, before and/or in performance of the ecotourism with utilization of the animals, employees of the tour planner/performer and its governmental supervisor may learn the management of the issues one by one. For example, the Master of Science in Wild Animal Health course organized by Zoological Society of London and the Royal Veterinary College, UK (Royal Veterinary College, 2009), which the present author has taken, has prepared a subject of the ecotourism related to wild animal health assessment. Such an educational system has been started in European countries, the U.S.A. and Australia.

Although there is not yet such a complete course in Japan, some applied zoological and veterinary universities/colleges have educated students partly as coordinators or managers to cope with some of the problems, and some of them have become professional leaders in ecotourism. By the way, the educational field is so attractive that it is highly competitive among candidates who select the subject of wild animal health. Since 2000, because of a decreasing total number of students due to a downsizing in Japan's young population, the management of Japanese universities has paid attention to the popular program for the survival of their own universities (Figure 14).

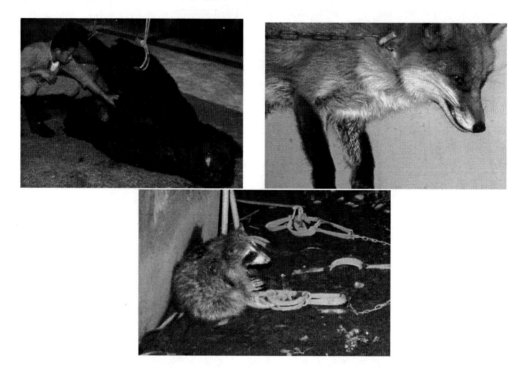

Figure 13. Terrestrial animals controlled in Hokkaido; Brown bear (top), red fox (top right), raccoon (bottom).

Figure 14. Radio telemetry trucking survey drill of the student short course (SSC) organized by the Japanese Society of Zoo and Wild Animal Medicine (JSZWM). The drill is highly popular for students.

Case Report of Educational Activities for Conservation Medicine Performed by Rakuno Gakuen University

Rakuno Gakuen University (RGU), is located in Hokkaido, the most northern part of Japan. RGU, established as an agricultural college in 1940, has 2 faculties of applied zoology and a veterinary school, and has contributed to the development of ecotourism in Hokkaido. Tourism is one of main industries of Hokkaido, because domestic and international tourists regard it as the place in Japan with the most wilderness. Actually, several zoological gardens, private companies, NPO, etc., offer tours for finding charismatic wild animals, e.g., sea eagles, Blakiston's owls, brown bears, whales, seals and so on, throughout the year, even in winter, although this season is very cool with deep snow in most regions of Hokkaido (Asakawa & Taniyama, 2005).

Recently, there have been suspicious infectious and parasitic diseases in wild and zoo/exotic animals since the 1990s—the period when ecotourism was just starting. Examples include echinococcosis in captive gorillas, fasciolaris in deer (Figure 19, middle), mange in raccoon dog (Figure 20), Mareck's disease in white-fronted goose, atoxoplasmosis and staphylococcosis in sparrows, and so on. Among them, some pathogens could infect each other among human, captive and wild animals, and it seems to have a negative impact on the development of ecotourism (Asakawa, 2007, 2008, 2009ab; Taniyama et al., 1996).

Figure 15. Landscape of Rakuno Gakuen University (top) , Wild Animal Medical Center (WAMC) located in the university (top right), and its staff (bottom).

Figure 16. Field survey in woods and sea coast near the WAMC. Collecting samples obtained from feral raccoons (top left and right) and stranded gray whale, one of the rare species in Japanese (bottom; photo by Dr. Hajime Ishikawa, Institute of Cetacean Reaerch).

In 2004, to provide facilities for conservation medical research and education, the Wild Animal Medical Center (WAMC) (Figure 15) was established in the Teaching Animal Hospital of the School of Veterinary Medicine (Asakawa & Taniyama, 2005). Principally, the main research activities of WAMC are veterinary medicine for wild and zoo animal medical practice, epidemiology on infectious pathogens of both humans and (captive and wild) animals, bio/chemical toxic agents, positive diagnosis of parasitic diseases etc. with zoo vets, university staffs, NGOs and students who are interested in ecotourism (Figures 16–18).

Because the present author who has been a wildlife helminthologist has managed WAMC as a director, most scientific papers which have been published in WAMC belong to the scientific field of helminthology (Asakawa, 2007, 2008, 2009ab) (Figures 19–20) and the Japanese Society of Zoo and Wildlife Medicine has designated WAMC as the Wildlife Helminthiasis Center since 2006. The designation has helped indirectly to accelerate making solid relationships between zoological gardens and aquariums' directors/wildlife officers and researchers/exotic veterinarians, etc., and the WAMC. Such relationships provide not only a clinical benefit with its positive diagnosis but also educational activities as byproducts of exchanging staffs of the organizations and university students. Anyway, some potential strategies including monitoring with consideration of ecology of the agents will be able to go on at the WAMC because the agents related to the diseases could infect not only humans but also captive animals.

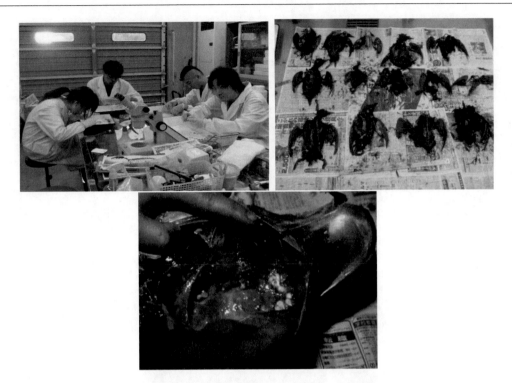

Figure 17. Laboratory work in the WAMC (top) and avian species. Oil stained sea birds in Shiretoko Peninsula (top right) and a case of aspergillosis (bottom).

Figure 18. Veterinary care in the WAMC (top left) with young hares (top right), and released kite (bottom).

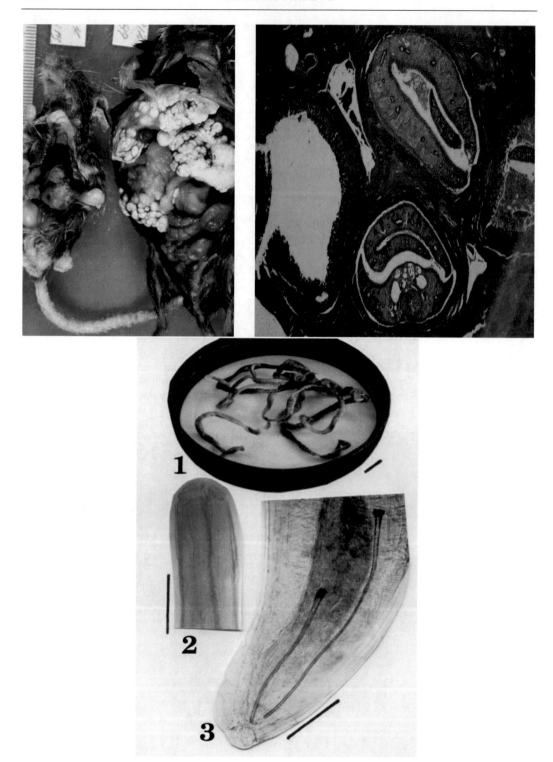

Figure 19. Wildlife helminthiasis found in the WAMC. Echinococcosis in a field mouse and a vole (top left; they are intermediate hosts), fasciolaris in deer (top right; histopathology), and *Anisakis* sp. from orca (bottom).

Figure 20. Mange in raccoon dogs (left) and its histopathology (right) found in the WAMC.

CONCLUSION

It is evident that an adequate utilization of wild animals for ecotourism is needed. Namely, this means that the wild animals are valuable tools for tourism. But, at the same time and place, wild animals are regarded as pests for agricultural and medical reasons, and so we are presented with the resources versus the issues for human society. Therefore, before and/or in performance of ecotourism with utilization of the animals, educational opportunities are needed. I introduced the ongoing monitoring system performed by the Wild Animal Medical Center (WAMC). Probably, this system will support the sustainable adequate ecotourism.

By the way, if we make the tourism sustainable, we have to keep educating staffs as well. For example, the WAMC is managed by veterinary university students supervised by the present author. So-called wildlife or nature education is one of the developing businesses in Japan. Students pay around 20,000 USD a year for tuition, but they seem to be absolutely satisfied with working with real wild animals, and even dead bodies. Finally, they will get job opportunities to become professional wildlife vets and/or scientists, and will help to progress the ecotourism related to wild animals in Japan. We, belonging to universities of veterinary or applied zoology, should discover a new scientific or business field between the ecotourism and wildlife education in the future, because this emerging new field will promote safe ecotourism.

ACKNOWLEDGMENTS

The present note was based on the data obtained from the research projects supported by the Global Environment Research Fund (F-062, 2006-2008) of the Ministry of the Environment, and a Grant-in-Aid (Nos. 18510205, 20380163) of the Ministry of the

Education, Science and Culture, Japan. I thank Dr. Hajime Ishikawa, Institute of Cetacean Research, Tokyo, for giving his permission to use his photograph.

REFERENCES

Aguirre, A. A., et al. (2002) *Conservation Medicine: ecological health in practice.* Oxford University Press, Oxford.

Asakawa, M. (2007). Annual report 2006 of the Wild Animal Medical Center, Rakuno Gakuen University. *J Hokkaido Vet Med Assoc, 51,* 7-17. (in Japanese).

Asakawa, M. (2008). Annual report 2007 of the Wild Animal Medical Center, Rakuno Gakuen University. *J Hokkaido Vet Med Assoc, 52,* 85-94.(in Japanese).

Asakawa, M. (2009a). Annual report 2008 of the Wild Animal Medical Center, Rakuno Gakuen University (1). *J Hokkaido Vet Med Assoc, 53,* 67-71. (in Japanese).

Asakawa, M. (2009b). Annual report 2007 of the Wild Animal Medical Center, Rakuno Gakuen University (2). *J Hokkaido Vet Med Assoc, 53,* 118-123. (in Japanese).

Asakawa, M. & Taniyama, H. (2005). Research and educational activities of the Wild Animal Medical Center in Rakuno Gakuen University—Past, present and future. *J Rakuno Gakuen Univ, 29,* 145-153.

Hayama, S. (2001) *Wildlife Issues;* Chijin-shokan Co., Tokyo,

Ministry of Health, Labour and Welfare of Japan (2009). Zoonosis: http:www.forth.go.jp/

Royal Veterinary College, Londin University (2009).

mhlw/animal/

http://www.rvc.ac.uk/Postgraduate/ Masters/MScWildAnimalHealth/index.cfm

Taniyama, H., et al; (1996) A natural case of larval echinococcosis caused by *Echinococcus multilocularis* in a zoo orangutan (*Pongo pygmaeus*). In Uchino, J. and Sato, N. eds., *Alveolar echinococcosis,* Fujishoin, Sapporo, 65-67.

In: Ecotourism: Management, Development and Impact
Editors: A. Krause, E. Weir, pp. 241-255
ISBN: 978-1-60876-724-3
© 2010 Nova Science Publishers, Inc.

Chapter 11

PAST LANDSCAPES FOR THE RECONSTRUCTION OF ROMAN LAND USE: ECO-HISTORY TOURISM IN THE ALGARVE

Eric de Noronha Vaz[1], João Pedro Bernardes[2] and Peter Nijkamp[3]*

[1]New University of Lisbon – Institute of Statistics and Information Management.
[2]University of the Algarve – Faculty of Human and Social Sciences.
[3]Free University of Amsterdam – Faculty of Economics and Business Administration.

ABSTRACT

Over the last 50 years, land use has dramatically changed. Over the past two decades, Remote Sensing imagery and its capacity to observe detailed land use patterns has facilitated a deeper understanding of historical land development patterns. Hence, the goal of this paper is to shed some light on the possibilities of recovering ancient landscapes, by using spatial analysis combined with statistical methodologies applied to archaeological Roman sites in Portugal. The investigation of Roman land use patterns in the Algarve is carried out using density patterns of site propensity based on geographic and topological characteristics. Such a methodology allows a more accurate assessment of what might have been past land use during the Roman period in the Algarve. This experiment is also useful to better comprehend and make a more appropriate interpretation of predictive modelling scenarios. In particular, in our case- study area, to have a share in the Algarve's archaeological legacy value may be very interesting to the tourist industry because of the possibility to explore more sustainable tourism options rather than the 'sun and beach' mass tourism offered traditionally in that region. This may lead to the development of an eco-history tourism product, by recycling existing built environments and creating an opportunity to generate revenues related to historico-cultural assets.

Keywords: Ecotourism, Algarve, GIS, Land Use, Survey data, Spatial Analysis, Cultural Heritage, Roman land use.

* Corresponding authors: E-mail: pnijkamp@feweb.vu.nl, Pn339ev; evaz@isegi.unl.pt; jbernar@ualg.pt

1. INTRODUCTION

For over two centuries, "Archaeology has possessed strong conceptual divides between data collection and data analysis, manifested most obviously between excavation and post excavation activities" (Conolly and Lake, 2006). Material evidence has led to collection of spatial data related to anthropogenic and archaeological subjects (Renfrew and Bahn, 2004). Archaeological material evidence, as is the case for archaeological sites with specific spatial characteristics, has a very unique spatial dimension. The combination of anthropogenic sites at a spatial level helps modern man to understand his origins: "(…) human behavior consists of people-artifact interactions at various scales, and then research questions in the social and behavioral sciences should be reformulated to include a more symmetrical understanding of people and artifacts. One can no longer be satisfied to analytically separate people (and the "social") from their material matrix. All human activities simultaneously involve interactions in the life histories of artifacts and participation in cadenas. Separating human behaviour from artifacts always results in neglect of the latter" (Walker and Shiffer, 2006).

The classical Roman Empire was well-established in the southern region of Portugal, the Algarve, where a rich historical and archaeological legacy remains. Since the 19th century, those studying the region have been interested in gaining a better understanding of the Roman socio-economic activity in the area. The region itself has been a cradle for past civilizations, where its favourable geographic location has led to commercial and agricultural benefits since the Neolithic period. By combining a large amount of (although scattered) site information, Roman land use becomes a source of archaeological insights with ancillary environmental characteristics.

Such environmental characteristics, as well as georeferenced site information, may easily be analysed by means of Geographic Information Systems (GIS). The combination of GIS-related logistic regression properties can reveal patterns of Roman land use. The use of such technologies to 'revive' past land use, may be very valuable both for historians wishing to better understand cultural complexity (Kvamme, 1990) and for the development of new tourism products, such as cultural heritage tourism. This agenda puts archaeology in perspective, not only as a historical domain but also as a sub-area of regional planning and urban growth.

There is a certain social efficiency in recovering the past to value the present. First, the roots of local and regional history often become better remembered, and, secondly, by sensitizing society to the existing heritage, and by offering interesting solutions to meso-economic problems, sustainable and more integrated directions of regional development may be achieved.

The circular flow model proposed by Tribe (1995) in Figure 1 clearly focuses on the consequences of tourism and the use of sinks/sources relating to environmental capacity. The circular flow model shows the consequences of permitting the accumulation of wealth from the production of goods and services and the exploitation of resources. The relationship between the production of goods and services and the utilization of resources necessary for this, comined with the scarcity of resources, defines the carrying capacity of the environment. Such consequences lead inevitably to land use change, pollution and the vulnerability of ecosystems, and thus sustainability is comprised.

The understanding of cultural legacy at the regional level starts with the application of spatial technologies in the context of detecting patterns of land use, in relation to the regional dimension of land use planning. Although usually left unconsidered for planning purposes, archaeology does have an important role and has long relied on survey data to facilitate the historic understanding of past civilizations. Thus, articulation of survey data brought from archaeology in the context of economic and spatial analysis is both an unprecedented and important task.

Predicting past land use scenarios unavoidably carries a certain degree of spatial uncertainty. However, surveyed archaeological site information not only allows the historical understanding of man's past activities to be questioned but also helps to recover local tradition and culture in a given region for a specific 'place in time'. By recovering historical tradition, it may be possible to revive the past, as well as to set in motion interesting trends for future sustainable development (Holtorf, 2008) in order to avoid excessive exploitation of economic resources.

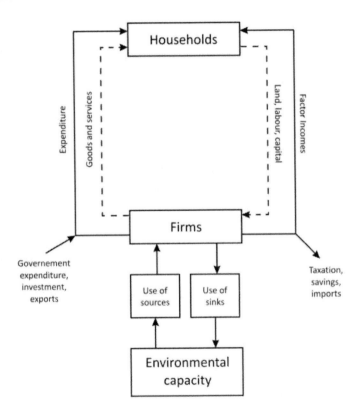

Figure 1. Environmental capacity and the circular flow model (adapted from Tribe, 1995)

2. THE HISTORICAL ALGARVE

The Algarve region comprises a total area of 4899 km^2 which represents 5.5 per cent of continental Portugal and is the most southerly region in Portugal. It is surrounded by the Atlantic Ocean to the South and West, and to the North a massive mountain range, the *Serra do Caldeirão*, separates it from the Alentejo. This basic morphology of the region has had a profound influence on its more temperate micro-climate compared with the rest of Portugal, contributing to a particular vegetation and wildlife in a unique habitat for many species. From a geomorphological perspective, the Algarve has three distinct layers of indigenous cultural, vegetative and ecological characteristics.

The location of the Serra do Caldeirão, is known as the Barrocal. As suggested by Malato-Beliz (1986) "(...) because of its climate and soil conditions, the Barrocal area has a very peculiar distinctive coverage, whose floral composition and grouping, if not exclusive, are certainly rare outside of this region." South of the Barrocal is the Interior, while the massively populated region along the coast is known as the Litoral.

The lack of transportation networks has to a certain extent meant that the degradation of the *Interior* and *Barrocal* has been avoided. However, since the 1960s the coastal region has been affected by the mass tourism industry. This has led to great landscape pressure and urban growth, resulting from population increases due to local economic prosperity and the availability of seasonal jobs. Consequently, a remarkable contrast is found in the Algarve: the southern Algarve is highly populated and has extensive urban areas. Influenced by the economic development in the Algarve, the original scenic landscapes that were once characterized by picturesque whitewashed houses are becoming forever lost as a result of unprecedented city growth (Vaz and Nijkamp, 2008). Nevertheless, some kilometres north of the long stretches of modern buildings, a more remote and ancestral Algarve beckons as an interesting opportunity to reshape the predominant hotel and tourist package offers.

As a result of its privileged geographical and topographic characteristics, the Algarve has been of great economic importance since pre-Roman times (Gamito, 1997). Its unique location as a port for the Mediterranean areas (including Northern Africa) with its moderate climate and its well-charted waters, which allowed easy access to the lush pastures of the area formerly-known as Lusitania, was already acknowledged centuries ago by Strabo (Strabo, 2007).

With its high Neolithic presence (Nocete et al., 2005; Ramirez et al., 2007) and several Bronze Age settlements, there has been archaeological interest in the region since the 19th century, first shown by archaeologists such as Estácio da Veiga who, among others, catalogued and described a wide range of archaeological findings in the region. The Algarve in the Roman period is well-documented (Santos, 1971; Alarcão, 1974; Teichner, 1994; Bernardes and Oliveira, 2002). The built-up heritage from the classical Roman period is still observable in the vicinity of the coastal cities. In the coastal areas many *cetarias* (rectangular stone vessels) have been found. These vessels once contained a typical Roman fish spice, *garum* (Curtis, 1991; Étienne and Mayet, 2002), widely produced along the Algarve, and exported throughout the entire Roman Empire. The production of *garum* in southern Hispania has been identified as a key element to the Algarve's economic success during the Roman period (Edmondson, 1990; Osland, 2006).

The former area of *Lusitania* prospered from the reign of Augustus until the end of the Antiquity. Major Roman *civitates* (cities) such as *Ossonoba* or *Cilpes* were fortified and reoccupied during the Moorish period. As a consequence of this heterogeneous mixture of styles, the Algarve shows a variety of Moorish, Roman and Christian heritage within its cities' urban limits. Former Roman cities such as *Ossonoba* and *Balsa*, as well as the ruins of *Milreu* in *Estoi* or the ruins found in Vilamoura (*Cerro da Vila*), were economically important during this period.

Also, the abundance of the classical Roman period is visible by the in rich legacy monuments. Many of the mosaics which adorn the monuments have nautical motifs, accompanied by a profusion of sea creatures and Gods. Such heritage presents a unique ecological vision of the Algarve as a coastal area of the past. Furthermore, it is endowed with an aesthetic dimension composed of the actual landscape together with its cultural archaeological heritage.

3. ARCHAEOLOGICAL INFORMATION SYSTEMS

Despite the rich historical legacy, past land use has not been much explored in the Algarve. However, the availability of archaeological catalogue and geo-information data, concerning the environment and supported by geo-statistical inference, enables a better understanding past land use patterns. As the causal relations between georeferenced sites are established, environmental and geographical characteristics can help to recover spatial dimensions of archaeological evidence.

As mentioned earlier, the large quantity of *cetarias* found in the Algarve region show that the region was once a proficient producer of *garum* (Silva, 2007). Overall, the Algarve in Roman times seems to have been an area of economic wealth, based on this production which was distributed to the entire Roman Empire, as well as being a place of leisure and worship of deities. Such socio-economic niches seem to be common throughout the entire southwest region of the Iberian Peninsula.

Understanding Roman land use depends on survey data resulting from almost two hundred years of Roman archaeological investigation in the Algarve. The distribution of material evidence results from the spatial location where the archaeological survey occurred, based on archaeological excavations. The collection of this spatial information has enabled a database to be compiled with 452 occurrences of archaeological sites excavated from 1910 up to 2006.

The archaeological sites were interpreted in our study by employing a GIS which uses the Universal Transverse Mercator (UTM) as a geographic projection. Georeferenced archaeological sites were classified into socio-economic categories of Ceramics, Mosaics, Coins, Iron, and Epigraphs. The combination of the spatial location of material evidence and environmental characteristics enabled a spatial assessment of Roman land use. Geographic Information Systems (GIS) have an important role in regional development and planning (Douven et al., 1993). Not only do GIS represent systems to access, analyse and represent data (Longley et. al. 2006), but they are also able to cope with different data sets which allows quantitative methodologies to be used within various human sciences (Wheatley and Gillings, 2002).

A further topic in which GIS is having great impact and which is considered to be as useful as radiocarbon dating (Westcott and Brandon, 2000) in archaeology. Since the beginning of processual archaeology, material evidence obtained from archaeological excavations has had a key role in the interpretation of material culture (White, 1959). Because of their inherent spatial character (Schiffer, 1972), past activities based on spatial archaeological data become easier to understand (Hodder, 1972). Technological advances, statistical approaches, survey methods, and available information have become more important supporting methodologies for 'quantifying archaeology'.

Although the consequences of environmental determinism are sometimes viewed with a certain scepticism (Burns, 2007), in a regional planning context, environmental determinism in archaeology may be overcome for the following reasons: (1) the possibility to observe past land use has shed light on road networks which lead to monuments of historic interest; (2) the context of historic urban and regional planning differs largely from traditional archaeological subjectivity; and (3) the articulation between tourism and archaeology or cultural heritage leads to a fusion of areas in which spatial environmental determinism already exists because of available infrastructures that complement the provision of the already available tourist industry.

Over the years, archaeology has greatly benefitted from spatial analysis and surveillance by Remote Sensing techniques, as well as Database management and GIS in general (Connolly and Lake, 2006). The ubiquity of areas in which archaeology benefits has such a broad spectrum that the correct manipulation of data and research of collected material is often complex. Such complexity involves many different actors with different needs and demands within the archaeological subject. Information should allow the creation of innovative scientific processes, involving different actors in the archaeological frame. In a combined information flux, anthropologists, conservationists, field archaeologists, GIS experts and cultural heritage managers, among many others, could work together to combine their information in an interdisciplinary way. Such an objective can only be achieved with a robust system that supports many different types of tasks and workflow levels.

The quantification of information in the human sciences is not always an easy process as quantifiable and technological processes are limited. However, some human sciences such as sociology, geography, anthropology and archaeology, have felt the need to dissociate themselves from the strictly qualitative sciences. Given the pragmatic character of real-world phenomena (whether past, present or future), nature retains certain aspects of quantitative relevance. Such aspects of quantification are being explored by a handful of what are known as human sciences, and have brought a convergence between mathematical, social and statistical methodologies.

Attempts to provide quantitative and qualitative integrated future knowledge have led to lively debates such as the Dahlem Workshops[1] where quantitative and qualitative information combined have set the tone for new paradigms of a common sustainable future (Costanza et al., 2006).

For archaeology an interest in quantitative and technological methodologies is justified by the possibility of quantifying material evidence (Doran and Hodson, 1975). With the evolution of archaeological science and GIS, the latter has developed into more user-friendly platforms which allow spatial interpretation. Nowadays GIS represent an important tool for analysis, comparison and the investigation of archaeological phenomena and information (Connolly and Lake, 2006). Thus, archaeological catalogues have developed from simple registries into large data containers with information that may be created, retrieved, eliminated and changed, and facilitated by GIS.

---

[1] Dahlem Workshop Goal: To understand better the dynamics between human societies and their environment by linking various forms of knowledge on human history and environmental change at multiple temporal scales (millennial, centennial, decadal and future scenarios.

The conditions for a database management system were established in the field of archaeology in order to enable the integration of information related to archaeological site phenomena. Nowadays, an archaeological database is not just advantageous for archaeological registry, but is also an important tool for information management and retrieval, thereby permitting the generation of a knowledge flow between the different actors engaged in the archaeological sciences. Technologically, archaeological information demands the physical storage properties of databases. The resulting databases with information centrally stored, keep data consistent and standardized over a multi-user support for data input and output.

The construction of an accurate and complete database is not always an easy task, as linking different actors is often not a standardized process and needs effective assembly. Henceforth, the relation between the abstract concepts of a logical archaeological database and the execution of operational support demands precise technical methods. Next, Section 4 explains the creation of such a framework for Portugal in an operational data experiment designed to identify Roman land use in the Algarve.

4. ENDOVELICO, A PORTUGUESE DATABASE MANAGEMENT SYSTEM FOR ARCHAEOLOGY

In 1989, the first attempt was made to create a map of archaeological findings. Nevertheless, it was only in 1995 that this map (Carta Arqueológica de Portugal) was actually compiled. This initiative became the responsibility of the Portuguese Archaeological Institute in 1997. Thus, as of this date, this map has been recognized as an important landmark in the present information to support archaeological preservation in Portugal (Divisão de Inventário do Instituto Português de Arqueologia, 2002). A contextual framework, driven by the main objective of the Portuguese Archaeological Institute to "*detect, protect and manage archaeological vestiges*" (Decree no. 117/97, May 14th, Paragraph 1A, Article 2), reinforced this achievement. As an important event in the national archaeological framework, the Archaeological map (*Carta Arqueológica Portuguesa*) became a recognized asset for the validation and confirmation of research and excavations.

The archaeological information available in the *Carta Aqueológica Portuguesa* is organized into a database named *Endovélico*. This database allows the addition of current research, as well as spatial validation of past site information. The context of information systems from an archaeological perspective generates synergy among institutions and stakeholders. Thus, *Endovélico* may prove to have a central role in archaeological preservation and archaeological excavation in Portugal. Moreover, it is important to provide a common ground for the ubiquity of archaeological information.

Figure 2 is a graphical representation of the conceptual workflow of all the attributes stored in the *Endovélico* database. The structural relations are separate from the occurrence of archaeological sites, and have a central role in the evolution of scientific as well as other important research. As sites are supported by bibliographic research, as well as fieldwork, people as well as institutions become an inherent part of the workflow process. Institutions, on the other hand, play an important role in proactively defining new projects to enrich the scientific work field and create new documents, reports or ancillary scientific processes, and, as a result, inherent spatial dimensions might be framed in a Geographic Information System. The location of institutions and people as well as the location of sites, share important spatial dynamics which are stored in the *Endovélico* and supply a coherent validation of Archaeological data, as facilitating intra-institutional cooperation.

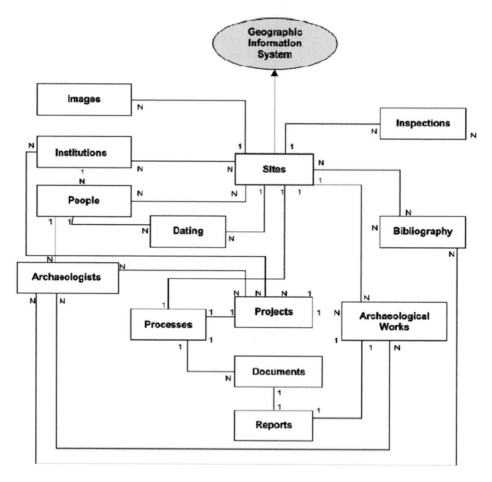

Figure 2. Simplified ER Diagram of Endovélico (adapted from Divisão do Inventário do Instituto Português de Arqueologia, 2002)

5. ROMAN LAND USE IN THE ALGARVE A PREDICTIVE MODELLING APPROACH

The Roman land-use prediction model for the Algarve was calculated by combining environmental variables with available archaeological material evidence. Furthermore, statistical inference on site location allowed a generalized land use propensity to be established (Kvamme, 1988).

After choosing a region of a total area of 5x5km, a digital elevation model was generated to allow the calculation of slope and direction. The cost surface corresponding to the prediction of higher Roman activity propensity was based on the combination of those variables within a quantification standard of site densities (Figure 3), brought from the *Endovélico*-confirmed regional data set.

As archaeological activity is supposed to reveal Roman behaviour, information regarding elevation from the digital elevation model (DEM) provided a solid methodology to calculate other environmental surfaces (Miller and Barton, 2008; Hayakawa and Tsumura, 2009). The variation of weights related to the presence or non-presence of Roman remains depending on spatial location permitted us to generate specific weights based on a logistic regression of weight behaviour throughout distances. The combination of those aggregated classes generated the propensity for the potential to find future archaeological sites and Roman land use.

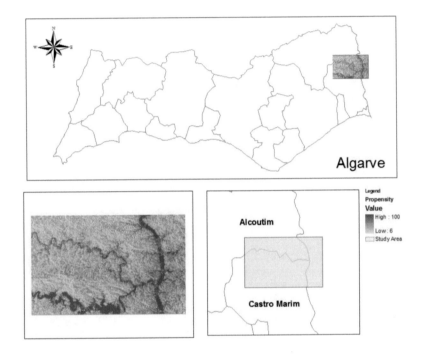

Figure 3. Overview of study area with propensity for Roman heritage

As may be observed in Figure 3, a greater potential for finding Roman remains exists in the area with low slope and lower elevation. Such conclusions are interesting, as this resembles contemporary settling preferences in contemporary urban growth, i.e. the vicinities of river basins or coastal shores, which establishes an interesting correlation between past and present human behaviour as well as the central role of past land use traditions.

The accuracy of the land use model was investigated in a more regional context, making the following assumptions: (1) Roman settlement preferences are linked to higher elevations and shade; (2) south or north facing locations are preferred for human activity; (3) and so is proximity to river basins and coastal bodies of water. A generalized propensity model was next established via the comparison of the generated 5x5 km model, within a lower resolution spatial area. NASA's Shuttle Radar Topography Mission (SRTM) digital elevation model (DEM) with 90m spatial resolution was used to calculate weights for comparable environmental characteristics. Table 1 shows a comparison of the accuracy and similarity of the observed sites in both scenarios.

Table 2. – Weight Matrix of variable criteria for site propensity

	High Spatial Resolution			
	Classified	Non Classified	Accuracy	Weight
Elevation (48-120m)	11	8	0.578947	79
Slope (0 - 33%)	14	5	0.736842	100
Aspect (North and South)	9	10	0.473684	64

A propensity map for regional comparison was generated by structuring a propensity equation with relative weights of elevation, slope, and aspect. The resulting formula may be expressed as follows:

$$P = (w_1X_1 + w_2X_2 + w_3X_3)/N,$$

where w1, w2 and w3 represent the relative accuracy for each of the variables, and where x1, x2 and x3 show the respective landscape variables used. It appears that most archaeological sites may be found in the 80-100% interval of the archaeological site potential (Figure 4), which supports the accuracy of generalizing local scale sites to a more regional scope of analysis.

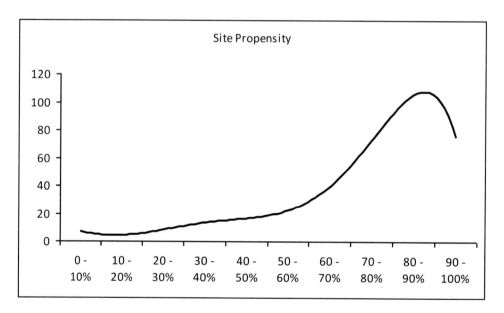

Figure 4. Overall site propensity for Roman sites in the Algarve

6. CONCLUSIONS ON ARCHAEOLOGICAL PREDICTIVE MODELS

By comparing the propensities generated by local and regional models in our study, it was possible to determine the influence of scale in the archaeological predictive context.

Comparing the model accuracy, we have witnessed the possibilities of combining local spatial strata into a more aggregated macro-analysis level. Our information combined stochastic methodologies leading ultimately to a generalized framework of Roman land use propensity. Some interesting questions were raised by this analysis: (i) possibilities of combining smaller and higher scales of study, as spatial patterns seem to be constant over regional territory for anthropologic behaviour. The use of smaller scales may further allow the break down of the areas into simpler and more homogeneous units which would lead to higher data consistency, although this issue is often neglected by the archaeological community (Bevan and Conolly, 2009); (ii) calculated cost surfaces of Roman land use have confirmed that Roman land use and settlement occur in proximity to river basins; (iii) the spatial orientation that human settlements might have had obviously plays an important role in geo-archaeological circumstances.

7. CONCLUSIONS ON POLICY CHOICES FOR ECO-HISTORY TOURISM

The Algarve has experienced a rapid increase in its tourist industry since the beginning of the 1960s. Exploration of the tourist product related to 'sol e praia' ('sun and beach'), strongly focused on the exploitation of coastal landscapes (Cunha, 1993), has inevitably led to an increasing fragility of littoral ecosystems. The increasing vulnerability of marine ecosystems has been brought to light in particular as a result of the rising number of hotels and resorts. However, the depletion of scarce ecosystems in order to create leisure products should be analysed critically from the perspective of the dynamics of the carrying capacity of the ecosystem itself (Tribe, 1995).

Tourism in the Algarve currently faces several competitors regarding tourist products, as low airfares encourage tourists to visit more tropical destinations, with unrivalled 'sun and beach' attractions. Choosing other tourist products such as historical tourism/cultural tourism relating to the rich fauna and flora of the region, would enable the Algarve to explore a new concept of eco-history tourism, which would provide a more competitive and less environmentally-exhaustive alternative. Clearly, the availability of a rich cultural heritage that is not located in the areas of current fragile coastal ecosystems brings an interesting opportunity to relieve tourist pressure on the littoral areas. The creation of new tourist attractions inherent to the richness of the region and based on existing and renewable resources seems to be an immediate answer to sustain tourism in the Algarve.

Thus, evidence of Roman land use in the Algarve and the existence of an abundant Roman historic legacy suggest that this regions should be promoted as a route of Roman past portrait in a typical Mediterranean landscape, and thus an opportunity for a new kind of tourist product[2]. Furthermore, recent studies (Campos Carrasco et al., 2008) describe the rich collection of Roman mosaics found in the southern part of the former region of Hispania (Algarve and South-Andalusia) which emphasizes the relevance of this area as one of the Roman Empire's poles of cultural heritage. If archaeology and the tourist industry were to collaborate in joint initiatives,

---

[2] A good example to illustrate the first steps in such a direction is the project MOSUDHIS ("Roman Mosaics in the southeast of Hispania: Andalusia and Algarve", European Community INTERREG III-A, Measure 2.4, Axis II, URL: http://www.cepha.ualg.pt/mosudhis/). By combining spatial information and touristic information within a framework of scientific archaeological research is developing a new type of touristic product.

then the role of scientific information would be to underpin the concept of eco-history tourism. This might represent a more ecological alternative by avoiding the consequences of the mass tourist industry and supporting an environmentally-benign, historical landscape.

This paper has suggested a new approach to define an innovative area for the tourist sector: eco-history tourism. On the one hand, this tourist product relies on scientific information (such as archaeological predictive models), and, on the other, factual information on archaeological sites (by use of databases) to confirm relevant patterns of past land use in regions. This information supported by scientific findings may help to market regions on the basis of their archaeological legacy, offering a cultural tourism alternative which is an interesting solution for developing conservation and cultural sustainability alternatives. In the Algarve, such a product would adapt quite well, given the already-existing tourism infrastructures. In regions such as the Algarve, with a diverse and attractive fauna and flora, ecotourism is likely to do well, while simultaneously offering a past identity to the region focused on the existing historic monuments and archaeological heritage.

The re-equilibrium of the asymmetric spatial properties of tourism in the Algarve demands new solutions to provide an attractive alternative to the mass tourism industry in the region. More attention to carrying capacity of existing infrastructures, whether natural or artificial (monuments and archaeological heritage), should be given (see also Coccossis, 2004). Lessons to be heeded are thus:

- Mass tourism exerts pressure on land use and affects natural and land resources. Therefore, the trade-off of providing a new tourist product in the Algarve related to ecotourism and cultural heritage may rebalance an already overexploited resource;
- A profound awareness of impacts is necessary to comprehend more fully the actual state of local and micro-scale degradation due to tourism in the Algarve. As the coastal area seems clearly affected, Pressure-State-Response[3] will lead necessarily to solutions which would spatially protect the resource.

The resources available in the Algarve are many, and policy options regarding sustainability must have consideration for the environment. This paper has demonstrated the possibility of bringing alternatives of sustainable tourism to the Algarve. As highlighted in the proceedings of *Património e Turismo* ('Heritage and Tourism', 1999) by the coordinator of the national increment programme of cultural tourism: *"Heritage tourism is a growing demand at national and European level that should be cherished and protected, while vitalized as an interesting alternative for tourism and development"*.

REFERENCES

Alarcão, J. (1974). *Portugal Romano* (Coimbra: Verbo).

---

[3] The Pressure-State-Response is an Environmental deterministic framework which measures existing environmental pressures (pollution, urban degradation, etc.), current state (How much pollution? What areas are degraded?), and policy responses (What can be done and how?) in a given location.

Bernardes, J. P. & Oliveira, L. (2002). A calçadinha de S. Brás de Alportel e a antiga rede viária do Algarve central (Faro: Universidade do Algarve).

Bevan, A. & Conolly, J. (2009). Modelling spatial heterogeneity and nonstationarity in artifact-rich landscapes, *Journal of Archaeological Science, 36(4),* 956-964.

Burns, G. (2007). *Predictive Modeling of Cultural Resources in the Theban Necropolis, Luxor Egypt,* Master thesis dissertation, Graduate School - College of Charleston.

Campos Carrasco, J. M., Fernández Ugalde, A., García Dils, S., Gómez Rodríguez, Á., Lancha, J. Oliveira, C., De Rueda Roigé, J. F. & And De La O Vidal Teruel, N. (2008). *A Rota Do Mosaico Romano, O Sul Da Hispânia (Andaluzia E Algarve) - Cidades E Villae Notáveis Da Bética E Lusitânia Romanas,* Faro: Departamento De História, Arqueologia E Património Da Universidade Do Algarve.

Coccossis, H., 2004, Sustainable Tourism and Carrying Capacity: A New Context. In H. Coccossis and A. Mexa (eds), *The Challenge of Tourism Carrying Capacity Assessment: Theory and Practice* (Aldershot: Ashgate). 3-15.

Conolly, K. & Lake, M. (2006). *Geographical Information Systems in Archaeology* (New York: Cambridge University Press).

Costanza, R., Graumlich, L. & Steffen, W. (2007). Sustainability or collapse: Lessons from integrating the history of humans and the rest of nature. In R. Costanza, L. Graumlich and W. Steffen, *Sustainability or collapse? An integrated history and future of people on earth,* Dahlem Workshop Reports, (Cambridge MA: MIT Press), 3-19.

Cunha, L. (1997). *Economia e Política do Turismo* (Lisbon: Mcgraw-Hill).

Curtis, R. I. (1991). Garum and Salsamenta. Production and Commerce in Materia Medica, *Studies in Ancient Medicine, 3* (Leiden: Brill).

Divisão Do Inventário Do Instituto Português De Arqueologia, (2002). Endovélico - Sistema De Gestão E Informação Arqueológica, *Revista Portuguesa De Arqueologia, 5(1),* 277-283.

Doran, J. E. & Hodson, F. R. (1975). *Mathematics and Computers in Archaeology* (Edinburgh: Edinburgh University Press).

Douven, W., Grothe, M., Nijkamp, P. & Scholten, H. J. (1993). Urban and Regional Planning Models and GIS, Research Memorandum 1992-74, (Amsterdam: VU University).

Edmondson, J. C. (1990). Le Garum en Lusitanie urbaine et rurale: hierarchies de demande et de production, *Les Villes de Lusitanie romaine: hierarchies et territories,* Table ronde internationale du CNRS (Talence, 8-9 decebre 1988). 149-206.

Étienne and Mayet, (2002). *Salaism et sauces de poisson hispanique* (Paris: Boccard)

Gamito, T. J. (1997). A cidade de Ossonoba e o seu território envolvente, *Noventa séculos entre a serra e o mar* (Lisbon: IPPAR), 343-360.

Hayakawa, Y. S. & Tsumura, H. (2009). Utilization of laser range finder and differential GPS for high-resolution topographic measurement at Hacituğrul Tepe, Turkey, *Geoarchaeology, 24(2).* 176-190.

Hodder I. (1972). Locational models and the study of the Romano-British settlement. In D.L. Clarke (ed.), *Models in Archaeology* (London: Methuen), 887-909.

Holtorf, C. (2008). Is the Past a Non-renewable Resource? In G. Fairclough, R. Harrison, J.H. Jameson and J. Shoffield (eds.), *The Heritage Reader* (Oxon: Routledge), 125-133.

Kvamme, K. (1988). Development And Testing Of Quantitative Models In J. Judge and L. Sebastian (eds.), *Quantifying The Present And Predicting The Past* (Denver: US Department of the Interior, Bureau of Land Management), 325-418.

Kvamme, K. (1990). The Fundamental Principles and Practice of Predictive Archaeological Modeling. In A. Verrips (ed.), *Mathematics and Information Science in Archaeology: A Flexible Framework* (Bonn: Holos-Verlag), 257-295.

Longley, P. A., Goodchild, M. F., Maguire, D. J. & Rhind, D. W. (2006). *Geographic Information Systems and Science* (2nd edition), West Sussex: John Wiley and Sons.

Malato-Beliz, J. V. C. (1986). O Barrocal Algarvio, *Col. Parques Naturais* **17** (Lisboa: Serviço Nacional de Parques, Reservas e Património Paisagístico).

Miller, A. & Barton, M. (2008). Exploring the land: a comparison of land-use patterns in the Middle and Upper Paleolithic of the western Mediterranean, *Journal of Archaeological Science, 35(5)*, 1427-1437.

Nocete, F., Saéz, R., Nieto, J. M., Cruz-Auñon, R., Cabrero, R., Alex, E. & Bayona, M. R. (2005). Circulation of silicified Neolithic limestone blades in South-Iberia (Spain and Portugal) during the third millennium B.C.: an expression of a core/periphery framework, *Journal of Anthropological Archaeology, 24(1)*, pp. 62-81.

Osland, D. (2006). *The early Roman cities of Lusitania* (Oxford: Archaeopress).

Patrimonio, E. & Turismo, (1999). Proceedings of the Patrimonio e turismo desenvolvimento e turismo: cicle de debates (Lisbon: Instituto de Financiamento e Apoio ao Turismo).

Ramirez, P. B., Behrmann, R. B. & Bermejo, R. B., (2007). Chronologie de l'art Mégalithique ibérique : C14 et contextes archéologiques, *L'Anthropologie, 111(4)*, 590-654.

Renfrew, C. & P. Bahn, (2004). *Archaeology: Theories, Methods and Practice* (London: Thames & Hudson).

Santos, M. L. E. V. dos, (1971). Arqueologia romana do Algarve, vol. I (Lisboa: Associação dos Arqueólogos Portugueses).

Schiffer, M. B, (1972). Archaeological context and systemic context, *American Antiquity, 37*, 156-65.

Silva, L. F. (2007). *Balsa, Cidade Perdida* (Tavira: Câmara Municipal de Tavira).

Strabo, (2007). *Geographica – Drittes Buch, Zweites Kapitel: Beschreibung des inneren Landes von Bätika oder Turdetanien* (Berlin: Marixverlag).

Swensen, G. (2006). Incorporating urban heritage into local community planning. In W. van der Knaap and A. van der Valk (eds.), *Multiple Landscape – Merging Past and Present* (Wageningen: Ponsen & Looijen), 157-170.

Teichner, F. (1994). Acerca da vila romana de Milreu/Estoi: continuidade da ocupação na época árabe, *Arqueologia Medieval, 3*, 89-100.

Tribe, J. (1995). *The Economics of leisure and tourism – Environments, Markets and Impacts* (Oxford: Butterworth-Heinemann).

Vaz, E. & Nijkamp, P. (2009). Historico-Cultural Sustainability and Urban Dynamics. In G. Maciocco and S. Serreli (eds.), *Enhancing the city, New Perspectives for Tourism and Leisure* (Berlin: Springer).

Veiga, S. P. (2005). *Antiguidades monumentais do Algarve*, (Coimbra: Universidade do Algarve).

Walker, W. H. & Schiffer, M. B. (2006). The Materiality of Social Power: The Artifact-Acquisition Perspective, *Journal of Archaeological Method and Theory, 13(2)*, 67-88.

Westcott, K. L. & Brandon, R. K. (2000). *Practical Applications of GIS for Archaeologists: A Predictive Modeling Kit* (London: Taylor and Francis)

Wheatley, D. & Gillings, M. (2002). *Spatial Technology and Archaeology: The Archaeological Applications of GIS* (London: Taylor & Francis).

White, L. (1959). *The Evolution of Culture* (New York: McGraw-Hill).

In: Ecotourism: Management, Development and Impact
Editors: A. Krause, E. Weir, pp. 257-260

ISBN: 978-1-60876-724-3
© 2010 Nova Science Publishers, Inc.

Chapter 12

EFFECTIVE MANAGEMENT DECISION-MAKING DEPENDS ON RIGOROUS RESEARCH

Ursula Ellenberg and Philip J. Seddon

Department of Zoology, University of Otago, Dunedin, New Zealand

ABSTRACT

Mainstream tourism eco-certification programmes focus with varying success on "brown" aspects of environmental management, such as energy efficiency, resource consumption and waste treatment, whereas the impacts of tourism on "green" aspects, i.e. on the species and habitats that attracted nature-based tourism in the first place, are still largely being ignored. As the growth of nature-based tourism is expected to continue, it is important not only for ecological but also for economic sustainability to minimise any associated negative human impacts. Currently, managers are forced to operate without the information necessary for appropriate and anticipatory management decisions. We believe that effective mitigation of potentially harmful effects that accompanies any human activity in natural environments will arise only from detailed site- and species-specific guidelines derived from rigorous research. Such research is resource hungry so it becomes increasingly important that costs will be borne by end users.

COMMENTARY

The impact of human disturbance on wildlife is often neglected when promoting "sustainable" tourism operations. However, even a one-off disturbance event can have devastating consequences; for example, approximately 7,000 King penguins died by asphyxiation when a single overflight by a Hercules aircraft caused a stampede on Macquarie Island (Rounsevell & Binns 1991; Cooper et al. 1994). The deaths resulted from large numbers of fleeing penguins piling up on top of each other against a natural barrier at one edge of the colony. While an extreme example, this event does illustrate that even without any bad intentions significant damage can be done. The effects of human disturbance in natural habitats have to be taken seriously and should be ideally managed via anticipatory decisions.

Although less conspicuous and thus often overlooked, the subtle accumulated effects of frequent low level human disturbance have potentially even more serious consequences than the single aircraft overflight mentioned above. The world population of Yellow-eyed penguins, for example, is currently estimated to be around 2,000 breeding pairs (Department of Conservation pers. comm.) and this species is an important flagship for nature-based tourism operations in New Zealand. We found unregulated tourism to be associated with reduced penguin reproductive success at frequently visited sites (Ellenberg et al. 2007). The cumulative effects of even minor human disturbance can cause lower fledgling weights which means chicks have reduce likelihood of surviving their first year at sea and recruiting into the breeding population (McClung et al. 2004; Ellenberg et al. 2007). For a more detailed review of human disturbance effects please refer to Seddon & Ellenberg (2008). Buckley (2004) provides a good and comprehensive overview of environmental impacts of ecotourism.

Natural habitats and the species therein are often taken for granted and subtle changes caused by human activities are not easily noticed. Few people are involved long enough with a given tourism operation that they would be aware of shifting species abundance or gradual habitat alterations. Baseline research providing information about the natural state of the system is usually unavailable and with a few exceptions little effort is made even to monitor the state of focal species from year to year. Associated species that may be less attractive as tourist attractions are often ignored even, though they may have important population strongholds in the area or play an integral part in ecosystem functioning. The tourists themselves will buy what they are sold, unaware of their impact which, in its true extent, is usually indiscernible for the short-term visitor – until their desired experience may have been degraded past the point of recovery.

Unfortunately, good intentions alone do not guarantee ecological sustainability. Recent research shows intuition provides a poor guide for managing human disturbance impact (e.g. Langkilde & Shine 2006). Disturbance stimuli that we, from a subjective human perspective, would consider to be low impact may be perceived quite differently by the affected animal. We were able to demonstrate that the slow and careful presence of a wildlife photographer was significantly more stressful to a nesting Yellow-eyed penguin than an entirely motionless human spending the same time at the same distance, or even a routine nest-check that involved lifting a bird up to view nest contents (Ellenberg & Seddon, unpublished data). Habituation to human disturbance is a complex issue that requires careful management and can by no means be assumed (Ellenberg et al. 2007; Ellenberg et al. 2009). Furthermore, even closely related species may respond very differently to human disturbance depending on a range of factors we are only now beginning to appreciate (Ellenberg et al. 2006; Seddon & Ellenberg 2008).

The accumulating effects of low level human disturbance events can be documented only via comprehensive research. We therefore urge tourism operators and those agencies or organisation charged with supporting or expanding the industry, to invest in rigorous research in association with nature-based businesses. Subtle changes frequently go unnoticed but can potentially have far reaching consequences: Seabirds, for example, live for a long time; the oldest recorded breeding Yellow-eyed penguin is currently at least 25 years of age. Seabirds are faithful to their breeding colonies and may return year after year despite previous breeding failure. Hence the loss of the next generation will be detected only years later once the aged colony starts to decline. By then management action may be too late; tourism will have destroyed its own base.

One has to keep in mind that human disturbance acts on top of other threats wildlife must face - and survival hasn't become any easier in recent decades. Human pressure on the world's ecosystems has considerably increased, with effects such as habitat destruction, pollution, introduced predators, over-use of natural resources, and climatic changes that perturb previously stable ecosystems. However, compared to many of these global threats human disturbance impact is relatively easily minimised. Local efforts will yield local rewards.

For ecological and thus economic sustainability, monitoring of disturbed and suitable control sites must accompany any nature-based tourism operations. Long-term population studies provide the data necessary to disentangle the confounding effects of human activity from those of other environmental variables. Such studies also allow for a better understanding of the secondary effects of human disturbance via complex ecological networks and multiple stressor interactions, and will detect other factors potentially threatening species (and tourism operations) early enough to allow for effective management action.

Measures of short- and medium-term physiological, behavioural responses and associated fitness consequences to a range of human disturbance stimuli will enable understanding of the proximate mechanisms of human disturbance effects. Experimental approaches in particular will provide managers with the reliable data necessary to develop appropriate and anticipatory site- and species-specific visitor management guidelines.

Finally, it is important to verify the efficiency of management guidelines currently in place. Management decisions, based on previous research, need to be re-assessed in terms of their effectiveness reducing human disturbance impact and in terms of visitor acceptance. Management needs to stay flexible and adaptive to be powerful.

Despite the current global economic recession the tourism industry continues to grow, and there remains a special emphasis on nature-based activities (ITB 2009) that will increase tourism pressure on the Earth's last wild areas. While current tourism eco-certification programmes may have the potential to eventually improve an operation's sustainability from a "brown" resource point of view, it is about time that the "green" aspects, the species and habitats that attracted the tourism in the very first place, are seen as an equally important resource and managed accordingly.

Rigorous research is needed to understand the nature of human disturbance related impacts. Only on the basis of hard data will conservation managers be able to formulate appropriate and anticipatory site- and species-specific visitor management guidelines. The complexity of ecological impacts or time and resources required to carry out the research necessary for appropriate control and management of human disturbance effects is still vastly underappreciated (Buckley 2004). The significant gaps in our knowledge need to be filled urgently, since tourism development and expansion will not necessarily wait for better guidelines. Rigorous comprehensive research is a wise and timely investment into the ecological and thus economical sustainability of nature-based tourism operations.

REFERENCES

Buckley, R. (2004). Environmental impacts of ecotourism. CABI, Wallingford, UK.

Cooper, J., Avenant, N. & P. Lafite. (1994). Airdrops and King penguins: a potential conservation problem at sub-Antarctic Marion Island. *Polar Record, 30,* 277-282.

Ellenberg, U., Mattern, T. & Seddon, P. J. (2009). Habituation potential of Yellow-eyed penguins depends on sex, character and previous experience with humans. *Animal Behaviour, 77,* 289-296.

Ellenberg, U., Mattern, T. Seddon, P. J. & Luna-Jorquera, G. (2006). Physiological and reproductive consequences of human disturbance in Humboldt penguins: The need for species-specific visitor management. *Biological Conservation, 133,* 95-106.

Ellenberg, U., Setiawan, A. N., Cree, A., Houston, D. M. & Seddon, P. J. (2007). Elevated hormonal stress response and reduced reproductive output in Yellow-eyed penguins exposed to unregulated tourism. *General and Comparative Endocrinology, 152,* 54-63.

ITB, (2009). World Travel Trends Report 2009. Downloaded from http://www1.messe-berlin.de/vip81/website/Internet/Internet/www.itb-berlin/pdf/Publikationen/worldttr 2009.pdf

Langkilde, T. & Shine, R. (2006). How much stress do researchers inflict on their study animals? A case study using a scincid lizard, *Eulamprus heatwolei. Journal of Experimental Biology, 209,* 1035-1043.

McClung, M. R., Seddon, P. J., Massaro, M. & Setiawan, A. N. (2004). Nature-based tourism impacts on yellow-eyed penguins *Megadyptes antipodes*: does unregulated visitor access affect fledging weight and juvenile survival? *Biological Conservation, 119,*279-285.

Rounsevell, D. & D. Binns. (1991). Mass deaths of King penguins (*Aptenodytes patagonicus*) at Lusitiana Bay, Macquarie Island. *Aurora, 10,* 8-10.

Seddon, P. J. & Ellenberg, U. (2008). Effects of human disturbance on penguins: The need for site- and species-specific visitor management guidelines. In: *Marine Wildlife and Tourism Management: Insights from the Natural and Social Sciences* (Ed. By Higham, J., and Lueck, M.), 163-181. Wallingford, Oxfordshire, UK: CAB International.

In: Ecotourism: Management, Development and Impact   ISBN: 978-1-60876-724-3
Editors: A. Krause, E. Weir, pp. 261-264   © 2010 Nova Science Publishers, Inc.

Chapter 13

QUALITY AND BUYING PROCESS IN RURAL TOURISM IN SPAIN

Rosa M. Hernández-Maestro

University of Salamanca - Administración y Economía de la Empresa, Campus Miguel
de Unamuno, Salamanca, Spain

ABSTRACT

Rural tourism in Spain has relied heavily on quality as a competitive strategy. However, some aspects of this sector make the buying process complex for consumers, which may compromise their ability to achieve their quality expectations. Facilities' variability in terms of their type and quality distinctions, as well as the important use of the Internet and the presence of illegal facilities, all contribute to this complexity.

COMMENTARY

Quality has become a key element for businesses because of its positive relationship with success. High-quality performance enhances business performance in both industrial and service sectors (Anderson et al., 1994, 1997; Behn and Riley, 1999; Smith and Wright, 2004; Valdés Peláez and Ballina Ballina, 2005). Different indicators of business performance relate positively to quality, such as sales or profits.

The process of obtaining positive business performance from the quality of an offering is represented in Figure 1. Customers' perceptions of quality, satisfaction and behaviour mediate the relationship between real or objective quality and business performance.

One sector that relies particularly on the effects of quality is rural tourism. In Spain, rural tourism has grown very quickly, increasing from 5,497 rural lodging facilities and 1,210,891 tourists in 2001 to 12,803 facilities and 2,626,821 tourists by 2008 (Spanish Institute of Statistics [INE], 2009). Quality in the Spanish rural tourism sector relates to several positive consequences. For example, Hernández-Maestro et al. (2009) find that a measure of rural lodging facilities' objective quality relates positively to tourists' perceptions of quality. Moreover, Valdés Peláez and Ballina Ballina (2005) confirm that the facilities that earn the quality brand "Casonas Asturianas" attain higher quality perceptions and business performance.

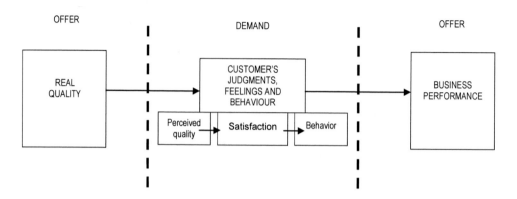

Figure 1. Consequences of quality

However, certain circumstances regarding rural tourism in Spain also can make a tourist's buying process complex, increasing the effort required to process and evaluate information and thus make an appropriate decision and ensure fulfilment of quality expectations (i.e., the degree and direction of the discrepancy between consumers' perceptions and expectations defines perceived quality; Parasuraman et al., 1985, 1988).

- First, the traditional variation in rural buildings remains, such that more than 30 different types of rural lodging facilities are officially recognized by Spanish legislation. A regional normative framework makes sense, because it has helped preserve the identity of each region, but it also creates confusion due to the multitude of types of lodging facilities. Some typologies differ only in name, whereas others imply differences in the type of buildings (e.g., regular house of traditional architecture in a town, building of historical value, or house on a farm), the range of services (e.g., some types must include the offer of complementary leisure activities, or restaurant services), and size (e.g., accommodate a maximum of 6 persons versus up to 60). These different typologies, both within and across regions, make the buying process more complex, even though 80% of rural tourists are domestic (Spanish Institute of Statistics [INE], 2009), so they should be more familiar than foreigners with the different types of traditional buildings.
- Second, many simultaneous quality classification systems and quality brands (e.g., Casonas Asturianas) have been developed by the regional normative frameworks and private associations. Unlike other European countries, such as Austria (which classifies the rural lodging facilities with flowers), France (ears of corn), or Germany (stars), Spain allows for several quality classification systems. Consequently, different indicators, such as the number of olives, ears of corn, or leaves, represent the facilities' quality. This context makes it difficult for tourists to become familiar with the quality distinctions or make comparisons among facilities, which further complicates their buying process. Furthermore, high perceived quality (after the

experience) cannot be ensured by the classification systems, few of which require regular inspections or audits after an initial review. Most of the quality standards also refer to tangible elements of the service, such as infrastructure and equipment (e.g., required room size, room amenities), without controlling for how the service is provided. In this regard, indicators referring to processes or management generally are not included, and the mystery shopping technique is rare.

- Third, the Internet plays an important role in the tourism buying process, and there are many rural tourism Web sites. These sites result from the regional normative frameworks and the development of private associations. They generally feature different designs, search options, types of facilities, and quality distinctions. Although the Internet makes it easy to access a multitude of information, the resultant information overload may produce more confusion for the tourist.
- Fourth, some facilities are not officially registered. The Internet grants access to unregistered facilities, and tourists may not be able to distinguish an official facility from an unregistered one. Illegal facilities do not even guarantee the minimum standards of quality with regard to safety, which deteriorates the rural tourism sector in general.

In conclusion, different typologies and quality distinctions, together with the important use of the Internet and the presence of illegal facilities, make it difficult for a consumer to accomplish a successful buying process and make a good decision. In this context, the tourist's familiarity may be a key variable to define different buying processes for rural tourism in Spain. Previous literature recognizes various consequences of a client's familiarity (Peracchio and Tybout, 1996). Particularly in rural tourism, Hernández Maestro et al. (2007) confirm that with greater familiarity, tourists' quality perceptions about their experience at a facility are less biased by their psychological state prior to the experience. Familiarity also should help the tourist understand the implicit promise established by the different facilities' typologies or different quality distinctions, how each quality standard compares with the others, and mechanisms to identify illegal facilities. Consequently, familiarity should have an important effect in terms of decreasing the tourist's uncertainty and favouring a better result through the confirmation of expectations.

REFERENCES

Anderson, E. W., Fornell, C. & Lehmann, D. R. (1994). Customer satisfaction, market share, and profitability: Findings from Sweden. *Journal of Marketing, 58*, 53-66.

Anderson, E. W., Fornell, C. & Rust, R. T. (1997). Customer satisfaction, productivity, and profitability: Differences between goods and services, *Marketing Science, 16(2)*, 129-145.

Behn, B. K. & Riley, R. A. J. (1999). Using nonfinancial information to predict financial performance: The case of the US airline industry. *Journal of Accounting, Auditing and Finance, 14(1)*, 29-56.

Hernández Maestro, R. M., Muñoz Gallego, P. A. & Santos Requejo, L. (2007). The moderating role of familiarity in rural tourism in Spain. *Tourism Management, 28*, 951-964.

Hernández-Maestro, R. M., Muñoz-Gallego, P. & Santos-Requejo, L. (2009). Small-business owners' knowledge and rural tourism establishment performance in Spain. *Journal of Travel Research,* 48(1), 58-77.

Parasuraman, A., Zeithaml, V. A. & Berry, L. L. (1985). A conceptual model of service quality and its implications for future research. *Journal of Marketing, 49(4)*, 41-50.

Parasuraman, A., Zeithaml, V. A. & Berry, L. L. (1988). SERVQUAL: A multiple-item scale for measuring consumer perceptions of service quality. *Journal of Retailing, 64(1)*, 12-40.

Peracchio, L. A. & Tybout, A. M. (1996). The moderating role of prior knowledge in schema-based product evaluation. *Journal of Consumer Research, 23*, 177-192.

Smith, R. E. & Wright, W. F. (2004). Determinants of customer loyalty and financial performance. *Journal of Management Accounting Research, 16*, 183-205.

Spanish Institute of Statistics (INE). www.ine.es

Valdés Peláez, L. & Ballina Ballina, F. J. (2005). La Calidad en el Turismo Rural: El Caso de las Marcas de Calidad Regionales. *Investigación y Marketing, 87*, 43-48.

INDEX

D

F

G

I

N

O

S

T

Y

Z